Teacher Education in CALL

Language Learning and Language Teaching

The *LL&LT* monograph series publishes monographs as well as edited volumes on applied and methodological issues in the field of language pedagogy. The focus of the series is on subjects such as classroom discourse and interaction; language diversity in educational settings; bilingual education; language testing and language assessment; teaching methods and teaching performance; learning trajectories in second language acquisition; and written language learning in educational settings.

Series editors

Nina Spada
Ontario Institute for Studies in Education, University of Toronto

Jan H. Hulstijn
Department of Second Language Acquisition, University of Amsterdam

Volume 14
Teacher Education in CALL
Edited by Philip Hubbard and Mike Levy

Teacher Education in CALL

Edited by

Philip Hubbard

Stanford University

Mike Levy

Griffith University

John Benjamins Publishing Company

Amsterdam / Philadelphia

∞™ The paper used in this publication meets the minimum requirements
of American National Standard for Information Sciences – Permanence
of Paper for Printed Library Materials, ANSI z39.48-1984.

Library of Congress Cataloging-in-Publication Data

Teacher education in CALL / edited by Philip Hubbard and Michael J. Levy.
        p.   cm. (Language Learning and Language Teaching, ISSN 1569–9471
; v. 14)
        Includes bibliographical references and indexes.
            1. Language teachers--Training of. 2. Language and languages--
        Computer-assisted instruction. I. Hubbard, Philip, 1952- II. Levy, Mike,
        1953- III. Title: Teacher education in computer-assisted language learning.

        P53.85.T385 2006
    418'007--dc22   2006045896
    ISBN 90 272 1967 2 (Hb; alk. paper)
    ISBN 90 272 1968 0 (Pb; alk. paper)

John Benjamins Publishing Co. · P.O. Box 36224 · 1020 ME Amsterdam · The Netherlands
John Benjamins North America · P.O. Box 27519 · Philadelphia PA 19118-0519 · USA

Table of contents

Foreword

Carol A. Chapelle
Iowa State University, USA

Decisions about the design of language-teacher education curricula and course content present challenges for most professors and lecturers in applied linguistics. The perennial issues include finding an appropriate balance between theory and practice, complementing knowledge transmission pedagogies with discovery-oriented projects, and selecting from the numerous approaches and important areas of applied linguistics those that will offer the most solid basis for practice and future development. These decisions have to be made within the cultural and academic context of the program and in view of the fact that students in such programs may go on to be classroom teachers, administrators, developers of learning and assessment materials, or experts in language and language policy in many other settings.

In some ways the issues associated with teacher education in computer-assisted language learning (CALL) mirror those in other areas of second-language teacher education. CALL, the strand of applied linguistics concerned with teaching and learning of second-languages through computer technology, is one of many areas that competes for a place in the curriculum. For many programs, the solution to the curriculum issue has been to leave it out and to advise interested students to take a general educational technology course. Twenty years ago this was a tenable solution, but second-language teachers today need to be able to choose, use, and in some cases, refuse technology for their students. Success in all three requires professional expertise beyond what they should have to pick up in self study.

Many involved in the education of second-language teachers recognize that their students need to have an understanding of issues and practices in technology use for second-language teaching and learning. This recognition, however, typically comes with some anxiety and uncertainty about precisely what and how to teach current and future teachers about technology. In many cases, teacher educators themselves have partial and fragile knowledge of the area of CALL. This fact is exacerbated by the scope and complexity of this area of research and practice, as well as the speed with which changes occur. How does one strike an appropriate balance between theory and practice in CALL? Moreover, what do theory and practice consist of in CALL? What is the professional knowledge base about CALL that should be transmitted to or discovered by students studying CALL in graduate programs? What technical knowledge does a language teacher need to engage in discovery work in CALL? What areas of CALL and approaches to CALL should be included?

Most applied linguists working in CALL would agree that all of these questions should be open to discussion, and fortunately this collection of papers takes the first step. No single textbook exists for teaching a CALL course. Instead, most professors and lecturers who teach CALL courses in graduate programs in higher education use a combination of books, articles, and software. This means that each instructor has to choose from the dozen or more recent books. Choices have to be made about how to author CALL materials as well as how much time to spend doing so. In addition, key papers have to be selected from at least five journals that publish research exclusively on CALL and from other journals that publish occasional papers on CALL. When I began teaching a CALL course over twenty years ago, the challenge was to find a sufficient amount and quality of professional literature directly pertaining to CALL. What a different problem we are faced with today! It is a problem faced not only in higher education but also throughout in-service and professional development courses.

Many of today's students are headed for careers that will put them in the position of needing different types of technology expertise as they work as teachers in language classrooms, directors of language learning centers, developers of CALL and computer-assisted assessments, researchers and teacher educators. These different roles they will take up suggest different learning needs. The educational programs discussed in this volume meet various needs by the way they place technology issues in the curriculum.

The papers open a much-needed discussion on the issues associated with courses and programs on CALL. They describe many of the options by drawing upon examples of curricula and courses in a variety of academic contexts, and discuss their consequences for the students. This volume will contribute greatly toward addressing today's problem of deciding how, when, what and why to teach about CALL in pre-service and in-service teacher education. It is a welcome addition to the professional literature in CALL.

Introduction

The growth of the Internet and proliferation of computers in school and home settings has led to a significant expansion of the use of technology in foreign and second language instruction. Increasingly, both language teachers in train- ing and practicing teachers will find themselves at a disadvantage if they are not <!-- handwritten annotation: quote --> adequately proficient in computer-assisted language learning (CALL). In-service and pre-service programs alike are recognizing the need for filling this gap, and work is being done independently by hundreds of trainers in this area. There are already CALL certificate programs, CALL courses as part of master's curricula in applied linguistics, second language acquisition, and language pedagogy, and even entire graduate programs dedicated to CALL. CALICO (Computer-Assisted Language Instruction Consortium) has a special interest group devoted to CALL teacher education, and the number of conference presentations in this area has grown noticeably in recent years. To date, however, there have been only a rela- tively small number of professional publications devoted to the topic, most notably a special issue of *Language Learning & Technology* in 2002 containing five articles exclusively from US institutions. We believe this area warrants considerably more professional – and international – attention, and the present volume represents a major step in that direction.

Woven throughout the chapters of the book are a number of recurring themes:

1) the need for both technical and pedagogical training in CALL, ideally inte- grated with one another;
2) the recognition of the limits of formal teaching because the technology changes so rapidly;
3) the need to connect CALL education to authentic teaching settings, especially ones where software, hardware, and technical support differ from the ideal;
4) the idea of using CALL to learn about CALL – experiencing educational ap- plications of technology firsthand as a student to learn how to use technology as a teacher;
5) the value of having CALL permeate the language teacher education curricu- lum rather than appear solely in a standalone course.

The volume has 20 chapters covering research and practice in this area, divided across five sections: foundations of CALL teacher education; CALL degree programs; CALL pre-service courses; CALL in-service projects, courses, and workshops; and alternatives to formal CALL training. In addition to the breadth of topics, the chapters also cover a range of levels, environments, countries, and languages. They provide practical information to readers, reporting on authors' experiences in a wide variety of teacher education programs and courses, along with the obstacles that have been or still need to be overcome. In many cases the papers describe how programs and courses have evolved over a number of years, and many of these chapters also involve qualitative or quantitative research to support the claims of the authors. We hope that the wide-ranging approach that this volume embodies will allow both teacher educators and language program administrators to find viable options for CALL education that will fit the needs of their teachers and the realities of their institutional environments.

Part I consists of three chapters on foundations of the field. It opens with a paper by the editors offering a brief overview of trends in CALL teacher education, along with a proposed framework for distinguishing institutional and functional roles reflecting types and degrees of expertise within the field. The other chapters in this section include a report of a survey of practicing teachers on the type and value of the CALL training they received, if any, in their professional degree programs and a description of a range of initiatives regarding technology standards for language teacher education, certification, and credentialing emerging from both professional and government entities.

Part II includes three chapters on CALL graduate degree programs: two in the UK and one in Australia. The focus in all three is on how these programs have developed and changed over the years in response to both the shifts in technology and the perceived needs of the students. The second and third chapters in this section have the additional themes of the reconstructive and transformational nature of technology education and project-oriented CALL, respectively.

Part III concerns pre-service CALL courses, typically within a general degree program in language teaching. This is perhaps the most significant area within the field due to the critical need for the present cadre of language teachers in training to become more technologically knowledgeable, prepared for a future in which the role of the computer in language teaching continues to evolve. These five chapters encompass a variety of viewpoints as to the content of CALL courses and the process through which students can gain their technological and pedagogical proficiency. The section includes chapters on learning to use common applications, programming of courseware, and courses taught both face to face and online.

Part IV focuses on in-service training. The five chapters here cover such topics as teacher training to develop a specific CALL activity or to use a particular online teaching environment, as well as a number of broader issues, including setting up CALL training programs at the national level. The courses and workshops described are from venues reflecting the international scope of the book – the US, Taiwan, Hong Kong, Ireland, and Russia.

Part V extends the notion of CALL education to alternatives beyond the formal level. These four chapters include the rationale and resources for communities of practice, academic and professional mentoring, learning CALL collaboratively at the program level, and preparing both pre-service and in-service teachers to become autonomous learners, noting that whatever they study today will soon be superseded as the technology is constantly changing.

We would like to express our gratitude for the patience and understanding of our families, in particular our wives Kathleen and Cynthia, the encouragement of Marc Weide and Graham Davies in moving this project forward initially, and the support of Kees Vaes at John Benjamins and *Language Learning and Language Teaching* series editors Jan Hulstijn and Nina Spada in bringing it to completion.

Philip Hubbard and Mike Levy
March, 2006

References

CALICO (Computer-Assisted Language Instruction Consortium). www.calico.org

Language Learning & Technology 2002. Special Issue on Technology and Teacher Education. Available at http://llt.msu.edu/vol6num3.

PART I

Foundations of teacher education in CALL

Preface to

The scope of CALL education

As editors of this volume, we have provided each chapter with a short introduction to help readers understand the purpose and context of the papers as well as their relationship to one another and to the overall world of CALL teacher education. In this, our own chapter, we introduce the current state of that world through an overview of four major trends relevant to it: the production of training materials for classroom teachers, the specialized literature on CALL teacher education, frameworks that link CALL practice to particular approaches, and the increasing use of online collaborative learning techniques. We note that the field of CALL teacher education has been growing rapidly in both size and importance, and that it would therefore be useful to begin looking at broad-based frameworks within which to develop, discuss, and evaluate alternative conceptions of what teachers and others should know and be able to do with technology in support of language learning. We offer a sketch of such a framework, one that seeks to define the scope of CALL education through distinguishing the institutional and functional roles of its participants. With respect to institutional roles, the framework covers not only pre- and in-service classroom teachers but also others involved in the field as CALL specialists and CALL professionals. In terms of functional roles, beyond the most common role of practitioner, it recognizes the roles of developer, researcher, and trainer, roles that can be and arguably are assumed by classroom teachers as well as specialists and professionals. Other key components of the framework include the distinction between CALL knowledge and skills and the importance of recognizing proficiency in both technical and pedagogical domains. Overall, the goal is to make a first step toward a descriptive mechanism that will provide CALL educators and other stakeholders with a tool to aid in determining the objectives and content of CALL educational initiatives.

The scope of CALL education

Philip Hubbard and Mike Levy
Stanford University, USA / Griffith University, Australia

Along with the growing influence of technology in language teaching and learning, there has been parallel growth in the development of course work to prepare language teachers to use the technology. Such preparation ranges from reading a single chapter within a comprehensive methodology textbook (e.g., Sokolik 2001) or participating in a one-time in-service workshop, through dedicated courses and seminars, CALL course series, CALL certificates, and even CALL graduate degrees.

As is often the case with new fields, this growth has generally been bottom-up and for the most part *ad hoc*. Over the years there have been a number of books and articles covering various aspects of CALL methodology, materials, and techniques. However, prior to the present volume, there have been only scattered attempts in the literature to characterize the knowledge and skills a language teacher or other educational adjunct, such as a technical support person for a language program, should have. As there is still considerable disagreement within CALL and language teaching in general about what constitutes optimal, or even acceptable, uses of technology, this absence is not surprising.

Some other areas of education have moved more decisively. ISTE (International Society for Technology in Education) has produced a set of guidelines for technological competence for both teachers (ISTE 2000) and elementary and secondary students (ISTE 1998). Guidelines such as these can inform similar enterprises in CALL, but language learning is broadly recognized as a unique field that should be wary of relying too much on generic educational criteria. Murphy-Judy and Youngs (this volume) describe developments in this area by other groups such as ACTFL (American Council on the Teaching of Foreign Languages) and the Council of Europe, but these are still in early stages. It is worth noting that there is a risk that such initiatives can be somewhat rigid, sometimes taking a "best-practices" approach that marginalizes alternative conceptualizations by institutionalizing certain prevailing views (see, for example, the critical review of the NCATE/TESOL Teacher Education Standards in Newman & Hanauer 2005).

[handwritten marginalia: "be critical of standards"]

There are valid reasons for promoting such standards in language teaching – indeed, they are what makes it possible for it to claim the status of a profession – but given the limitations of our current state of knowledge with regard to implementing technology in this domain, the results of such enterprises for CALL must be scrutinized with a particularly critical eye even as they are welcomed.

While the focus of the present book is on teacher education, it is assumed that CALL education as a whole should have a wider mission, to prepare not only classroom teachers but also others that are involved in the integration of technology and the language learning process. In line with that position, this chapter broadly outlines the larger scope of CALL education, introducing a framework for distinguishing elements of CALL expertise in a form that is comprehensive at a relatively general level but that offers the necessary structure for going into greater detail as desired. It begins with the assumption that a useful approach to describing expertise is in terms of *roles* played by the individual within the field, as it is the individual that we are ultimately educating.

This approach is inspired by concepts from an area of social psychology known as role theory (Biddle 1986). Although it has since been superseded by experimentalist approaches and social identity theory in mainstream social psychology (Schmidt 2000), "role" remains at the very least a compelling pre-theoretical notion. It captures the intuition that we view ourselves and others in terms of expectations built around roles and the labels that accompany them. We believe that by characterizing CALL education in this manner, we can provide a useful framework, even a nascent heuristic, for solving the problem of determining what teachers and others in given settings ought to know with respect to applying computer technology in language learning.

This is not the first attempt to use roles as a defining construct in language teaching. Indeed, the recent literature of language education is replete with references to the roles of the teacher, particularly to the teacher as a guide or facilitator. At the descriptive level, the widely-cited framework of Richards and Rodgers (1982) characterizes the *design* of a language teaching method largely in terms of the roles of the teacher, the students, the syllabus, and the materials. Interestingly, in characterizing the roles of humans engaged in the use of technology here, we are by extension characterizing the roles of the technology itself. In this sense, the current framework may be seen as a relative of earlier frameworks the two of us offered independently: the methodological framework in Hubbard (1988, 1992, 1996) and the tutor-tool framework in Levy (1995, 1997).

We begin with a brief overview of some trends in CALL education to provide a context in which to interpret the place of the proposed framework. We then introduce the framework itself, distinguishing two types of roles: *functional* and *institutional*. Functional roles – practitioner, developer, researcher, and trainer – describe what one does in relation to CALL; institutional roles – classroom teacher (at both pre-service and in-service stages), CALL specialist, and CALL professional – relate to the anticipated responsibilities and expected levels of expertise within an organization. Taken together as two dimensions, we believe they can help coherently characterize the knowledge base and skills needed to fulfill the expectations of a given position in an educational setting. In doing so, they provide a structure for conducting needs analyses and creating sets of learning objectives for specific role combinations that can then serve to inform CALL education curricula. The framework can also be used as a tool to aid in developing and interpreting evaluation rubrics for certification and other standards or simply to describe qualifications for the purposes of informally assessing CALL proficiency or creating job descriptions.

It should be noted that the goal here is not to attempt to specify what the content of any particular CALL education initiative should be. Our aim is the more modest one of laying out the scope of the field and offering a general plan for the conceptual space within which such decisions can ultimately be made by individual teacher educators and professional entities.

The state of CALL teacher education

As the other chapters in this book make clear, there is tremendous variety in the form, content, and intensity of teacher education in environments around the world. Some of these, as in the ISTE standards, are quite explicit and internally consistent (though often quite general as well). However, to date, no one has offered a comprehensive approach of the type we envision. Instead, we can recognize four general trends in CALL education:

1) the production of training and support materials directly oriented toward classroom teachers;
2) a small but growing literature in CALL teacher education itself at the levels of both research and practice;
3) frameworks that attempt to define CALL practice on the basis of principles derived from particular language teaching approaches, especially those supported by SLA (second language acquisition) research;
4) the use of online collaborative learning techniques in CALL teacher education with a growing interest in the quality of the transfer of skills and expertise from formal courses to the language classroom.

The first trend is particularly apparent in textbooks aimed at introducing newcomers to the field. Recent examples include an edited volume on teaching with technology (Lomicka & Cooke-Plagwitz 2004) and books by Beatty (2003) and Egbert (2005) for CALL in general and Warschauer, Shetzer, and Meloni (2000) for the Internet specifically. Besides these printed texts, the ICT4LT (Information and Communications Technologies for Language Teachers) website (Davies 2006) offers 16 online training modules aimed at in-service teachers, providing free materials equivalent to a good-sized textbook. Begun in 1998, it is still being regularly expanded and updated at the time of this writing.

The second trend is reflected in the growing production of research and practice articles aimed directly at teacher educators. Davies (2003) provides a fairly comprehensive overview of some of the issues involved in technology training for both online and offline language teaching, as well as a discussion of initiatives to address them. In addition to the chapters in the present volume, the most notable collection of CALL teacher education papers is found in a special issue of *Language Learning & Technology* (September, 2002). Among the five papers there is one by Egbert, Paulus, and Nakamichi offering the following set of questions to guide research in the area of technology and teacher education:

- How do teachers learn about CALL-based activities?
- How does what they learned in their coursework impact their current teaching contexts?
- What factors influence whether they use computers in their classrooms?
- How do participants continue to acquire and master new ideas in CALL after formal coursework ends (professional development)?

(Egbert, Paulus, & Nakamichi 2002: 109)

Questions like these can provide direction to those seeking insights into the critical area of the *processes* of CALL teacher education. As such, they complement the framework proposed below that focuses on content and objectives.

The third trend in CALL education is one which characterizes CALL in terms of a given language teaching approach or set of related approaches. The advantage here is a clear linkage to the non-CALL aspects of teaching, supported by currently accepted theory and a significant research base. An early example is found in Underwood (1984) for communicative CALL. More recently, we have seen connections between SLA theory and research leading to characterizations of general principles which can be used to inform CALL course objectives. Possibly the most comprehensive work oriented toward teacher education is Egbert and Hanson-Smith (1999). In addition to structuring this edited volume around eight generalizations relating to optimal language learning derived from SLA research, they provide guiding questions and tasks, making the volume useful not only as a professional reference but also as a course textbook. Chapelle (2001) has also become an influential source for many current students of CALL. Her widely-cited framework offers a set of six general criteria for the design and evaluation of CALL tasks (in the areas of language learning potential, meaning focus, learner fit, authenticity, impact, and practicality), each of which can be expanded to themes in a CALL course directly connected to SLA research findings. Doughty and Long (2003) present a set of conditions to describe optimal practice in distance education settings, again drawing from SLA research findings, incorporating 10 principles of task-based learning adapted to the specific CALL area of online teaching. Although practice-oriented, it is clear that their principles could form the core of a training program in distance language education.

The fourth trend encompasses the evolving processes of CALL teacher education and a concern with the degree to which trainees can successfully apply the ideas and skills they learn through books, articles or formal courses to the language classroom (see Nunan 1999; Egbert et al. 2002). Collaborative learning and communities of practice facilitated through e-mail, chat and discussion groups can help teachers make this link (Hanson-Smith, this volume), as can CALL courses themselves embodying a significant online component (Cooke-Plagwitz 2004; Bauer-Ramazani, this volume). For language teaching and CALL, experiencing the use of these tools first hand can help bring home the strengths and limitations of the individual technologies for learning. Discussion groups and learning communities can also be formed, both within pre-service and in-service groups and beyond so that peers may share experiences and practitioners may be effectively linked with trainees. This kind of interaction can help trainees better understand and engage with the complexities and contradictions that can arise with the regular use of technology in language learning. Also, this kind of interaction can provide a valuable check for teacher educators who tend to operate in relatively well-resourced conditions in university environments where general levels of funding and support are strong. In these circumstances, language teacher trainees can sometimes reach the conclusion that technology always works and technology support is always readily available. Real conditions can be very different, and trainees need to engage with some of the complexities and tensions that often exist. School environments provide an example because time and resources tend to be strictly limited or variable. Individual schools often have systems that are idiosyncratic, notably in relation to technology infrastructure (e.g., how security is handled), technical support, and scheduling.

A variety of approaches are being developed to help the trainee experience authentic contexts and conditions. These include situated learning (Egbert et al. 2002; Weasonforth, Biesenbach-Lucas, & Meloni 2002) and critical incidents (Tripp 1993). Situated learning is concerned with how learning occurs in everyday settings (see Egbert, this volume). From this perspective, human knowledge "develops in the course of activity" and is viewed as, "a capacity to coordinate and sequence behavior, to adapt dynamically to changing circumstances" (Clancey 1995:49). Situated learning can be very helpful for thinking about the realities of actual practice. The use of a critical incidents file can likewise be valuable for professional development with a focus on practice (Tripp 1993:68). A log or journal of critical incidents encountered in the classroom, when subsequently analyzed systematically, can feed back into learning what is necessary to ensure an informed approach if a similar situation or event should occur again. These kinds of techniques are quite pertinent for the CALL classroom where the language teacher has to be prepared for the unexpected.

Language teachers and learners operate within a set of interrelated constraints. These constraints, often associated with the limited time and resources available to the teacher and the student, typically include the number of contact hours predetermined for a course, lesson times and durations, preparation time, access to new technologies and to software development budget, technical support, ancillary learning materials, and so on. All of these, in one way or another, directly impact on the teacher in the classroom. The language teacher needs to be able to identify and to understand the impact of authentic constraints and to be able to work creatively within them. To conceptualize language teaching or CALL without such constraints and to assume "ideal conditions" – as is often the case with theoretically derived models of language teaching and learning – is to miss the point as far as successful planning and implementation is concerned in real educational settings. In this context, working to an ideal without boundaries or restrictions really does not teach very much. That is why the best pre-service and in-service professional development courses build authentic constraints into the tasks trainee language teachers are required to complete. Then, later, novice teachers will be in a much stronger position to operate within the constraints that will inevitably impinge on their work during their professional lives.

In contrasting the present approach with these trends, in particular with the third and fourth ones, it should be emphasized that ours is a *descriptive* rather than a *prescriptive* framework and thus is designed to be open and flexible. In the framework itself, we are not making claims about what should or should not be the content of any given CALL education initiative. This is an important distinction because the majority of CALL frameworks presented recently have not been descriptive. We readily acknowledge that being prescriptive is not necessarily a negative point and do not intend the term "prescriptive" to be pejorative in this context. Clearly, Egbert and Hanson-Smith (1999), Chapelle (2001), and Doughty and Long (2003) present coherent and defensible frameworks that link the evaluation of CALL applications, activities, and tasks to widely accepted findings in second language acquisition research and theory. However, "widely-accepted" must be recognized as a time-bound concept, not to be confused with "true", a fact too often ignored in education but acknowledged with refreshing directness in the opening of the final paragraph in Doughty and Long (2003:68): "Given the checkered history of prescriptions for language teaching, the likelihood that all 10 TBLT MPs [task-based language teaching methodological principles] will turn out to have been well founded is minimal."

Using an appropriately designed descriptive tool, we believe it is possible to effectively characterize the various current views of language learning and CALL as well as to accommodate, and even support, the development of future competing ones. In that sense, our approach is not meant to supplant prescriptive ones but rather to allow for development and comparison among them.

A role-based framework for CALL education

As noted in the introduction, we propose that a framework for CALL education can be built on the concept of roles. The version presented here is a major elaboration of one introduced in an editorial in *Computer Assisted Language Learning* (Hubbard 2004). Before discussing the details, we would like to be clear about a couple of starting points in this approach beyond the fact that it is primarily descriptive.

First, our framework is for education and training *across* the field of CALL – it is not limited to classroom language teachers, although that is a key part of it. In this sense, we diverge from scholars such as Bax (2003), who seems to reduce CALL to classroom linkages. While his concept of "normalization" as the path for the future of CALL has an obvious appeal to teachers, we regard a situation where "the technology is so integrated into our lives that it becomes invisible" (Bax 2003:25) as one that limits both the conception and the development of CALL as a legitimate academic field (see Levy & Stockwell 2006). For example, when we look through the contents of major international CALL journals such as *ReCALL*, *CALICO* or *Computer Assisted Language Learning*, we see that CALL is given a broad interpretation that reaches well beyond classroom language teaching. It involves research and development of a wide range of products including online courses, programs, tutors, and tools. It also includes discussion of the use of generic tools for language learning purposes such as the word processor, email, chat, and audio- and video-conferencing programs. In research, it seeks to evaluate emergent technologies such as speech recognition applications, broadband audiovisual technologies, online teaching systems (with human tutors), and mobile technologies. In practice, it considers task and activity design, website design, evaluation, and classroom management as well as practical techniques for teaching and introducing students to CALL. The common thread is that technology is being employed in some form for language teaching and learning.

We favor the term "CALL" for this work because of its now well-established presence in the discourse surrounding the topic, and because we believe there is a benefit in having a focus which rests on the technology itself, especially with regard to teacher education. We have not yet reached a point, especially in university or school settings, where the technology is invisible. It is highly visible with respect to such matters as access and availability, new technologies, technology breakdown, evaluation, quality of online materials, and variable levels of expertise across faculty and students. In all these matters, we feel there are considerable benefits in having a special focus. In fact, if there is not a special focus, there is the very real danger that new technologies (both hardware and software) will be either blindly accepted or rejected without an informed and careful critical review or evaluation (see Levy and Hubbard (2005) for more on this topic).

Second, we would like to like to point out that our overall conception of CALL education and training is not limited to classroom, workshop, or other formal interactive settings (such as online courses). Our approach also embraces community of practice, mentoring, apprenticeship, courseware-based and even autodidactic settings, all of which are touched on in other chapters in this volume. This is especially important for the CALL specialist and professional roles we introduce below, as there are fewer opportunities for formal education at these levels.

The goal of any course of study, formal or otherwise, is achieved through both content and process, which ideally combine to induce changes in the learners that conform to the stated learning objectives. While acknowledging the crucial role of process, our framework in its present form focuses largely on content. There are two pairs of elements of importance in determining content, both clearly relating to learning objectives. The first involves the classic distinction between what the learner should know and what the learner should be able to do: in simple terms, knowledge and skills. The second is an area crucial for the CALL domain, namely the distinction between *technical* knowledge and skills that are necessary for the competent operation of the computer technology, and *pedagogical* knowledge and skills involving the computer technology's impact on a learning environment and its appropriate and effective integration into the teaching and learning process. The importance of technical knowledge is emphasized in Hegelheimer (this volume), who describes the structure and impact of a technical skills course that provides a foundation for integrating technology in courses throughout an MA/TESL program. While some may argue that technical skills can dominate too much, without a sufficient technical foundation it is unlikely that pedagogical points can be effectively dealt with. It is abundantly clear that teachers get frustrated when they are unable to get a piece of equipment or application to work and have no conception of how to fix it, or when they are simply intimidated by the length of time it would seem to take to integrate some otherwise promising application into their course. The absence of a basic technical foundation in their training exacerbates this situation, and therefore it is reasonable to expect CALL teacher educators to at least consider providing such a foundation.

Figure 1 illustrates the role-based approach with a matrix that places institutional roles in rows and functional roles in columns, allowing the base concepts of the framework to appear in a form that is readily conceivable. For a given setting, the cells on this matrix would of course need to be specified more rigorously through a hierarchical layering that could eventually get down to the level of bits of relevant information and micro-skills in a way that could be accommodated by a textbook or detailed course outline.

Functional roles

As noted previously, functional roles refer explicitly to what one does. Figure 1 recognizes the following functional roles: practitioner, developer, researcher, and trainer.

Practitioners are those who apply their knowledge and skill directly in the performance of their institutional roles. In particular, the traditional role of a teacher is linked to practitioner. As Freeman notes in making the case for teacher research in language learning, "Teachers are seen – and principally see themselves – as consumers rather than producers of knowledge. Other people write curricula, develop teaching methodologies, create published materials, and make policies and procedures about education that teachers are called upon to implement" (Freeman 1998: 10). There are two points to be made here. First, as consumers, teachers need to be informed and critical. They need to be able to understand frameworks for evaluating CALL in its many forms, especially language learning websites, CALL tasks, and learning environments involving a variety of technologies. Teachers need to know why they do what they do, using pedagogical approaches that are intentional and well-considered. They need to be able to make informed judgments on the suitability of the tool for the task; for example, knowing what kinds of language learning goals and tasks may appropriately include the use of chat or email. This also involves an appreciation of strengths and limitations of the technology options at hand. Second, in line with Freeman, we want to identify teachers

Institutional roles	Functional roles			
	Practitioner	Developer	Researcher	Trainer
Pre-service classroom teachers	X	X	X	X
In-service classroom teachers	X	X	X	X
CALL specialists (expert/adjunct)	X	X	X	X
CALL professionals (expert/adjunct)	X	X	X	X

Figure 1. A role-based framework for CALL education showing institutional roles (rows) and functional roles (columns). X includes both the technical and pedagogical knowledge base and skill set for the given role combination (see Figure 2).

as having the potential to be much more than consumers, if they are given the opportunity. We want them to be regarded as having the capacity for research and development in CALL and performing in functional roles beyond practitioner. But for these roles they will need training.

Developers are those who are actively engaged in the creation of something new or revision or adaptation of existing work. Although "developer" has most often been used in the literature to label those who produce CALL software, it is intended here to refer also to those who construct language activities and tasks involving the computer in a significant way. That is, we see developer as a role linked to implementations of the computer as both tutor and tool (Levy 1997).

Researchers in this context are those who attempt to discover new information relating to CALL or to pursue evaluation of the success of a CALL initiative. In the first case, we can include the more traditional "library" type of research (now predominantly online) – namely, the discovery and collection of relevant published information previously unknown to the individual regardless of the fact that it may have been known to others: this is of particular relevance to classroom teachers. The more active, productive type of research can be done across a range from informal (reflective or action research) to formal. The key is the pursuit of discovering something new or of validating or rejecting something previously proposed.

Trainers are those who are acting to build CALL knowledge and skills in others, rather than just language knowledge and skills. This role accommodates both formal and informal training, mentoring, and assisting of students and colleagues not subsumed by the previous roles. For teachers, this includes CALL learner training, both technical and pedagogical, of the type described in Kolaitis, Mahoney, Pomann and Hubbard (this volume), as well as assisting other language teachers, given the likelihood that recent graduates with CALL training will find themselves in a position as "expert colleague" in their language programs. Not surprisingly, for CALL specialists and professionals (see below) trainer is likely to be a more emphasized role in their institutional settings.

Because functional roles refer to actions, they can be dynamic, and it is common for one person to shift functional roles fairly quickly, often in an integrated fashion linked to a specific activity or task. For example, a classroom teacher as a *developer* might create a new CALL task requiring students to employ the web to gather information, comprehend it, and use a discussion board or other collaborative online space to interpret and synthesize it for a group project, such as a WebQuest (Chao, this volume). As a *practitioner,* the teacher would determine how to integrate this task into the course, present it to the students, organize groups, set expectations, manage their progress, and provide feedback on their final product. As a *trainer* the teacher would provide students with any needed instruction in the technical operation of the computer application as well as strategy training on how to connect their actions to learning objectives (Kolaitis et al., this volume). As

a *researcher*, the teacher could review the postings on the discussion board, looking for new or previously identified structures, lexis, or interactional patterns that
may inform later activities in the class or future versions of that task. From the
teacher education perspective, it is important to work toward the provision of the
underlying knowledge and skills that the teacher needs in order to accomplish the
preceding tasks in those four roles.

Institutional roles

While functional roles are relatively dynamic, institutional roles are typically more
stable and refer to situations or settings. As the term implies, institutional roles are
often reflected in job titles or descriptions, but even when they are not, they can
represent collections of expectations held by supervisors or colleagues as well as by
those one serves. This is particularly true of the CALL specialist.

Classroom teachers, with respect to CALL, are those who use the computer
in some way to promote, manage, or assess their students' learning. Note that
"classroom" is used in its broadest sense here to subsume language teaching in
a traditional physical space, a computer lab, a mix of physical classroom or lab
and online, or entirely online. A distinction often made for educational purposes
is that between *pre-service* teachers (those who are in a course or certificate, or
degree program but are not yet teaching) and *in-service* teachers, those who are
receiving their CALL training while actively engaged in classroom language teaching). This distinction can be significant for a number of reasons and in fact is a
structural division of the present volume. In particular, in-service teachers

1) have a current class or classes they are teaching that can provide a context
   for interpreting and even applying what they are learning (see Egbert (this
   volume) for a discussion of situated learning for teachers);
2) have experience in the teaching role that they can build on during course work;
3) are often not learning CALL in a degree or certificate program where they are
   also learning other elements of language teaching (second language acquisition theory, classroom methodology, etc.).

It is worth noting that in practice, the pre-service/in-service distinction may be
blurred. Pre-service and in-service teachers may be combined in a single class,
particularly in the online setting. It is also common to have students in pre-service
degree programs who have language teaching experience or who may have taught
some other subject mixed in with those who are true teaching novices. We might
refer to the former as "between-service." In some of these cases, they may still be
teaching actively while they go through the program.

CALL specialists represent a particularly interesting category, since recognition of their existence is arguably the best evidence for an identifiable discipline of

CALL. To characterize the difference between classroom teachers and specialists, we need to diverge briefly to a discussion of *shallow* vs. *deep* knowledge and *limited* vs. *elaborated* skill sets.

Motivational and personality factors aside, classroom teachers with a broad knowledge base are assumed to be more effective than those without it. That is why we have teacher education programs and certification procedures. However, in order to achieve this breadth in the limited time available for institutional education, we expect much of this knowledge to be relatively shallow compared to that of experts. For example, any well-trained language teacher today should have some understanding of pronunciation, including the inventory of sounds in the target language and their realizations in various phonological contexts; basic rhythm, stress, and intonation patterns; common problem areas for students; and the factors that influence pronunciation development so that they can have realistic expectations for student progress (Goodwin 2001). Similarly, we expect their skill sets to include the ability to analyze learners' speech and identify some of their more obvious problems, along with the ability to suggest appropriate techniques for drawing learners' attention to pronunciation and improving it. An adequate teacher preparation program should provide for most, if not all, of this general competence.

We would expect more from someone labeled a pronunciation *specialist*. We would assume that a pronunciation specialist would have a much deeper knowledge of phonological processes in the target language and an understanding of ways in which phonological theory and linguistic research could be relevant to learning. We would also expect a stronger base in pronunciation research literature of both developmental processes and effective teaching techniques for different types of learners. The skill set would be similarly elaborated, with both higher analytical and higher diagnostic proficiency, the ability to create or adapt materials rapidly, and a wider repertoire of techniques and the know-how to apply them appropriately and assess their effectiveness.

In comparison, a *CALL* pronunciation specialist would ideally inherit the characteristics of a pronunciation specialist in general *and* have additional skills and knowledge relevant to CALL. The latter would include knowledge of available CALL pronunciation software and its usefulness, an understanding of the strengths and limitations of automatic speech recognition in support of pronunciation development, familiarity with computer hardware and software applications that provide visual displays and effective techniques for utilizing them with students, a strong foundation in CALL pronunciation literature, and so on.

Before leaving the specialist category, we would like to cover one other important distinction: *expert* vs. *adjunct*. An expert is a specialist with a primary attachment to language learning and teaching. An adjunct specialist on the other hand is a somewhat nebulous category meant to accommodate someone with deep knowledge and an elaborated skill set that is relevant to a CALL specialization but who may have quite shallow knowledge in second language learning and teaching, computer applications, or both. For the pronunciation specialist example, this could include phonologists or phoneticians applying themselves to a CALL pronunciation project, programmers with expertise in speech recognition or visualization, or speech therapists. These adjunct specialists have long been part of CALL development teams, and the interdisciplinarity they represent is a frequently-cited hallmark of the field. Levy (1997:49–50), for example, presents a list of 24 disciplines and fields with relevance to CALL, and given the growth of CMC (computer-mediated communication) and the web since that time, this list could undoubtedly be expanded. A formal recognition of the functional and institutional roles of adjuncts, coupled with a means of identifying their specific knowledge and skill sets, would go a long way toward offering a more coherent account of the relationship between CALL and its associated fields.

Finally, *CALL professionals* are those recognized as having 1) broad understanding of CALL as a whole, with a knowledge base and skill set in many CALL areas at least equivalent to that expected for teachers; 2) relatively deeper knowledge and more elaborated skill sets in multiple areas, most likely with one or more demonstrated specializations; 3) most prominently, a clear commitment to CALL as a primary area of professional development as evidenced by knowledge of the history and literature in the field, and/or activity in CALL conference presentations and publications outside of a single specialization. More relevant here, from the CALL education perspective, producing a CALL professional is the likely objective of an appropriately focused master's or doctoral program in the field, and we would expect a number of faculty engaged in such programs to be CALL professionals themselves. The term "CALL professional", like teacher and specialist, is intended as an institutional role label; however, it should be recognized that the impact of a CALL professional is likely to extend beyond the individual institution.

Interestingly, CALL professional can be considered largely a derivative role. That is, once we have determined technical and pedagogical knowledge and skill sets for pre-service and in-service teachers and for a range of specializations, we will have produced most of what is needed to educate and recognize the CALL professional. For that reason, we concentrate more on the other three institutional roles in this chapter.

Filling in the matrix

As mentioned previously, the institutional-functional role pairs (X's in Figure 1) are characterized by two domains, technical and pedagogical, each having a knowledge and a skill component. These are laid out in more detail in Figure 2:

	Technical	Pedagogical
CALL Knowledge	Systematic and incidental understanding of the computer system, including peripheral devices, in terms of hardware, software, and networking.	Systematic and incidental understanding of ways of effectively using the computer in language teaching.
CALL Skill	Ability to use technical knowledge and experience both for the operation of the computer system and relevant applications and in dealing with various problems.	Ability to use knowledge and experience to determine effective materials, content, and tasks, and to monitor and assess results appropriately.

Figure 2. Technical and pedagogical knowledge and skills for CALL.

note that in both cases, these are specific to language teaching. We can consider the pedagogical column to be related to what Shulman (1986) calls "pedagogical content knowledge," which represents not only an understanding of the subject matter – language in this case – but also an understanding of the specific ways in which to teach that content to others effectively, i.e., how to teach language using technology.

A few comments are in order here. First, note that these descriptions are quite general as they must encompass not only the obvious teaching aspects but also other institutional roles. Second, although knowledge and skill are separated here, in many instances in practice they are combined into behavioral or "can do" objectives. This is presumably because knowledge is sometimes accepted as important only to the extent that it moves from declarative (what we call "knowledge" here) to procedural (i.e., skills). We believe, however, that there is much to gain by separating them. In particular, at the technical level it is all too common to learn a fixed sequence of actions that produce a desired result (e.g., saving a file; sending and receiving email, attaching a data projector to a laptop…) only to be left helpless when something goes wrong because of a lack of foundational knowledge as to what that sequence actually represents in terms of interacting with software and hardware. Third, we acknowledge with the term "incidental" the practical point that not everything of value that is learned is integrated readily into a system. This seems to be particularly true of technical skills and knowledge.

As presented here, the framework is still at its broadest level. Because our goal is not prescriptive and space is limited, we will not attempt to provide specifications for the cells in the Figure 1 matrix. However, even its present form, the framework can offer guidance to others who wish to address such details. For example, for those who have already developed CALL teacher education courses, it offers input into an evaluation rubric for course content. Specifically, it invites considerations 1) of both knowledge and skills; 2) in both technical and pedagogical domains; 3) in the context of the institutional role or roles the students will be playing; and 4) importantly, with a recognition of the range of functional roles the students will play: practitioner, developer, researcher, and trainer. For those who are planning courses, or who are engaged in developing certification guidelines or standards, by its structure it implicitly recommends considerations across that same range of areas, some of which might otherwise be overlooked. It further suggests that a way to generate ideas for content and objectives is to start with identification of the expected knowledge and skills needed to fulfill predicted functional and institutional roles. Although we have not discussed it here, such expectations could be derived through a formal needs analysis. Finally, for those who by choice or necessity are learning about CALL independently, it provides a means to structure learning about the field in a reasoned fashion.

Discussion

We recognize that our approach does not characterize all the necessary elements of CALL education in a straightforward way, so in this section, we would like to clarify several points and acknowledge a few limitations. First, we have separated roles here that could arguably be seen as "blended" (for instance, some might want to define a trained, competent practitioner as one who already *is* a capable developer, researcher and trainer as well). We believe that making these roles discrete allows them to be characterized more readily. Second, while there is something of a hierarchy implied in our institutional dimension, it is not the case that we would expect those at the "higher" levels to inherit all the properties (skills and knowledge) from the lower ones. For instance, one could be a CALL professional but still lack some of the detailed knowledge and skill of an in-service classroom teacher or a CALL specialist. Third, we have referred to the institutional roles of CALL specialist and CALL professional, but not to "CALL" classroom teacher. This is because in most cases CALL is only a part, sometimes a very small part, of what classroom teachers are expected to do. While we see CALL as being a primary or even the defining quality of the institutional role for the specialist and professional, the classroom teacher requires a more flexible characterization.

Four limitations should be mentioned. As noted previously this framework does not address the process through which CALL knowledge and skills are developed in the individual. Other chapters in the present volume deal with this critical issue. However, arguably once the knowledge and performance objectives are clarified, the development and evaluation of effective paths toward them is a much easier task. Second, for the purposes of exposition and simplicity, we have limited ourselves to a four-by-four, two-dimensional matrix. A multi-dimensional one is possible, and cases could no doubt be made for additional institutional roles (e.g., administrator, private tutor) or functional roles (e.g., assessor, language informant). Third, we have focused on technical and pedagogical skills and knowledge only, without considering other aspects of teaching roles that are enhanced by the computer, e.g., record keeping, communication with colleagues (when not directly related to the aforementioned functional roles), communication with parents, administrators and other non-student stakeholders, etc. Finally, while we have addressed the institutional roles of pre- and in-service teacher, CALL specialist, and CALL professional, we have not touched on the institutional role of "student". It is not clear whether the framework should attempt to accommodate this directly or simply specify student technical and pedagogical knowledge and skills indirectly through the teacher's role as "trainer". However, a comprehensive description of technology in language education would need to address the learner's role in some fashion. It is interesting in this regard that ISTE apparently began with technology standards for students (ISTE 1998) before specifying them for teachers (ISTE 2000).

We believe that these limitations are acceptable at this initial stage in making the problem of determining CALL education tractable. Ultimately, a framework is only valuable to the extent that it is usable, and we are comfortable at this point with the tradeoff between completeness and practicality that the present proposal affords.

Future developments

There are two key characteristics to the preceding proposal that we feel are as important as the machinery of the framework itself: breadth and openness. By allowing for a broad conceptualization of CALL (i.e., anything involving computers – in all their manifestations – as an identifiable actor in the language learning arena), we have created a structure that we hope will be able to encompass not only current settings and utilizations but also those for the foreseeable future. By working toward openness, taking a descriptive rather than prescriptive approach, we have presented a structure consistent with the philosophies manifested in our previous publications (notably Hubbard 1996; Levy 1997) – one that encourages a wide range of alternatives in a forum where they can be readily compared and contrasted.

The framework presented here represents a proposal for what we see as a fruitful direction for ourselves and others to continue exploring, expanding, and refining. By using the constructs above – functional roles, institutional roles, technical and pedagogical domains, deep and shallow knowledge, limited and elaborated skillsets – we have outlined a set of considerations through which to construct both questions and tentative answers relevant to the area of the content and objectives of CALL education.

Finally, although our goal here was to present a proposal for characterizing CALL education in terms of roles, there is a possibility for taking this conceptualization further. To the extent that the classification matrix turns out to be useful in describing its intended target, it offers the potential for a substantial piece of a descriptive theoretical framework or metatheory for CALL. The ostensibly missing elements, notably the learner and the learning environment, are crucial considerations for the competent practitioner, researcher, developer, and trainer, and thus will need to be incorporated in the role expectations. Once these roles are described in a more detailed fashion – in particular the expected or ideal characteristics for a range of CALL specialists – we may find that we have described a lot of what is needed to account for CALL as a whole.

References

Bax, S. (2003). CALL – Past, present, and future. *System, 31*, 13–28.

Beatty, K. (2003). *Teaching and Researching Computer Assisted Language Learning.* London: Pearson Education.

Biddle, B. J. (1986). Recent developments in role theory. *Annual Review of Sociology, 12,* 67–92.

Chapelle, C. (2001). *Computer Applications in Second Language Acquisition: Foundations for teaching, testing, and research.* Cambridge: CUP.

Clancey, W. J. (1995). A tutorial on situated learning. In J. Self (Ed.), *Proceedings of the International Conference on Computers and Education* (Taiwan) (pp. 49–70). Charlottesville, VA: AACE.

Cooke-Plagwitz, J. (2004). Using the Internet to train language teachers to use the Internet: A special topics course for teachers of German. In L. Lomicka & J. Cooke-Plagwitz (Eds.), *Teaching with Technology* (pp. 65–71). Boston, MA: Heinle.

Davies, G. (2003). Perspectives on offline and online training initiatives. In U. Felix (Ed.), *Language Learning Online: Towards best practice* (pp. 193–214). Lisse: Swets & Zeitlinger.

Davies, G. (Ed.). (2006). *Information and Communication Technologies for Language Teachers (ICT4LT).* Slough: Thames Valley University. Available at http://www.ict4lt.org.

Doughty, C. & Long, M. (2003). Optimal psycholinguistic environments for distance foreign language learning. *Language Learning & Technology, 7* (3), 50–80.

Egbert, J. (2005). *CALL Essentials: Principles and practice in CALL classrooms.* Alexandria, VA: TESOL.

Egbert, J. & Hanson-Smith, E. (Eds.). (1999). *CALL Environments: Research, practice, and critical issues.* Alexandria, VA: TESOL.

Egbert, J., Paulus, T., & Nakamichi, Y. (2002). The impact of CALL instruction on classroom computer use: A foundation for rethinking technology in teacher education. *Language Learning & Technology, 6* (3), 108–126.

Freeman, D. (1998). *Doing Teacher Research: From inquiry to understanding.* Pacific Grove, CA: Heinle.

Goodwin, J. (2001). Teaching pronunciation. In M. Celce-Murcia (Ed.), *Teaching English as a Second or Foreign Language* (third edition) (pp. 117–138). Boston, MA: Heinle.

Hubbard, P. (1988). An integrated framework for CALL courseware evaluation. *CALICO Journal, 6* (2), 51–72.

Hubbard, P. (1992). A methodological framework for CALL courseware development. In M. Pennington & V. Stevens (Eds.), *Computers in Applied Linguistics* (pp. 39–65). Clevedon: Multilingual Matters.

Hubbard, P. (1996). Elements of CALL methodology: Development, evaluation, and implementation. In M. Pennington (Ed.), *The Power of CALL* (pp. 15–32). Houston, TX: Athelstan.

Hubbard, P. (2004). Guest editorial (untitled). *Computer Assisted Language Learning, 17* (1), 1–6.

ISTE (1998). *National Educational Technology Standards for Students Booklet.* Eugene, OR: International Society for Technology in Education.

ISTE (2000). *National Educational Technology Standards for Teachers Booklet.* Eugene, OR: International Society for Technology in Education.

Levy, M. (1995). Integrating CALL: The tutor and the tool. In A. Gimeno (Ed.), *Technology Enhanced Language Learning: Focus on integration, proceedings of EuroCALL '95* (pp. 239–248). Valencia: Universidad Politécnica de Valencia.

Levy, M. (1997). *CALL: Context and conceptualization.* Oxford: Clarendon Press.

Levy, M. & Hubbard, P. (2005). Why call CALL 'CALL'? (Guest editorial). *Computer Assisted Language Learning, 18* (3), 1–6.

Levy, M. & Stockwell, G. (2006). *CALL Dimensions: Options and issues in computer assisted language learning.* Mahwah, NJ: Lawrence Erlbaum.

Lomicka, L & Cooke-Plagwitz, J. (Eds.). (2004). *Teaching with Technology.* Boston MA: Heinle.

Newman, M. & Hanauer, D. (2005). The NCATE/TESOL teacher education standards: A critical review. *TESOL Quarterly, 39* (4), 753–764.

Nunan, D. (1999). A foot in the world of ideas: Graduate study through the Internet. *Language Learning & Technology, 3* (1), 52–74.

Richards, J. & Rodgers, T. (1982). Method: Approach, design, and procedure. *TESOL Quarterly, 16* (2), 153–168.

Schmidt, M. (2000). Role theory, emotions, and identity in the department headship of secondary schooling. *Teaching and Teacher Education, 16,* 827–842.

Shulman, L. (1986). Those who understand: Knowledge growth in teaching. *Educational Researcher, 15,* 4–14.

Sokolik, M. (2001). Computers in language teaching. In M. Celce-Murcia (Ed.), *Teaching English as a Second or Foreign Language* (third edition) (pp. 477–488). Boston, MA: Heinle.

Tripp, D. (1993). *Critical Incidents in Teaching: Developing professional judgement.* London: Routledge.

Underwood, J. (1984). *Linguistics, Computers, and the Language Teacher: A communicative approach.* Rowley, MA: Newbury House.

Warschauer, M., Shetzer, H., & Meloni, C. (2000). *Internet for English Teaching.* Alexandria, VA: TESOL.

Weasonforth, D., Biesenbach-Lucas, S., & Meloni, C. (2002). Realizing constructivist objectives through collaborative technologies: Threaded discussions. *Language Learning & Technology, 6* (3), 58–86.

Preface to

Assessing CALL teacher training

What are we doing and what could we do better?

In recent years in CALL, there has been much anecdotal evidence to suggest that language teachers who wish to learn more about the uses of technology in language learning are not able to locate the appropriate formal courses or programs to help them. As a result, language teachers are often compelled to take one of two alternatives, or both, to acquire some of the requisite skills. The first alternative is to attend short, generic courses on new learning technologies, or introductory courses on a particular piece of software, for example a new or upgraded e-mail application, or a learner management system (LMS) that the institution has chosen to adopt, such as a *Blackboard*. The second alternative is to "do it yourself", for example through asking colleagues, through attending workshops at CALL conferences, or by joining a discussion group where more experienced members of the group answer specific questions. Though these alternatives have their place and value, they have their limitations too. To explore this problem, Greg Kessler collected data from practicing teachers, teacher trainers, and teacher education program coordinators through an online survey, focus groups and interviews. In analyzing the findings, he sheds light on trends and patterns of activity in teacher education and CALL. He also provides more detail on how motivated language teachers respond to prevailing conditions, how they compensate for the lack of formal courses, and the many ways in which they seek to educate themselves. On the basis of the data collected, he concludes the chapter with a series of recommendations for both pre-service and in-service teacher training and support.

Assessing CALL teacher training

What are we doing and what could we do better?

Greg Kessler
Ohio University, USA

The use of CALL in language programs has become a standard and expected part of a curriculum. ESL and EFL programs find the use and knowledge of CALL to be essential to effective instruction (Warschauer & Healey 1998). This understanding is also reflected in employment practices. For example, of the 15 job postings on TESOL's Career Center (accessed March 22, 2006) that targeted master's prepared ESOL teachers, nine (60%) listed training or experience with CALL, online delivery, or educational technology as a required or desirable attribute. However, training continues to predominantly be acquired in an informal or ad hoc manner through conference workshops, in-services, personal reading and other forms of self-edification. It seems that formal language teacher preparation programs have largely neglected to equip their graduates with the related knowledge and skills they need to enter today's technologically advanced language classroom. A visit to 50 North American TESOL graduate program websites in early 2004 revealed that only eight had any mention of CALL as a component within their coursework. Only three of these included a CALL course among requirements (Kessler 2005).

Research has attempted to identify the success of individual CALL teacher training courses (Egbert, Paulus, & Nakamichi 2002). However, the literature contains no evidence of an attempt to identify the extent of CALL training across the field. Further, none have identified the value assigned to such teacher preparation. This study uses an online survey to investigate the extent to which CALL has been incorporated as a component of language teacher education as well as the levels of satisfaction of those who receive this training as a part of language teacher preparation. Further, additional investigation through focus groups and individual interviews provides insight into what may contribute to the overall lack of CALL training. Finally, potential solutions for improvements based on these qualitative inquiries and personal observations will be explored. While this investigation was primarily concerned with training that occurs in North American

TESOL masters degree programs, it is likely that the findings are relevant to other degree programs as well as programs in other geographic areas.

Before discussing the present study, it is worth reviewing the literature for insight into what CALL training might entail. There has been wide support for teachers to learn to use technology over the past twenty years. The development of basic computer skills, such as keyboarding, mouse skills and working with menus, has been incorporated into many teacher training technology courses within colleges of education (NCATE 2004). Other skills identified as necessary for professional purposes include using software for record keeping, research, and maintaining electronic communication (Grau 1996). Familiarity with a variety of approaches to electronic communication, such as email, discussion boards and file sharing, are identified as contributing to successful collaboration with colleagues and mentors for pre-service and novice teachers. The ability to effectively use the Internet is also considered essential, and in particular the use of computer mediated communication (CMC) systems and course management systems (CMS) has been recognized as important in today's academic environment (Thomas, Clift, & Sugimoto 1996; Fotos & Browne 2004). Attention is also given to the development of more sophisticated skills, such as video teleconferencing and development of web-based materials. Some have acknowledged the proliferation of Weblogs, Chat and other forums as well as the general move to distance or distance enhanced learning (Son 2002). Daud (1992) insists that teachers understand that expectations should be reasonable. He suggested that many teachers new to the use of technology "expect the computer to handle all of their students' problems" (Daud 1992:69). There continues to be an attitude among the unprepared that the use of computers is either fully successful or fully unsuccessful.

While there are many important decisions surrounding the implementation of technology, decisions related to exactly what skills and software teachers are or should be learning in technology courses dominates much of the literature (Hargrave & Hsu 2000). Many have pointed out the importance of conducting technology training as part of language teacher preparation. Researchers have offered guidelines for those engaged in such training (Levy 1996; Hubbard 1996). While these guidelines share many characteristics, there are some distinctions worth noting. There is universal agreement that teachers must be able to evaluate materials. Chapelle (2001) identifies a method that may be used to evaluate CALL tasks, including aspects of theory and research, learner fit, meaning focus, authenticity, and practicality. Levy (1997) suggests that teachers need ongoing support to effectively implement, and appreciate, CALL. Chapelle and Hegelheimer (2004) recognize the need for teachers to be familiar with a variety of information regarding basic computer, hardware, software and lab operation in order to make informed decisions regarding CALL use. They also stress that teachers need to be aware of the variety of potential tasks and associated research. Kolaitis, Mahoney,

Pomann and Hubbard (this volume) address the variety of crucial issues related to learner training. Fotos and Browne (2004) identify the variety of language skills related to CALL use and training.

Why should we be concerned?

While these extensive guidelines have been suggested, there appears to be a lack *lack* of training within language teacher preparation. Some acknowledge that a variety of limitations make it impossible to truly incorporate everything in the short amount of time allowed for CALL (Hatasa 1999). It has been suggested that the greatest restriction on technology-enhanced instruction is the lack of adequate teacher training for such use (Butler-Pascoe 1995; Egbert & Thomas 2001). Clark and Gorski (2001) point out that teachers who have recently learned to use technology often use it in ways that detract from instruction. One of the predominant problems they observed is the inability to identify when *not* to use technology; when it would be more appropriate to rely on traditional techniques. For example, having students interact with one another in real time through web-based discussion boards when they are physically in the same location may complicate and detract from opportunities for authentic communication.

A general lack of technical skills has been identified among teachers who are both in the field and in training (Brinkerhoff, Ku, Glazewski, & Brush 2000; Burke 2000). Murray (1998) indicates that prior assessment will inform trainers of teacher technology courses. However, ranges are likely to be vast and complicate training procedures. Abdal-Haqq (1995) argues that the needs of teachers in training are often not met by the technology training programs due to the outdated nature of the technology they tend to utilize. In these courses students are likely to learn using older technologies and programs and therefore not be prepared to integrate newer technologies that would best serve their students' needs into their own classrooms.

In addition to recognizing the lack of access to newer technology, it has been *continued training* suggested that technology courses may not be sufficiently integrated into teacher preparation programs. Instructional technology cannot be treated as only part of a teacher preparation program, but must be ongoing in order to be successful (Northrup & Little 1996). Halttunen (2002) echoes this call for integration while adding that teachers also require ongoing retraining as new technologies and materials become available.

It has also been suggested that a sense of intimidation continues to be prevalent among users of technology who are not integrally motivated. Teachers who are not inclined to utilize technology often react negatively to situations which require them to do so (Egbert & Thomas 2001). It may seem obvious that our personal use of computers will positively influence our professional use of computers. However, the context and expectations may be quite distinct. This assumption would support the long held fallacy that any native speaker can teach grammar without explicitly studying grammar. Just like the teaching of grammar, the utilization of CALL requires an intimate and extensive knowledge of technology that is pedagogically focused and informed by the literature. Our knowledge and use of CALL should not rely solely on the skills we acquire as we dabble in personal use of the Web, email and online chatting.

Toward the end of the century trainers began to identify a growing potential for CALL. Many observed the effects of the introduction of CALL on the teachers' role in the classroom. Some suggested that automated "teacherless" CALL should serve as the ultimate ideal while others recognized a growing need to prepare teachers to utilize CALL most appropriately (Davies & Williamson 1998; Barnes 1997).

Jones (2001) suggests that CALL agendas are in many cases self destructive, relying so heavily on self-access and autonomy that the language community becomes alienated from the use of CALL. He makes anecdotal reference to language centers that barely function due to the lack of human intervention in the learning process. Consequently, he argues that CALL agendas realign themselves with the idea that teachers are needed to "drive the CALL process" (Jones 2001:365). The author goes on to conclude that it is not only the responsibility of researchers within the field of CALL, but also administrators and faculty that must act in a deliberate and inclusive manner to respond to this growing dilemma. Thus, teachers must be trained explicitly in CALL in order to be prepared to make important decisions regarding the manner of implementation. Davies and Williamson (1998) conversely argue that CALL needs to aspire to a goal in which a teaching and learning process is implicit and the teacher is "built in." They suggest that CALL serving as a medium of instruction is no more than an "Electronic Chalkboard." Ultimately, they suggest that teachers and developers should approach development not in terms of what a computer can do, but in terms of what a human can do. This dichotomy has existed since the introduction of CALL. However, researchers have yet to investigate the influence of these two camps on the development of new CALL professionals.

Another frequently addressed issue is the willingness of teachers to continue using technology in a pedagogic manner once training has ceased. Technology training programs often incorporate funding that allows participants to have access to resources for the duration of the course or some limited time that follows. Once these resources become unavailable the teachers often neglect to continue practicing the technology related skills they have learned (Butler-Pascoe 1995). It has been suggested that there is little impact of technology teacher training programs on how teachers think about and implement technology in the classroom (Cuban 1986; Feiman-Nemser & Remillard 1996). Research has suggested that teachers tend to practice very little of what they receive in technology training programs once they begin teaching unless they had already been technologically inclined prior to the technology training course. They are more likely to further their development by gathering information from colleagues than any other formal method of training (Egbert et al. 2002). Similarly, Galloway (1997) found that most teachers surveyed learned to use computers on their own or with the help of friends and colleagues outside of the classroom and not as a result of their formal training. In response, attempts have been made to identify potential alternative approaches to technology training.

While there may be many reasons that technology becomes unused or underused, access to resources is most often identified as the reason that technology for instruction remains unutilized. Resources include hardware, software, time and technical, emotional and curricular support (Egbert et al. 2002; Schrum 1999). Many attempts at introducing instructional technology into the curriculum involve making those resources necessary for the current project available to the participants; however, when the introductory project is complete the resources are no longer available, thus leaving the faculty in a position that discourages use of technology (Barnes 1997).

Perhaps the most widely recognized factor influencing access to technology is the digital divide. ESL communities, generally built on a multicultural model, are certainly subject to the negative impact of this phenomenon (Clark & Gorski 2001). While there is ongoing debate about the existence and state of the digital divide, it is important that teachers utilizing technology be aware of current conditions.

A number of barriers have also presented themselves in the specific context of CALL teacher preparation. Egbert et al. (2002) studied the use of CALL by teachers who had completed a CALL course. Teachers often continued to rely upon the skill and knowledge related to technology that they had acquired in their personal use. Despite being confident and capable with the technologies, teachers were not likely to implement these newly learned practices due to a number of other factors. These impediments included time, curricular and administrative restrictions as well as an insufficient amount of resources.

Joffe (2000) identifies myriad potentials for CALL practitioners to receive training through distance education. This context can increase the potential for interaction among cultures, thus providing language teachers with valuable cultural insight. She further suggests that participation in distance education as a teacher in training would positively enhance the teacher's ability to implement CALL in the classroom.

The aim of the current study is to begin to identify teachers' perceptions of CALL preparation and how such preparation may relate to practical usage. This preliminary study focused on two research questions: 1) How satisfied are teachers with the CALL preparation they receive? 2) What could be done to better prepare teachers for their professional use of CALL?

Methodology

This study consisted of three distinct components: survey, focus groups and interviews. This variety of collection techniques was chosen in an exploratory manner. Consequently, all three forms of information gathering were intentionally broad and preliminary in order to allow the path of inquiry and topics to arise that may have been unanticipated by the researcher (Patton 2002).

The 32 question survey (Appendix A) was available online between December 2003 and February 2004. The survey was completed by 240 graduates of North American TESOL master's degree programs. Since all of the participants have graduated from MA programs and taught language, they should all be familiar with the language teaching field in general and specifically familiar with the CALL related demands and experiences that may accompany the authentic teaching environment. Surveys were distributed through the NetTeach, TESL_CALL, CALICO and LLTI lists and collected through a web-based interface. Each of these lists functions as an informal means of communication among language teachers interested in CALL. This purposeful sampling of CALL-centric online communities should reveal insight about CALL training (Patton 2002). Due to this approach, however, it is impossible to determine the response rate. While this approach may have led to a skewed sample (namely, those on the lists who for whatever reason decided to respond), it was chosen to address a large group of specific CALL practitioners. Further, since these individuals are active in the use of CALL, they are more likely to have sought out training than others in the greater language teaching community. The questions addressed general satisfaction with CALL preparation, identification of successful types of CALL preparation, and open-ended opportunities to guide further inquiry.

In addition to this survey, a focus group was conducted to identify themes, trends and concerns of those involved in conducting CALL teacher training. While preliminary questions (Appendix B) helped direct the focus group, the structure emerged as the discussion progressed. The focus group included eighteen individuals who were all involved in CALL training. Fifteen were faculty at universities and the others taught at private language schools. The focus group was arranged as a discussion session at the 38th annual convention of TESOL in Long Beach, California, entitled, *What can we do to prepare better CALL practitioners?* The fifty-minute discussion allowed participants to share their experiences and perspectives regarding CALL teacher training as both trainers and trainees. An online

discussion forum was also created to extend this dialogue and six of the participants chose to continue to share information through this forum. All participants
were actively involved in CALL teacher preparation ranging from in-service and
workshop training to full courses.

The third form of information gathering involved interviews with TESOL
teacher trainers. Three individuals were chosen to represent three distinct TESOL
programs in different regions of the United States. These individuals shared their
perspectives about CALL as a component of their TESOL training programs. Appendix C presents the springboard questions that initiated these interviews. These
interviews revealed perceptions of a deficiency in CALL preparation as well as
potential causes of this deficiency. Themes for further exploration and potential
solutions to this perceived problem were also explored. The interviews were also
conducted at the 38th annual TESOL Convention. The results of these inquiries
are included in the discussion that follows the survey results.

Survey results

The results reveal a general dissatisfaction with, and lack of, CALL training. There
is also evidence that many have relied upon alternative sources of information for
their CALL preparation as has been noted by others (Robb, this volume). Finally it
appears that many have even engaged in formal training outside of their language
teacher preparation programs in order to compensate for this deficit.

Some respondents suggested that they had graduated (as one stated), "Before
CALL became in vogue," and therefore, some of the survey questions were inappropriate. These individuals began using technology for instruction between ten
and twenty years ago. It is worth noting that CALL preparation was already a matter of discussion and teacher preparation as early as the 1970s, albeit on a limited
scale (Delcloque 2000). Since the literature suggests that CALL preparation began
to be a fully recognized and significant component of teacher training in the early
1990s, the results of those who have taught for more than ten years were compared to those who have taught for less than ten years (unfortunately, the survey
did not ask for a specific graduation date). None of these resulted in a statistically
significant difference between the groups, so here the results are combined. Survey
results are described below.

In response to the prompt, *My Degree Program Taught Me To Effectively Teach
With Technology*, nearly 77% of respondents chose either somewhat ineffective
(25%) or extremely ineffective (52%). The other 23% felt that such preparation
was either somewhat (15%) or extremely effective (8%).

18% of respondents felt that the courses in technology for teaching they had
taken were always relevant to future teaching experience. The largest group, 43%,

Table 1. Technology related coursework in degree program

Number of courses	How many courses did you take in your degree program that focused on technology?	How many courses did you take in your degree program that involved any training for teaching with technology?	How many courses focused on using technology for teaching were required in your program?
0	56.7%	60.8%	79.2%
1–2	27.5%	25.9%	14.1%
3–4	5.0%	6.2%	1.7%
5–6	5.8%	2.7%	3.3%
7 or more	5.0%	4.4%	1.7%

Table 2. General perception of formal CALL training

	Would you have benefited from more instruction regarding teaching with technology?	Have you taken courses outside of your degree program to learn more about teaching with technology?
Yes	87.5%	91.7%
No	12.5%	8.3%

felt that these courses were sometimes relevant and 38% of all respondents felt that these courses were never relevant.

Similarly, respondents felt that the amount of time devoted to learning about CALL was deficient. 84% of all respondents agreed that the amount of time was either insufficient or extremely insufficient. 13% thought the amount of time was perfect and 2% thought it was either excessive or extremely excessive.

Table 1 presents the coursework of the respondents, and it is interesting to see a reflection of the general lack of coursework there. The most disconcerting results are reflected in the required CALL coursework. 79.2% were not required to take a course regarding teaching with technology while 56.7% took no classes that focused on technology. With 60.8% having never taken a course that involved any CALL preparation, it is no wonder that there is such reliance upon alternative forms of preparation.

The results presented in Table 2 suggest that those who claim that they would have benefited from more instruction have taken action to compensate for the inadequacy of their degree program preparation. Beyond the informal practices that are assumed to fill this gap, conventional technology courses also appear to serve as a means of further instruction in this area. Contrary to the assumptions that there is obviously more effective and extensive CALL training than in the past, these results indicate that it may only be expectations that have increased.

Table 3. CALL in the workplace

	Is the use of technology encouraged at your school?	Does your school offer incentives for teachers who use technology for teaching?	Does your school offer incentives for teachers who use technology who use technology who develop technology for teaching?
Always	43.8%	51.7%	41.7%
Sometimes	47.5%	43.3%	50.8%
Never	4.2%	5.0%	7.5%

The results in Table 3 further support the assumption that CALL is valued as a component with language teaching programs. This assumption does not appear to be supported by the majority of teacher training programs. Consequently, the proposed study is intended to determine the perceived importance of this type of training with such programs.

Again, these results support the assumption that CALL is valued as a component with language teaching programs, an assumption that does not appear to be supported by the majority of teacher training programs.

While it may be surprising to discover the lack of training that is apparent in this investigation, it is not surprising that many language teachers have found the wherewithal to become "self-trained" in CALL. It is also not surprising that the group of CALL practitioners surveyed appear to be extremely active. They identified the alternative means by which they obtain training, information and currency regarding CALL through both a set of predetermined selections as well as an open-ended question. It is difficult to determine the exact cause and effect relationship, but the lack of formal preparation and the reliance upon informal alternative sources definitely coexist. As Robb (this volume) elaborates, many have become reliant on alternative sources of information. A number of respondents indicated utilization of the following resources for their CALL preparation:

- Listservs (240)
- Professional Conferences (220)
- Web Sites (210)
- Colleagues (180)
- Journals (160)
- University Courses (145)
- University Libraries (140)
- Public Libraries (95)

It is certainly encouraging to see the extent to which these individuals are engaging in self-directed lifelong learning, but such supplemental reliance may not be effective without a foundation of CALL theory, methodology, principles and practices. While this dedication is certainly impressive, it is hardly the ideal. Technology related courses in departments of computer science are likely to be so technical that they are accessible to only a very select group of language teachers. This type of instruction is also likely to result in a greater rift between the CALL "experts" and others.

Focus group results

A focus group served as the second source of information for this study. According to members of the focus group, much of what seems to be taking place in the name of CALL teacher training would qualify as training in digital literacy. They claim that they are often charged with the task of training colleagues in basic computing skills and software to perform such common tasks as word processing, spreadsheet use and presentation preparation. While such tools can certainly serve an instructional purpose in the language classroom, this context is apparently not being presented to a majority of TESOL MA graduate students. It is worth noting that none of the members of the focus group recalled receiving significant CALL training in their formal teacher preparation.

Focus group participants recognized that while there are signs that more of this digital literacy oriented training is occurring within graduate programs (from what they see of recent graduates), such training is still predominantly done in an ad hoc or informal manner. In many cases it seems that attempts to introduce technologies such as course management systems are aimed at training for faculty across the university spectrum. These opportunities may enhance faculty awareness of resources, but do not allow for focus on the use of such tools with a language learning context.

Those in the focus group who have learned to develop materials using an authoring system complain that the focus has been solely on the system in question with little to no attention paid to the universality of such tasks. Learning universal skills can help us to prepare for future generations of software and solutions. The learning of such universal skills can also help to inform us about the decision-making processes in a CALL environment. The more familiar we are with available options and alternatives for CALL use, the better our decision-making will be. Therefore, focus group members agreed that CALL practitioners should be as comfortable and familiar with CALL materials as they are with traditional materials.

Many in the focus group also recognized a problem of contextualization. They felt that much of what occurs in ad hoc CALL training is not reinforced with pedagogic and linguistic support. For example, a collection of web-based resources may be presented as useful without much elaboration regarding the learner variables that may influence their appropriateness.

Most in the focus group were pleased that their CALL labs were being used on a regular basis. However, some complained that this use is generally limited to word processing tasks. Other forms of CALL are often overlooked or neglected.

Some in the focus group recognized a need for autonomous and self-directed learning. Consequently, they suggested that creating conditions which support such learning may be the most effective solution.

Finally, the focus group unanimously agreed that group CALL projects involving a broad cross-section of faculty are often the most successful approach to introducing CALL. Such situations have been recognized as contributing to a high quality of materials as well as an increased confidence and interest in CALL among faculty. Faculty who are less inclined to pursue the development or use of CALL materials on their own are often eager to work with others who can share their CALL expertise. Further, content experts often contribute in unexpected ways to such projects.

Interview results

Each of the three interviews, while brief and preliminary in nature, contributed to a better understanding of the lack of formalized CALL training. The interviews with coordinators of teacher preparation programs indicated that there is a general reluctance for faculty to engage in CALL training unless they identify themselves specifically as CALL specialists. None of the individuals interviewed considered themselves to be such a specialist. Statements such as, "CALL is out of my grasp" and "We don't have a specialist" dominated the interviews. While all of those interviewed felt confident using technology for their own purposes and felt essentially informed about CALL practices, none were willing to engage in CALL training. They felt that such training was out of their reach.

Further explanations regarding insufficient CALL training included: lack of funding to expand programs, too many other issues that require attention, and a widespread belief that those who are interested in CALL will simply "pick it up." Further, two of these representatives stated that although they would appreciate the addition of a CALL component, it was an unlikely addition in the near future. They wish that they would be able to offer CALL training since they seemed to consider it a positive recruiting tool. This apprehension for non-experts to engage in CALL preparation is evident at the language teaching level as well. In order for teachers to be able to effectively identify, select and integrate CALL materials, they must be comfortable with the materials in the same way they would be with traditional print materials. However, if only those who are highly motivated to learn about CALL are doing so, it is unlikely that CALL practice will become successfully integrated.

A follow-up study is currently being conducted to determine the value placed upon CALL as a component within TESOL masters programs. Further research could investigate specific aspects of CALL teacher training. As CALL teacher preparation is beginning to receive more attention, we are likely to see vast improvement in the deficiencies noted here. Investigation into the ongoing development of CALL teacher preparation would thus be beneficial.

What could we do better? Some recommendations

This investigation resulted in a number of recommendations for both preservice and inservice teacher training.

Involve a specialist

The ideal solution for a teacher education program would be to add a CALL specialist to your faculty. With the competitiveness of the language teacher training job market, it is certainly reasonable to require any new faculty member to have some preparation to serve as a CALL resource for a program. This does not require that such a person have specific training as a CALL specialist, but at least an inclination and background. Just as faculty often teach subjects peripheral to their expertise, CALL should be targeted as a professional area of focus. Language programs with CALL-competent faculty are often the envy of those without. When computer labs function smoothly, student and faculty fears are quelled and CALL operates as a supportive and appropriate component of the curriculum, all who are involved are more likely to appreciate CALL as an enhancement. When any of these factors are neglected, CALL continues to be viewed negatively.

At the teacher training level it is important that any introduction of CALL training that occurs must be integrated in the overall program. If it is not possible to establish dedicated CALL courses, an attempt should be made to establish some CALL component within methodology or pedagogy courses.

Involve all stakeholders

All teacher preparation faculty should be conscious of CALL practices to some degree just as all teacher preparation faculty should understand how to work with a variety of methodologies.

By involving, and preparing, all stakeholders in the decision-making process we are likely to experience a more successful and positive response to the use of

CALL. Make technology resources available to teachers in preparation. It would be wise to involve all stakeholders in the CALL activities of any language programs on your campus or in your community, providing them with information about any training in the local community as well as local and national conferences. It appears that many language teachers do not receive such opportunities until they are faced with technology related tasks.

Provide incentives

At the pre-service level it is important to inform future teachers of the importance of CALL within language instruction. Such incentives as heightened employment prospects can suffice. At the inservice level, we can offer release time, financial compensation and recognition.

Keep use relevant

Technology trainers may realize that alternative options best meet the needs and attitudes of some teachers in training. It may be necessary to utilize project-based learning within a school or department or establishment of collaborative team-work as a substitute for more formal classroom training. Further inquiry into the use of these alternative approaches may prove beneficial.

Those who are not completely confident in their technology use have often found it easy to dismiss CALL as the realm of gadgets and geeks, but it needn't be that way. As familiar as email and the Internet are these days, all educators should be familiar with a breadth of CALL activities. Most of today's CALL solutions require very little technology background in order to find success.

It is clear that CALL use is becoming more prevalent within language programs, particularly as programs gravitate toward the web. Teachers need to become more proficient in their understanding of CALL methodology, practices, history and possibilities. Decisions influencing CALL use should be informed by an understanding of pedagogy and technology and how the two merge. Further, teachers need to be willing to experiment with approaches to determine which may work best for the teachers they are training. Such decisions may be informed by further study of current and emerging instructional technology practices. Research into the perceived effectiveness of various CALL training methods and approaches is crucial to improving our understanding of how training may best be conducted. Such research will contribute to the establishment of best practices for all aspects of CALL implementation.

References

Abdal-Haqq, I. (1995). Infusing technology into pre-service teacher education. ERIC Digest 389699. Available at http://www.ed.gov/databases/ERIC_Digests/ed389699.html.

Barnes, S. (1997). Integrating technology and media into regular classrooms to facilitate inclusion: Preservice/inservice training of rural educators. ERIC Document Reproduction Service No ED406124I.

Brinkerhoff, J. D., Ku, H.Y., Glazewski, K., & Brush, T. (2001). An assessment of technology skills and classroom technology integration experience in preservice and practicing teachers. Paper presented at the Society for Information Technology & Teacher Education 2001, 12th International Conference 1866–1871. Norfolk, VA: Association for the Advancement of Computing in Education (AACE).

Burke, J. (2000). New directions – teacher technology standards. SREB Educational technology cooperative. Available at
http://www.sreb.org/programs/EdTech/pubs/NewDirections/NewDirections.pdf

Butler-Pascoe, M. (1995). A national survey of the integration of technology into TESOL master's programs. In D. Willis, B. Robin, & J. Willis (Eds.), *Technology and Teacher Education Annual* (pp. 98–101). Charlottesville, VA: Association for the Advancement of Computing in Education.

Chapelle, C. (2001). *Computer Applications in Second Language Acquisition.* Cambridge: CUP.

Chapelle, C. & Hegelheimer, V. (2004). The language teacher in the 21st century. In S. Fotos & C. Browne (Eds.), *New Perspectives on CALL for Second Language Classrooms* (pp. 297–313). Mahwah, NJ: Lawrence Erlbaum.

Clark, C. & Gorski, P. (2001). Multicultural education and the digital divide: Focus on race, language, socioeconomic class, sex, and disability. *Multicultural Perspectives, 3* (3), 39–44.

Cuban, L. (1986). *Teachers and Machines: The classroom use of technology since 1920.* New York, NY: Teachers College Press.

Daud, M. (1992). Issues in CALL implementation and its implications on teacher training. *CALICO Journal, 10* (1), 69–78.

Davies, T. & Williamson, R. (1998). The ghost in the machine: Are 'teacherless' CALL programs really possible? *Canadian Modern Language Review, 55* (1), 7–18.

Delcloque, P. (2000). The history of CALL. Available at http://www.history-of-call.org.

Egbert, J., Paulus, T., & Nakamichi, Y. (2002). The impact of CALL instruction on language classroom technology use: A foundation for rethinking CALL teacher education? *Language Learning and Technology, 6* (3), 108–126.

Egbert, J. & Thomas, M. (2001). The new frontier: A case study in applying instructional design for distance teacher education. *Journal of Technology and Teacher Education, 9* (3), 391–405.

Feiman-Nemser, S. & Remillard, J. (1996). Perspectives on learning to teach. In F. B. Murray (Ed.), *The Teacher Educator's Handbook: Building a knowledge base for the preparation of teachers* (pp. 63–91). San Francisco, CA: Jossey-Bass.

Fotos, S. & Browne, C. (2004). The development of CALL and current options. In S. Fotos & C. Browne (Eds.), *New Perspectives on CALL for Second Language Classrooms* (pp. 3–14). Mahwah, NJ: Lawrence Erlbaum.

Galloway, J. P. (1997). How teachers use and learn to use computers. In *Technology and Teacher Education Annual*, 857–859.

Grau, I. (1996). Teacher development in technology instruction: Does computer coursework transfer into actual teaching practice? Paper presented at the Annual Meeting of the Southwest Educational Research Association, Dallas, TX. (ERIC Document Reproduction Service No. ED394949)

Halttunen, L. G. (2002). Palomar College: A technological transformation. *Community College Journal, 73* (2), 26–31.

Hargrave, C. & Hsu, Y. (2000). Survey of instructional technology courses for pre-service teachers. *Journal of Technology and Teacher Education, 8* (4), 303–314.

Hatasa, K. (1999). Technological literacy for foreign language instructors and a web-based tutorial. In R. Debski & M. Levy (Eds.), *WORLDCALL: Global perspectives on computer-assisted language learning* (pp. 339–354). Lisse: Swets & Zeitlinger.

Hubbard, P. (1996). Elements of CALL methodology: Development, evaluation, and implementation. In M. Pennington (Ed.), *The Power of CALL* (pp. 15–32). Houston, TX: Athelstan.

Hubbard, P. (2004). Learner training for effective use of CALL. In S. Fotos & C. Browne (Eds.), *New Perspectives on CALL for Second Language Classrooms* (pp. 45–67). Mahwah, NJ: Lawrence Erlbaum.

Joffe, L. (2000). Getting connected: Online learning for the EFL professional. ERIC document number 447298.

Jones, J. (2001). CALL and the responsibilities of teachers and administrators. *ELT Journal, 55* (4), 360–367.

Kessler, G. (2005). Computer Assisted Language Learning Within Masters Programs for Teachers of English to Speakers of other Languages. PhD dissertation, Ohio University. Available at http://gregling.net/kessleretd.pdf.

Levy, M. (1996). A rationale for teacher education and CALL: The holistic view and its implications. *Computers and the Humanities, 30,* 293–302.

Levy, M. (1997). *Computer Assisted Language Learning: Context and conceptualization.* Oxford: Clarendon Press.

Murray, L. (1998). CALL and web training with teacher self-empowerment: A departmental and long-term approach. *Computers & Education, 31* (1), 17–23.

NCATE (2004). NCATE standards. Available at http://www.ncate.org/standards/.

Northrup, P. & Little, W. (1996). Establishing instructional technology benchmarks for teacher preparation programs. *Journal of Teacher Education, 47* (3), 213–222.

Patton, M. (2002). *Qualitative Research and Evaluation Methods.* London: Sage.

Son, J.-B. (2002). Online discussion in a CALL course for distance language teachers. *CALICO Journal, 20* (1), 127–144.

TESOL Career Center (March 22, 2006). Available at: http://www.vv-vv.com/tesol/R45975OR.cfm?A=List&SToken=93459913

Thomas, L., Clift, R. T., & Sugimoto, T. (1996). Telecommunication, student teaching, and methods instruction: An exploratory investigation. *Journal of Teacher Education, 47* (3), 165–174.

Warschauer, M. & Healey, D. (1998). Computers and language learning: An overview. *Language Teaching, 31,* 57–71. Available at http://www.gse.uci.edu/markw/overview.html.

APPENDIX A

Survey questions

1) How many years have you taught language?

    0–1
    2–5
    6–9
    10–15
    15 or more

2) In which of the following settings do you currently teach?

    (Choose Up To 5)
    Intensive English Program (in North America)
    Post Matriculation University Program (in North America)
    Language Program Overseas
    K-12
    Other

3) What language(s) are you currently teaching?

    (Choose Up To 8)
    English
    Spanish
    French
    German
    Russian
    Japanese
    Chinese
    Other

4) How many hours per week do you currently teach?

    0–5
    6–10
    11–15
    16–20
    21 or more

5) Is the use of technology for language instruction encouraged at your school?

    Always   Sometimes   Never

6) Does your school offer incentives for teachers who use technology for teaching?

    Always   Sometimes   Never

7) Does your school offer incentives for teachers who develop technology for instruction?

    Always   Sometimes   Never

8)   How long have you been using technology for teaching?

   0–1 year
   2–5 years
   6–10 years
   11–15 years
   16 or more years

9)   How confident do you feel using technology for instruction?

   Extremely confident
   Somewhat confident
   Not sure
   Somewhat unconfident
   Extremely unconfident

10)   Which is the highest degree you hold?

   PhD in Linguistics
   PhD in Modern Languages
   PhD in Education
   MA in Linguistics
   MA in Modern Languages
   MA in Education
   Other PhD
   Other MA
   BA
   Language teaching certificate

11)   To what extent did your degree program prepare you for teaching with technology?

   Very prepared
   Somewhat prepared
   Neutral
   Somewhat unprepared
   Very unprepared

12)   How many courses did you take in your degree program that focused on using technology for teaching?

   0
   1–2
   3–4
   5–6
   7 or more

13) How many courses did you take in your degree program that devoted more than 20% of the time to issues regarding teaching with technology?

    0
    1–2
    3–4
    5–6
    7 or more

14) How many courses did you take in your degree program that involved any training for teaching with technology?

    0
    1–2
    3–4
    5–6
    7

15) How many courses focusing on technology for teaching were required in your degree program?

    0
    1–2
    3–4
    5–6
    7 or more

16) My degree program taught me how to effectively teach with technology

    Strongly Agree
    Agree
    Disagree
    Strongly Disagree

17) How would you best finish this sentence? The extent of time devoted to learning about teaching with technology in my degree program was:

    Extremely excessive
    Excessive
    Perfect
    Insufficient
    Extremely insufficient

18) Do you feel you would have benefited from more instruction in your degree program regarding teaching with technology?

    Yes   No

19) The technology for teaching courses that I took were relevant to my future teaching experience:

    Always   Sometimes   Never

20) Have you taken classes or attended conference workshops outside of your degree program to gain more knowledge about using technology for teaching?

Yes   No

21) Do you feel that you are capable of keeping up with the rapid pace of technological growth?

Always   Sometimes   Never

22) How do you currently stay informed about CALL approaches, techniques and or methods?
23) Have you presented at professional conferences on topics related to CALL?

Yes   No

24) Which professional organizations do you belong to?
(Choose Up To 10)

CALICO
ISTE
MLA
TESOL
EUROCALL
IALL
IFETS
AACE
ACTFL
LLTI

25) What challenges do computers present for language instructors?
26) What is most promising about using technology for language instruction?
28) Why do you use technology for instruction?
29) What was your first experience using CALL as a teacher?
30) Which of the following do you utilize for your knowledge of CALL?
(Choose Up To 8)
Journals

Professional Conferences
Listservs
University Courses
Public Libraries
University Libraries
Colleagues
Web Sites

31) Would you mind answering follow up questions about CALL teacher training?

Yes   No

32) If you found any of the questions confusing, please comment on them here.

APPENDIX B

Questions for focus groups

What kind of CALL training did you receive as a graduate student?
What kind of training did you not receive that you believe you would have benefited from?
How have you attempted to stay informed of CALL?
What kind of training do you provide for your colleagues?
What barriers to CALL do you face in your current environments?
What kind of training do you dream of?

APPENDIX C

Interview Questions

What CALL training does your TESOL program offer?
What CALL training does your TESOL program require?
Do you believe that this is sufficient?
What technology for teaching skills would you like your graduates to have?
What concerns do you have about CALL regarding your graduates?
What do you think we can do to improve CALL training?

Preface to

Technology standards for teacher education, credentialing, and certification

The role of technology standards in teacher education and CALL is an important, but complex issue. It is important because technology standards help those involved in CALL to recognize distinct levels of proficiency and skill, and through explicit, shared guidelines, teacher education courses can make their learning goals and outcomes more explicit: this is of special importance with regard to formal accreditation. However, the role of technology standards may also be problematical because standards may suffer from being too prescriptive and narrowly defined, or alternatively, they may be too general and vague. Overly prescriptive standards can have a strong and detrimental impact on creativity in CALL and provoke a negative reaction because teachers and students feel their hands are tied whenever they want to try something new; on the other hand, standards that are too general and vague may provide so little direction that they are of no practical value. Like the temperature of the porridge in Goldilocks and the Three Bears, technology standards have to be "just right" to be acceptable. This chapter by Kathryn Murphy-Judy and Bonnie Youngs charts the path of technology standards in CALL in three geographical regions of the world. It begins by describing the history and development of standards in the United States as they relate to foreign-language education and technology. Particular quotations from the relevant standards documents help illuminate the discussion. Then three specific examples concerning the implementation of technology standards are given at three levels: at a university level in the United States; at a national level in Colombia, South America; and across the Common European Framework. These examples emphasize the importance of recognizing goals and contextual factors in developing technology standards.

Technology standards for teacher education, credentialing, and certification

Kathryn Murphy-Judy and Bonnie L. Youngs

Virginia Commonwealth University, USA / Carnegie Mellon University, USA

Introduction

Standards of learning and related assessments of learning outcomes are impacting education worldwide, from early childhood classrooms all the way to accomplished teacher certification. To ensure that teachers are able to guide their students to desired learning outcomes, commensurate standards for university teacher education programs, accreditation criteria, and processes for teacher preparation programs, in addition to state licensure for teachers, re-certification and national professional certification are being elaborated. In foreign language education, given the emphasis on communication and the opportunities for computer-assisted learning, technologies play an ever-increasing role in learning standards. Thus, appropriate and skillful integration of computer-assisted language learning (CALL) figures into the standards for teacher preparation and the institutions that educate, license, and re-certify teachers.

As new technologies continue to impact educational theories and practices, the technology standards for language learning and teaching are designed not to turn classrooms into a series of mass-produced, undifferentiating experiences, but rather offer "models to be followed" that are meant to promote creativity, individual expression, and critical thinking. In the learning standards described below (mainly sample learning scenarios and progress indicators), a variety of learner-centered experiences of CALL emerge that demand higher-order CALL knowledge and experience from the teachers in order to achieve the learning outcomes. The role of technology standards in teacher education and professional certification is explored in this chapter, first by tracing their development across the entire scope of foreign language teacher education in the United States. It expands to a comparison of three sets of standards for teacher education and technology on three different continents: in a U.S. public university; at the national level in Colombia, S.A; and across the transnational Common European Framework. All three examples underscore how "un-standardized" these standards are meant to be. Yet, even though the standards are leading toward better teaching and learning of foreign languages, and even though the technologies are more accessible and better integrated, a major problem still persists, at least in the United States.

The history and development of learner standards of foreign language education in the United States

The development of standards of learning has arisen from ever-improving educational theories, methods, and practices over the last century. A watershed moment in foreign language education in the United States occurred in the late twentieth century when emphasis shifted from learning about a language as a system to learning how to communicate. The pragmatic realignment of emphasis away from "what learners knew about" a language toward "what they could do with" the language (American Council on the Teaching of Foreign Languages Teacher Standards Writing Team 2002: 7) was paralleled in other disciplines like math and science. Concomitantly, emphasis shifted in assessment to showing evidence of successful performance.

By the early 1980s in the United States, however, a serious disconnect was apparent in the teaching-learning dyad. In 1977, President Jimmy Carter noted that he was "particularly concerned with the decline in foreign language and area studies in the U.S." when Senator Paul Simon brought it to his attention. He continued, noting that "[i]t appears that this decline is due to complex factors which cut across various economic, social, and educational issues." He therefore established the Commission on Foreign Languages and International Studies (Brod 1977). Dr. Richard Brod, addressing the Commission in October 1978, asked, "How can the educational process in foreign language study be converted from one that measures (and rewards) time spent to one that measures proficiency attained? What can be done to standardize the evaluation of student achievement in order to avoid loss of time and effort and motivation when students transfer from one educational level to another? How can such efforts toward standardization be applied to the preparation of foreign language teachers for schools and colleges?" (Brod 1979: 7). Although the change of guard from Carter to Reagan in 1980 slowed the momentum launched after the Commission Report, *Strength through Wisdom: A Critique of U.S. Capability. A Report to the President from the President's Commission on Foreign Language and International Studies* (November 1979), the move to create proficiency oriented testing continued and led eventually to the creation of national standards and performance indicators (Schulz 1981).

In 1983 the National Commission on Excellence in Education, under President Ronald Reagan, published the report, *A Nation at Risk*, in which U.S. national security was viewed as threatened by an increasingly mediocre educational system. Early in his office, President George Herbert Bush organized a national panel to address this perceived national threat to security. By 1991, the panel produced the *National Education Goals Report: Building a Nation of Learners*. From it and a related demand for accountability arose the standards movement (Marzano, 1998: 1–2).

One of the first steps toward standardization and accountability in language education came out of the collaboration of educators, the American Council on the Teaching of Foreign Languages (ACTFL), and government agencies, including the Interagency Language Roundtable (ILR). In 1986, they produced the first set of language proficiency guidelines. The ACTFL Proficiency Guidelines, a descriptive metric intended to guide proficiency in multiple languages, included listening, speaking, reading, and writing performance at four levels: Novice, Intermediate, Advanced, and Superior. After some ten years of reorienting the entire range of language education toward proficiency indicators and performance driven goals, objectives, and outcomes, the field moved toward the articulation of standards of learning. Concurrently, other disciplines, mathematics, science, social studies, and language arts, were producing their national standards within most of the fifty states. For foreign languages to maintain (and in some instances to fight for) their place in a standards driven arena, language educators needed to delineate clear, attainable, mutually agreed upon goals and learner outcomes. Endeavoring to produce learner standards from kindergarten through post-secondary education (K-16), the National Standards in Foreign Language Education Collaborative Project, a consortium of nine language associations endorsed by 46 state and national organizations, presented its *Standards for Foreign Language Learning: Preparing for the 21st Century* in 1996, and in 1999, the *K-16 Standards for Foreign Language Learning in the 21st Century*.

Learner and teacher education standards development vis-à-vis technology

All the major standards documents mention the role of new technologies in student learning. The ACTFL foreign language learning standards, for example, assume that "language and culture education … is tied to program models that incorporate effective strategies, assessment procedures, and technologies. …" (National Standards in Foreign Language Education Project 1999: 7). A sample Minitel Project (using the French telephone-informatic network called the Minitel) that depends heavily on Internet technology targets five standards and all the while

> ...exemplifies how technology facilitates language learning and plays a role in mo-
> tivating students to use the foreign language with peers. . . . What is clear is that
> technology will play a critical role in bringing native speakers and current infor-
> mation from the culture into the classroom.
>   (National Standards in Foreign Language Education Project 1999: 86–87)

In the elaboration of the framework for the communicative modes, technologically mediated communications, such as email (interpersonal), non-print and
recorded materials (interpretive), and presentational media, either implicitly or
explicitly indicate the use of new technologies (36–37). In the chapter on Standards
for Russian Language Learning, a Sample Progress Indicator includes "[s]tudents
use interactive technology (e.g., e-mail, interactive television links) to exchange
perspectives and opinions on a variety of topics of interest such as school, travel,
music, and politics" (National Standards in Foreign Language Education Project
1999: 400). The actual delineation of technology-specific standards, however, was
left to the National Education Technology Standards Project (NETS), the roots
of which are found in the work of the International Society for Technology in
Education (ISTE). Their work first produced learning standards germane to all educational levels and then quickly ratcheted up to teaching and teacher education
standards.

Yet, well in advance of the adoption of these many learning standards, foreign language educators who recognized the importance of kindergarten through
university programmatic coherence were focusing on teacher education. For example, before the 1999 adoption of the national standards, Gail Guntermann
(1993: 213–227) and June K. Phillips (1998: 5–6), among others, were noting that
teacher education candidates would need the advanced high proficiency level in
speaking, listening, and reading, and the advanced level in writing to be able to deliver the upper level standards driven curricula in the kindergarten through high
school (K-12) levels. Indeed, this movement can be observed as early as 1988 in
the ACTFL publication of the provisional *Program Guidelines for Foreign Language
Teacher Education*, which served post-secondary teacher education programs until
1998 when ACTFL joined with the National Council for Accreditation of Teacher
Education (NCATE). Specific to the role of technology in the field, in the 1997
ERIC Digest, "Professional Development of Foreign Language Teachers," Joy Peyton notes "[k]nowledge of the various technologies and how to integrate them
into their instruction" as essential for foreign language teachers (Peyton 1997). By
2004, the concerted efforts of ACTFL, NCATE, and ISTE led to a comprehensive
albeit separately articulated array of initial teacher preparation standards in which
new technologies play a significant role.

Teaching and teacher education standards

Teacher education from pre-service preparation through advanced professional development requirements is overseen by a variety of educational agencies in the United States. Each addresses technology standards. Beginning with the National Council for Accreditation of Teacher Education (NCATE), the agency that reviews the majority of U.S. teacher education programs, teacher preparation candidates are now required to have knowledge of the use and application of technology in foreign language classrooms. Additionally, a general knowledge of the field of second language acquisition (SLA) includes learning about research on the use of technology to teach and learn languages. Given the current state of many teacher preparation programs, it has become a distinctive challenge to prepare pre-service teachers and to provide ongoing professional development once they are in the field. ACTFL has worked diligently with other national groups to align teacher career preparation and continuing professional development opportunities, mindful of the integration of new technologies in the learner standards and the K-12 performance guidelines. For example, for pre-service teachers, the NCATE standards require a specific level of knowledge in order for candidates to obtain certification. Teacher preparation programs are re-vamping their curricula and assessments to re-align with these new standards, which were used for their program reviews beginning in 2004.

Thus NCATE, in collaboration with ACTFL, reviews teacher education programs with respect to teacher candidate preparation. These accreditation standards were once prescriptive but now emerge organically from each institution's own individualized and contextualized conceptual framework. The technology aspects of the standards, thus, guide rather than constrain. Teacher education programs are evaluated according to the *Program Standards for the Preparation of Foreign Language Teachers* (2002). The instructions state that teacher preparation programs must submit their reports based on relatively new guidelines intended for use for K-12 and secondary certification programs. Item 7 of the Standards document states that programs must provide: "Opportunities for candidates to experience technology-enhanced instruction and to use technology in their own teaching" (American Council on the Teaching of Foreign Languages Foreign Language Teacher Standards Writing Team 2002: 24). Additionally, technology use for personal professional development is included in these standards: "Candidates maintain and enhance their [language] proficiency by interacting in the target language outside of the classroom, reading, and using technology to access target language communities" and furthermore "[c]andidates learn about target language varieties through interaction with native speakers outside of class and by accessing authentic target language samples through a variety of means such as technology" (American Council on the Teaching of Foreign Languages Foreign Language Teacher Standards Writing Team 2002: 31, 35).

There are multiple examples of when, how, and how well teacher candidates are expected to use technology and technology-enhanced language learning in the teacher preparation standards document (American Council on the Teaching of Foreign Languages Foreign Language Teacher Standards Writing Team 2002: 24). The criteria for performance rating are: Approaches Standard, Meets Standard, Exceeds Standard. The three examples given here are at the level of "Meets Standard".

> Standard 2.b., "Candidates...enrich classroom content with texts and topics valued by the culture...taken from literature and other media" (39).

> Standard 4.b., "Candidates provide opportunities for their students to connect to target-language communities through a variety of means such as technology and authentic materials" (49).

> Standard 4.c., "Candidates use their knowledge of standards and curricular goals to evaluate, select, and design materials, including visuals, realia, authentic printed and oral materials, and other resources obtained through technology" (50).

It is expected that every graduate of an NCATE accredited teacher education program will attain the level of "Meets Standard" for almost all rubrics upon graduation.

The next stage in teacher preparation is licensing. The Interstate New Teacher Assessment and Support Consortium (INTASC) developed a document outlining requirements for teachers to obtain their licensure and recertification, again, with technology requirements. The document, *INTASC Standards for Licensing Beginning Foreign Language Teachers*, dovetails with the ACTFL standards document for teacher preparation (2002) in that the INTASC standards

> ...address foreign language teachers' knowledge of their content, and their ability to adapt instruction to individual learner diversity, create learning environments, use teaching strategies, foster communication, plan instruction, assess learners, function as reflective practitioners, and relate to the communities in which their schools are located.
> (American Council on the Teaching of Foreign Languages Foreign Language Teacher Standards Writing Team 2002: 16)

The ten core principles of INTASC align with the six standards of the ACTFL/ NCATE program standards, overlapping multiple times (American Council on the Teaching of Foreign Languages Foreign Language Teacher Standards Writing Team 2002: 17).

Principle #4 of the INTASC standards describes explicitly the need for teachers to "...base their instructional strategies on principles of language learning and can explain, in general terms, how their strategies relate to second language acquisition theories and research" (INTASC 2002:20). Addressing technology, this principle suggests that teachers

> ...provide learning experiences that encourage students to make inferences from a variety of materials and media resources... [they] incorporate technology into their instruction. They are familiar with educational applications of technology and can use technology as a tool to develop and assess language proficiency, cultural understanding, and critical thinking skills. Teachers know how to embed technology into instruction, prepare students for its use, and integrate it into their lessons and curriculum. They use technology appropriately to enhance instruction and/or conduct assessments including the use of the Internet and other multimedia applications.   (INTASC 2002:23)

The National Board for Professional Teaching Standards (NBPTS) targets teachers later in their professional career development. ACTFL, working with NBPTS, requires teachers to submit portfolios to become board certified, and once again, skillful manipulation and integration of technology is part of these board certification requirements. The rationale for board certification is to urge language teachers to become respected members of the teaching community. Indeed, foreign language teaching was one of the last content areas to post board certification standards. As with NCATE and INTASC, aligning the ACTFL teacher education standards with the NPBTS standards permits a longitudinal view of teacher professional development. The NBPTS lists five core propositions:

1. Teachers are committed to students and their learning.
2. Teachers know the subjects they teach and how to teach those subjects to students.
3. Teachers are responsible for managing and monitoring student learning.
4. Teachers think systematically about their practice and learn from experience.
5. Teachers are members of learning communities (NBPTS 2004:17–18).

Furthermore, the NBPTS standards elucidate the need for knowledge of second language acquisition theory:

> V. Knowledge of Language Acquisition: Accomplished teachers of world languages other than English are familiar with how students acquire competence in another language, understand varied methodologies and approaches used in the teaching and learning of languages, and draw on this knowledge to design instructional strategies appropriate to their instructional goals.   (NBPTS 2004)

not required

And, although there is no specific rubric for technology, examples abound for its uses. Under "Instructional Resources", one finds:

> Accomplished teachers expand their base of instructional resources by using technology to support sound teaching practices and to offer students opportunities to explore important ideas, concepts, and theories. For example, students at all levels

can use multimedia systems to create projects in the target language. Or, a teacher might use a foreign-language news broadcast as the basis for a lesson or lessons that could vary according to the language competence of the students.

(NBPTS 2004: 51)

The emphasis is on appropriate choice of materials to suit diverse learning needs and competent integration into a well-designed curriculum. The yearlong process of board certification costs dearly in both time and money. Yet, the portfolio performance assessment is rigorous and demonstrates a teacher's mastery of the content area, pedagogical acumen and prowess, and skilled integration of learning resources.

In this suite of standards, then, learning about second language acquisition theory and technology use is ensured by teacher preparation oversight agencies from the very beginning of a teacher's career to its culmination. While it is evident that many national organizations have shown their commitment to teacher development and career preparation, and while the use of technology is perhaps not as explicit as it could be, the many mentions of technology prove that teacher preparation programs must consider integrating into their curricula information regarding the use and application of technology to the teaching and learning of foreign languages, all resting solidly on second language acquisition theories. While teacher preparation programs cannot ignore teacher education standards for new and continuing teacher preparation, neither can a teacher ignore learner standards and use technology indiscriminately and still achieve certification, licensure, and board certification.

Standards: Technology and research initiatives

Two initiatives are worthy of mention here, as they relate to both learner and teacher standards development. First, the primary goal of the ISTE NETS Project is to enable stakeholders from preschool through high school to develop national standards for educational uses of technology that assist school improvement in the United States. The NETS Project defines standards for students, integrating curriculum technology, technology support, and standards for student assessment and evaluation of technology use. Obviously, its integration necessitates teachers prepared in technology use and capable of delivering the requisite learning to students.

The second initiative, the New Visions in Action project, was begun in 1998 by ACTFL and the National K-12 Foreign Language Resource Center (NFLRC) at Iowa State University. New Visions is an innovative series of goal areas that both involve and impact the entire academic foreign language community in the

United States. Four task forces were identified through an arduous process: foreign language teacher development; teacher retention and recruitment; curriculum, instruction, articulation, and assessment; and research. These four areas are intended to address key obstacles of foreign language education in the United States, develop the field of foreign language education, and allow a broader audience of learners to participate in the positive experience of foreign language education.

Additionally, all four areas relate to the discussion of teacher candidate preparation. The research task force aligns closely with the idea that teachers are researchers, and that at their core, teachers who are trained, perhaps in Action Research, can be their own advocates as they explore different teaching techniques and assess the learning of their students, noted explicitly for example, in the IN-TASC Standards document regarding teachers as "reflective practitioners" and the NBPTS Principle #4, above. Further advantages to this focus on research will be quantitative studies intended to educate publics and governments about the positive impact of learning foreign languages. If teachers learn to reflect critically on their own teaching, following the required path encouraged by NCATE, INTASC, and NBPTS, then throughout their careers, they will remain informed advocates of foreign language learning. Furthermore, with respect to technology, teachers who are better able to review and assess teaching and learning via technology will continue to grow not only in the field, but be able to grow the field as well, leading to more and better uses of technology in the foreign language classroom.

Standards in action: Three models

In this section, three examples of technology standards in foreign language teacher education are presented. The first occurs in a major U.S. public university that juggles issues of local autonomy with national oversight, across some five educational and professional agencies. The second is the top down standardization articulated and overseen by the national Ministerio de Educación of Colombia, S.A. The third is the necessarily non-prescriptive Common European Framework from the Council of Europe that offers a menu of suggested strategies to negotiate the cultural and linguistic pluralities of its many member nations.

An American University

Virginia Commonwealth University (VCU) is a large, urban institution of 28,000 students (as of 2004) located in Richmond Virginia. VCU is the largest producer of teachers in central Virginia and its School of Education ranks in the top fifty nationwide in teacher education. The School of World Studies is home to majors in French, German, and Spanish, and minors in Italian and Latin. VCU underwent a university-wide Southern Association of Colleges and Schools (SACS) accreditation review in 2004 and will undergo its NCATE accreditation review in the School of Education (SOE) in 2006. Thus, a climate of teaching and learning standards and assessment currently permeates the university. Other local factors that tie into the climate of standards and specifically the role of technologies are the long-standing Virginia standards for foreign languages, codified in 2000; the current LinguaFolio Project led by the Virginia Department of Education; and the Henrico County Public Schools Computer Initiative whereby every secondary student uses a laptop for learning.

For the 2006 NCATE review, the division of Teaching and Learning of the SOE has produced its new conceptual framework, revising the 2001 framework, "Teacher as Decision Maker" to that of the "Educator as Critically Reflective Practitioner." To respond to the NCATE expectation of evidence of a commitment to technology (www.ncate.org/standard/unit_stds/ch2.htm), the VCU document states:

> Candidates are expected to be able to utilize technology with students in whatever ways are appropriate to their roles. As evidenced in class syllabi, most course work within programs has technological components or assignments and several classes are offered in part or wholly on line.

Technology is also viewed as an important tool in ensuring the support of diverse student learning and as a mechanism for motivating learning for all students (Section 3, p. 6).

In its clinical evaluation instrument, one of the rubrics under "Planning for Instruction" is "Uses instructional strategies, resources, and technologies to make learning accessible for all students," for which reaching the target means that the student teacher "[u]ses multiple instructional strategies, resources, and technologies in units of instruction that promote student understanding for all students" (3). Minimal revamping of the required "Methods of Teaching Foreign Languages" course (TEDU 543) will be needed to support the technology expectations as it was originally designed by a CALL expert.

Although VCU benefits from a somewhat unique situation technologically, difficulties in teacher preparation arise elsewhere, for the largest problem in the United States in the creation, deployment, and assessment of language and technology standards is not the availability of hardware, software, and trainer expertise, but rather, the level of linguistic proficiency of the teaching corps. This problem harkens back to former President Carter's recognition of the lamentable state of foreign language acquisition in the United States. The challenges of aligning federal and state regulations notwithstanding, perhaps the single most determining factor is that of ensuring that college graduates attain the requisite linguistic proficiency levels necessary for language teaching. Standards and federal laws will not suffice as long as foreign language education is touted as core but treated as ancillary.

Still, communication technologies and media may actually prove the inroad to facilitate contact with languages other than English, as U.S. young people freely and willingly cross language borders. The Center for Applied Linguistics (CAL) digest article "What We Can Learn From Foreign Language Teaching In Other Countries" (Pufahl, Rhodes, & Christian 2001) underscores the efficacy of this direction. Besides recognizing the importance of early language learning in public education, the report notes that many countries (notably Canada, Denmark, and Thailand) support the comprehensive use of new technologies in the classroom. Access to information and entertainment, and interaction and collaboration with native speakers and their cultures are the two highlighted facets of technological intervention. The media are later connected to "project-oriented learning that emphasizes the use of authentic materials through technology." The article cites two important lessons to be learned:

- identifying how technology can improve language instruction. A major question remains about how successful technology is in improving foreign language instruction. We need specific research on how technology can best be used to increase students' proficiency in other languages.
- improving teacher education. The United States needs to conduct a more in-depth investigation into how some countries are recruiting high-caliber students into teaching and providing top quality in-service and pre-service training.

It is to be hoped that the standards movement will facilitate the United States' move toward more and better linguistic and cultural competencies. Yet, it is the information technologies that have the greater potential, at this time, for facilitating them.

Colombia, South America

The importance of this example is the national, top-down priority given to linguistic multi-competence and information technologies. Colombia is a country whose government promotes foreign language education, and despite long-standing economic, political, and social difficulties, the Colombian government has had a national policy of bilingual education for over a decade. It had, in fact, tied language education to technological media in its 1997 policy, *Bilinguïsmo y Nuevas Tecnologías*. Today, the standards for teacher education are fully elaborated and the national website is ready to enter data from assessments. As far as technology and language education are concerned, the Ministry of Education includes an entire website space on these topics, notably its *Serie lineamientos curriculares*,

Idiomas Extranjeros: Las Nuevas Tecnologías en el Currículo de Lenguas Extranjeras.
The document explains the "new world order" in relation to language and technology and the implications for education (i.e., the impact of European educational systems on the modernization and globalization of Colombia's mass education), providing three sections on teacher technological competencies needed to educate in this environment, the major foci of which are reading hypertexts and the use of televisuals. Much is made of self-actuated learning through progressive CALL programs, undoubtedly in light of the purchase and implementation of *English Discoveries* software for all English as a Foreign Language (EFL) classrooms nationwide, begun in 1998. It was expected that the program would serve first to improve educators' language and soon after they would teach using the multimedia software. The use of technologies is coalesced with more or less constructivist notions of language learning and acquisition with the final and most fully articulated section on the use of televisuals (*Televisión: Usos Didácticos*).

Since the late 1990s, many public and private agencies have promoted teacher education in language and technologies. Nearly all the major universities' foreign language departments hold conferences and workshops (e.g., Universidad Javeriana, Universidad de Cauca, Universidad Autónoma de Bucaramanga, among many others), as do the Fulbright office in Bogotá, the Conexiones group in Medellín (EAFIT University), ICETEX, the Institutos Colombo-Americano, textbook companies from Europe and the United States, and the British Council, to name but a few. These endeavors continue across the entire country as more and more schools receive hardware, software, and most importantly teacher training in CALL. The national priority given to foreign language education is validated and supported by technology and teacher training resources.

The European Union

The Council of Europe has articulated its Common European Framework, the goal of which is a plurilingual and interculturally adept European Union (E.U.). Part of its mission is:

> (F17) To take such steps as are necessary to complete the establishment of an effective European system of information exchange covering all aspects of language learning, teaching and research, and making full use of information technology. (2)

The framework offers an open and flexible menu of learning and teaching goals in order to suit the wide variety of E.U. realities and needs. Still, throughout the document, there are many references to new media and technologies as part of the common European present and future educational arenas. For example, learner goals make frequent mention of information technologies:

4.4.3.2 Written interaction
Interaction through the medium of written language includes such activities as:

– passing and exchanging notes, memos, etc. when spoken interaction is impossible and inappropriate;
– correspondence by letter, fax, e-mail, etc.;
– negotiating the text of agreements, contracts, communiqués, etc. by re-formulating and exchanging drafts, amendments, proof corrections, etc.;
– participating in on-line or off-line computer conferences. (82)

4.4.3.3 Face-to-face interaction may of course involve a mixture of media: spoken, written, audio-visual, paralinguistic (see section 4.4.5.2) and para-textual (see 4.4.5.3). (82)

4.4.3.4 With the increasing sophistication of computer software, interactive man-machine communication is coming to play an ever more important part in the public, occupational, educational and even personal domains. (82)

As part of the learner "ability to learn" one notes:

Skills and know-how: e.g. facility in using a dictionary or being able to find one's way easily around a documentation centre; knowing how to manipulate audiovisual or computer media (e.g. the Internet) as learning resources. (12)

Teachers, therefore, are asked to reflect on :

6.4.2.4 What use can and should be made of instructional media (audio and video cassettes, computers, etc.)?
a. none;
b. for whole-class demonstrations, repetitions, etc.;
c. in a language/video/computer laboratory mode;
d. in an individual self-instructional mode;
e. as a basis for group work (discussion, negotiation, co-operative and com-petitive games, etc.);
f. in international computer networking of schools, classes and individual students. (145)

Although the framework avoids dictating any specific technology standards, the document is infused with references to technologies: radio, television, tapes, film, email, CDs, and other digital and networked media. Since each country has sovereignty over its educational system and teacher preparation, the framework tends rather to let the common reference levels for outcome-based proficiency assessments guide toward valid and meaningful criteria across all borders.

The Council also offers the Portfolio and its related Passport:

> The European Language Portfolio is a document in which those who are learning or have learned a language – whether at school or outside school – can record and reflect on their language learning and cultural experiences.
>
> The portfolio contains a language passport which its owner regularly updates. A grid is provided where his/her language competences can be described according to common criteria accepted throughout Europe and which can serve as a complement to customary certificates. The document also contains a detailed language biography describing the owner's experiences in each language and which is designed to guide the learner in planning and assessing progress. Finally, there is a dossier where examples of personal work can be kept to illustrate one's language competences.

What is especially important in this Portfolio and Passport program is its very delivery through the website of the Council of Europe. It also offers a guide for teachers and teacher trainers, and provides standards of learning and teaching languages that will eventually facilitate, sometimes technologically, the flow of trans-European Union communications and communicators.

Conclusion

Learner and teacher education standards have become the norm in public education in the United States and beyond. Although the United States may be a global forerunner in developing and applying standards and integrating new technologies into the equation, it lags woefully behind in articulating a national policy on the need and support of foreign language education. Other countries, like Colombia, and transnational unions, like the Council of Europe, are openly committed to plurilingualism and interculturality. U.S. language educators and associations have made herculean efforts to bring the educational system linguistically and culturally into the global 21st century, but without top-down support and valorization, their success will continue to be limited. It is to be hoped that the 2005 Year of Languages momentum in the United States will have finally produced a national language policy to support and foster foreign language learning for its citizenry.

Yet, while waiting for a U.S. national policy and the eventual spread of improved communication skills and understanding worldwide, educators around the world must keep endeavoring to share knowledge and best practices. Current technology practitioners familiar with the how and why of technology can advocate for foreign language and technology learning and teaching standards. By making the standards outcomes explicit, we can advance assistive technological skills and integrative strategies. Part of this work includes designing professional presentations, courses, workshops, and articles around the learner and teacher preparation standards. Providing information to new and continuing teachers, encouraging our colleagues to support and adhere to standards in our foreign language classrooms, all of this will only enhance our opportunities to improve the state of foreign language education in our respective countries.

References

American Council on the Teaching of Foreign Languages (1988). *Program Guidelines for Foreign Language Teacher Education.* Yonkers, NY: ACTFL.

American Council on the Teaching of Foreign Languages Foreign Language Teacher Standards Writing Team (2002). *Program Standards for the Preparation of Foreign Language Teachers (Initial Level-Undergraduate & Graduate) (For K-12 and Secondary Certification Programs).* Yonkers, NY: ACTFL.

Brod, R. I. (1977). Back page: Presidential Commission on Language and Area Studies. *ADFL Bulletin, 9* (1), 50.

Brod, R. I. (1979). Strengthening language instruction in the United States. *ADFL Bulletin, 10* (3), 7–8.

Commission on Foreign Languages and International Studies (1980). Strength through wisdom: A critique of U.S. capability. A Report to the President from the President's Commission on Foreign Language and International Studies, November 1979. *Modern Language Journal, 64* 9–57.

Council of Europe. *Common European Framework.* Available at www.culture2.coe.int/portfolio/documents/0521803136txt.pdf.

Council of Europe. *The Portfolio and its Related Passport.* Available at www.culture2.coe.int/portfolio.

Council of Europe. *Teachers and Trainers Guide.* Available at www.culture2.coe.int/portfolio//documents/ELPguide_teacherstrainers.pdf.

Division of Teaching and Learning, School of Education, Virginia Commonwealth University (2004). *The Educator as Critically Reflective Practitioner: NCATE continuing accreditation resource manual.* Richmond, VA: In-house manual.

Guntermann, G. (Ed.). (1993). *Developing Language Teachers for a Changing World.* In the *ACTFL Foreign Language Education Series.* Lincolnwood, IL: National Textbook Co.

Henrico County Public Schools I-book Initiative. Available at http://www.henrico.k12.va.us/iBook/.

Interstate New Teacher Assessment and Support Consortium (INTASC). (2002). *Model Standards for Licensing Beginning Foreign Language Teachers: A resource for state dialogue.* Washington, DC: Council of Chief State School Officers. Available at http://www.ccsso.org/projects/interstate_new_teacher_assessment_and_support_consortium/Projects/Standards_Development/.

International Society for Technology in Education (ISTE) -NETS website. NETS project main page. Available at http://cnets.iste.org/nets_overview.html.

International Society for Technology in Education (ISTE) -NETS website. *Educational Technology Standards and Performance Indicators for All Teachers.* Available at http://cnets.iste.org/teachers/t_stands.html.

Marzano, R. J. (December 1998). *Models of Standards Implementations: Implications for the classroom.* Washington, DC: Office of Educational Research and Improvement report. *ERIC* ED 427 088.

Ministry of Education, Colombia, South America. Available at http://www.mineducacion. gov.co/proyectos_men/REPORTE_GRAFICA/repo_grafi.asp?codi_poli=3&codi_proy=239.

Ministry of Education, Colombia, South America, *Serie lineamientos curriculares, Idiomas Extranjeros, "Las Nuevas Tecnologías en el Currículo de Lenguas Extranjeras."* Available at http://www.mineducacion.gov.co/index2.html.

National Board for Professional Teaching Standards (NBPTS). (2004). *World Languages Other Than English Standards.* Available at http://www.nbpts.org/standards/stdsoverviews.cfm.

National Commission on Excellence in Education (April 1983). *A Nation at Risk: The imperative for educational reform.* Available at http://www.ed.gov/pubs/ NatAtRisk/index.html.

National Education Goals Panel (1992). *National Education Goals Report: Building a nation of learners.* Available at http://www.negp.gov/reports/99rpt.pdf.

National Education Technology Standards (NETS). Available at http://nets.org.

National K-12 Standards for Foreign Language Education Project (1996). *Standards for Foreign Language Learning: Preparing for the 21st century.* Yonkers, NY: ACTFL.

National Standards in Foreign Language Education Project (1999). *Standards for Foreign Language Learning in the 21st Century.* Yonkers, NY: ACTFL.

NCATE (2004). *Program Guidelines for Foreign Language Teacher Education.* Available at http://www.NCATE.org.

New Visions in Action. ACTFL. Available at http://www.actfl.org.

Peyton, J. K. (1997). Professional development of foreign language teachers. *ERIC Digest* ED 414768.

Phillips, J. K. (1998). Changing teacher/learner roles in standards-driven contexts. In J. Harper, M. Lively, & M. Williams (Eds.), *The Coming of Age of the Profession: Issues and emerging ideas for the teaching of foreign languages.* Boston, MA: Heinle & Heinle.

Pufahl, I., Rhodes N. C., & Christian, D. (September 2001). What we can learn from foreign language teaching in other countries. In *CAL Digests*, available at http://www. cal.org/resources/digest/0106pufahl.html.

Schulz, Renate A. (1981). Searching for life after death: In the aftermath of the President's Commission on Foreign Language and International Studies. *ADFL Bulletin, 13* (1), 1–6.

Teacher Education Accreditation Council, U.S. Department of Education. Available at http://www.TEAC.org.

Virginia Department of Education. *Foreign Language Standards of Learning.* Available at http://www.pen.k12.va.us/VDOE/Instruction/Language/#flsol.

Virginia Department of Education, LinguaFolio Project. Available at http://www.pen.k12. va.us/VDOE/Instruction/Language/linguafolio/index.shtml.

Part II

CALL degree programs

Preface to

Matching language and IT skills
The life-cycle of an MA programme

At first glance it may appear unusual to read about the rise *and fall* of an MA program focusing on CALL. Surely, if a program could not be continued, it must be for good reasons – insufficient students, lack of qualified staff, shifting priorities in the educational environment; and perhaps there is little to be gained by dwelling on such facts. In this chapter John Partridge amply demonstrates this is not the case, and that there is much to be learnt by recording the history of a CALL program. Further, the telling of this story re-emphasises the critical importance of teacher educators in CALL. Without those who are properly trained as CALL specialists, we are going to be ill-prepared to serve the next generation of language teachers who need to be able to handle new technologies with skill and confidence. We can learn much from experienced CALL practitioners who have had sustained and in-depth experience in the planning and teaching of CALL courses and programs, for example a deeper understanding of the many roles that technology can play, the ways in which CALL might be presented to match the needs of students with different backgrounds, experience and goals, and the importance of financial aspects and forward-planning. Also, it is worth remembering that though a course or program may cease, the students go on, and the benefits of good training may continue to be felt into the future as graduates pass on their knowledge and expertise to others. In sum, this chapter offers much wisdom and practical advice to all those who are involved in teacher education and CALL.

Matching language and IT skills

The life-cycle of an MA programme

John Partridge
University of Kent, England

Introduction

The MA in Applied Language Studies: Computing (ALS:C) ran successfully at the University of Kent from 1993 to 2002. It was forced to terminate not because of any endemic fault or a failure to recruit but because of the attrition of appropriately qualified staff, to a great extent as a result of financial strictures and early retirement. Over nine years some 60 to 70 graduates from a wide range of nationalities enhanced their careers in the language-teaching profession, embarked on careers in FL materials design, IT management, website design, film-subtitling, and lexicography, to give a representative sample, and/or went on to study for doctorates in educational technology and applied linguistics.

CALL was formally instituted at the University of Kent in 1989 in the form of a small dedicated self-access computer lab (for brief accounts see Shaw 1991, 1992), but it soon became evident that possession of equipment was not the automatic solution to all the problems of language-learning and language-teaching, nor would it cheaply replace language teaching staff, popularly but erroneously perceived to be expensive. To be effective in the area, teachers need to keep up with the capacities of the new technology, not necessarily as programmers, but as practitioners competent in its practical application. Then as now there was a need for a formalised body of training information to ensure continuity of supply of practitioners capable of exploiting the benefits of IT for language purposes. Linguists needed an insight into the workings and products of IT to complement their linguistic and pedagogical skills. This chapter covers the development of such a course of study, paying special attention to areas of component courses, the financial metric, staffing, equipment, and technical support, offering insights into problems experienced and possible solutions.

Rationale

The programme was conceived as a realistic and practical hands-on course of study in applications, to supplement languages graduates' knowledge of their chosen language with the advantages offered by information technology and to advance the languages/IT synergy. Whilst neither a course in pedagogy nor offering a pedagogical qualification, it would offer career progression in language teaching and open up opportunities in other areas, e.g., language software creation, network design and management, website design and management. It would encourage individual and team work in research and development. The average eight hours per week of formal instruction over 24 weeks would be supplemented by at least 32 hours hands-on work per week. Although, not surprisingly, reviews showed the need for periodic revisions, it was consistently successful in all of these areas.

Target group and entry qualifications

The target group of potential students were in-service graduate language teachers seconded by their school or educational authority, translators or linguists seeking to broaden their professional horizons, or language practitioners with appropriate professional experience. They would not necessarily be drawn primarily from English native speakers – over the years students came from Cyprus, France, Germany, Greece, Ireland, Italy, Japan, Spain, Taiwan and Thailand as well as the UK, Canada and Ireland – although with English as the *lingua franca* it was imperative that all applicants had a strong command of both spoken and written English. It was also strongly recommended that students should in addition to their chosen degree language have a good command of at least one European language other than English, as the expertise of the teaching staff centred mainly round Dutch, French, German, Italian, Russian and Spanish. This proved somewhat difficult for candidates from Asia, who struggled at times with example material, but ultimately acquitted themselves well. These criteria came to vary sometimes according to candidates' individual strengths. The age profile dropped rapidly as employers became increasingly reluctant to second their employees and the tendency was for students to be self-financing, applying for a place immediately after taking their first degree or after relatively few years in employment.

Candidates were assumed to have no previous experience or ability in IT, and all initial IT-based modules were designed on this basis. From the outset it was stressed that this was a course in applications and that an IT background was not essential for those wishing to exploit rather than create technology. Indeed, candidates with IT qualifications were discouraged from applying unless they had a very strong language commitment.

Concept of CALL

From the beginning a deliberately wide concept of CALL was adopted (see Levy 1997), one envisaging a holistic attitude to language learning. The approach was not restricted to 'classical' dedicated CALL programs of various kinds, such as multiple choice questions, cloze exercises, true-false and comprehension questions, and drag-and-drop exercises; these programs tend in many ways to replicate and automate practices which can be performed, more arduously, with pen and paper. Instead the totality of the experience was to include such traditional language skills and applications as translation, interpreting and linguistic analysis, and also to employ the mundane yet inherently linguistic aspects of office technology: word-processing, e-mail, and language tools (fonts, grammar- and spell-checkers, thesauri, etc.). Their use for the linguist was to be practically evaluated, as were the potentials and the practicalities of a dedicated CALL lab. Those working within a language professional's framework, it was felt, should have an insight into how language processing is performed by machines, so as to be able to give realistic, realisable computational tasks to the programmers translating their materials into applications, or at least so as to be able to discuss them. As the majority of incoming students came from mainly literary backgrounds, this also included an introduction into linguistic methodology and typology. Constituents of CALL would thus be viewed evaluatively from the outside, and productively from the inside.

The teaching team

The original teaching team began with the explicit intention of combining the insights of linguists and language practitioners with the techniques and resources of IT specialists in a concrete, practical, realistic and meaningful way. From the start it was agreed that this was an essentially non-technical humanities project which would only draw on the technical expertise of Computing staff when it could not provide it itself.

The main core were teachers of languages (EFL, French, German, Italian, Russian and Spanish with a few fortuitous admixtures, including Breton, Dutch, Japanese and Swahili) and/or linguistics. IT knowledge and background varied widely. A leading member of the team was a specialist in the French Renaissance and a skilled programmer with expertise in creating bibliographical databases and CALL programs. Another was a Hispanist who later wrote the Spanish CALL program *¡Escuchame!*. One member of the team was a Germanist specialising in language teaching methodology and the application of CALL; another, the course director, a Germanist theoretical linguist with some IT training. Other team members had basic word-processing and e-mailing skills including one, a loudly self-professed technophobe, who was committed to advancing the cause of languages. A limited amount of technical teaching was brought in from Computing: this included a whole desktop publishing course (quickly dropped), principles of networks, and natural language processing. Later, a member of the Computing staff, a graduate in German and French with a postgraduate qualification in translation retrained in computing, came in to teach natural language processing through PROLOG and authoring in *Macromedia Director*. As the embodiment of the combination of IT and languages, she proved an ideal member of the team. We also had the advantage of having as external examiner a prestigious CALL expert, now an ex-president of EUROCALL. Essential to the whole enterprise were our two highly skilled, helpful and resourceful laboratory technicians.

It became increasingly clear that the strength of the team as a whole lay in its diversity. Each step of the process of staff attrition meant a diminution of expertise which could not be resolved by the remainder of the teaching team taking over where departing members had left off, and the end came when the whole programme depended ultimately on one person (the author).

The planning process and its outcome

A number of factors decisively influenced the planning of the programme:

a) the idealistic, as sketched above: the wish to create a course to combine the skills and insights of the worlds of languages and IT;
b) the material: possessing almost by chance a CALL lab and the need to exploit it productively and imaginatively;
c) the mercenary: the advantages in terms of income and prestige of running a unique graduate course with perceptible future prospects;
d) serendipity: the presence in the same place of a number of like-minded individuals; and
e) luck: the fortunate constellation of the foregoing factors and the chance meeting between an until then unenthusiastic Vice-Chancellor and a Minister of Education extolling the use of IT in the humanities, which led to the establishment of the first lab.

As a result of these factors a one-year programme (see Table 1) emerged, consisting of eight one-unit modules taught over two terms and a two-unit dissertation module extending over the third (summer) term and the long summer vacation; all elements were compulsory,

Thought had further to be given to recruitment strategies: an original advertisement through the Linguist List elicited a response from the British Council, which gave support by supplying CALL-related literature surplus to its own requirements and including the degree programme in its circulations; UKC's Inter-

Table 1. The original format of the programme: Note that the coursework element had to be passed before proceeding to the project/dissertation

Module	Term	Units
Software Evaluation 1: CALL	winter	1
Software Evaluation 2: Translation	winter	1
Utilities 1	winter	1
Description of English	winter	1
Desktop Publishing	spring	1
Software Design and Implementation	spring	1
NLP and Language Typology	spring	1
Utilities 2	spring	1
Project/Dissertation	summer + long vacation	2
	(total)	10

national Office was also particularly useful for recruiting in Greece and the Far East. EU-sponsored ERASMUS-Socrates exchange relations with other European universities were also instrumental in attracting candidates. Advertisements placed in graduate employment journals and similar media did not prove particularly productive. However, publicity is critical for such programs, and time and money invested in careful design and presentation is well spent.

Components and contents of the programme

Principles and practices

Work in the first term was primarily evaluative, to establish critical principles and practices. After demonstrations of various types of software, students were required to perform their own hands-on analysis, to be researched, implemented, written up and presented, with the stress on how any given software could be employed in the language context, even though maybe not specifically designed for it. The Term 2 course *Software Design and Implementation* built on the insights of these evaluation courses, with students creating their own programs using an authoring application.

Software Evaluation 1: CALL
In this course students were given a generic introduction to CALL programs, e.g., cloze, mazes, true/false questions, multiple choice questions, etc. They were then required to evaluate and write critical reports on CALL programs held in house or available elsewhere, after creating exercises for themselves (see Hubbard 1987, 1988). These were then marked as part of the assessment procedure on the basis of their stated purpose and their success in achieving it. At first this was done purely

in the form of a written paper, but at a later stage, with an increasing attrition rate amongst teaching staff, students were required to give a presentation using exercises they had created themselves using commercial or downloaded programs, as well as submitting a written report. Besides being more economical with staff time, this had the advantages of making students design exercises with a stated purpose and evaluate their own as well as the program's efficiency. They also developed presentational skills which were adopted for Software Evaluation 2. In addition, at a later stage, from the later 1990s onwards, students were encouraged to compare 'classical' CALL (free-standing CALL via floppy disks, CD-ROM and entire program downloads) and online language learning, and to evaluate their relative strengths and weaknesses, e.g., instant versus delayed response, asynchronous learning, limited or potentially limitless breadth of coverage, real-time scheduling considerations and the desirability or otherwise of possibly more personal treatment.

Software Evaluation 2: Translation Software

The modernist view of the language teacher has tended to sheer away from translation as a language learning exercise, but the view was strongly maintained that translation offers a route to learning in both the source and the target (typically native) language through structural comparison, vocabulary and stylistic equivalence and can offer a quick breakthrough in comprehension impasses. Accordingly students were encouraged to use CD and online dictionaries (for example *Euro-DicAutom*) and to test online machine translation (MT) systems (e.g., *Babel Fish*, *Logos* and *PROMT*) by feeding their own texts into demonstration versions of commercial programs and examining the results to establish the *modus operandi* and the capabilities of the system. This had the effect of partially dispelling the idea that MT was a pointless exercise, as the approach allowed the tools to fit the level of the task, as reflected in the practices of professional translation agencies (For a similar, but literature-based, point of view, see Eco 2003). At a later stage it was also possible to encourage students to 'post-edit the source text' (Somers 1997) to enhance and augment the performance of the translation machine, thus to realise that such systems do have their uses. Such an exercise has the pedagogical advantage of making students look closely at style and structure in both source and target languages. Finally *Systran 4* was settled on as house program for MT and *Babylon* as a TSR (terminate and stay resident) fast word translation reference program, but students were also encouraged to look for and test systems offered on the Net. Towards the late 1990s, far from rejecting IT as a translation tool, but seeing it as a highly productive supplement to human translation, Translation Memory programs were introduced. Students were shown how they can increase translation consistency by replicating previous translations of a given word or expression, expanding vocabulary and grammatical awareness by making entries into a translation glossary and pairing terms, and preparing pre-translations of texts currently being processed and those of a similar nature which might be presented later. After problems in installing and running *Trados*, *Déjà Vu X* was selected as the house program.[1]

Utilities 1

Part of the wider concept of CALL was the awareness that generalised utilities can also be employed for language teaching purposes or more broadly for the purposes of the language practitioner. Two sub-courses were devoted to these areas. The first one dealt evaluatively with word-processors. Even towards the end of the programme's life some incoming students were still not fully conversant with these and needed supplementary help. The second covered grammar- and spell-checkers. This work became an important analytical exercise for deducing functional principles and how they can be used in language instruction. In fact, they are very useful in promoting linguistic examination and speculation, particularly when used in conjunction. The heavily documented interactive language learning potential of e-mail was also examined. At an intermediate stage, although students had long been using the Net in information and program searches, additional courses on information retrieval from CD-ROMs and specialist online databases were offered by the Library Information Service. Also, in the late 1990s and early into the present decade students were focused by the methods and resources of the *WELL (Web Enhanced Language Learning Project)* onto specific potential uses of the Web for language purposes. Towards the end of the term an introduction was made to Web authoring, using both hard-coded HTML and programs such as *FrontPage* and *DreamWeaver*. From the pedagogical as well as professional point of view the insights gained in all three evaluative modules fed into the Software Design and Implementation module and the final project/dissertation.

Description of English

As many course participants came from a background of literature rather than linguistics, it was important that they received a grounding in linguistic methodology and terminology. With English the only common language of course members, this module served that purpose, providing a terminological and conceptual basis for those looking forward to a career in EFL and for those wishing to deal with other, mainly European, languages. It served as a unifying supplement to the other course modules, in particular providing an analytical tool based on Systemic-Functional principles (cf. Halliday 1985) for software design and some of the theoretical underpinnings for the module in natural language processing and language typology.

Natural Language Processing and Language Typology

In this module students were first introduced to computing algorithms for dealing with linguistic material. Pinker (1994) provided additional conceptual backing and Crystal (1995) a compendium of factual information on languages and linguistics. As basic NLP models were based on English, a contrastive strategy was adopted. This was worked through for Romance and Germanic and over the years for a variety of arguably more 'exotic' languages. Typological rules were refined and translated into pre-code algorithms for the structures of these languages, and assessment was carried out by analysis of a fragment of the language of preference for submission to a programmer, to program the programmer, so to speak. In its earlier days the module was rounded off with a worked case study of a CALL program for Dutch given by a linguist member of the Computing staff, who later replaced it with a popular short hands-on course in PROLOG for linguists (cf. Matthews 1998) This element was illustrative rather than didactic, and students were not required to write PROLOG programs as part of assessed work.

Desktop Publishing

This was a course 'borrowed' from the final year options of Computing Science. It was taught and assessed over one term, and examined in the summer but proved not to be of any particular benefit for linguists, and was dropped from the programme after two years. ALS:C students lacked the prerequisite experience in computer science and were in need of a less theoretical applications course. It was very successfully replaced by an in-house innovation, Computers and Corpora (see below).[2]

Computers and Corpora

This course proved to be the ALS:C programme's most acclaimed and distinctive module in terms of the provision of powerful tools for the linguist.

A language teacher developed the course in-house, and it introduced students to extant corpora and showed how they might exploit them via concordancers for generating materials in a number of linguistic fields, including grammar, cross-language and cross-cultural equivalences (parallel corpora) vocabulary and institutional materials primarily, but with many further possibilities (e.g., see Aarts & Meijs 1984; Dodd 2000; Sampson 1992). The principles and practice of corpus creation were dealt with in detail, so that students might create materials suited to their own specifically defined purpose. Ultimately the course was taught on an intensive basis by an ALS:C graduate now working as a lexicographer for a leading German dictionary publisher and following an ALS:C PhD programme. Although the ALS:C MA programme is now defunct, this course is still on offer as an option on Humanities MA programmes, as its usefulness is not restricted to linguists.

Software Design and Implementation

This Term 2 module, based on the principles and insights from the first term's evaluative modules, made a significant contribution to materials creation. It conformed to the principle that the degree programme should be application-, not programming-based, and that students should not have to follow a discipline which might not suit them. However, it was felt that students should have some idea of programming concepts, provided in a short, non-assessed element of BASIC. This helped when, after units on sound and image capture and the software lifecycle, they were introduced to authoring programs and encouraged to design and implement under supervision their 'mini-project', the negotiated assessment work for the module. This incorporated all elements in the module in a coherent piece of linguistic teaching material. Initially the authoring program used was *Guide*, developed by a member of the Kent computing staff, but ultimately overtaken by large-scale commercial programs. Thereafter *Delphi* and *Authorware* were employed as authoring platforms, with *Delphi* the more popular. In the last instance, *Macromedia Director* was used as the authoring program. The difficulties and high costs for licensing and upgrading *Director* were however giving cause for concern by the time ALS:C was terminated, and anyone contemplating moving into this pedagogically rewarding area of CALL materials production is advised to approach the question of a platform with extreme caution – or employ web techniques with the contingent caveats on fallibility, corruption and time-lag between submission and response.

Utilities 2

This module was arguably somewhat amorphous and diffuse, but a legitimate justification for its existence was that it prepared students in the differing aspects of the use of technology in the organisational and administrative roles of the language professional. Students were introduced to the internal workings of the computer, file formats, spreadsheets and bibliographical software. As a major part of CALL activity is based on networked laboratories, students were introduced to the basic theories and practice of networks (cf. Williams 2001), which along with a hardware review and considerations of CALL lab design formed the major thematic thrust of the module. In the preparation of the assignment, to design a CALL lab, students were encouraged to prepare their best and worst possible scenarios, taking into account all aspects of hardware, software, the physical environment, staffing and budgetary constraints, the basic thrust being: "What is essential? What can you afford? What can you do without? What can you compromise on? Do you really need it? Don't buy what you don't need." (See Needs analysis and the financial metric.)

Project/Dissertation

On successful completion of the eight-unit coursework component, students proceeded to the double-weighted project/dissertation element, extending from the end of the second term to the submission date shortly before the beginning of the next academic year. During this period students worked on researching, implementing and documenting a language-based project and then wrote it up. The topic, to be approved by a supervisor, could be selected from any of the coursework areas including orthodox CALL, a viable Web site, an algorithmic analysis of a linguistic problem, machine-aided translation, a dedicated corpus or an extensive software review for example, technical staff providing intensive but regulated input. The pedagogical aim was that students should produce a meaningful, integrated and useful piece of work demonstrating their understanding of and facility with the separate elements of the program involved

Degree programme, final form

The degree programme in its final configuration is shown in Table 2. All courses were obligatory. The mode of assessment for each course is displayed in the third column. Asterisks indicate courses taken in the first year if the degree was followed over two years in part-time mode, which allowed for half the number of courses followed by the full-time contingent to be taken each year, in exactly the same timetable slots, as teaching time was at a premium, so no allowance was made for the difference in mode. The dissertation element was formally taken in the summer after the successful completion of coursework. The part-time option, designed for students still in employment, was only exercised by three students, two

Table 2. Final configuration of MA in Applied Language Studies: Computing degree programme

Module	Term	Assessment	Units
*Software Evaluation 1: CALL**	1	Presentation and essay	1
*Software Evaluation 2: Translation**	1	Presentation and essay	1
Utilities 1	1	Essay	1
Description of English	1	2 linguistic analyses	1
*Computers and Corpora**	2	Design/create a corpus	1
Software Design and Implementation	2	Design and implement a program ('mini-project')	1
NLP and Language Typology	2	1 typological analysis	1
*Utilities 2**	2	Design a CALL Lab	1
Project/Dissertation	3	Design and implement an extended program/ review the field	2
		(total)	10

of whom completed entirely successfully, the other withdrawing early because of private commitments.

The above schema differs from the original only in that Desktop Publishing was replaced by Computers and Corpora and the addition of presentation as an assessment method. This does not imply that the programme remained inflexible during most of its existence. Rather it was a structure which stood the test of time, with modifications being made to the internal composition of individual constituents in the light of the prevailing situation without the whole framework requiring radical revision.

Reasons for changes

It would be tempting to assume that development proceeded at a measured, steady pace or in distinct, deliberate phases: this would unfortunately be erroneous. In terms of the technology available and students' familiarity with it one is to an extent dependent on the outside world as well as internal constraints and institutional policy. For example, at the beginning of the programme some students needed quite intensive training in word-processing, which was provided by a support unit attached to the Computing Department. After about two years the decision was made that such facilities should not be restricted to particular programmes of study but should be made universally available across the campus, so support was withdrawn and ALS:C staff took over the job of teaching word-processing. Although by the mid-1990s school students were coming to higher education with quite considerable IT skills, this took some time to filter through to the graduate intake, but by the millennium the word-processing course had shrunk from five weeks to two, with the occasional remedial session where necessary.

Similarly, when the programme began, the World Wide Web was very much in its infancy. It was extremely time-consuming and at times difficult to get browsers to function; now this facility is taken for granted. Courses in HTML gave way to swift classes, almost asides, on the use of *FrontPage* and *DreamWeaver*, with online self-administered courses becoming available on the campus net.

A further example is instructive. In the early 1990s hypertext was an exotic concept with great potential. A Hypertext Support Unit was set up by the University and provided invaluable help with authoring systems until the facility was extended across the campus and withdrawn from the ALS:C programme. As a result, ALS:C staff again shouldered the burden. After that came a rather patchy supply of authoring teaching until it was possible to hire a member of the Computing staff (see The teaching team) to continue with *Director* until her home department could spare her no longer. In addition, the costs of updating *Authorware* and acquiring sufficient licences for *Director* were becoming prohibitive towards the end of the life of ALS:C. One staff member was able to fill in with *Delphi*: the approach might be best described as patchwork rather than design, but nevertheless it was successful in the short term. Some students took on the considerable task of learning *Director* practically unaided, and through sheer determination achieved impressive results.

Another controlling factor was finance. After our first forays into CALL and the first software acquisitions, it soon became clear that software was not always reliable, it was generally expensive, and could be a constant drain on resources, if viability was to be maintained. With increasing interest in the programme, the lab originally allotted had become too small. A new drive in the mid to late 1990s resulted in additional money for software and the conversion of a language lab to a postgraduate CALL lab. However, sadly, the impetus was not maintained. The lesson that a constant watch has to be kept on software capability and compatibility was hard learned. The delicate balance between obsolescence and keeping abreast of, if not ahead of, technological developments is crucial in keeping degree programmes viable and attractive; and both hard- and software cost money. A case in point is that of interactive whiteboards. A local infants' school with 270 pupils has currently five of these. The university programme with responsibility for the evaluation of technological language teaching aids for over 500 students was allowed none. Visiting school students and teachers are not impressed.

Some lessons learnt

Needs analysis and the financial metric: Humans, machines or books?

A firm principle underlying the degree programme was that of needs analysis in the context of a financial metric. Most educational institutions are subject to financial constraints, and it is essential to maintain a hard-headed attitude in terms of hardware and software acquisition. This principle was built into the Software Evaluation 1 and 2 and the Utilities 2 courses, and the methodological commitment to them became almost a mantra:

- What is the job to be done, and what is the best tool to do it, under optimal, and minimal, conditions?
- Is it necessary to have the ultimate in available hardware and software? Is it necessary to adopt a technological solution at all? A vicious cycle operates between hardware and software: more advanced hardware often demands more advanced software, often rendering extant hard- and software obsolete or useless, whilst at the same time accelerating costs.
- Is it necessary to have the newest software when it may be more effective and cheaper to use say a dictionary or grammar exercises?
- How are resources, both human and technological, best used?

A frequently quoted rationale is that unlike humans, computers do not get bored and can keep on doing repetitious routines forever – or until they crash. So application of the machine to such tasks may release the teacher to perform tasks best suited to humans. A good example is provided in the interactive oral side for example, though spectrographs and intonation contour graphics programs undoubtedly have their merits.

In confronting such considerations students are forced to look at available resources and differential solutions. Larger and better-endowed institutions may be better able to make more intensive, thus more cost-effective, use of expensive software than smaller ones, who are unable to exploit the high potential turnover. This applies in particular to translation software, but even so the software needed to train a usually relatively small number of teachers is more economically used by large numbers of language-learners in the school context. Of course, if both purposes can be served more or less simultaneously, the problem becomes less acute. As new developments in hardware and software spiral in their functionality and compatibility, they make increasing demands on each other, and on the user's budget. Machines wear out or suffer terminal crashes, and a constant program and budget for maintenance and replacement is indispensable. However, this all comes at a price, so a consideration of durability, compatibility and robustness must form a part of long-term strategy.

Common sense and flexibility

In terms of life skills one might say that many of the lessons learnt in creating and maintaining the CALL-based programme outlined above have been in the application of common sense and the constant need for a mixture of determination, focus and flexibility. Staff learn this lesson in teaching and maintaining the programme in all its aspects and students in keeping an eye on the instructional purpose, yet being willing to adapt to circumstances, for example when a particular strategy fails to deliver. It has been said that computers only solve the problems they create, and then not all of them.

This vigilance extends materially over staff support as well as financial and pedagogical parameters. Continuity figures highly in staffing practices, particularly when, as in this case, the operation functions not as part of a dedicated institutional machine, but as a result of the concerted efforts of a team of committed individuals. The initial concept and teaching team depended primarily on languages academics from the basically IT-competent to the expert. All shared a vision of how IT could help the linguist. Equally the programme could not have functioned without dedicated technicians, whose contribution to student learning, particularly in the project implementation stage, was inestimable. Any diminution of such human resources, particularly on the technical side, is life-threatening to such a programme as ALS:C and these circumstances ultimately proved its downfall.

A carefully coordinated and efficient operation such as this also necessitated tight control of the curriculum. All component modules were obligatory, with no programme-internal options to dilute recruitment to individual modules and thus decrease economic viability. In a more widely drawn context in which various separate but cognate degree programs are run in parallel, controlled cross-fertilisation would be a possibility. For example, one ALS:C module is still available to students on literary MA courses, and when MAs in applied linguistics and professional translation were still extant they were able to subscribe to IT courses offered by ALS:C, for example Computers and Corpora, NLP/Typology and Software Evaluation 2 (translation technology), thus spreading the financial burden and making software purchase and use more cost-effective.

Much play has been made in this paper of the notions of needs analysis and discernment, and this can be seen clearly in respect of the rise of the Internet. Whilst the Internet has without any doubt made a vast amount of invaluable information freely available and favoured the openness, flexibility and teamwork which were the guiding spirit of the programme, it has also given access to inferior, even pernicious, material and increased the need for discerning evaluation. It has also, sadly, engendered a blind faith in the innate value of Internet-derived material, and encouraged and facilitated plagiarism. Thus precisely the rationale which underlay the programme needed to be brought to bear in assessing the various vices and virtues of CALL and Net materials, especially by carefully checking sources.

Assessment and student support

It was clear from the outset that the success of a programme is not purely dependent on constituent courses but also on the morale of its participants. With goodwill a small teaching team with relatively small student rolls in an institution which takes good care of its students is well equipped to keep a watchful eye on them in terms of individual and academic needs. Though personal, medical and financial problems did arise, student attrition remained at a very low level overall. This approach was found useful in identifying students with particular weaknesses who could be helped before things went irremediably wrong.

Transparency

One of the guiding principles of the MA programme was that at all times a policy of openness and full information was observed. All students had access to the university's support, welfare and leisure facilities. The comprehensive course handbook covering details of course and student life was issued to all students at the beginning of the academic year, and comments and feedback were always welcome. It was for example frequently necessary to explain to students how the various elements of the programme fitted together – a task often only fully completed in the final dissertation stage when everything came together, as it invariably did. There was a permanent facility for discussion in the form of a weekly forum, with content determined by students (perhaps discussion of course content or progress or some topic considered interesting or promising). In addition, at the end of the programme of instruction, an open discussion was conducted between students and the external examiner in the absence of the teaching staff. The results were then reported back to the teaching staff by the external examiner, and a suitable response was made in accordance with the recommendations.

Assessment

The principle of transparency outlined above was reflected in the assessment policy. With the exception of the Description of English module, assessment was by negotiated assignments, on the principle that students would be more committed to and motivated by work they had themselves designed and researched, rather than by being put through a standardised set of formal exercises. Students came to one of the course team and worked out an assignment and approach, which was agreed to and signed off on by all parties. They then received individualised and differential help. Some found the apparent freedom of negotiated assignments unnerving and intimidating, but it was always possible to agree on a topic. As submitted coursework was marked three times, and detailed reports were written by examiners at each stage of the process, it was also possible to ensure transparency in awarding the final mark.

The entries in Table 2 for the two software evaluation courses show the introduction of presentation[3] of worked programs and subsequent evaluation as an assessment procedure, primarily for reasons of staff availability and economy. However, presentation also proved highly successful as a pedagogical method. It cut marking time and with two instructors writing a combined report almost instantly after the presentation session dramatically speeded up the return of feedback to students.

Pedagogically, presentation as a skill in itself also involved other students in their coursemates' work, as they were challenged to respond to the presentation and encouraged to collaborate and learn from each other. Another advantage was in gauging other students' comprehension and ability to manipulate the material. This illustrated the bilateral nature of presentation. However, presentation skills and subject comprehension had to be assessed and appear separately in the joint report. An extension of this practice might well have been peer assessment, but even group presentations were assessed separately for each member, as experiments in other programs had revealed an unwillingness to mark fellow members of the group down. Course participants quickly realised, however, that while clearly each had individual strengths and weaknesses, it was more productive for all concerned to employ their strengths for the communal good. This positive principle emerged saliently in the project/dissertation stage.

A final comment

The ALS:C degree programme produced many successful graduates. Some used the programme as a springboard to advance in their already chosen careers; others branched out in new directions; and yet others (a gratifying ten percent) went on to Ph.D. programmes. It was a worthwhile and rewarding undertaking, which produced capable and enthusiastic graduates who continued to spread their expertise; it also brought in revenue and acclaim to the host institution. However, in a very true sense its fate is a case study in betraying the very principles it espoused. The re-examination of needs and objectives and the maintenance of a view to the future lapsed under the pressures of immediacy and the short term. Key staff resigning or retiring were not replaced. Pleas that new, incoming staff should have IT capability, if not necessarily expertise, were ignored. The programme could be revived, dusted off, updated and run again, but like all successful enterprises, the mechanisms which led to its success require constant maintenance and attention. Perhaps that is the greatest lesson of all.

Notes

1. Future extension of a programme of this sort would include an examination of the principles of localisation and its attendant software: increasing globalisation demands that provision of language products and services be adapted to both local and global arenas.

2. Subsequently DTP rapidly became such a commonplace that the course became obsolete shortly afterwards. It indeed became a generally recognised factor that technology hailed in its early years as ground-breaking became accepted facts of life, no longer at the cutting edge.

3. Parenthetically, display, originally regarded as the prerogative of the teacher rather than the student, had indeed been a problem, both physically and financially. The idea of transferable generic skills did not feature highly when the programme was in its infancy, and presentation technology was by no means as advanced and accessible as it is today. The use of a large panoramic monitor controlled from a master console was ruled out not only on budgetary but also on constructional grounds: a) despite its size it would still not be visible to all in the long tube-like room allocated to CALL and b) despite the lab being in a new building there was no assurance that because of its size and weight it would not cause either the wall or ceiling on which it would be mounted to collapse! The solution was to use on/off signal splitters limiting monitors to displaying only material relayed from the control. The advent of affordable data

projectors while solving the display problem exposed a further one. Unless a very high intensity projector was used, curtains had to be closed to exclude external light, and it became difficult to take readable notes. Another problem, that of theft, was if not obviated at least diminished by bolting the projector, lighter than a monitor, to the ceiling.

References

Aarts, J. & Meijs, W. (Eds.). (1984). *Corpus Linguistics*. Rodopi: Amsterdam.

Authorware. Available at http://www.macromedia.com.

Babel Fish. Available at http://babelfish.altavista.com

Babylon. Available at http://www.babylon.com

Crystal, D. (1995). *The Cambridge Encyclopædia of Language* 2nd ed. Cambridge: CUP.

Déjà Vu. Available at: http://europa.eu.int/eurodicautom/

Director. Available at http://www.macromedia.com.

Dodd, W. (Ed.). (2000). *Working with German Corpora*. Birmingham: University of Birmingham Press.

Eco, U. (2003). *Mouse or Rat? Translation as negotiation*. London: Phoenix.

EuroDicAutom. Available at http://www.europa.eu.int/eurodicautom/

Halliday, M. A. K. (1995). *An Introduction to Functional Grammar*. London: Arnold.

Hubbard, P. (1987). Language teaching approaches, the evaluation of CALL software, and design implications. In W. Flint Smith (Ed.), *Modern Media in Foreign Language Education: Theory and implementation* (pp. 227–254). Lincolnwood, IL: National Textbook Company.

Hubbard, P. (1988). An integrated framework for CALL courseware evaluation. *CALICO Journal, 6* (2), 51–72.

Levy, M. (1997). *Computer-Assisted Language Learning: Context and conceptualization*. Oxford: Clarendon Press.

Logos. Available at http://www.logos.it/lang/transl_en.html

Matthews, C. (1998). *An Introduction to Natural Language Programming through PROLOG*. London: Longman.

Pinker, S. (1994). *The Language Instinct*. New York, NY: HarperCollins.

PROMT. Available at http://www.promt.ru/

Sampson, G. (1992). Analysed corpora of English: A consumer guide. In M. C. Pennington & V. Stevens (Eds.), *Computers in Applied Linguistics* (pp. 181–200). Clevedon: Multilingual Matters.

Shaw, D. J. (1991). A new CALL laboratory at the University of Kent. *ReCALL, 4*, 2–4.

Shaw, D. J. (1992). Setting up a new CALL Lab at the University of Kent. In C. Davis & M. Deegan (Eds.), *Computers and Language* (pp. 21–26). Office for Humanities Communication Publications, no. 2.

Somers, H. (1997). A practical approach to using machine translation software: 'Post-editing' the source text. *The Translator, 3* (2), 193–212.

SYSTRAN. Available at http://www.systranbox.com

TRADOS. Available at http://www.trados.com

WELL Project. Available at http://www.well.ac.uk/

Williams, R. (2001). *Computer Systems Architecture: A networking approach*. London: Addison-Wesley.

Reconstructing practice

Language teacher education and ICT

When programmes or courses in teacher education and CALL are described and presented, there is a tendency for the products to govern the processes. Thus, typically, a course description will elaborate on the aims and objectives, the intended learning outcomes, the topics covered week by week, the contact hours and organisation, and the assessment, but aside from rather general statements on how learning will be facilitated, matters of process tend to be left implicit. In contrast, this chapter by Diane Slaouti and Gary Motteram brings the learning process to centre stage in the design of a CALL training programme. In this case, conceptually, articulation of the processes leads to identification of the products (e.g., content), rather than vice versa. Specifically, the authors use the concept of reconstructive processes to capture and describe the ways in which a CALL training programme operates. The chapter features a number of narratives from a sample of graduate teachers which detail their goals and expectations. These narratives illustrate the diversity of backgrounds and the quality of the experience for participants. This is followed by an in-depth discussion of reconstructive processes, especially with regard to the ways in which metacognitive awareness and reflection on learning may be encouraged. Implications for teacher educators' own reconstructions of practice are also considered, with a particular focus on the design of CALL teacher education programmes as the technology continues to develop and evolve.

Reconstructing practice

Language teacher education and ICT

Diane Slaouti and Gary Motteram
University of Manchester, UK

This chapter explores the ways in which a particular training programme conceptualises reconstructive processes (Biggs 1999; Freeman 1993; Johnson & Golombek 2002; Shulman 1986) with respect to language teachers who are keen to develop their skills with educational technologies. It develops a picture of the knowledge base that we believe informs a course such as this, and considers the processes through which teachers take ownership of that knowledge. It draws on data from narrative research carried out with a sample of graduate teachers. The teachers were invited to tell their stories about how they came to us for their professional development, their expectations, the ways in which the course impacted on their thinking and what they have done since they graduated. This narrative data, collected during September 2004, was interrogated for themes that will emerge as we explore the various aspects of the programme and the teacher education process. We will use extracts from the teachers' narratives in this chapter, referring to each by country and year of graduation.

Background

The MA in Educational Technology and TESOL at Manchester University has been running in various forms since 1992, both as an onsite degree and by distance. During this period, although the structure of the degree has remained broadly the same, the content has changed dramatically. This evolution reflects changing technologies, evolving teacher knowledge and skills, and an element of tutors' reconstruction of practice as the course is informed by our thinking about and research into teaching and technology.

Our students are practising teachers, with a minimum of three years experience. Although there is some variation, they typically have a first degree, usually in a language or education discipline, and a teaching qualification. They come from a variety of educational cultures with often very different ideas about the processes of education and the development of language teaching skills and practices. The sample of twenty teachers in this study reflects the range of profiles. Regions included South America, Southeast Asia, Europe, and the Middle East. Three were current students at the time of the study; the rest graduated between 2001 and 2004. Students who studied in different modes were also represented (10 on-site in Manchester and 10 by distance learning). Whilst current working context was not a criterial factor for selection, the sample provided a representative range (teaching young learners or in primary and secondary state schools, working with adults in private language schools, company contexts and higher education, working in teacher education).

As regards motivations for joining the programme, teachers cite career advancement and/or enthusiasm based on recent experience of technology use or expectations of a role for technology with which they are perhaps not yet familiar. These motivations and how they impact on the course itself will be explored in more detail presently. They are also teachers with a growing and often well-established experience of teaching, learners, and their contexts but for whom technology use may be an innovation. They come with a variety of expectations of what they will learn and how. The tutors also bring their own ideas about what and how concepts and materials should be presented, the types of skills that should be developed, and what the participants should know when they graduate.

The programme is constructed around four core technology modules with a further two being chosen from electives with a more general ELT orientation. The four technology modules are:

Computers and video in the language classroom (CVLC)
Computer assisted language learning (CALL)
Multimedia in language education (MLE)
Computers, language and context (CLC)

The first of these (CVLC) takes the teachers' experience of their language teaching contexts and situates technology within those familiar schema. Teachers consider not only how generic tools such as wordprocessors, the WWW, computer mediated communication, or specific resources or applications might be integrated into their practice, but also how the use of such tools impact on our views of the development of language and literacy. The 'classroom' in this unit has increasingly moved from the four walls that many teachers inhabit before coming to us, to the virtual, and this has been a key reconstruction of context evident through developments in programme design. The CALL module develops teachers' awareness of computer-based task design by providing them with the skills to create their own materials. Here much debate has been evident as to programming environment and this still continues. The aim is to develop transferable skills rather than 'teach programming'. MLE extends the materials design and development strand by both furthering the skills teachers are in command of (digitising and manipulating video content, integration of different tools within an online teaching environment) and by facilitating critical engagement with the nature of multimedia 'texts' and their impact on second language learning (interrogating aspects such as feedback approaches, interactivity, and multimedia annotations). The final module, CLC, encourages teachers to 'stand back' from the more practical developments of CALL and MLE, and to consider the changing landscape of teaching with technology, of being a teacher online and its implications for their and their learners' roles, for teacher development and for research.

We will outline how these modular components are informed by an understanding of professional need, of a knowledge base for language teacher education and ICT, and of the processes that aim to facilitate meaningful engagement with their content.

Starting points: Language teachers, ICT and professional development needs

Like many others on professional development programmes, the teachers bring with them an existing knowledge base and an expectation that this will be augmented. This is informed by the aspects of their teaching lives that Freeman (1989:40) describes as 'idiosyncratic and individual': familiar classroom contexts, experience of learners in specific cultural settings, and local expectations in terms of curriculum, teaching and testing approaches. In short they bring a rich tapestry of existing experiences and beliefs about teaching. They also have a desire to re-construct themselves as teachers and to augment their practice through the use of technology. They want to develop skills and competences with regard to manipulating the technologies themselves and to building up techniques that allow them to use technology for pedagogic purposes, to manage learning in increasingly diverse classrooms, both physical and virtual, and to create learning materials to 'fill' those electronic spaces. These perspectives are evident in the teacher narratives. These expectations might be defined by intrinsic or extrinsic motivations,

> I felt instinctively that the ELT sector would increasingly embrace technology and that this, therefore, was a burgeoning sector, and one I wished to be involved in ... I was particularly pleased that there was a practical component to the course and that I would learn how to create my own educational software materials.
> [Scandinavia 2002]

> My authorities expected teachers to be able to exploit effectively the equipment being acquired at that time.
> [Mexico 2003]

or by a preparedness for change:

> At first I was a bit afraid of the technology, being completely ignorant about computers. But I thought the challenge was good and achievable. ... one way or another, I would have faced technology in my career as a teacher. I had already come into contact with computers as a BA student and educational material developer. But I thought I was repeating the same behaviourist programming I saw in other materials.   [UK 2004]

For some the use of ICT is a complete innovation in their teaching practice, although they may use ICT as a tool themselves; others have begun to use some ICT in their teaching and are looking for a deeper understanding of its application; still others arrive with advanced programming skills, but may have less experience of thinking about pedagogic rationales for the use of ICT. What is evident here is that they recognise that their practice needs reformulation and re-focusing and that they come to the course anticipating that they will be different by the end of it.

All of the teachers in our study talk of skills in conjunction with knowledge development, and recognise context as a mediating force. Some of their reflections provide clues to the type of knowledge and skills enhancement they are looking for:

> [I hoped] the programme would develop my knowledge and skills in this area, so that language learning would be a more "real-life" activity.   [Greece (1) 2004]

> I didn't know how I was going to achieve it but I believed that I was going to learn practical pedagogical techniques, different ways of teaching, how to incorporate technology into my teaching. In other words, I was thinking of applied knowledge.   [Mexico 2003]

> I knew that I wanted to combine theoretical knowledge with practical and to be able to use my teaching context while doing so.   [Israel, current]

> I was highly enthusiastic about learning more about the area of CALL as I was feeling myself insufficient, feeling the need to learn more and that I have almost no knowledge and very limited skills in using the technology. I wasn't confident in the area and I was always afraid of taking responsibility on my own. [Cyprus 2002]

Applied knowledge, real life activity in language learning, theory and practice, knowledge and skills are some of the ways in which the teachers articulate their thinking with respect to their desire to *reframe their experience* (Shulman 1986). How we satisfy each individual's skills needs is a particular challenge. As Levy (1996) points out, it is unreasonable to expect to cover all possible technologies in all possible scenarios. We would agree with his argument for a more generative approach, providing a foundation for ongoing professional development beyond the boundaries of a course defined by time and will show that not only was change in evidence during the course itself, but also as our graduates continued with their careers.

The knowledge base for language teacher education and ICT

Various writers view teaching as a knowledge-based activity (Shulman 1986; Hegarty 2000; Turner-Bissett 1999, 2001). Shulman (1986) is oft cited for his work in establishing categories of knowledge for teachers and for coining specifically the notion of pedagogic content knowledge which 'is the blending of content and pedagogy into an understanding of how particular topics are transformed, organised, represented and adapted to varying interests and abilities of learn-ers.' (Turner-Bisset 1999: 12). Shulman established categories of content or subject knowledge, general pedagogic knowledge (the knowledge that transcends specific topic knowledge e.g. classroom management), curriculum knowledge, knowledge of learners, knowledge of educational contexts, and knowledge of education ends (e.g. views of education as having moral purpose, of facilitating lifelong learning, of empowering minority groups).

The thinking underlying the programme design can be articulated in relation to these categories of knowledge.

Content knowledge
In our Master's programme teachers explore approaches to teaching and learning with ICT (substantive knowledge), for example, developments of technology in behaviourist, communicative, constructivist, and social constructivist paradigms.

Part of teacher learning also relates to 'scholarship on the nature of knowledge' in the field (Shulman 1987: 9). Shulman refers to this as syntactic knowledge and includes developing an understanding about approaches to research and debates around research paradigms that inform our thinking about language learning and teaching and about the role of ICT.

General pedagogical knowledge
Here we explore what craft knowledge informs the way in which teachers inte-grate and manage ICT within their classrooms, both physical and virtual. This includes the ability to exploit generic tools and to design dedicated learning ma-terials. As technology increasingly becomes an integral or 'normalised' (Bax 2003) aspect of teaching in some contexts, then we would argue that this is becoming fundamental.

Curriculum knowledge

This involves asking questions about curriculum design and the role of ICT. We consider whether there is such a notion as an ICT curriculum as we consider a developing understanding of digital literacy. We debate what might be an optimum match between curriculum and ICT resources or ICT facilitated approaches.

Knowledge of learners

We are interested in what learner factors impact on appropriate methodology with ICT. These might be cognitive factors, e.g. relating to how learners learn or acquire language, and empirical factors, including gender, age, computer use and efficacy, and interests.

Knowledge of educational contexts

The relationship between contextual factors such as technology infrastructure and support, computer setting (e.g. lab versus single machines), and ICT use is part of the discussion, as is how virtual learning environments are impacting on teaching and learning, and what institutional directives are driving these developments.

Knowledge of educational ends

We consider philosophical or moral debates about the use of technology in teaching and learning e.g. inclusive practice, globalisation effects, or debates about access to the knowledge economy.

This taxonomy provides a useful framework for thinking about language teacher education and ICT, and the principles exemplified here underlie all the modules described earlier. However, key to an understanding of how teachers interpret learning content is the need to recognise our personal knowledge base (Clandenin & Connelly 1987; Verloop, van Driel, & Meijer 2001).

> This personal knowledge of each teacher is highly determined and "coloured" by his or her individual experiences, personal history (including learning processes), personality variables, subject matter knowledge, and so on. This personal knowledge base is the teacher's filter for interpreting new information.
>
> (Verloop et al. 2001:443)

Freeman and Johnson (1998:405) emphasise the dangers of an approach to teacher education that encourages teachers to 'substitute received knowledge for [a] fundamental need for cogent analysis and self understanding.' The teacher is not an empty vessel into which knowledge is poured but an active participant in its construction, filtering that knowledge as it is explored (Johnson 1999; Shavelson & Stern 1981) and then embedding it in existing schemata, or adjusting schemata to take on these new ideas. Specific research into teacher use of ICT by Gobbo and Girardi (2001:80) identified the way in which 'behaviours and strategies in teaching and managing the classroom were influenced by interacting factors like the level of competence with ICT and teaching epistemology.' Teachers need to interpret what they 'learn' in relation to their cultural and teaching contexts, to their beliefs, to their expectations, and to their needs. We believe this stance is especially important when what is being 'learned' links technology skills, theory and practice, but it may result in certain tensions as we reconcile our own training agenda and the perceived needs of our teachers. We have to constantly lay ourselves open to the questioning and debate that accompanies critically interrogating roles for technology in different contexts.

Towards reconstruction

Thus far we have recognised not only a knowledge base that cuts across the fields of language teaching and ICT in language teaching research, but also our teachers' existing rich personal knowledge. We acknowledge the needs of our teachers with respect to the interplay between skills and theory. Most importantly we recognise learning as a process that allows for teachers to explore their understanding, to develop a layer of knowledge that allows for the transformation of learning during the programme (Biggs 1999; Marton & Saljo 1976) into learning over time.

We identified earlier how teachers talk about their expectations of their teacher education experience with respect to *applied knowledge,* but as Freeman (1993) suggests, the relationship between teacher education and action is a complex one.

One of our teachers identified the potential danger of inadequate recognition of this:

> [Many] CALL courses for teachers are carried upon the assumption that the theoretical knowledge of the changes the computer imposes on the roles of the teachers and learners, the increase of teachers' awareness of these roles and their ability to evaluate designed materials within their context, make them capable of obtaining these roles within their practice, which is not true as this theoretical knowledge sets the foundation for practice but doesn't equal or replace it.   [Oman 2002]

This reflection is an interesting one as it demonstrates a development in awareness that perhaps contrasts with the earlier evidence of expectations of the course. Expectations of *change* and *different ways of teaching* become tempered by reflections that begin to recognise that there are mediating factors. This and the following two extracts also illustrate an important observation that reconstruction of practice involves varied outcomes that are evidenced not only in teacher action but also in teacher thinking.

> I would say that the major contribution of this program ... is the fact that I have much more insight into technological issues... I'm much less technophobic and

willing to face a challenge which involves either technological matters or pedagogical ones. I feel more confident about myself as a person who understands the
world around him and is capable of adapting to change.   [Israel, current]

Technology definitely has its place in language learning. I'm thinking of offering a
course online, being aware that many students simply do not have time to come to
classes, especially if they are from different places... It would be ideal if a teacher
could introduce elements of synchronous teaching/learning too but that seems
to be a financial problem (buying expensive software) but I believe one can do
also with a simple web page and emails for a start, offering some kind of asynchronous teaching. However, although the literature shows DLL is good for adult
and mature students, in my opinion CALL cannot completely replace f2f teaching,
particularly if you're dealing with younger and less motivated students.
                                                                [Slovenia 2003]

Through their narratives, our teachers have also contributed to our understanding
of the reconstructive process. We have identified characteristics of this particular
teacher education programme that appear to facilitate this.

Reconstruction: A situated experience

Freeman (1996: 90) argues that knowledge of teaching is created in relation to an
individual teacher's reality:

Knowing how to teach does not simply entail behavioural knowledge of how to
do particular things in the classroom; it involves a cognitive dimension that links
thought with activity, centring on the context-embedded, interpretative process
of knowing what to do.

Acceptance of this *cognitive dimension in context* also means recognition of the social context of teaching, one in which learners, other teachers, institutional figures,
governmental agents, parents, and professional bodies all play a part. In a programme focusing on technology, the context can be a powerful mediating force as
local perceptions about ICT, institutional infrastructures, and learner experience
all exert an influence. Distance learning possibilities suggest that teachers might
be able to try out their learning more immediately than those studying *away* from
context. However, whatever the mode of study, 'situated technology experiences'
(Egbert et al. 2002) need to be facilitated through programme design.

   We cannot map the precise needs of every teacher onto every learning experience on every module. However, we can constructively align (Biggs 1999) learning,
teaching and assessment as a set of interwoven elements that allow for teachers
to make learning more personal. This diagram illustrates the interaction between
outcomes, process and assessment for the CLC module.

Learning Outcomes for Computers, Language and Context
➤ Develop an ability to think critically about developments in the use of technology in the ELT field
➤ Understand issues relating to effective use of technology in distributed learning
➤ Understand the impact of technology on roles of teachers and learners in online and independent learning contexts
➤ Identify teacher development needs with respect to technology in widening educational contexts
➤ Have a general understanding of approaches to researching technology in context

Learning & Teaching Processes (to allow students to achieve intended outcomes)

Online input: distance learning and the impact of technology on flexible learning and implications for learner autonomy; the nature of teaching and learning online; the demands of changing technological horizons on teacher development; the nature of research into online learning.

Group problem solving; online discussion in synchronous and asynchronous tools; individual and group enquiry; reflective tasks; diaries/learning logs/BLOGs; data analysis using technologies e.g. concordancers

Assessment (of intended outcomes)

a) A reflective review of learner experiences over the module, analysing learning log and electronic discussion data gathered throughout the module

b) An in-depth critical review of an area of interest or of specific relevance to the student and consideration of implications for practice

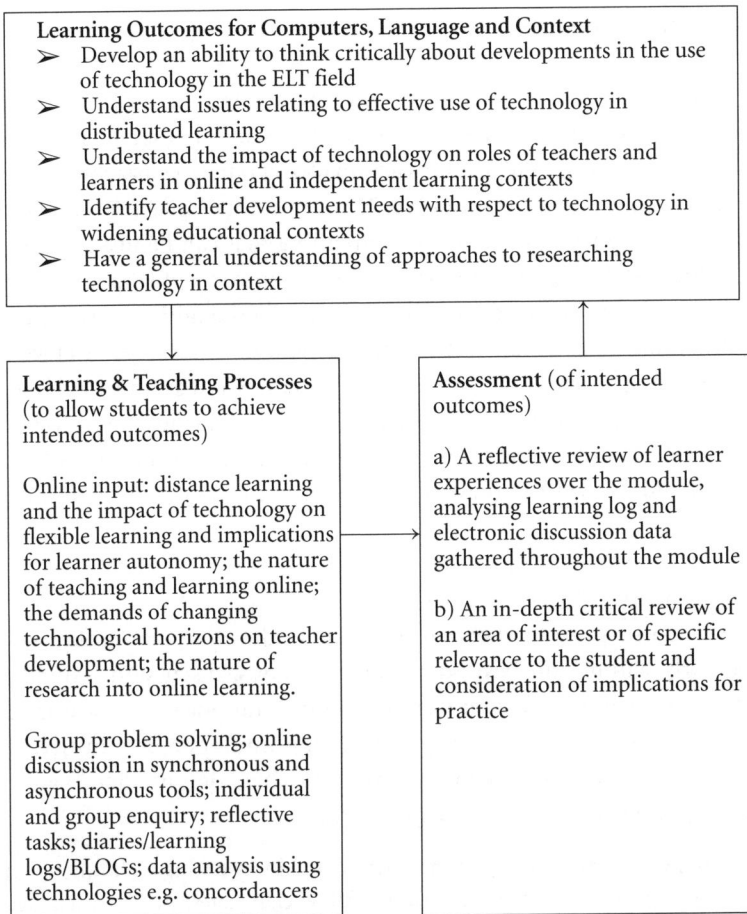

Figure 1. Syllabus design: Interactions between outcome, process and assessment.

The linkages between the learning outcomes, the learning and teaching processes, and the assessment promote reconstruction. The topics encourage the students to look critically at their own practice and the assignment includes both personal reflection as well as a critical review of an aspect of the input that they relate directly to their own practice.

In more recent years, teachers onsite have experienced this module in the same way as those studying by distance: totally online with no face-to-face encounters. This is one example of how we have also reconstructed our practice in line with our belief that teachers need to learn *about* online learning *through* online learning; that is, through a situated experience. This process is ongoing and other modules are changed as necessary to reflect our own as well as our students' changing perspectives.

Reconstructive processes

As tutors embedded in our own socio-cultural contexts, we can never truly understand the detail of our students' teaching worlds and this again emphasises the importance of an interpretative approach involving reflective practice. Herein lies a challenge. Zeichner and Liston (1996:9) observe that 'reflection involves intuition, emotion, and passion and is not something that can be neatly packaged as a set of techniques for teachers to use.' To help us in conceptualising how we embed reconstruction in such a course, we make use of the notion of metacognition that Shulman indicates as key in the development of knowledge. Metacognition underlies teaching, learning, and assessment processes and as time has gone by, we have become stronger in our conviction that this lies at the heart of reconstructive processes. Metacognitive awareness embodies *reflection*, *recognition* and *conscious articulation*, and we will use these terms to demonstrate the different aspects of reconstruction.

Encouraging metacognitive processes
It will be of no surprise to experienced teacher educators that group work features regularly within and beyond teaching sessions: discussion around issues; exploration of learning software; justification of a rationale for software design. However, reflecting and consciously articulating one's practice, justifying what one does, is not necessarily second nature to teachers despite their own roles in encouraging learners to interact in classrooms.

> Groupwork was inspiring to me. I wasn't used to working with others or talking about my assignments openly to my fellow classmates. At first I felt weird and suspicious in a way, wondering what if someone steals my idea (that's another element of Greek education) but then I realised how well I could communicate with others, how it helped me to see the pros and cons of my ideas and how good I felt not being competitive but ready to help and to be helped. [Greece (2) 2004]

It is noticeable that this teacher's attitude to reflection was changed by the tasks she was asked to engage in. She identifies not only the sharing aspect of group work but also the development of transferable skills such as problem solving or software design tasks, as well as the effect on her own thinking processes, helping to '*see the pros and cons of [her] ideas.*'

Our teachers frequently talk of standing back from tasks they are asked to undertake. One identified how she was lacking the confidence to know that her developing ideas might work because technology had been used so infrequently in her context. Listening to others is seen as a key process in reassuring her:

> Through reflection, I had the opportunity to express my feelings, become aware of my teaching situation and its implementation into my teaching situation and

thinking of the way to adapt it into my own teaching situation. My reflection as well as hearing from classmates on practice helped me a lot to change my way of thinking in a positive way and start to think more positively and more widely with confidence.   [Greece 2003]

Computer mediated communication (CMC) is frequently mentioned in the narratives as the teachers talk about this 'listening and sharing' process. Over time there has been increased use of CMC tools such as discussion lists, forums, and blogs in both distance and onsite modes, and we have used our own electronic communities as a source of shared understanding about the role of such tools in effecting deeper learning (e.g. Motteram 2001; Slaouti 2001). This *record* of dialogue appears to play an increasingly fundamental role in facilitating the reflection that is part of reconstruction. In their narratives teachers refer both to episodes when a specific task was centred on forum negotiation and exchange, and to using such evidence as a source of personal reflection on learning.

One teacher who participated in a forum exchange identified changes in her thinking which interestingly had implications for her views on interaction more widely than the specific online context within which this occurred:

> As the course progressed, I increasingly valued the contributions of my peers and this made me think that as a teacher, I had not really cultivated or seen the value of peer interaction; beyond seeing it as an opportunity for spoken English practice.
> [Israel, current]

Specific experiences of technology in use (e.g. teachers working through task sequences as learners or designing multimedia materials for specific learners, groupwork exploiting the CMC tools they are considering) are referred to frequently, and thoughts on learning through these processes provide evidence of a good deal of personal meaning-making, reflecting Wegerif et al.'s (1999) 'dialogue from within.' Here are another teacher's reflections on a synchronous seminar experience:

> I joined the next synchronous meeting. The connection was working this time. However, the conversation was too fast to follow. I had to scroll the window up and down to try to get some understanding. . .then I missed the action! I started to think about how I avoid these problems if I wanna apply synchronous modes with my students. It's essential to make sure that access to the tool won't be a problem for them, then the number of participants for each synchronous meeting should be controlled, I think 6 is the maximum. What's more, as we can see from the logs, there's a lot of work for teacher. . . The teacher's role seems to be more important and complicated in distance learning than face-to-face learning.
> [Argentina, current]

The type of reflection illustrated here in many ways characterises the knowledge that experienced educators may feel for their subject, that is the knowledge that is intuitive, beyond content, pedagogy, or curriculum. It is the knowledge of what works in what contexts, which is often difficult to pin down other than situating teachers in relevant learning experiences whilst building technology confidence.

Conscious articulation over time

Freeman (1991) cites Shulman (1988: 3) on the central role of encouraging teachers to ask:

> 'How do I know what I know? How do I know the reasons for what I do? Why do I ask my students to perform or think in particular ways?' The capacity to answer such questions not only lies at the heart of what we mean by becoming skilled as a teacher; it also requires a combining of reflection on practical experience and reflection on theoretical understanding.

This can be a long process and many of the extracts from our data so far cited have been expressed in terms of learning or realisations over time. One of our teachers was explicit about her gradual surfacing of understanding:

> I think this realization that I could have passed more of the learning responsibility over to the students, in part characterizes my thinking. A combination of course units, both technology-related and focussing on ELT made me reconsider the role I played as a teacher. When I was teaching, I didn't consider my approach to be teacher centred; I prided myself on my limited 'teacher talk time'. In retrospect, it probably was. My Presentation, Practice, Production approach didn't provide students with sufficient opportunity to explore and discover aspects of language themselves. The knowledge gained in that first term gave me ideas as to how that might be done via technology and the scope it offers for more student centred learning.   [UK 2004]

Also significant in this extract is the reference to the identification of an inter-action between 'technology-related' and 'ELT' content. The teacher narratives all refer to similar interplays. The balance between the technology-specific and ELT-generic is a particular challenge, that is, how do we achieve the best fit. However, this conscious strategy not to divorce acquisition of technology skills from applied practice permeates all programme content, including materials development modules, where teachers do need to build new technological skills sets. This can cause some tension as we negotiate teacher expectations and build the requisite skills sets with a group of teachers increasingly arriving with diverse levels of expertise. In the early stages of the programme we often find ourselves rationalising the chosen balance with teachers responding to queries such as 'Why aren't we learning how to use x software?' 'We need to spend more time learning how to program y.' However, the narratives suggest that views of this balance are a key reconstruction in teacher thinking over time.

> ...then I started seeing this programme differently. As I've previously mentioned, my goal was to learn how to incorporate technology into my teaching procedure but then, that changed. I was more interested to learn why I should use it, how to evaluate a piece of software, what my pupils can gain out of it. [Greece (1) 2004]

Such retrospective understandings of the programme's impact are important to annual discussions about revisions and focus.

Reflection on apprenticeship

The interweaving of theory and practice through the experiential is one approach to encouraging teachers to engage with their own beliefs about teaching and learning. An area that emerged strongly from the narrative data was the teachers' talk about 'apprenticeship' (Lortie 1975; Lave & Wenger 1991; Johnson 1999). This Greek teacher wrote a few months after finishing the programme:

> By carefully observing your teaching, I learnt more than I thought. Even now that I am in a school where access to technology is limited, I tend to use a lot the way you helped us learn. You know, in Greece, learner autonomy is hard to be achieved; teachers are expected to deliver knowledge and only few parents and teachers accept the fact that learners are in position to argue with the one who provides knowledge. But, I try to make them think, argue and justify their view, and work on their own. I try to make them feel independent and in charge of their own learning just like you did with us.   [Greece (2) 2004]

Others at distance saw this apprenticeship in their interactions with the learning materials themselves. In many ways we realise that we demonstrate through our own practice much of what is tacit to ourselves as teacher educators and that reconstruction of practice is a mutual endeavour. Experiential approaches in which tutor and students are partners seem to facilitate this process and these are a significant part of the programme's content and practice.

Assessment as a metacognitive process

A pleasing surprise to us in the narrative data was the extent to which teachers recognised the very specific role that assignments and the dissertation, possibly the most challenging aspects of their experience, had played. Looking back, one affirmed:

> As a graduate I am now the last to jump into any new fashionable technology before reflecting on the real possibilities it may have, and the impact it will have on my students. I think I gained that from the various assignments I had to deliver in which critical thinking and justification was required.   [Oman 2002]

Another referred to assignment and dissertation writing and associated formative feedback as 'awareness-raising activities and procedures' and recognised the power of the writing process:

> Sometimes I felt that I was "lost". In particular, when I had to decide upon the teaching-learning context in my assignments, the appropriacy of various applications and their rationale (for instance, choosing frameworks), it was very challenging. But, at the same time it was an intriguing experience. Although in some assignments I didn't do very well, I learnt that by putting down my thoughts, some things became clearer.   [Greece (2) 2004]

The ways in which assessment, teaching and learning processes and learning outcomes interrelate are important to a situated approach. Figure 1 illustrated one example. Learning processes, which include experiencing online learning, group interactions around ideas, and designing, trialling and evaluating learning materials for specific learners, provide both an opportunity to develop an applied understanding and a source for reflection and analysis. Assignment briefs which invite teachers to work with these experiences as part of the assessment stage seem to result in them contributing to learning in their own right.

Assignments are highly contextualised. An analysis of the teaching context into which any technological intervention is going to be introduced foregrounds all assignments. A demonstration of critical understanding of the theory (the notion of critical understanding being difficult for many to grasp in the early pieces) informs an applied example of practice: a piece of computer based learning material, an outline of a teaching session into which technology is integrated, or a presentation of principles for the development of ICT initiatives.

Assessment criteria should reflect the importance of encouraging teachers to challenge, to critique, to justify their approach in the light of what they have been exploring. Whilst evidence of practical ICT skills should clearly be expected on such a degree, it is these interpretive skills that are transferable; that is, they move beyond the boundary of a course that has to make specific decisions about which technologies to use, technologies that may not be exactly those that teachers will encounter in the future.

Identifying reconstruction

Because teachers' starting points are so varied, satisfying expectations can only be achieved through encouraging individual engagement with what are essentially group processes, developing an awareness of self. The programme is also clearly informed by what we as teacher educators feel should be present. Our own sense of self and our beliefs about teaching and learning inform our expectations about outcomes and processes. Occasional tensions between what the teachers expect and what we expect of them surface: the technology skills/theory balance, the dependency/independency continuum, and the specific technologies we have chosen to focus on or learn how to use. We are also on occasions disappointed that technology seems to be made to fit the straitjacket of teaching approaches that in themselves require critical reflection. The technology thus takes some precedence over the analysis of appropriate methodology. But perhaps this is a rather constrained view of reconstruction. It is not always easy to pin down precisely when reconstruction happens, nor how, for any individual, it relates to specific components or approaches. The individuality of reconstruction is reflected in the themes explored in this chapter, but equally in different accounts of specific episodes of learning and significance. There seem to be elements of the course that, with hindsight, have struck a particular chord and had specific impact on each person. This surfaced both through reflection on the nature of learning during the course and through reflections on what has happened since, on how teachers have or have not implemented technology in their practice, on their beliefs about technology and learning.

Probing this element of retrospective reflection through the narratives provided a picture of how reconstruction is a process that, if triggered, moves beyond the boundaries of a programme allowing teachers to better understand their own development needs. As observed by one:

> This comes as an afterthought. I was conscious at the time that I needed further training, but today I know exactly what my necessity was.   [UK 2004]

Our first narrative extracts in this chapter indicated expectations of developing knowledge and skills, of taking away informed ideas to the teachers' contexts. There is evidence of all of these. However, as we looked in more detail for evidence of what that learning had been and how it had occurred, there was a strong sense of questioning about technology that is congruent with an interpretative approach to teacher development. A recurring reconstruction in thinking might be described as one of informed scepticism.

> When I applied for an ICT position with a reputable ELT organisation, I was asked if the course had a practical component to which I replied "yes, I have created three software projects during the course". It turned out that they meant face-to-face teaching practice. What struck me about this interchange was that practical experience in the classroom seemed to be more highly valued than an interrogation of pedagogical theory in relation to technology. Yet it seems to me, from the experience and knowledge gained on the course, that to successfully introduce technology into a classroom scenario, and to create successful software, you really have to know why you are using the technology, who you are doing it for, how best

> to go about it; learning theory is the best place to start. It is not a matter of simply transferring lessons in a face-to-face context to software.   [UK 2003]

The question about what a language teacher education and ICT programme should address continues to be posed. The global impact of technology has caused our own reconstruction of practice with respect to the design of our programme. Technologies are still ever changing as is teachers' personal experience of those technologies. As teacher educators we have to be confident in our belief that the decisions we make about programme content are well-founded. Yet we constantly debate what the next delivery of the programme should provide and how it should do so. These two elements, constant dialogue around the knowledge base that informs our domain and recognition of the processes that we have described as reconstructive, appear to be pivotal in ensuring that healthy questioning continues to empower language teachers engaging with the potentials and challenges of technology to language education.

References

Bax, S. (2003). CALL – past, present and future. *System, 31*, 13–28.

Biggs, J. (1999). *Teaching for Quality Learning at University*. Milton Keynes: SRHE and Open University Press.

Clandennin, J. D. & Connelly, M. F. (1987). Teachers' personal knowledge: What counts as personal in studies of the personal. *Journal of Curriculum Studies, 19* (6), 487–500.

Egbert, J., Paulus, T., & Nakamichi, Y. (2002). The impact of CALL instruction on classroom computer use: A foundation for rethinking technology in teacher education. *Language Learning and Technology, 6* (3), 106–126. Available at http://llt.msu.edu.

Freeman, D. (1989). Teacher training, development and decision making: A model of teaching and related strategies for language teacher education. *TESOL Quarterly, 23* (1), 27–45.

Freeman, D. (1991). To make the tacit explicit: Teacher education, emerging discourse and conceptions of teaching. *Teaching and Teacher Education, 7* (5–6), 439–454.

Freeman, D. (1993). Renaming experience/reconstructing practice: Developing new understandings of teaching. *Teaching and Teacher Education, 9* (5–6), 485–497.

Freeman, D. (1996). Redefining the relationship between research and what teachers know. In M. K. Bailey & D. Nunan (Eds.), *Voices from the Language Classroom* (pp. 88–115). Cambridge: CUP.

Freeman, D. & Johnson, K. E. (1998). Reconceptualizing the knowledge base of language teacher education. *TESOL Quarterly, 32* (3), 397–417.

Gobbo, C. & Girardi, M. (2001). Teachers' beliefs and integration of information and communications technology in Italian schools. *Journal of Information Technology for Teacher Education, 10* (1&2), 63–85.

Hegarty, S. (2000). Teaching as a knowledge-based activity. *Oxford Review of Education, 26*, 451–465.

Johnson, K. E. (1999). *Understanding Language Teaching: Reasoning in action*. Toronto: Heinle and Heinle.

Johnson, K. & Golombek, P. (2002). *Teachers' Narrative Inquiry as Professional Development.* Cambridge: CUP.

Lave, J. & Wenger, E. (1991). *Situated Learning: Legitimate peripheral participation.* New York: CUP.

Levy, M. (1996). A rationale for teacher education and CALL: The holistic view and its implications. *Computers and the Humanities, 30* (4), 293–302.

Lortie, D. (1975). *School Teacher: A sociological study.* Chicago, IL: University of Chicago Press.

Marton, F. & Saljo, R. (1976). On qualitative differences in learning – 1: Outcome and process. *British Journal of Educational Psychology, 46,* 4–11.

Motteram, G. (2001). The role of synchronous communication in fully distance education. *Australasian Journal of Educational Technology, 17* (2), 131–149. Available at http://www.ascilite.org.au/ajet/ajet.html.

Shavelson, R., & Stern, P. (1981). Research on teachers' pedagogical thoughts, judgments, decisions, and behavior. *Review of Educational Research, 51,* 455–498.

Shulman, L. S. (1986). Those who understand: knowledge growth in teaching. *Educational Researcher, 15,* 4–14.

Shulman, L. S. (1987). Knowledge and teaching: Foundations of the new reform. *Harvard Educational Review, 57,* 1–22.

Shulman, L. S. (1988). The dangers of dichotomous thinking in education. In P. Grimmet & G. Erickson (Eds.), *Reflection in Teacher Education* (pp. 31–39). New York, NY: Teachers College Press.

Slaouti, D. (2001). Student 'voices' and course development: Reading the signs on a distance course in educational technology. *Association of Learning Technologies Journal, 9* (1), 62–72.

Turner-Bissett, R. (1999). The knowledge bases of the expert teacher. *British Educational Research Journal, 25* (1), 39–56.

Turner-Bisset, R. (2001). *Expert Teaching: Knowledge and pedagogy to lead the profession.* London: David Fulton.

Verloop, N., van Driel, J., & Meijer, P. C. (2001). Teacher knowledge and the knowledge base of teaching. *International Journal of Educational Research, 35* (5), 441–461.

Wegerif, R., Mercer, N., & Dawes, L. (1999). From social interaction to individual reasoning: An empirical investigation of a possible socio-cultural model of cognitive development. *Learning and Instruction, 9* (6), 493–516.

Zeichner, K. M. & Liston, D. P. (1996). *Reflective Teaching: An introduction.* Mahwah, NJ: Lawrence Erlbaum.

Theory and practice in teaching project-oriented CALL

Project-oriented learning is widely recognized as a pillar of modern educational practice, particularly in constructivist approaches. It has appropriately emerged as one of the central themes of this volume, being found in one form or another in a number of chapters. In this one, Robert Debski introduces us to the rationale and implementation of project-oriented learning in a CALL course at the University of Melbourne. As a sub-theme, he discusses the place of CALL as an academic discipline, and more specifically as a design science, showing how the project-centered approach can provide an important theoretical concept to support the field's development. The chapter begins by noting how CALL matured in the 1990s from being primarily practice-oriented to embracing theory and research perspectives more broadly. Debski then leads us on a journey into the theoretical domain with a discussion of the underpinnings of project-oriented learning, which he relates to a particular brand of constructivist theory linked to MIT educator Seymour Papert called "constructionism". Constructionism is based on the notion that the synthesis and integration of new knowledge can be effectively achieved through the creation of a product. Moving from theory to practice, Debski provides a detailed account of a CALL course project to build a support website to prepare students from Japan for their cultural experience in Australia. The chapter is also important for its description of the structure of the CALL Master's program and the CALL track of the applied linguistics MA program at Melbourne, a description that includes some enlightening data from a survey of the course expectations of six student groups there from 1997–2004.

Theory and practice in teaching project-oriented CALL

Robert Debski
The University of Melbourne, Australia

Introduction

Offering credit CALL courses at the tertiary level is becoming increasingly popular. Typing "Introduction to CALL" as a query in Google returns hundreds of hits today and one learns that CALL as an academic subject is offered by the Dublin City University, Cambridge University, and the Monterey Institute of International Studies, to name only a few academic institutions. As courses in CALL are offered at the undergraduate, postgraduate certificate/diploma, and masters levels, clear principles and benchmarks for CALL education need to be developed and shared by institutions around the world.

The topic of introducing theory in CALL courses and achieving the right balance between theory and practice is important, especially for courses at the masters level, which in most disciplines focus on the synthesis of practice, theory generation and research. The chapter proposes that project-oriented learning goes a long way towards integrating theory and practice in the teaching of CALL (see also Levy 1997) in a way that is the most useful to CALL understood as a design science (Levy 2002). Such a view of CALL is in consonance with the conceptualization of educational technology as a design science, not a natural science, since the phenomena that it studies are the products of human conceptions and devices (Glaser 1976 cited in Kozma 1994).

The present chapter analyses an application of project learning in the Master of CALL program at The University of Melbourne. It demonstrates that this pedagogy offers learning opportunities unavailable in more traditional syllabus-driven courses, and has the potential to introduce rationalization of practice in the context of meaningful projects. Also, the emphasis on projects oriented to real-life audiences contributes to strengthening CALL and presenting it in the home university as an area supporting language teaching, and to building links with the language profession outside the university.

Rationalization and teaching

CALL had its beginnings as a label describing the practices of teachers sharing a fascination with developing digital technologies and a vision of using them for the benefit of language learning. Following a period dominated by practical projects and classroom reports, the late 1990s introduced an era of rationalization of the discipline. The development of CALL from a practical discipline to a theoretical science can be explained by the theory of rationalization, which proposes that individuals, in order to achieve their goals, choose their means methodically and rationally (Weber 1947). Accordingly, to develop a better understanding of their intuitive practices, CALL practitioners have turned to theories from cognate disciplines such as second language acquisition, educational psychology, or media research. Today, it may seem that the effort of recent years to develop CALL as an academic discipline based on a solid empirical foundation has been successful. Even a cursory look at leading CALL periodicals tells one that they contain more research-based papers than practical reports. The new millennium has brought an explosion of works developing research agendas for CALL, either by conceptualizing it as a sub-field of second language acquisition (SLA) (e.g., Chapelle 2001) or emphasizing it as an arena of enquiry in its own right (e.g., Levy 2000; Hubbard 2003).

The development of CALL as an academic discipline introduces new issues that require attention. Firstly, Weber's rationalization theory suggests a paradox in that the drive to achieve goals through rational action may result in erosion of values. Accordingly, the drive to theorize CALL might be seen as jeopardizing the focus on practical knowledge derived from classroom experience. There is evidence that classroom experience has always been a source of momentum for the development of CALL. For example, the early teaching experiments with telecollaborative CALL (Barson, Frommer, & Schwartz 1993; Kern 1996; Barson & Debski 1996) have made a significant impact on the discipline, but they were undertaken before the existence of a complete theoretical apparatus explaining their desirability. They were based on intuition and fascination with emerging technologies. Rationalization of CALL therefore may be seen as sacrificing the intuitions of creative teachers that lead to successful practices, but which are difficult to explain and formalize by the application of currently available scientific rigor. Secondly, rationalization means the development of a specialist language and discourse. Many recent CALL publications address issues of learning and teaching languages with computers using specialist and hermetic language that makes it difficult, if not impossible, for teachers to draw practical conclusions and develop classroom applications. Thirdly, the teaching of CALL as a science has moved to academic departments which emphasize the theoretical basis of disciplines and often do not possess the infrastructure and technical support necessary to introduce practical components in their programs. It is well known that teaching CALL through practical projects is resource-hungry, and low student enrollments, which are to be expected in a niche area such as CALL, often make it difficult to justify more expensive hands-on pedagogies.

This chapter proposes that a good balance between theory and practice in a CALL course can be achieved by engaging CALL students in meaningful projects aimed at real-life audiences in and outside the university. The next section provides a discussion of project-oriented learning, which is followed by a description of the Melbourne University Master of CALL program.

Project-oriented learning

In the project-oriented classroom, students are challenged to *get real*, which must manifest itself in interacting with real people and issues, and in students' taking responsibility for their learning. The principal role of the teacher is to assure the success of student-led enterprise and to engineer learning opportunities, just as the role of a skilful manager is to ensure that work gets done on time and to the client's satisfaction, and that all the team members utilize the best of their talent and enthusiasm.

While recognizing the importance of course content, project-oriented learning does not see it as an organized repertoire of units to be systematically practised. Instead, it asserts goal-oriented, meaningful activity as the force guiding the assimilation of course content, which should be practised as opportunities arise and always with reference to goal-oriented activity. The course is thus defined as a malleable entity identifying actors – both human and artefact – goals, and actions related to an activity at hand. Such actors could be audience, advisory committee, sponsors, software, and hardware. Goals and actions can be such as developing understanding of a theory or selecting development tools best matching the achievement of specific goals.

Project-oriented learning draws on a number of compatible learning concepts that could be together named as constructivist. One understanding of constructivism is that it is a theory that asserts that "human knowledge – whether it be the bodies of public knowledge known as the disciplines or the cognitive structures of individuals or learners – is constructed" (Phillips 1995:5), and as such cannot be transferred from reservoirs of knowledge directly and unaltered into the human mind. The concept of constructivism eludes a clear definition and the range of constructivist authors is wide. Piaget (1980) associates learning with feedback received from actions and therefore concrete materials that can be manipulated have an important role in learning. Vygotsky (1978) links knowledge acquisition to social processes by asserting that knowledge arises in social interactions before the individual internalizes it. Dewey's (1960: 196) views on learning connect knowledge acquisition to directed action:

> If we see that knowing is not the act of an outside spectator but of a participator inside the natural and social sense, then the true object of knowledge resides in the consequences of directed action.

A theory drawing on all the above concepts and most directly explaining the benefits of project learning, however, is *constructionism* (Papert 1980, 1993), a concept based on constructivism to which it adds the idea that people construct new knowledge with particular effectiveness when they are engaged in constructing personally-meaningful products (Kafai & Resnick 1996). Constructionism thus incorporates elements of humanistic psychology by acknowledging intrinsic motivation and self-edification as important drivers for education.

The CALL program

The academic program in CALL at The University of Melbourne was established in 1997 and housed in the Horwood Language Centre (HLC). At first offered at the Postgraduate Diploma level, in 2000 the program was upgraded to a Master of CALL that can be completed either by coursework or coursework and minor thesis. Today, students with an honours degree or equivalent work experience can complete the program in one year. The Centre also offers a Postgraduate Certificate in Arts (CALL), which can be completed in one semester of full-time study and can lead to the Master of CALL for high-achieving students. The coursework and minor thesis option of the masters program opens admission to the PhD program to students with no research experience.

The Centre currently offers seven postgraduate subjects in CALL: "Introduction to CALL", "Introduction to CALL: Project", "Research and evaluation in CALL", "Online language learning", "Current issues in CALL", "CALL software design and implementation", and "Minor thesis". The development of subjects has been informed by an annual survey of student needs. Students can also take complementary subjects in second language acquisition, language testing, or research methods in the Department of Linguistics and Applied Linguistics. In 2002, a CALL stream in the applied linguistics program was established for students wishing to take subjects in CALL. Overall, enrolments have been adequate in those CALL subjects that are listed both in the Master of CALL and the Master of Applied Linguistics (CALL) programs, whereas some of the other subjects have suffered from low student numbers. This may necessitate a further integration of the CALL program with the program in applied linguistics and/or offering more CALL subjects as core or optional subjects in the applied linguistics program in the near future.

Placing the program in the language centre has presented a number of advantages, two of which are relevant for the present discussion. Firstly, easy access to expert technical staff has assisted the program's focus on practical, real-life applications. Secondly, the Centre's links with the language departments have assisted the CALL students in undertaking joint-projects with language teachers resulting in the development of useful CALL materials for specific audiences. Two issues have emerged in this area, however, having financial implications and requiring organizational adjustments. Firstly, engagement of the Centre's technical staff in the CALL program has been regarded by the university as not always directly relevant to the Centre's core mission. It is worth noting that, until recently, "support" provided by the Centre was understood as provision of day-to-day technical assistance, language media handling, and laboratory maintenance. Secondly, working with CALL students on projects presented an additional workload for the language teachers. Consequently, only teachers who managed to obtain some form of support, e.g. teaching relief, could participate in the CALL projects. The program has also suffered from the Centre's ambiguous status as a service and academic unit.

Transformation of the program

Educating the "CALL Expert" (or "CALL Professional": see Hubbard and Levy, this volume) is an explicit aim of the Master of CALL program. As outlined in the course objectives, the "CALL Expert" will have the requisite skills to provide leadership for teachers and other experts working on CALL innovations.

A questionnaire administered to students taking "Introduction to CALL" in 1997, 1999, 2001, 2002, 2003 and 2004 displays a variety of expectations students had after joining the program (Table 1).

As revealed by the questionnaire, enhancing one's own repertoire of teaching practices and acquiring skills in designing and developing software, virtual classrooms and online courses have by far been the most important objectives for students. Obtaining knowledge in order to share it with other teachers in the workplace, as a consultant or coordinator, and to be able to justify the use of computers to others have emerged as the third most important motivation. This was closely followed by an expectation of becoming more computer literate, employable, and more knowledgeable about software in order to make informed selection decisions. A smaller number of students joined the course to satisfy their curiosity of

Table 1. Course entry expectations of CALL students in years 1997, 1999, and 2001–2004 (N = 69)

Student Expectations	No.
Using CALL	33
Be able to use CALL in the classroom	
Incorporate CALL into own teaching	
Developing materials	27
Learn to design and create CALL Websites and applications	
Learn how to collaborate with software designers	
Develop educational software	
Learn how to deliver online courses	
Set up virtual classrooms	
Disseminating CALL knowledge and skills	11
Be able to teach/lecture in CALL	
Be able to support other teachers	
Be able to justify the use of computers	
Become a CALL consultant	
Become a CALL coordinator in a school	
To offer assistance, advice, support to students	
Acquiring computer literacy	9
Upgrade general computer skills	
Get familiarized with technical terminology	
Evaluating CALL materials	7
Know better what software is available	
Be able to evaluate CALL	
Find out how CALL can promote autonomous learning	
Changing career	7
Build a basis for another career	
Become more employable	
Joining an educational courseware developer	
Establish a partnership/business in language Websites	
Conducting research	5
Continue research in CALL	
Design software for research purposes	
Formulate a coherent picture of the discipline	
Bring knowledge about CALL to the home country	3
Teach a language course with an IT focus	1

CALL as an academic discipline, to conduct research, and to bring CALL expertise to their home country.

The same questionnaire has also recorded a change in the student perception of their computer skills at the time they commenced their studies. A section in which students were asked to assess their skills on a Likert scale of 0–5 (0-never done before; 5-expert knowledge) demonstrates that student computer skills, their

Table 2. Change in computer skills of students entering the CALL program

Computing Skills	1997 (N = 10)	1999 (N = 8)	2001 (N = 10)	2003 (N = 13)	2004 (N = 13)
General computer skills	2.3	2.9	4.1	3.5	3.8
Word processing	2.8	2.9	4.1	3.8	3.8
Web	1.1	2.9	4.1	4.1	4.1
Web creation	0.2	0.7	2.4	1.5	1.5
Image editing	0.8	0.8	1.2	1.3	2.2
Programming	0.1	0.0	0.5	0.5	1.0

familiarity with Web browsing, Web development, and image editing at the time of entry to the program have been increasing steadily (Table 2).

The above results show how the assessment of student needs and the change in their skills have made it necessary to move the program towards employing modules of project-oriented learning. The results indicate that, today, our students expect a practice-oriented course with some coverage of theory and research, and they are increasingly better equipped with relevant computer skills to undertake projects that are more than academic exercises. They still however require the assistance of expert technicians with more advanced programming aspects of their projects.

The next sections describe a specific application of project learning undertaken in 2004 in one of the subjects offered as part of the CALL program, and analyse the learning outcomes.

The subject

"Online Language Learning" is offered as a core subject within the Master of CALL at the University of Melbourne.

Subject objectives

The HLC runs short programs in English language and Australian culture for groups of students from Japanese universities. As the programs did not have any Web presence, the lecturer proposed development of a Website for the Centre's Cultural Programs as a subject project.

The subject involved four contact hours per week (a 2-hour seminar and a 2-hour tutorial) over a twelve-week semester. In the seminars, aspects of second language acquisition were discussed vis-à-vis examples of practical CALL applications. The purpose of the tutorials, on the other hand, was to explore a gamut of electronic tools, and identify such that could be used to develop a working model of an online community for the benefit of the Cultural Programs.

Procedures

The seminars took place in a wireless laptop-based classroom. Each seminar involved introduction of a CALL/SLA issue, a group discussion of readings, a discussion of the implications of the concepts introduced by the reading for the ongoing project, and a project progress report. The workshop part of the subject took place in a PC laboratory and involved a survey of online communities and communicative tools, meetings with the coordinator of the Cultural Programs to determine the scope of the project, working on the project specifications, and developing the project.

Assessment

The assessment was constructed to give students marks for individual as well as group work and contained the following elements:

a. A written assignment of not more than 4000 words (30%).
b. Presentation of a topic different than the topic of the essay subsequently written up (1000 words) (20%).
c. A working model of a Website and a written specification and rationale (collective mark) (20%).
d. A written summation of one's personal contribution to the project (20%).
e. A verbal presentation on online communication tools (10%).

Deliverables

In the course of the subject, the students created a comprehensive Website for the Cultural Programs. Another deliverable was a 26-page Project Specification. The specification contained information on the background of the project, a needs analysis and a rationale for the project, and technical specifications and suggestions for future applications and development.

The students also wrote essays on issues related to the project. The following are examples of the essay topics proposed by the students: "The roles of the computer in intercultural language learning", "Autonomy and its importance in telecollaborative language learning", and "Investigation of pedagogical theories supporting the construction of an e-learning environment". Finally, they each wrote 2–3 page reflections describing the contributions they had made to the project and what they had learned in the subject.

The Project Specification and Student Reflection documents are used in the next section of the chapter to describe the learning outcomes of the subject.

PROJECT

Reflection on Theory ←···→ Reflection on Design
(2-hr seminars)   (2-hr workshops)

Figure 1. Learning theory-in-practice.

Discussion of learning outcomes

Learning theory-in-practice

As they engaged in their project, the students were challenged to make decisions about the design of the Website and to support those decisions with relevant theory and research. The project thus functioned as an interface linking the two parts of the course and a stage where reflection on theory and design could crystallize into educationally desirable solutions (Figure 1).

In the Project Specification, the students explain the decisions they have made about the functionality and design of the Website. The rationale for the project was based on their conviction that it would be beneficial for the Japanese students who come to Melbourne for five weeks to engage with the Australian culture and the Australian variety of English before their arrival and to remain in contact with them after departure. This notion was developed after discussing in the classroom O'Dowd's (2000) report on an intercultural videoconferencing project and the phenomena of "cultural shock" and "intercultural learning". The students started thinking that electronic communication might be helpful in overcoming cultural shock by extending cultural contact through purposefully designed tasks. They also became keen on creating facilities that could be used to develop an online community where past and future students from Japan and their Australian partners could organize events, meet, and exchange views. In such a community, the study of a foreign culture would be closely linked to reflection on your own culture, appreciation of similarities and differences, and could be enhanced by online exchanges of information. Influenced by the literature on intercultural learning, they proposed that the HLC program change its name from "Cultural Programs" to "Intercultural Programs", a name in their opinion better reflecting the process of cultural learning that could be enabled by the online community they were building.

In order to implement the community, they had to review community-building tools and the rationale behind using them. This is how a student described this process:

> [...] we deliberated on some computer-mediated [communication] tools we might want to use in our project and allocated a tool for each member to research on. I researched the pedagogical rationale for using blogs and wrote a short piece justifying the use of blogs and uploaded it to Vicnet.   (June)

Vicnet is a free, Victorian government Web portal that the students chose for setting up a bulletin board facility to negotiate the outcomes of their project. They investigated several other platforms, but chose Vicnet because it had no distracting advertisements, was easy to navigate, and had a facility for setting up communities. The lecturers and the coordinator of the Cultural Programs were invited to join the discussions. The group generated over 130 messages in the course of the semester.

The students drew the rationale for establishing *Our Community* from research into group dynamics. They concluded from it that in addition to "breaking the ice", the CMC environment that they were building would provide the opportunity to establish "group familiarity" and "group cohesion" (Mukahi & Corbitt 2004), which are necessary for the creation of a successful online community for the students before they arrive in Australia. They further speculated that there was some advantage in engaging the students in both face-to-face and CMC interaction because they had access to evidence that groups of students who have had the opportunity for both CMC and face-to-face outperformed the other groups in finding solutions and derived greater task satisfaction (Mukahi & Corbitt 2004). They also were introduced to literature (Weininger & Shield 2003; Roed 2003) demonstrating that "many types of learners perform better in a CMC environment rather than the traditional classroom" (Project Specification).

Vygotskyan concepts of "zone of proximal development" and "scaffolding" were also discussed. The students hypothesized that participants who lacked certain skills on their own might perform better in a social context provided by others who had the necessary knowledge through the process of scaffolding, which is the dialogic process by which one learner assists another to perform a new function by simplifying, promoting and maintaining interest in the task, and marking the critical features and discrepancies between what has been produced and the ideal solution. The Project Specification shows that in their consideration of scaffolding, they drew on Donato (1994), describing the collective scaffolding leading to acquisition by groups of students performing an oral task and Swain and Lapkin (1998), who have noted learners' ability to internalize grammatical features that they initially constructed collaboratively by performing a task.

Discussion of literature on cultural stereotypes led the group to develop a section called *Fun Facts* with interesting facts about Australia. This is how the students described the purpose of this page:

> This section was conceived and written to present a sample of stereotypical aspects about Australian culture and society, as well as emphasizing the multicultural nature of Australia. Particular attention was given to allay preconceived stereotypes and to encourage these to be challenged during the students' stay in Australia.
>
> (Project Specification)

Discussion of tandem learning literature (Schwienhorst 1998) in turn led the students to speculations about how the community they had built might be used in the future:

> Upon return to their country, students could be encouraged to maintain connections to *Our Community* through a tandem learning program which matches an Asian student who wants to learn English with an Australian student who wants to learn the Asian student's language. (Project Specification)

Authenticity

Students were profoundly aware of the audience they were creating the site for. First, an overall site metaphor was developed after an examination of the educational objectives of the Cultural Programs:

> Given these guidelines, the site was constructed using the concept of the students experiencing "The Journey". Essentially, the students would be able to gain a taste of the Australian experience through a "slide show" of events of the Summer InterCultural Program. (Project Specification)

Their design decisions were driven by their assessment of the audience:

> Given the target audience, it was deemed appropriate that the site be picture driven and colourful with the English wording being at the intermediate level. (Project Specification)

In their reflections they noted that many issues had cropped up which would not have been considered had the project not been authentic:

> Many matters arose concerning the confidentiality of students, the displaying of staff contact details on Websites, the image the project coordinators wish to disseminate about the course, the intended audience of the site, and concerns related to project marketing and pitch. (Anne)

The students also negotiated the choice of best possible technological tools for the development of their project:

> My original intention was to use Macromedia Flash to create the slideshow but after discussions with the other group members, it was thought that using Macromedia *Dreamweaver* would be a better choice. (June)

Roles and skills practised

The students assumed different roles and developed a range of skills. This is how three of them have described in their reflective journals the roles they adopted in the project and the skills they developed as, respectively, Coordinator and Liaison, Technical Leader, and Graphical Designer.

The student who became the Coordinator and Liaison reported that it was necessary that one group member should have a total overview of the project and be able to act as a transmitter of content and ideas between group members. In this role, she reports on coordinating the project, chairing meetings, allocating duties, highlighting and resolving conflicts, liaising with the clients, reporting to the project sponsor, transmitting content and ideas between different group members, devising concept maps for the site using *Inspiration*, and developing future directions for the project.

A student whose skills in *Dreamweaver* and other Web design tools were the most advanced in the group assumed the role of the Technical Leader. He described himself as the general architect of the Website. As Technical Leader, he developed a concept map of the site using *Inspiration*, created most of the Website, liaised with the students developing the other parts of the Website to preserve consistency of design, introduced and implemented the idea of developing 360-degree picture panoramas of several places in Melbourne and the University campus using *PhotoStitch*, and taught several other team members various *Dreamweaver* functions.

The role of Graphical Designer emerged when "it was decided later that it would be easier if Andy were to be in charge of the overall Website design while I worked on designing the homepage graphics and the slideshow on the Journey" (June). In her role, the Graphical Designer worked on site templates with the Technical Leader and designed all site graphics using Macromedia *Dreamweaver*, *Fireworks*, and *Flash*.

Peer support

It was inspiring to see that the students who had the least technical skills of the groups felt supported by the team, as illustrated by the following report:

> I really enjoyed working as a team member with a real professional group. It might be a shame to confess that I was the least qualified of those (professionals), but I can be very proud to work with them [...].   (Adam)

The same student commented on the complementary skills of the team. In his opinion, every member of the team "was really a (wiz) at certain skills as though destiny assembled them to complement each other and carry out this project successfully".

Student satisfaction

In their overall assessment of the course, the students emphasized satisfaction from working collectively with a group of dedicated people towards a worthy goal, as illustrated by the following statement:

> I feel I made a substantial contribution to the success of this worthy University project. Through cooperation and collaboration we were able to achieve something we can all be proud of.   (John)

However, some students expressed disbelief whether such a gratifying experience could be repeated in a university context:

> [...] all I can say [is] that I don't think such experience with such group will happen again regarding productivity and team soul.   (Adam)

Conclusions

The present chapter has demonstrated that work on a CALL project that is directed at an authentic audience can serve as a bridge linking the theoretical and practical aspects of a CALL subject to support *theory-in-practice* learning. In such an approach, the interplay between theory and practice is mediated by the pursuit of optimal solutions to a practical problem at hand. In the analysed example, the project became a conceptual space for the implementation of theory-inspired solutions as well as a motivator for the assimilation of theoretical knowledge. Theories and examples of best practice were reviewed in the seminar part of the subject, and students explored in more depth those aspects of theory and research which informed the specific project objectives. The project management process exposed those junctions where practice had to be informed by theory so that educationally desirable decisions could be made: for example once the students decided that they wanted to establish a learning community to overcome "cultural shock", they had to review community-building tools and make decisions about which of them best matched their goals. In CALL understood as a design science, principles can be taught as part of the design cycle aimed at producing pedagogical artefacts that are meaningful to students and useful in social contexts outside the classroom.

Theory-in-practice learning suggests however that the class will necessarily emphasise theories and research directly contributing to the project, perhaps at the expense of those which are less directly relevant. To overcome this limitation, project learning at Melbourne is implemented only in some subjects, while other subjects assure a systematic coverage of material. Also, the teacher's role is to develop the ability to establish connections between student projects and the requisite formal knowledge, and to manage the occurrence and constant appeal to theoretical principles, as they are not guaranteed by a linear syllabus.

The students were profoundly aware of the audience of their project throughout its duration. Decisions regarding design were made in consultation with the sponsors and clients, a process emphasizing to students the relationships between theoretical knowledge and practice, and, first of all, the social constraints that exist in applying theoretical solutions to real-life problems. For example, the class spent a considerable amount of time discussing the impact of their Website on marketing the courses to Japanese universities. The students realised that the Website must be pedagogically sound as well as presenting the program as attractive and worth applying for.

The students assumed roles and practiced skills that they would not be able to develop in a more traditional class. The development of those roles and skills was linked to the specific needs of the project and helped students understand their natural strengths and what roles they could play in CALL projects in the future. A number of students also commented on either receiving support from classmates or providing support to colleagues. Overall, they were satisfied with the experience, and in their evaluations they have emphasized the personal and professional gratification they achieved by making a contribution to a real-life audience.

Experience with project learning demonstrates however that sharing of responsibilities and developing roles in the project does not always go as smoothly as reported in the present chapter. Some students may not understand the rationale behind project learning and may expect more support from the teacher. Projects often polarize the class, so that highly motivated students end up doing most of the work, leaving few learning opportunities to those who are less motivated or do not see how they can contribute. The teacher plays an important role here as a manager of the learning process, a fair arbiter that resolves conflict and engineers and sustains learning opportunities for all the participants. The teacher may have to negotiate learning contracts with students outlining their engagement and personal objectives. Another important role of the teacher is to listen to students and deal in a supportive manner with project ideas.

Project-oriented learning has become a permanent feature of CALL courses at the University of Melbourne. Students work on individual or group projects for their own schools or language departments in the university. In the second semester of 2004, a group of students developed a Website for ethnic language schools, a seriously under-resourced sector of Australian education. Several months prior to the class, the lecturer had conducted a workshop for a group of ethnic school teachers and collected a few dozen email addresses. The CALL students were challenged to communicate with the teachers to find out what they could develop for them. In the theoretical part of the course, among other topics, the students were studying topics of bilingualism and language maintenance in order to establish what support technology could provide to minority language learning and teaching. Such projects are a good illustration of the "relate-create-donate" principle (Shneiderman 1997: vii), as they help teachers develop an understanding of technology as a tool that can be used to solve real social issues. Such educational approaches become important in today's world when people are challenged to harness technological advancement to solve issues of global ecology and diversity.

In 2005, CALL students developed a Website for the HLC Introductory Academic Program (IAP) and participated in the pilot implementation of *Blackboard* and the *Wimba* "building block" for *Blackboard*. Plans are being made to provide partial scholarships for students with strong technical skills who would come to Melbourne University to study and work on language projects under the supervision of academic and technical staff and receive academic credit for their efforts. Teachers who apply project-oriented approaches must use their connections within and outside the institution to look for projects that could inspire their students and develop new contexts for students to study CALL theory.

The need to improve the status of CALL and those who research and study it is still apparent. Today, it is clear that improving the status of CALL is as much about consolidating its scientific foundation as it is about strengthening it as an area of teaching and learning. Foremost, CALL must be cautious not to distance itself from the language teaching profession by focusing too strongly on earning a respectable place in academia alongside literary and cultural studies and second language acquisition research. The increasing rationalization of CALL may lead the discipline to an estrangement from its primary client base, practicing or trainee teachers, in turn leading to low enrolment and the decline of the discipline. Project-oriented learning seems to be a pedagogy that suits the advancement of CALL understood as a design science and is helpful in maintaining the necessary rationalization of CALL without sacrificing the practical dimension of the discipline.

References

Barson, J., Frommer, J., & Schwartz, M. (1993). Foreign language learning using email in a task-oriented perspective: An interuniversity experiment in communication and collaboration. *Journal for Science Education and Technology, 2*, 565–583.

Barson, J. & Debski, R. (1996). Calling back CALL: Technology in the service of foreign language learning based on creativity, contingency, and goal-oriented activity. In M. Warschauer (Ed.), *Telecollaboration in Foreign Language Learning: Proceedings of the Hawaii symposium*, Honolulu, HI: University of Hawaii, Second Language Teaching and Curriculum Centre.

Chapelle, C. (2001). *Computer Applications in Second Language Acquisition: Foundations for teaching, testing, and research*. Cambridge: CUP.

Dewey, J. (1960). *The Quest of Certainty*. New York, NY: Capricorn.

Donato, R. (1994). Collective scaffolding in second language learning. In J. Lantolf & G. Appel (Eds.), *Theoretical Framework: An introduction to Vygotskyan approaches to second language research*. Norwood, NJ: Ablex.

Hubbard, P. (2003). A survey of unanswered questions in CALL. *Computer Assisted Language Learning, 16* (2–3), 141–154.

Kafai, Y. & Resnick, M. (Eds.). (1996). *Constructionism in Practice: Designing, thinking and learning in a digital world*. Mahwah, NJ: Lawrence Erlbaum.

Kern, R. (1996). Computer-mediated communication: Using e-mail exchanges to explore personal histories in two cultures. In M. Warschauer (Ed.), *Telecollaboration in Foreign Language Learning*. Honolulu, HI: University of Hawai'i Second Language Teaching and Curriculum Center.

Kozma, R. (1994). Will media influence learning? Reframing the debate. *Educational Technology Research and Development, 42* (2), 7–19.

Levy, M. (1997). Project-based learning for language teachers: Reflection on the process. In R. Debski, J. Gassin, & M. Smith (Eds.), *Language Learning through Social Computing*. Applied Linguistics Association of Australia. Occasional Papers No. 16.

Levy, M. (2000). Scope, goals and methods in CALL research: Questions of coherence and autonomy. *ReCALL, 12* (2), 170–195.

Levy, M. (2002). CALL by design: Discourse, products and processes. *ReCALL, 14* (1), 58–84.

Mukahi, T. & Corbitt, G. (2004). The influence of familiarity among group members and extraversion on verbal interaction in proximate GSS sessions. In *Proceedings of the 37th Hawaii International Conference on System Sciences*. Available at http://csdl2.computer.org/persagen/DLAbsToc.jsp?resourcePath=/dl/proceedings/&toc=comp/proceedings/hicss/2004/2056/01/2056toc.xml&DOI=10.1109/HICSS.2004.1265149.

O'Dowd, R. (2000). Intercultural learning via videoconferencing: A pilot exchange project. *ReCALL, 12* (1), 49–61.

Papert, S. (1980). *Mindstorms*. London: Harvester Press.

Papert, S. (1993). *The Children's Machine: Rethinking school in the age of the computer*. New York, NY: Basic Books.

Phillips, D. C. (1995). The good, the bad, and the ugly: The many faces of constructivism. *Educational Researcher, 24* (7), 5–12.

Piaget, J. (1980). The psychogenesis of knowledge and its epistemological significance. In M. Piatteli-Palmarini (Ed.), *Language and Learning*. Cambridge, MA: Harvard University Press.

Roed, J. (2003). Language learning behaviour in a virtual environment. *Computer Assisted Language Learning, 16* (2–3), 155–172.

Schwienhorst, K. (1998). Matching pedagogy and technology: Tandem learning and learner autonomy in online virtual learning environments. In R. Soetaert, E. De Man, & G. Van Belle (Eds.), *Language Teaching On-line* (pp. 115–127). Ghent: University of Ghent.

Shneiderman, B. (1997). Foreword. In R. Debski, J. Gassin, & M. Smith (Eds.), *Language Learning through Social Computing*. Applied Linguistics Association of Australia. Occasional Papers No. 16.

Swain, M. & Lapkin, S. (1998). Interaction and second language learning: Two adolescent French immersion students working together. *Modern Language Journal, 82* (3), 320–337.

Vygotsky, L. S. (1978). *Mind in Society: The development of higher psychological processes*. Cambridge, MA: Harvard University Press.

Weber, M. (1947). *The Theory of Social and Economic Organization*. New York, NY: Oxford University Press.

Weininger, M. & Shield, L. (2003). Promoting oral production in a written channel: An investigation of learner language in MOO. *Computer Assisted Language Learning, 16* (4), 329–349.

PART III

CALL pre-service courses

When the technology course is required

Although many language teacher education programs now offer some form of a technology training course, that course is all too often an elective rather than a required part of the curriculum. In addition, if an appropriately skilled faculty member within the program is not available, the students may need to go outside the department, getting a course focused on something other than language teaching and learning applications. Finally, even when such courses are taught within the language teacher education program, they may be taken as late as the final semester, making it impossible to integrate the new technological proficiency into the parts of the training process that have already passed. In this chapter Volker Hegelheimer argues for a promising new approach for master's-level teacher training: to introduce technology knowledge and skills comprehensively through a foundational course at the beginning of the student's program. In that way, the technology knowledge and skills gained can be linked specifically to applied linguistics and language teaching applications and used throughout the remainder of the student's coursework. In addition, faculty teaching other courses in the program can assume a reasonable and more uniform level of technological proficiency that can aid them in expanding technology use in their subjects. Hegelheimer describes the implementation of his course, "Introduction to Computers in Applied Linguistics," in the MA TESL program at Iowa State University. He relates class activities both to general course goals and to the transfer of skills and knowledge to other classes in the program and in the students' own language teaching. He supports his discussion with comments gleaned from both students and faculty about the impact of the technology course on the overall program. His arguments and examples provide a convincing case for infusing technology throughout the curriculum.

When the technology course is required

Volker Hegelheimer
Iowa State University, USA

> The way that students will learn to do applied linguistics with technology is by
> learning applied linguistics through technology. (Chapelle 2003:31)

Preparing language teachers for the 21st century: Problems and solutions

Even though future language teachers will most certainly not be replaced by computers, computer-using language teachers will replace those teachers who do not
use computers. At its core, the answers to the basic question as to how language
teachers of the 21st century are to be trained will undoubtedly contain the words
"technology" and/or "computers." An ensuing question then is: How do we best
prepare language teachers for future careers in which technology will play a central
and constantly changing role?

While teacher trainers frequently realize that technology is crucial for teachers,
teacher training programs in general have been slow to respond with the necessary
curricular innovation. A problem with many current teacher training programs is
that computer and technology courses are either not required, taught by faculty
outside the department with very little relevance to language teaching, or occur
relatively late in the training so that the skills learned and knowledge gained do
not become an integral part of the program.

Clearly, the profession pays homage to technology and numerous ESL and
EFL job descriptions ask for technology savvy teachers (Kessler, this volume), yet
technology is still not as integrated as it should be. Thus, one could conclude that
many teacher training programs may not be effectively preparing their students
for their role as technology-using language teachers. One possible new approach
addressing these issues is to embark on curricular innovation and to include a
mandatory technology course early in a teacher training program. In this chapter,
one such approach is outlined, and its effects on the curriculum, the students, and

other faculty within the same program are discussed, followed by suggestions and insights based on interim reflections on the new curriculum.

A novel approach to language teacher training

Realizing the vital role of technology in language teaching, the faculty in the M.A. program in Teaching English as a Second Language/Applied Linguistics (TESL/AL) at Iowa State University (ISU) engaged in curricular reorganization in late 1997 to better reflect the expressed need for greater integration of technology into the M.A. program. Below, after presenting the revised curriculum and the newly required technology course, the connections between the new course and established M.A. courses are discussed in light of the transfer of skills. This discussion is augmented by student feedback.

The revised curriculum

The curriculum leading to the M.A. in Teaching English as a Second Language/Applied Linguistics at ISU now includes prerequisites, core requirements, and areas of concentration, culminating in a thesis project in the area of concentration (Table 1). The newly added technology course, *Computer Methods in Applied Linguistics*, is one of the prerequisite courses. The premise of the curricular revision process was to integrate technology more fully and to establish a technology foundation for language teachers not only early on in the curriculum, but also one that is focused on teaching English as a Second Language rather than advising students to take a technology elective in other departments. Consequently, the course had to be offered at the beginning of the program and be taught by a TESL/AL faculty member. The content of this course, which will be discussed in greater detail below, had to address what the faculty felt was necessary and beneficial knowledge and skills that could be used throughout the rest of the curriculum, including in courses that do not lead to a CALL specialization. However, as is the case in many programs, the perceived need for technology integration varies from faculty member to faculty member. In particular, faculty members who have been teaching courses for years (or decades) a certain way are frequently unaware of the benefits technology can hold. Therefore, when approached as to what skills they feel should be taught in the introductory computer course, they did not always have a clear idea of what is possible with technology and did not request that certain skills be included in the computer methods course. Thus, innovation and curricular change occurred through the students who came into the other courses with a fairly good understanding of technology and applied the skills they learned

Table 1. The M.A. TESL/Applied Linguistics curriculum at ISU

Prerequisites	Core Requirements	Areas of Concentration & Courses	Independent Research
– English Grammar – Introduction to Linguistic Analysis – **Computer Methods in Applied Linguistics**	– Sociolinguistics – Grammatical Analysis – Second Language Acquisition – TESL Methods & Materials – Second Language Testing – Practicum	CALL – Computer-Assisted Language Learning – Instructional Technology Language Assessment – Discourse Analysis – Assessment Practicum English for Specific Purposes – Discourse Analysis – English for Specific Purposes Literacy* – Literacy: Methods and Materials – Teaching Composition – Teaching ESL Listening and Speaking Literature in ESL**	Thesis research
3 credits can be used for the M.A.	18 credits	6 credits	3 credits

Note.
*The first course is required, others can be chosen from a list.
**Electives are chosen from the course offerings in literature.

to class work, which is illustrated in the section outlining the connection between the curriculum and the new requirement.

The required technology course

Since the fall semester of 1999, the M.A. curriculum has included a prerequisite computer methods course in which students are introduced to the use of technology in language teaching and research as well as classroom management. The course, *Introduction to Computers in Applied Linguistics* (English 510), is aimed at equipping graduate students with the basic computer and technology skills necessary for the (English) language teacher in the 21st century early in the M.A. program. It is designed to provide students with the opportunity to 1) increase their familiarity with computers in general, 2) explore and describe current and potential applications of computers for teaching, testing, research, administration, and CALL, 3) create web pages that complement language teaching, and 4) conduct statistical and linguistic analyses of various data.

To achieve these objectives, a two-pronged approach synthesizing practice and theory is taken. During the hands-on portion,[1] students are introduced to basic teacher tools (word processing, spreadsheet, and presentation applications, e.g., the *Microsoft Office Suite*), management tools (database applications, e.g., *FileMaker Pro*), development tools (WYSIWYG editors, animation applications, graphic applications, e.g., *Macromedia Studio MX 2004*), and research tools (concordancing, data gathering, and statistical analysis applications, e.g., *MonoConc Pro, Camtasia*, and *SPSS* or *MS Excel*, respectively). In addition to the practical components of the course, theoretical aspects revolving around the use of computers in language teaching are introduced through selected readings, which are discussed in an online forum one week prior to the in-class presentation. Plus, since most enrolled students also teach a variety of ESL and first-year composition courses in the computer classroom, the course is aimed at supplying the students with knowledge and skills that could be integrated into their own classroom teaching. Since its inception in 1999, of the approximately 80 students who have completed the course, few actually went on to concentrate on CALL, but all mastered the basics of technology and its use in the language classroom. How this course connects with other courses in the curriculum is outlined next.

The technology-curriculum connection

While the prerequisite course provides a foundation, the technology skills are ideally continually reinforced through the use of technology in the M.A. students' own teaching and in other M.A. TESL graduate courses. Table 2 outlines the goals, the related class activities, and the transfer of the goals (and skills) to other classes.

Following the curricular reorganization efforts, integration of technology in other graduate courses can proceed based on the assumption that students enrolled in subsequent semesters have acquired essential technology skills, which they are encouraged to employ in completing class tasks. This, however, is but one aspect of how a technology course can have an affect on an entire program. Given that technology permeates the profession (Chapelle & Hegelheimer 2004), the goal of an M.A. program in the 21st century should perhaps focus on empowering future teachers to successfully and competently implement technology in their classroom practices. Rather than focusing on what M.A. graduates should be able to do upon graduating, it may be time for teacher training programs to be evaluated in terms of how they integrate technology. While a lot of work remains to be accomplished, the attempts of the M.A. program at ISU are outlined in Table 3. Technology currently plays an integral part in several graduate courses. For example, corpus linguistics is introduced in the introductory linguistics course and covered in greater detail in *Grammatical Analysis*. Multimedia web development is initially covered in *Computer Methods for Applied Linguistics* and then

Table 2. Course goals, activities, and skill transfer

Goals	Class Activities	Transfer (to other classes)
Increased general computer familiarity	Semester-long use of computers and technology during class meetings in computer classroom Required in-class *PowerPoint* presentations of related articles and online resources	Search for information and materials online Final presentations of projects in computer classroom using *PowerPoint*.
Basic knowledge of current and potential applications of computers for teaching, testing, research, administration, & CALL	Grade and attendance management unit Introduction to quiz generating tools (e.g., *Hot Potatoes, CourseBuilder*) Introduction to screen capturing application Course readings and online discussion	Course and grade management of their own classes Generating interactive activities & assessments as part of other assignments in graduate courses
Ability to create functional web pages that complement language teaching	Creation of professional homepage Skill consolidation activity Web-based teaching unit	Class homepage development for their own classes Ability to put information online (including assignments and activities as part of other graduate courses)
Ability to conduct statistical and linguistic analyses of various data.	Introduction to basic descriptive statistics using *MS Excel* Introduction to corpus linguistics and the use of corpora and concordances	Computing test statistics in Language Testing course Consumption of research articles in all courses Analysis of learner language

revisited in *Language Testing*, when students work on implementing computer-assisted language testing (CALT) activities. Similarly, the introduction to the use of applications to compute statistics (e.g., *MS Excel* and *SPSS*) in the introductory technology course prepares students to apply and extend this knowledge as part of generating test statistics. Students specializing in CALL take two courses, a CALL seminar and a course in instructional technology, in which technology plays an integral role.

When asked about the role technology plays in other graduate classes, M.A. students noted that technology certainly does play a role. This role varied from being able to facilitate data analysis to conducting research to creating online materials and web pages, as can be seen by these comments on the role of technology in data analysis and content creation:

Table 3. Technology integration in the M.A. curriculum

Type of requirement	Course in the M.A. curriculum	Technology thread
Prerequisites	English Grammar	
	Introduction to Linguistic Analysis	Introduction to corpus linguistics
	Computer Methods in Applied Linguistics	Complete course
Core	Sociolinguistics	
Requirements	Grammatical Analysis	Corpus linguistics, computational analysis of texts
	Second Language Acquisition	Learner corpora, technology-mediated SLA tasks, individualization
	TESL Methods and Materials	
	Second Language Testing	Testing data analysis and computer-assisted language testing (CALT)
	Practicum	
Areas of Concentration*	CALL	
	Computer-Assisted Language Learning	Complete course
	Instructional Technology	Complete course
Independent Research	Thesis Research	Research investigating CALL

* Only one area of concentration (CALL) is listed here for demonstration purposes. Other areas include Language Assessment, English for Specific Purposes, Literacy, and Literature in ESL. See Table 1 for a complete list.

> For the 517 [Second Language Acquisition] project, we were viewing the video mediated through a computer, utilizing [technology] there. We had a video that was stored on a CD and we viewed [and analyzed] it through QuickTime player of students interacting, performing a computer-based task.
> (KR)

> We're supposed to give a workshop about how to use media and computer [in 518, TESOL Methods]. It turned out to be the use of internet. We gave the audience the opportunity to see websites and analyze, to evaluate whether this website is good or not. It turned out to be very useful because we learned a lot from the readings [in 510].
> (NI)

However, as the following comment illustrates, technology frequently played a number of roles, extending beyond courses and relating to teaching as well, which is very encouraging since students were able to "practice what was preached" in English 510.

> I used [technology], in my studies, then I used it first of all for my grading. I used Excel for grading sheets. I used my web development skills with Macromedia Dreamweaver to create, to expand my website. So, I created some of the class websites for all of the classes I have taught so far. Also for 526 [seminar course on Computer-Assisted Language Learning], I put some of the materials online. As for the teaching, I have found some activities that are online and used them with my students. (MG)

Interestingly, students realized that they were now being held responsible for knowledge some of the instructors assumed of the students. For example, one instructor took it for granted that the students would have the necessary skills to create web pages to post information:

> Student: We didn't receive instruction about how to do the webpage or develop the quizzes on the computer, but the assignment stipulated that we do both.
> Researcher: Was it expected that you know?
> Student: Yeah. (KR)

Maybe English 510, which met in a computer lab at all times and made extensive use of technology, heightened students' awareness of technology and, when a lack of technology integration was perceived in other graduate courses, there was somewhat of a let-down, as is expressed by this student comment:

> Unfortunately, not all the classes I have taken required us to use the use of our website and things. I think that has to do with the way the instructors are teaching. (MG)

It was not only students who were more aware of technology. Faculty who teach subsequent courses noticed that the use of technology to complete assignments and to give in-class presentations or workshops in general increased. One faculty member remarked that it has become almost a given that students effectively utilize *PowerPoint* during their presentations:

> A relatively minor, but real, thing I've noticed is that when students give reports in class, *they use PowerPoint as a matter of course.*
> (FM1,[2] emphasis added)

Other faculty members also regard the technology course as a contributive factor towards increased professionalism, including the creation of technologically advanced class projects and their effective integration into students' teaching practice, as these two comments suggest:

> We [a group of three faculty members who team-teach] were all very impressed this semester with the TA's final projects which incorporated visual,

oral and electronic communication. The assignment is a collaborative project in which students create a unit that they will be able to use in [English] 105 [the second semester of first-year composition]. In particular, the unit that [one group of three students who were in 510] created on gender stereotyping was extremely well-done, and I know that they were working on that unit for [510]. I have also observed all three of them teaching this semester, and they were using materials from the unit very effectively. I know that without your class, they would not have had the technical skills needed to design such an effective web-based unit. In general, I see a higher facility and comfort with the technology, and I know the TAs feel it is important too.   (FM2)

In 518 (Methods and Materials), the benefits of 510 are enormous. The students in the class do workshops on how to teach particular areas (e.g., writing, vocabulary, etc.). The way they approach the workshops frequently shows evidence of the skills that they gain in 510. One group addressing how to teach vocabulary, for example, had us looking at CALL sites (using clear guidelines) and used pretty sophisticated Power Point to teach it. Probably the workshop that shows the greatest influence is the one on teaching using computers and media. Rather than the general kinds of stuff that I would probably do, the workshop consistently provides practical, clear, detailed activities that teach us about using corpora, what makes CALL exercises effective, how chat can work in a class, and other 510 topics. It's the students who have been in 510 (or even those who are in it concurrently) who drive this particular workshop. I find that I always learn a lot.   (FM3)

However, the impact of English 510 on other courses was not universal, indicating that the approach taken at ISU is merely at the beginning stages of its development and that continued refinement and collaboration among the faculty members is needed. One faculty member, while supportive, pointed out that the skill set does not fully transfer to her class:

Many of my students have already taken English 510 when they take English 516 [Grammatical Analysis]. In spite of the fact that I know that you introduce concordancing in 510, I have to introduce the use of Monoconc for linguistic analysis in detail all the same. Many students seem to have completely forgotten about concordancing. Some of them might not have taken the course, or just a couple might be taking it simultaneously (they are both taught in the fall) but for those who are in their second year (which is what it should be for 516), that is what happens. The rest of the course deals with linguistic analysis and there are no other programs that 510 could help with.   (FM4)

The impact on students

The impact of the course has been investigated through surveys and interviews with students. Results suggest that 1) students are not only more computer-literate and able to construct instructional web resources, which is the aspect of the course students are most excited about, but also more adept at using and critically evaluating technology in their teaching; 2) students are creating extensive projects of immediate usefulness to their teaching assignments; and 3) graduates of the program are successful at securing jobs in part due to their familiarity and expertise with technology.

Computer literacy

Increased computer literacy is a key component in elevating the qualifications of all students. In particular, students enrolled in the M.A. program are typically required to teach three courses per academic year, and most of the enrolled students teach composition courses either to first-year students or to non-native speakers of English. To the surprise of many, the writing courses frequently meet in computer classrooms. While the technology course helps alleviate the initial hesitance toward using computers in teaching, a seminar and mentoring in addition to the prerequisite computer methods course are offered.

A snapshot (Hegelheimer 2004) of the development of 22 first- and second-year M.A. students[3] in terms of their computer skills, their perception of the potential usefulness of technology in language teaching, and their attitudes towards computers and computer-assisted language learning in general reveals the following positive insights, all hinting at increased computer literacy. Not surprisingly, the perceived computer proficiency of the 22 participants increased significantly ($p < .001$) over the course of the semester in which they took the computer methods course. Figure 1 shows the responses to a questionnaire asking the students to rate their expertise using a scale from 0–6, whereby 0 indicates non-use, 1 and 2 beginning knowledge, 3 and 4 intermediate knowledge of an application, and 5 and 6 advanced expertise. The responses illustrate students' self-assessment indicating improvement in all skills and applications (except for database development).[4] In addition to increased computer skills, the students also had the opportunity to reflect on applications and skills they find to be important for future language teachers. When asked about the importance of specific applications for language teachers, the M.A. students' responses showed an increase only for word processing, spreadsheet, and presentation applications (*MS-Word*, *Excel*, and *PowerPoint*, respectively). For all other applications (web and database development, concordancing, WYSIWYG editors such as *Macromedia Dreamweaver* and *Macromedia Flash*), students consistently assigned less importance after the end of the course.

Skills Development

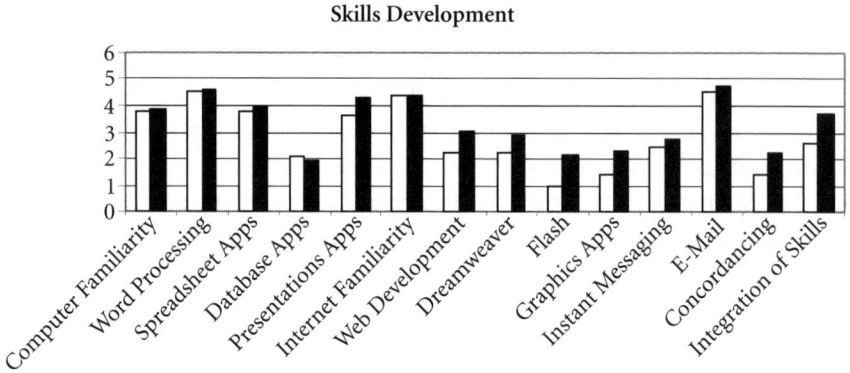

Figure 1. Self-assessment of expertise prior to and post-instruction.

This possibly reflects an initial assumption of beginning teachers that the less-known applications are judged to be more important initially and that learning about these applications helps future teachers realize that despite their usefulness, these programs may not be as important as knowledge of the basics. This also shows increased confidence and a sense of reality – being able to judge what is really important.

Similarly, the results indicate an improved attitude towards computers in general and towards the use of computers in language teaching. While positive to begin with (mean 7.28, SD 1.3 on a 10-point scale), the students' attitude towards utilizing computers in language teaching increased to 7.73 (SD 1.43), suggesting their first semester in the M.A. program did not exert a negative influence. Rather, the responses suggest the opposite.

Even more encouraging than the survey responses were responses to questions posed during a follow-up semi-structured interview. The students indicated not only that they felt more able to effectively utilize technology in their teaching, but also that they were more innovative in terms of conceptualizing novel ideas for teaching, even though they listed lack of time as a major factor preventing them from actually developing some of these resources.

> I had plans, I was thinking initially about using FileMaker Pro and make a database that was for my 101 class because we had to work with vocabulary and had to learn a lot of vocabulary items. I was thinking about making a database so they could all access and use it. Unfortunately it didn't work out because just of the lack of time. (ML)

When asked about her use of technology, one student responded that it had been increasing. Moreover, she became more of a risk-taker, as this comment illustrates:

> ...because I had 510 in my first semester, I was able to use more applications [in my] teaching and as a student I've used mostly [...] word processing. But also I am more willing to experiment or enhance what I am doing with charts or graphs. I did a [...] corpus project [for another class] and I [was] wondering how else I could do this, i.e., to explain this data. [so] I went right into [Microsoft] Excel, punched [the data] in and did a line graph to display what I did and it took no time. That's the kind of stuff that [I could do] because I had that class (510) the first semester. [...] So had I not had that in the first semester [it] would have been different.   (BD)

Increased confidence played a role as well, confidence not only about technology itself, but also about how technology might be utilized in a classroom setting, which is very important because as mentioned most of the M.A. students are also required to teach 1–2 sections of academic writing. The following two comments are indicators for increased confidence in finding and selecting useful online activities, ability to use the web as a source for communicating expectations in teaching, and confidence about using a computer classroom.

> In Malaysia, if I ever used a computer, there were programs and it would jumpstart for students, that's it. We did nothing creative. Now, I look for files for students to use to read, and make links for them to check the internet to get ideas, find quizzes online for them to do in class. I'm more confident now.
>   (JK)

> I guess the biggest change is with computer and internet use. *I have to teach in a computer lab next semester and if I had had to do that this past semester I would have hated it, but now I'm looking forward to it*. I'm starting to see how I can use the computer in a class room and how it could be useful and not distracting. When I came in I didn't think a writing class should be taught in a computer lab but now I can see how it's more helpful. I'm just more comfortable with it and I see that I can use it for more things than before. Now I also think, 'Oh I can put that on my website.' Of course I never would have thought that before for students who have access. Just thinking of the computer differently than before, more as a tool.   (SC, emphasis added)

Teaching and development

Of central importance to the successful use of key concepts and applications is the inclusion of projects. Consider this scenario:

> Four weeks before the end of their first semester, students in an M.A. program in Teaching English as a Second Language are working on their final projects for one of the prerequisite courses. One group of students has

checked out digital video cameras so they can take original footage of driving in a medium-size Midwestern city in the U.S. This is their second attempt to take video that is of a high enough quality to be used in their final project, an online resource for adult non-native speakers of English who are working towards passing the drivers' license test. Two members of the same group are working on creating a *Flash* interface to add interactivity so users can explore names of crucial car parts and other related vocabulary items. Another group member is taking digital images of the car parts to be illustrated in the project. Search functionality is included using a web-enabled database (*FileMaker Pro*) and self-testing is going to be an option available for users, who can work through quizzes created using *Hot Potatoes*. Three weeks later, the files for the web-based teaching unit, created using *Macromedia Dreamweaver MX*, are assembled to form a coherent unit (Figure 2). These students exhibit technical know-how language teachers of the 21st century might be expected to exhibit. While know-how is important, equally, if not more important, is knowing why and when to use technology. This particular online unit draws on research findings in second language acquisition, addressing some methodological principles for task-based language learning outlined by Doughty and Long (2003). Multiple sources of input (written, oral), comprehension checks, and the use of authentic video for illustration purposes are but a few of the areas addressed.

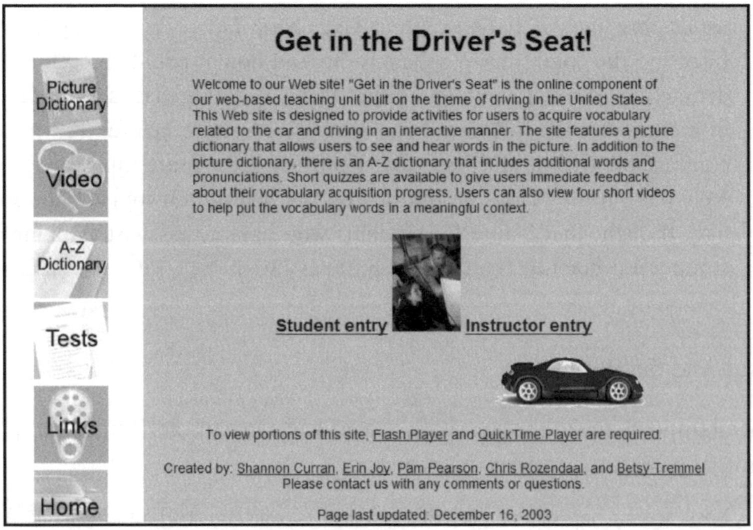

Figure 2. Student project "Get in the Driver's Seat!"

While this scenario of students working on a web-based teaching unit should not be novel, what is noteworthy is the fact that all students completed a comprehensive web-based teaching unit. Frequently, this is done during their first semester, which means the students know how to work with computers and are capable of using various software applications, including web design software used to produce web-based materials as they go on to the next courses.

Research findings thus far have not been promising when looking at the impact CALL courses have on actual technology use in teaching after graduating (Grau 1996; Egbert, Paulus, & Nakamichi 2002). Lack of time, support, and/or resources were frequently mentioned reasons for the inability to implement CALL in the classroom more frequently. One identifiable reason is the mismatch between the resources available during and after graduate work, which made it impossible for projects created by teacher-education students to be used in actual classrooms (Wentworth 1996). One promising approach to help remedy this problem, advocated by Fisher (1999) and Smerdon et al. (2000), is to use situated learning contexts (see also Egbert, this volume). In this model, teacher-trainees develop for a particular context and know what is and what is not available in terms of resources and facilities. Similarly, the projects completed as part of the required technology course in the M.A. curriculum are designed to engage students in project-based learning (Debski, this volume), whereby the projects should address a real need in the community and be used in subsequent semester. As such, the projects have real audiences and address real needs. In the fall semester of 2004, one project was designed to be used in first-year composition classes, paying special attention to enrolled non-native speaking students. Another project addressed the need for younger learners to be able to negotiate an American library. For the latter project, a mystery theme was chosen to enhance the appeal for the target audience. As with other tangible results, motivational issues are at play as well. Unlike in many other courses, where, granted, students learn crucial aspects of second language learning, the technology course provides them with the practical skills to create something concrete and usable. This, in turn, can provide a very positive attitude toward teaching, learning, and the M.A. program of their choice.

Marketability

A third, no less important effect the required technology course has had is related to securing jobs. Feedback from graduates from the program suggests that the skills they acquired as part of the required course have helped them get hired. One former student indicated that he felt he was chosen over another candidate for a full-time job at a community college because of his additional qualifications in the use of technology for language teaching. Equally helpful is the requirement to construct an initially modest, yet scalable professional homepage early on in the program. Being able to showcase an online portfolio with links to one's own materials or to relevant web sites can be the last piece of evidence needed to get a job offer. Even while still in graduate school, several other students reported tangible benefits from taking the course. Some were international students who had not been offered teaching assistantships. After completing the course, they were able to secure jobs in the form of research assistantships in large part because they had acquired valuable skills such as web design and multimedia development, skills that transfer to work in other disciplines. Other students who have gone on to pursue a Ph.D. in applied linguistics, for example, mentioned specifically that the knowledge they had gained put them at a distinct advantage over other incoming Ph.D. students with very little to no expertise in the area of technology. Clearly, all these students had to be qualified language teachers and excellent aspiring researchers first, but the point again is that knowledge of technology has become such an integral part of teachers and researchers of the 21st century that it should be taken into consideration in programs that train students to become the teachers and researchers of the 21st century. This is especially true for situations where seasoned teachers make up a large portion of the teaching staff. The expectation for recent graduates often includes the assumption that they will share their technology expertise with the staff and train them.

Insights and suggestions

There is broad agreement that future teachers should attain the ability to conceptualize, create, and make available good (online) theory-based language learning tasks. Subsequently, using a combination of judgmental and empirical methods (e.g., Chapelle 2001), future teachers need to be able to evaluate whether the tasks achieve their hypothesized (language learning) effect, and if learner behavior and feedback necessitates task modification. This interplay results in an iterative process including the conceptualizing, creating, uploading, testing, and modifying of tasks. Thus, it requires repetition, and students who have a handle on the technology can engage in this iterative process using new information they acquire in the subsequent graduate courses. As new insights about language learning and teaching surface, the students are now free to expend their energy on the content of tasks and projects, knowing that they have already grasped much of the delivery potential inherent with the web. To achieve this, several areas need to be addressed. Based on our experience, in addition to curricular reorganization, which required the collective and collaborative decision-making process in designing the new curriculum, the successful integration of a technology course hinges on the availability of a dedicated space, appropriate equipment, and expertise, with space appearing to be more crucial than up-to-date equipment and expertise. After that, the long process of working with faculty who are not very excited about technology and may resist technology integration in their courses can become a secondary focus.

As was the case for the M.A. program at ISU, convincing the departmental and college-wide decision makers often takes time and perseverance. After several years of unrelenting efforts, the faculty at ISU started out with a former office equipped with three computers on which relevant linguistics software was loaded so students could use this "research lab" outside of class. Using a pre-existing open computer classroom did not turn out to be a desirable option, in part due to the fact that students really needed access at all hours to specialized software (e.g., concordancers, corpora, web development software, and multimedia applications) to complete the various class projects. The availability of a larger space and the department's commitment of resources (approximately $18,000) turned into a dedicated applied linguistics computer research laboratory with 16 computers and a projector, a research facility that can also be used for holding graduate classes. While the importance of a computer lab is undisputable, what has proven to be even more crucial is the fact that the computer lab is only used by students in applied linguistics; plus, it is available to students year-round. As such, the lab has become a place for commiserating (especially students who are enrolled in English 510), community-building, and expertise-sharing. Thus, even though the computers cannot be upgraded on a regular basis due to budgetary concerns, the mere existence of such a lab has been more beneficial than could have been estimated. This lab space is becoming even more important with the beginning of a new Ph.D. program in Applied Linguistics and Technology in the fall semester of 2005 as it can serve as a synergistic place where practice and research meet.

New software applications that hold potential for language teachers and applied linguists or new versions of such applications are released almost daily and it is not feasible for faculty members, whose primary means for getting tenure and promotions are peer-refereed research publications, to keep up with the latest technology. Hence, another potential roadblock may be the lack of expertise on the side of the faculty to teach a course on technology. Despite recognizing the potential of newer web animation applications such as *Macromedia Flash* or web database connectivity using *ColdFusion* and *MYSQL*, the level of expertise of the current faculty is clearly limited. One possible temporary solution employed in our program is to tap into the expertise of Ph.D. students or advanced M.A. students in other areas, such as Rhetoric and Professional Communication. Inviting students who have expertise in those areas to conduct workshops in classes and asking them to be available for out-of-class consultations may be the solution.[5] That way, they gain valuable teaching experience while helping new students. The other alternative, i.e., to knowingly restrict teaching to the applications faculty know, would be a disservice to students who seek to be trained as language teachers of the new millennium.

Returning to Chapelle's (2003) quote, "The way that students will learn to do applied linguistics with technology is by learning applied linguistics through technology" (31), a continuing struggle remains to appeal to colleagues who are teaching in the same M.A. program. While often excellent scholars and teachers, they may be hesitant towards the use and integration of technology. Gradual and consistent illustrations and faculty training have had positive effects. More frequently, though, it is the technology-savvy students who act as change agents by making an impression on these faculty members when they give presentations, work on projects, or showcase materials they have developed, and thereby encouraging faculty to realize the potential and become interested in technology themselves.

In sum, students who are not even thinking about technology when entering a degree program in language teaching, but are required to learn about technology and able to implement technology throughout their M.A. program, can leave the program as competent technology-savvy teachers. This becomes a very real possibility – and should be the norm in the 21st Century – when the technology course is required.

Notes

1. Common reactions from outside faculty members in other disciplines who hear about the approach include doubt that the actual teaching of technology skills warrants inclusion in a graduate program. Comments such as "We don't teach applications; we focus on theory. Our students must learn applications on their own" reveal a common attitude which may be related not only to the conviction to teach transferable theory, but also to the frequent inability to teach applications. While more could and should be said about this particular point, it can quickly lead to controversy and antagonism and will therefore not be developed further in this chapter, but relegated to continued professional discourse.

2. FM = faculty member – four out of six faculty members responded to an inquiry regarding their perceived impact of 510 on their courses.

3. As background information, the students queried entered the program with the clear primary goal of becoming teachers. Teacher training, materials development, and research were less important (in that order). Their vision of technology for language learning was mediated by the fact that 10 had never used technology for teaching and the others had mainly used computer technology to create documents and handouts. The primary reason for the non-use of technology in teaching was lack of access, illustrating the all-too-frequent discrepancy between what is available at universities and many other places, including schools in the U.S. and large parts of the world.

4. In the semester the survey was conducted, database development was only briefly introduced in class and covered in greater detail through workshops for students interested in this area. Mostly group members in charge of this aspect of the final project participated in these out-of-class workshops.

5. Ph.D. students who have given 1–2-week workshops on *Flash* or web databases were willing to share their expertise voluntarily. However, they received remuneration when funds were available.

References

Camtasia (2002). Okemos, MI: Tech Smith.

Chapelle, C. A. (2003). *English Language Learning and Technology: Lectures on teaching and research in the age of information and communication.* Amsterdam: John Benjamins.

Chapelle, C. A. (2001). *Computer Applications in Second Language Acquisition: Foundations for teaching, testing, and research.* Cambridge: CUP.

Chapelle, C. & Hegelheimer, V. (2004). The English language teacher in the 21st century. In S. Fotos & C. Browne (Eds.), *New Perspectives on CALL for Second Language Classrooms* (pp. 299–316). Mahwah, NJ: Lawrence Erlbaum.

Doughty, C. & Long, M. (2003). Optimal psycholinguistic environments for distance foreign language learning. *Language Learning & Technology, 7* (3), 50–80. Available at http://llt.msu.edu/vol7num3/doughty/default.html.

Egbert, J., Paulus, T., & Nakamichi, Y. (2002). The impact of CALL instruction on classroom computer use: A foundation for rethinking technology in teacher education. *Language Learning and Technology, 6* (3), 108–126. Available at http://llt.msu.edu/vol6num3/egbert/default.html.

FileMaker Pro (2005). Santa Clara, CA: FileMaker.

Fisher, T. (1999). A new professionalism? Teacher use of multimedia portable computers with Internet capability. Paper presented at SITE 99. ERIC Document No. 432268.

Get in the Driver's Seat. Available at http://www.tesl.iastate.edu/510/F03/wbtubackup/wbtu.htm.

Grau, I. (1996). Teacher development in technology instruction: Does computer coursework transfer into actual teaching practice? Paper presented at the annual meeting of the Southwest Educational Research Association. ERIC Document Reproduction Service No. ED 394 949.

Hegelheimer, V. (2004). CALL and teacher training: A chance to reflect on what should be taught and why. Paper presented at CALICO 2004, Pittsburgh, June 08–12, 2004.

Macromedia Dreamweaver MX (2003). San Francisco, CA: Macromedia.

Macromedia Fireworks MX (2003). San Francisco, CA: Macromedia.

Macromedia Flash MX (2003). San Francisco, CA: Macromedia.

Microsoft Office Suite (2002). Redmond, WA: Microsoft.

MonoConc Pro (2002). Houston, TX: Athelstan.

Smerdon, B., Cronen, S., Lanahan, L., Anderson, J., Iannotti, N., & Angeles, J. (2000). *Teachers' Tools for the 21st Century: A report on teachers' use of technology.* Washington, DC: National Center for Education Statistics.

SPSS (2002). Chicago, IL: SPSS Inc.

Wentworth, N. (1996). Educational technology: From curriculum course to the classroom. *Technology and Teacher Education Annual, 1996,* 335–358.

Teaching the creation of software that uses speech recognition

Historically in CALL, developments in the field prior to the 1990s were often driven by teacher-programmers, who linked their classroom experience to the creation of tutorial software in which the computer had an identifiable teaching role. Although today many language teachers use technology primarily as a tool to get students to communicate in the target language or to put them in contact with authentic language content, interest in tutorial uses of CALL has remained strong, as evidenced by the thousands of teachers who have downloaded the *Hot Potatoes* program (University of Victoria, Canada) for authoring web-based exercises. In this chapter, Maxine Eskenazi and Jonathan Brown describe a course module created to help CALL students learn how to develop effective software that uses a particularly promising technology for language learning: automatic speech recognition. The course is taught in the final semester of a two-year Master's in CALL program at Carnegie Mellon University aimed at creating CALL professionals who can take leading roles in implementing language learning technology in their institutions. Eskenazi and Brown give a detailed description of the course, walking the reader chronologically through it and providing the rationale for both the content and process along the way. Rather than drawing primarily from second language acquisition theory and research as many other chapters do, they lead their students through linguistic and technical considerations and introduce them to other disciplines such as cognitive learning theory, which touches on universal elements of how humans process text, audio, and graphic information. Throughout, they stress the importance of understanding the strengths and limitations of speech technology in order to create successful instructional software. Their work is particularly valuable to those contemplating training in CALL software development, especially software using speech recognition, both for the experiences that the authors share and for the links to student project examples and support materials they provide.

Teaching the creation of software that uses speech recognition

Maxine Eskenazi and Jonathan Brown
Carnegie Mellon University, USA

Introduction

After receiving an increasing number of student requests for a program that would deal in detail with computer-assisted language learning and determining that there would be jobs for students who had this background, the Modern Languages Department and the Language Technologies Institute at Carnegie Mellon created the Master of Computer-Assisted Language Learning (MCALL) program. This program was designed to produce graduates who can create language learning software, run a language lab, and teach about CALL. It comprises a core curriculum with courses on second language acquisition, natural language grammars and lexicons, and a course called Language Technologies for CALL. This course, taken in the last semester of the two-year program, brings the students from the theory they have seen in other core courses to the actual design of small portions of systems, which in turn leads up to a summer research project of making a language tutoring system. The course has always appealed to students outside of the MCALL program as well. It is regularly attended by Master's and PhD students from the Language Technologies Institute.

The course was created for several reasons. First, with a wider background in CALL, the students should be more desirable when looking for jobs. Second, the CALL professional at present is completely dependent on the software that is available – there is no chance to have something tailored to the needs of their specific class. Thus software that has some positive points, but several drawbacks, has to be accepted as is, and extra time is required to adjust teaching to palliate the weak elements. Another problem for the CALL professional at present is that, without knowing about how the software was created and what principles were adhered to, it is difficult to judge the relative value of a potential purchase as well as how to make the best use of it. Knowing about the state of the art in CALL software and being able to have a vision of what it may become in the future gives the CALL professional the skills to judge a proposed software purchase not just at present, but as the technology evolves going forward. In fact, most of the techniques that are shown to the class are still upstream from being commercialized. Finally, the possibility of making one's own software for specific needs with freely available components enlarges the tools that the CALL teacher and the language lab director have at hand. Although these points specifically justified the present course, they provide important arguments for such a class in any program seeking to educate CALL professionals.

The goal of the course is to teach what constitutes good language learning software and how CALL students can create their own (CALL using language technologies will be called CALLLT hereafter and the *students* in this class – as opposed to the language *learners* – will be called *students*). The course is divided in three parts, and a piece of software is produced in each of the three parts. After the first part, using speech recognition, which is described in this chapter, students also use a grammar checker to create a writing tutor and natural language processing to create a reading tutor. In the first third of this course, students also learn the basics about language technologies for CALL systems.

This chapter provides a detailed description of the module of the course the authors were involved in, which focuses on understanding speech technologies and developing a piece of software utilizing them. In addition to the obvious technical expertise students learn, key course elements include providing the relevant historical background for appreciating the advantages and limitations of speech recognition systems in language learning, introducing students to a research-based framework of design principles aligned with cognitive learning theory (Clark & Mayer 2003), and involving outside experts as guest lecturers. Additional areas of importance covered are assessment, links to language learning research and immersion issues, and critiquing of commercialized CALL systems, all of the preceding culminating in the production of a tutorial application consistent with the tenets of project-based learning (Debski, this volume).

Introducing CALLLT to the students – the historical context

There are three parts at the beginning of the course, historical context, the principles of interaction and the assessment of systems. The course begins by placing CALLLT courseware in its historical context, starting with the first system that used automatic speech recognition (ASR), the IBM Speech Viewer system in the 1970's (Coursant-Moreau, Crepy, & Destombes 2002: 127), then the later systems that listened to students, but provided no feedback (Syracuse Language Systems 1994: 1), and finally, with the improvement of ASR, CALL systems that responded to multiple choice answers (Bernstein 1994: 37). At first, only one answer was right – the user had to try again if they got it wrong. Eventually, systems presented three or four correct choices, with each choice taking a dialogue in a different direction.

> S: Where would you like to go?
> U: I want to go to the zoo.
> S: We can take the bus.
>
>   OR
>
> S: Where would you like to go?
> U: I would like to go to the library.
> S: Let's walk there.   (S = system and U = user).

Finally, more recent systems that use natural language grammars, information retrieval, and machine translation techniques are discussed. Students are assigned the readings referenced above and encouraged to find other articles to share with the class. They are referred to the limited number of resources that are available so far. These are: the proceedings of the INSTiL/ICALL conference on NLP and Speech Technologies in Advanced Language Learning Systems, the proceedings of the Association for Computational Linguistics/Human Language and Technologies conference (ACL/HLT) and the online journal, *Language Learning & Technology*. The first two describe implementations with little reference to second language learning findings or to cognitive science.

Advantages and limitations of using language technologies in CALL systems

The next class deals with the advantages and limitations of using language technologies (specifically speech processing) in CALL systems. The advantages include the following:

- the learner can get feedback from the CALLLT system as to what was wrong and how to improve it;
- the CALLLT system is available when the learner needs it;
- the learner has privacy when using a CALLLT system, thus being able to make mistakes without losing face in front of others;
- lessons provided by a CALLLT system are individualized to each learner's needs;
- the CALLLT system provides a variety of voices for the learner to hear and imitate;
- the CALLLT system provides much more speaking practice than in a classroom situation.

The advantages are illustrated by a demonstration of the instructor's *Fluency* software.

CALLLT system limitations are due to the fact that the language technologies do not produce perfect results at present, as demonstrated by the instructor. The students are shown how to palliate the flaws of the technology by using smart engineering, for example, so that when making their software, they choose the vocabulary of their exercises to include words that are phonetically very different. They are also shown how to bring out the strong points of the technology, using, for example, duration information. The latter is reliably detected by ASR systems and can be used for purposes such as showing a learner when to hesitate less, removing unnecessary pauses to make more fluent speech. The goal is to keep system errors to a strict minimum by avoiding the weak points of the ASR so that learners' self-confidence and faith in the reliability of the system is maintained. To achieve this, examples at several levels are presented in the context of speech recognition: interface properties, semantic choices, sentences, and phonetics.

Decisions about the design of the *interface* also need to take into consideration the error introduced by the ASR. Students are shown that allowing free speech, that is, the ability to say anything at any time, generates a high error rate. So, successful use of ASR entails being able to predict what the learner will say and matching that with what the learner does say. The learner can read from the screen, or have a constrained task so that the speech that is elicited is highly predictable (S: who prepares the food in a restaurant? A cook or a plumber? U: A cook OR U: A cook does). Thus, determining whether the incoming speech matches the expected right answer is easier than determining what was actually said.

Students are shown that several levels of language are involved in human and machine recognition of spoken language. Amongst those levels are semantics and phonetics. At the *semantic* level, the use of free speech would allow a student to express any ideas on any topic, but a speech recognizer performs much better when the semantic domain is restrained and already modeled in the system. For example, asking a student to talk about what they did the day before would have less predictable content than asking whether they think it is good to rent an apartment on their own or live with other students while studying abroad.

On the *phonetic* level, several regularly-observed errors in the functioning of most present state-of-the-art recognizers are demonstrated to the students and the way to deal with them is described. For example, the first few sounds in an utterance (preceded by silence) are often poorly recognized, so sounds or words that are being focused on should not be located there if possible. We can choose a word that has the target sound at the beginning and make it appear later in the utterance. Another common problem is that, although vowels are usually fairly well detected, consonants don't fare as well. Extensive additional processing would be necessary to change this (Eskenazi & Pelton 2002), so if the system is not designed for phonetic correction, it is a good idea to choose words that are as phonetically different from one another as possible. Finally, phones in stressed syllables are easier to recognize than those in unstressed syllables since the places of articulation are usually more fully attained.

System planning – principles and design

The basics of good CALLLT courseware design start with design principles that are true for tutoring systems in any domain. An invited lecture during the second week of class deals with this. This is followed in the same week by specifics concerning language learning systems. In the third week the basic parts of a system (the interface, curriculum, and learner modeling) are presented as well as proper system assessment.

This course does not adhere to any specific theory of language learning. The systems that are demonstrated and referenced are built from observation of data that has been gathered either in tutoring situations or in interactions with a computer. Many systems, including the ones built by the instructor, are aimed at being testbeds for ways to improve language learning and thus are made to be as flexible as possible. For example, the validity of explicit as opposed to implicit training is a current debate. Systems may allow for words or sounds to be emboldened to show new items (a new sound, a new word) or not. They may show explicit explanations as to how to correct an error or leave the learner to figure out how to correct it.

Principles of good interaction

General principles
A key part of the course is the introduction to students of cognitive learning theory and the software design principles derived from it. Until quite recently, CALL specialists and cognitive theory specialists had little knowledge of one another's work. Cognitive theorists tested their hypotheses on more heavily-structured fields like math and science, where knowledge representation is more straightforward. After successes in those areas they are now looking at knowledge representation in less structured fields such as language learning. On the other hand, within CALLLT, although there are specialists who have a background in language learning (taught it, or studied its processes), many come solely from language technologies areas, such as automatic speech processing. The latter often create systems that use language technologies correctly for language learning, but that either ignore cognitive theory or use it without realizing that they are. Although it is important for CALLLT specialists and cognitive theory specialists to have knowledge of one another's work, this course does not espouse any specific cognitive theory or contain

detailed explanations of any cognitive theory. Instead, the CALLLT course instructor and guest lecturers focus on specific instructional design principles supported by experimental results. For example, language learning has "gone multimedia", but ignores the experimental work by Clark and Mayer (2003) that shows that concurrent perception of information through two channels affords more learning than through one channel at a time. So, the CALLLT creators who produce a system offering one button to hear a word pronounced and another to see a picture or cartoon representing the word should be aware that Clark and Mayer showed that it would be more effective to present just one button, where the word is heard as the image is seen. This is known as the Contiguity Principle. They also showed that using a single modality to give two different types of information at the same time impedes learning. For example, illustrating a word while showing a headcut of how to pronounce it divides the student's visual attention. This is known as the Split-Attention Principle. Clark and Meyer have a cognitive theory of multimedia learning, based on Paivio's (1986) dual coding theory and theories on working memory (Baddeley 1992) and cognitive load (Chandler & Sweller 1991), with which these research findings are consistent. However, the CALLLT instructor focuses on the principles and research findings, not the cognitive theory. Fortunately recent conferences, such as CALICO, show a new trend where some of the more classical CALL conference presentations refer to such principles and cognitive theory work.

Another feature that accompanies this part of the course is the use of outside experts as guest speakers. In the past, the CALLLT course instructor presented the general principles. However, with ever closer ties to the CMU experts from that field, it became logical to have them teach this material directly. Ken Koedinger, a recognized expert in intelligent tutoring, teaches a guest lecture on instructional design principles. He starts with an explanation of basic research findings concerning student interaction in intelligent tutoring systems, such as those that provide the basis for the Contiguity and Modality Principles (Clark & Mayer 2003). He then goes on to describe the importance of careful learner modeling and the positive effects of tailoring curriculum to individual learners. To illustrate this, Koedinger describes and demonstrates work that he and his colleagues have carried out in *ACT-R* on model tracing (monitoring a learner's progress through a problem solution) and on knowledge tracing (monitoring the learner's knowledge from problem to problem) (Koedinger, Anderson, Hadley, & Mark 1997: 30). In *ACT-R*, knowledge is represented as a series of skills and subskills, and so the learner's progress can be monitored individually as the skills are mastered (or not). The choice of what is presented next to the learner is based on this learner model, and the problems that can be presented next are represented as a series of skills. One is then presented with the task of matching the learner's skills with the underlying skills of the problems, building on the learner's prior knowledge. Students are expected to perform similar learner and problem modeling when they build their pieces of educational software, although the software they use to build their tutors does not impose the *ACT-R* (or any other) model.

The explicit presentation of these principles in this course is essential for the student. As we can see in the examples above, although some principles seem evident, others are not intuitive. In addition, because many of these principles have been derived through studies in other areas of learning and in specific conditions, some of these principles still need to be validated for language learning.

Results related to language learning
The students' attention is then drawn to research results that relate to language learning in particular and have been used and tested in the instructor's English pronunciation software, *Fluency* (Mayfield-Tomokiyo, Wang, & Eskenazi 2000). For example, after close observation of system users, the ability of the learner to make correct navigation choices during the use of software (vs. letting the software decide for the learner) has been examined. Another example of results communicated to the class is a study of people reading aloud that found that one out of every two people who were asked to read ten sentences aloud from a newspaper could not accomplish this task correctly (Lamel, Gauvain, & Eskenazi 1991). More recent experimentation has shown learners to be poor judges of which voice, given a choice of several, would be the best for them to imitate (Probst, Ke, & Eskenazi 2002:161). Students are thus shown that the learner does not always make decisions in their best interest. They also learn that all speakers of a language cannot be presumed to possess all basic language skills, such as reading aloud.

Beyond these results, the following issues are discussed:

- Language learners must *produce* large quantities of language on their own, be it spoken or written. Producing language is the way to demonstrate that something has been learned.
- Learners must *be exposed to* large quantities of oral and written language produced by many different native speakers. The learner who listens to only one speaker is unable to build a mental representation of the variability amongst the many speakers of the language.

Immersion issues

The students discuss what constitutes immersion in the first and second weeks of class. A popular theme through the 1990s, it promotes the belief that a language learner who is immersed in the country where the language is spoken learns the fastest. Much recent language learning software has been made to look and feel as if the learner were in the target country. This sometimes results in a very seductive system that is void of content. Class discussion centers on: "Can we imitate immersion, can we do better than immersion?" The students get a list of characteristics of immersion and add others, stating whether CALL software can embody those characteristics.

The characteristics presented include:

Constant exposure: the learner is constantly exposed to the target language (as opposed to twice a week for an hour). The advent of the personal computer allows our systems to be available whenever the learner wants, and as often as the learner can use them, at a lower cost than for an individual tutor.

Immediate, real feedback: as discussed above, our systems can provide this, just like a native speaker who hears something erroneous will often offer correction before continuing a conversation.

Culture immersion: can we do more than just show differences? Can we also explain different mentalities?

Idioms: when they are not immersed, speakers don't tend to use idioms. Can we show how to use them in a natural way that does not force too many on the learner at one time (list learning)?

Real speed: an immersed learner has to keep up with the pace of a real conversation. Can we slowly increase the pace so that it gets fast enough to make the language gestures become automatic?

Real need to use the language, real tasks: in immersion, the learner needs to use the language to survive; we probably can't imitate this (although the learner does need to speak well enough to get a passing grade!).

Combination of all levels of language all the time: in immersion, all levels of language come into play at the same time. This may not be good to imitate since research has shown that focusing the learner on one thing at a time makes for more successful learning (Newell & Simon 1972).

After the students add to the list, they discuss whether our systems can do better than immersion. The recurring right answer is that the computer's advantage is more *memory*, recall of exactly what the learner has done each time he/she has produced some language and how correct that was. With this excellent memory, our systems should be able to afford more individualized coursework, by choosing the next best thing to do based on a global and very accurate view of the learner's past work and remediating precisely when it is necessary.

Commercialized CALL systems

The discussion on immersion gives the students some concrete ideas for the tutors they will create. In order to contrast the theory they have seen up to this point with the reality of existing commercial systems, in their next assignment, they use and critique existing systems.

The instructor brings commercial software to the second session of class, and each student chooses one or two pieces of software to take home. The software offered here is often for English mother tongue students learning such languages as Spanish or French, but there are also Chinese mother tongue learning English systems as well as Spanish mother tongue learning English systems. The students are expected to spend several hours with the software, learning to use it, possibly for a language they don't know. They are given a list of 15 points to be covered in the critique that they are to give as a *PowerPoint* presentation to the whole class. These points include topics such as the appeal and ease of use of the software, the pedagogical goals, the technologies employed in the software, how feedback is given, how learners are assessed or guided, and whether the student would buy this software themselves if they needed to learn the target language. In addition, the students must complete another homework assignment with the same piece of software, trying to map the curriculum content and its structure. The students find that some software has few skills to teach in a maximum of about two hours while other software can provide as much as 100 hours of curriculum on just one goal (learning verb tenses, for example). The focus then changes to the tutor they are going to create. They start to define a goal, what the tutor will teach. Then they make a diagram of the curriculum that their complete system would have (although they will only be making two exercises).

Parts of a CALLLT system

Following the critique of commercial language learning software, the students are ready to start designing their own systems. They use the *Cognitive Tutor Authoring Tools* which we describe below. This makes system creation much easier, but they still need to know how a system designed "from scratch" functions. The background of most of the students is second language acquisition with very little computer science, so the use of these tools has enabled students (who would otherwise spend an inordinate amount of time just trying to program simple items) to concentrate on content and the overall interface. Students with more computer science background are encouraged to add modules as time allows. The work of each student is judged on the points described below. Due to the differing backgrounds of the students, an individual student is always judged according to what the instructor believes that individual is capable of, not in comparison to others in the class.

The students are given a list of types of exercises and can add to it. Some types are: multiple choice, reordering lists, matching, fill in the blank, and role-playing. The list is ordered from passive activities (multiple choice) to active ones (role-playing). The students find out that some very appealing activities cannot yet be implemented (e.g., open-ended discussion).

The students then create a flowchart of a sample system. They learn about the place of intelligent tutoring in the overall scheme of things and about deciding which skills to teach. They try to chart a complete curriculum.

Actual system creation

At this point, the students are ready to put what they have learned into practice. They are introduced to the authoring tools. To enable the reader to better follow this part, we will walk through the creation of a sample exercise using the tools and describe some of the types of language-learning exercises the students have built during the course.

Since speaking practice is an important part of learning a new language, students are asked to create language-learning exercises which provide more opportunities for learners to speak the language by using the speech recognition functionality. These can be at levels of language learning going from lexicon to culture. Because it is difficult to create exercises from scratch, students use the *Cognitive Tutor Authoring Tools*, the *Sphinx-2* speech recognition system, and a set of utilities for integrating the authoring tools and the speech recognition system. In addition to aiding in the mechanical process of creating tutors, these tools, especially the authoring tools, can also assist in exercise design fundamentals like cognitive task analysis and curriculum creation.

Cognitive Tutor Authoring Tools

The *Cognitive Tutor Authoring Tools* (CTAT) have been built by researchers at Carnegie Mellon University and Worcester Polytechnic Institute. They are designed to ease the development of intelligent tutors (Koedinger, Aleven, & Hefferman 2003: 455). A subset of these tools allow for the creation of "Pseudo tutors". Pseudo tutors exhibit the normal behavior of intelligent tutors but do not require the designer to perform any Artificial Intelligence (AI) programming (Koedinger et al. 2004) and thus make tutor creation more universally accessible.

Pseudo tutors are created in two steps. First, a designer creates the exercise interfaces using a GUI (graphical user interface) builder. This process involves dragging and dropping special interface widgets (interface control components, such as buttons) onto the exercise window. These widgets allow for a variety of different types of activities to be created. After creating the interface, the designer can model student behavior within that interface. The designer does this by demonstrating the correct and incorrect steps students may take when completing the exercise, using a special program called a Behavior Recorder, which automatically creates behavior graphs based on the designer's actions. The designer can also directly modify the behavior graph to mark certain paths as incorrect, to add feedback such as help and error messages, and to annotate the graph with skill labels. When this step is completed, a student is able to use the tutor exercise and receive feedback based on correct or incorrect actions. This feedback simulates the feedback resulting from model tracing and knowledge tracing in a full intelligent tutor (Anderson, Corbett, Koedinger, & Pelletier 1995: 167; Corbett & Anderson 1995: 253) without requiring Artificial Intelligence programming.

Sphinx-2 Speech Recognition System

Sphinx-2 is a real-time, large-vocabulary, speaker-independent speech recognition system, available online under a free and open source license (Huang et al. 1992: 137; Sphinx Project Page). *Sphinx-2* comes fully trained: the students can use it without modification. However, our students are expected to provide the system with a language model and a pronunciation lexicon. These can be easily created using the online *Sphinx Knowledge Base Tool* (Sphinx Knowledge Base Tools). This tool takes as input a sentence corpus, a file composed of all the possible sentences a student is expected to speak in the exercise. The tool outputs a language model file (which words can follow which other words) based on this corpus, as well as a pronunciation lexicon consisting of all of the words used. Additional words can be added if necessary, using the *CMU Pronouncing Dictionary*. The walk-through example below shows the details of this process.

Integration components

The third tool provided allows the speech recognition system to be integrated with the authoring tools. It consists of a recording and recognition component and a tutor integration component. The former component provides methods for recording the user's speech and interfacing with *Sphinx-2* to handle the recognition task. There is also a method for comparing the list of possible user utterances returned by *Sphinx-2* to the list of utterances the user was expected to speak during this exercise, to determine which, if any, of these utterances were spoken. The second component, the tutor integration component, is implemented as a template for creating speech-enabled exercises. This template includes the elements used to start and stop recording, using the recording and recognition component to record the user's speech and handle the recognition task. The template also includes code for sending update events to the authoring tools, so that the authoring tools can respond to user input as they do in tutors without speech functionality. These components are described more fully in a technical report and are freely available online (Sphinx2-CTAT; Brown 2004).

Walk-through of example exercise

Using the above-described tools, students are expected to build two different speech-enabled tutor exercises during the course. In this part, after showing the process of creating a simple exercise, examples of the students' work will be described. The exercise is the first part of a dialogue focused on politeness. The learner is presented with three sentences, one of which is impolite and thus considered incorrect. The other two are both correct and provide the start of two different paths in the full dialogue. To give a response, the learner clicks the record button, speaks the sentence, and clicks the stop button. The text of the learner's choice then appears in a textbox on the screen, and the learner receives appropriate feedback.

First the interface is created. As mentioned earlier, exercise designers were given templates from which to start, with the event handlers for the start and stop buttons. The designers must add all of the interface elements needed for their exercise to this template. In this exercise the following must be added:

- a number of labels for the problem directions and sentence choices,
- two buttons for starting and stopping recording,
- a textbox for the user response to appear in.

The text of the labels for the sentence choices is set to the following possible utterances for this exercise:

> "I would like a table, please."
> "I would like a seat by the window."
> "Give me a table."

The first two sentences are designated as correct and the last sentence is designated as incorrect. To add the buttons, two JButton widgets can be dragged onto the interface window. Finally, designers must add the textbox. This textbox is dragged onto the interface window. Figure 1 shows the completed interface.

The last step of the interface design process is to define the variable *currentAnswerChoices*, which holds the possible answer choices that the learner completing the exercise is expected to speak. The template includes a place for this to be defined. In this exercise, it is defined as follows:

```
currentAnswerChoices = new Vector();
currentAnswerChoices.add("I would like a table, please.");
currentAnswerChoices.add("I would like a seat by the window.");
currentAnswerChoices.add("Give me a table.");
```

The main elements of the interface have now been created. When the user of this exercise presses the start button, the recording process begins. When the stop button is pressed, recording is finished, and the audio file of the recording is provided to the speech recognition system. The event handler for the stop button waits for the recognition to finish, and then retrieves the list of the utterances from the recognition component. This list consists of the most likely utterances that the learner spoke, as computed by *Sphinx-2*. Finally, this list is compared with the list of expected user utterances in *currentAnswerChoices*. The result of this comparison is either one of the sentences in *currentAnswerChoices*, or it is an error message. The error message can be "NotHeard", if the recognizer did not hear any words spoken in the audio file, or it can be "NotUnderstood", which means the recognizer heard some words, but the output of the recognizer could not be matched to any of the possible answer choices. The exercise designer is expected to handle these error messages and give appropriate feedback to the user. The textbox is then given the value of this utterance, and an update event is sent to the authoring tools.

Although the interface design is then complete, designers must perform one more step before demonstrating user behavior. The speech recognition system must be provided with a language model and pronunciation lexicon. As mentioned, these files can be automatically generated using the online tool (Sphinx Knowledge Base Tools). This tool requires a sentence corpus file as input, i.e. a text file with one possible learner utterance per line. In this exercise, it consists of three lines, one for each answer choice. Punctuation is removed from these sentences so that the program can read them. Once this file has been uploaded to the tool, the language model files and pronunciation lexicon are downloaded and saved in the *Sphinx-2* configuration directory.

Student designers can now run the exercise and demonstrate learner behavior: this is what they must explain and then present in class. The Behavior Recorder is used for this. It automatically creates the behavior graph as the correct and incorrect actions are demonstrated. In this simple exercise, five actions must be demonstrated. The first two actions are correct actions, corresponding to the user choosing one of the first two options. The next action is an incorrect action, corresponding to the user choosing the third option, which was deemed incorrect because it is impolite. The last two actions handle the two possible error messages, "NotHeard" and "NotUnderstood". All of these actions are demonstrated directly in the interface just built by typing the sentence or error message into the textbox. After trying each of these five actions, the designer directly modifies the behav-

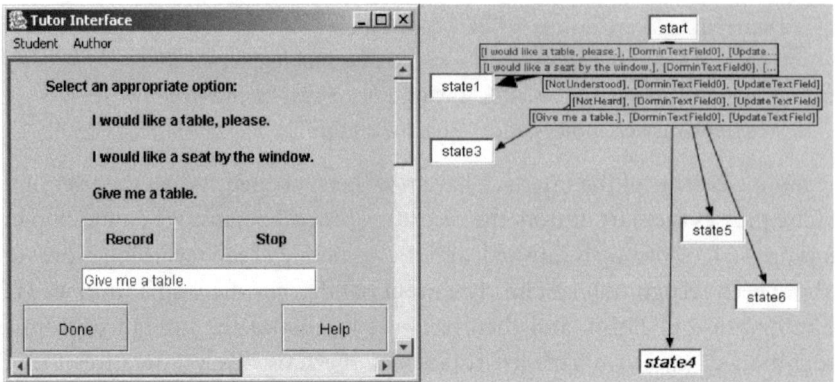

Figure 1. Exercise Interface and Behavior Graph.

ior graph, marking the last three as incorrect paths, and adding help and error messages. Figure 1 also shows the resulting behavior graph.

Other exercises built by the CALLLT students

Some of the exercises that the students in the class have built are either available for download or have screenshots available for download on the Sphinx2-CTAT Connection Utilities webpage. The exercises test various elements of the language such as formation of plurals, adjective ordering, active to passive conversion, and the use of prepositions, interrogative pronouns, and specific vocabulary. For these exercises, speech was used to ask questions about an upcoming party, describe pictures, compose sentences from certain words, navigate using a map, and solve a mystery. It is also possible to create activities like these to focus on higher-level material, such as politeness or other aspects of culture.

Assessing CALLLT systems

In this final part, the class examines system assessment: How do we know that the system is functioning correctly? How do we know that the system is helping the learners? Finally issues concerning human experimentation are addressed. With few systems in existence just a few years ago, there was not much to compare and assessment was often limited to whether a given teacher *liked* a piece of software for use in a given class (a very subjective judgment). With more and more software being available, classrooms being better equipped in terms of computer facilities, and teachers being more aware of the use of both of these, the issue of assessment of CALLLT software has become a major concern.

When a system has been created, it must be tested – every part of the curriculum is tried with every possible interface option. This debugging cycle is experienced first hand during the students' software creation.

After the system has been reasonably debugged, it is tested to see if it actually helps learners. The concepts discussed include *control group* and *test material being separate from training material*. Several methods of presentation, pretesting and posttesting, continual testing, AxB tests, etc. are presented. Finally there is a discussion of statistical significance.

CALL systems are always tested on human subjects, which evokes issues linked to human experimentation. The class is made aware of issues of privacy of information, of informed consent, etc., and the students are encouraged to take the online human subject experimentation training required for anyone conducting human experimentation. Finally the students are shown how to apply for Internal Review Board approval.

Conclusion

The general background and the use of the CTAT authoring tools bring the students' background in line with the research going on in the Pittsburgh Science of Learning Center (NSF-funded Center at Carnegie Mellon and the University of Pittsburgh, http://www.learnlab.org, established in 2004). These students are encouraged to take courses taught by others in the Center, such as those on intelligent tutoring. This also blends with other courses in the MCALL program. For example, the software assessment presentation is often used in SLA classes to analyze the curriculum of current software as well as to see what, if any, SLA theories have been employed.

The limitations encountered in this class come in the form of the students' backgrounds. The diversity in their backgrounds is a plus for the course, as we see them develop interesting pieces of software. However, although very limited programming knowledge is required, that small amount is essential for successful completion of the course. Students with language teaching backgrounds and no computer programming experience may not want to take this type of course.

The course lends itself to online presentation and will be gradually adapted to the online style of teaching so that it can reach a larger audience. The basic material can be offered as well as an assessment of the software that is created as a hand-in to the instructor.

Even if a student does not want to have a career in software creation, the firsthand experience in this course gives them a better understanding of what constitutes a good piece of CALLT software. In their teaching careers, in work in language labs, or elsewhere, the ability to assess new software is important. They will be choosing which software to buy, using it, or competing with it. They may also be called upon to make recommendations to others. The use of language technologies for CALL systems constantly changes, with new and exciting applications appearing regularly, and the students' experience makes them capable of understanding these changes. The course described in this chapter is flexible, and accommodates such changes as well. It strives to define what good CALLLT software is and allows its students to discover this first hand.

Hands-on experience, whether it be in creating software or, in other cases, in using many different types of software, is an excellent teaching mechanism. Students learn by doing, answering their own questions either by trying out commercial software or experimenting with something of their own creation.

References

Anderson, J. R., Corbett, A. T., Koedinger, K. R., & Pelletier, R. (1995). Cognitive tutors: Lessons learned. *The Journal of the Learning Sciences, 4* (2), 167–207.

Association for Computational Linguistics/Human Language and Technologies conference (ACL/HLT). Available at http://www1.cs.columbia.edu/~acl/.

Baddeley, A. (1992). Working memory. *Science, 255,* 555–559.

Bernstein, J. (1994). Speech recognition in language education. In *Proceedings of the Computer Assisted Language Instruction Consortium CALICO '94 Symposium* (pp. 37–41).

Brown, J. (2004). Integrating tools for the creation of speech-enabled tutors. *CMU LTI Technical Report* CMU-LTI-04-186.

Chandler, P. & Sweller, J. (1991). Cognitive load theory and the format of instruction. *Cognition and Instruction, 8,* 293–332.

Clark, R. C. & Mayer, R. E. (2003). *e-Learning and the Science of Instruction.* San Francisco, CA: John Wiley & Sons.

CMU Pronouncing Dictionary. Available at http://www.speech.cs.cmu.edu/cgi-bin/cmudict/.

Corbett, A. T. & Anderson, J. R. (1995). Knowledge tracing: Modeling the acquisition of procedural knowledge. *User Modeling and User-Adapted Interaction, 4,* 253–278.

Coursant-Moreau, A., Crepy, H., & Destombes, F. (2002). Lipcom: An IBM research project to help reception of speech by deaf persons. In *Proceedings of the 7th International Conference on Computers Helping People with Special Needs – ICCHP2000* (pp. 127–134).

Eskenazi, M. & Pelton, G. (2002). Pinpointing pronunciation errors in children's speech: Examining the role of the speech recognizer. *Proceedings of the Pronunciation Modeling and Lexicon Adaptation for Spoken Language Technology Workshop*: Estes Park, Colorado. Available at http://www.iscaspeech.org/archive_papers/pmla/pmla_048.pdf.

Huang, X., Alleva, F., Hon, H.-W., Hwang, M.-Y., Lee, K.-F., & Rosenfeld, R. (1992). The SPHINX-II speech recognition system: An overview. *Computer Speech and Language, 7* (2), 137–148.

Koedinger, K. R., Aleven, V., & Heffernan, N. (2003). Toward a rapid development environment for cognitive tutors. In U. Hoppe, F. Verdejo, & J. Kay (Eds.), *Artificial Intelligence in Education, Proceedings of AI-ED 2003* (pp. 455–457). Amsterdam: IOS Press.

Koedinger, K., Aleven, V., Heffernan, N., McLaren, B. M., & Hockenberry, M. (2004). Opening the door to non-programmers: Authoring intelligent tutor behavior by demonstration. *Proceedings of the Seventh International Conference on Intelligent Tutoring Systems (ITS-2004)*.

Koedinger, K. R., Anderson, J. R., Hadley, W. H., & Mark, M. A. (1997). Intelligent tutoring goes to school in the big city. *International Journal of Artificial Intelligence in Education, 8*, 30–43.

Lamel, L., Gauvain, J. L., & Eskenazi, M. (1991). BREF, a large vocabulary spoken corpus for French. *Proceedings of EUROSPEECH-91*.

Language Learning and Technology Online Journal. Available at http://llt.msu.edu/.

Mayfield Tomokiyo, L., Wang, L., & Eskenazi, M. (2000). An empirical study of the effectiveness of speech-recognition-based pronunciation training. *Proceedings of the International Conference on Spoken Language Processing ICSLP2000*.

Newell, A. & Simon, H. A. (1972). *Human Problem Solving*, Englewood Cliffs, NJ: Prentice-Hall.

Paivio, A. (1986). *Mental Representations: A dual coding approach*. Oxford: OUP.

Probst, K., Ke, Y., & Eskenazi, M. (2002). Enhancing foreign language tutors – in search of the golden speaker. *Speech Communication, 37* (3–4), 161–173.

Sphinx Knowledge Base Tools. Available at http://www.speech.cs.cmu.edu/tools/.

Sphinx Project Page. Available at http://www.speech.cs.cmu.edu/sphinx/.

Sphinx2-CTAT Connection Utilities. Available at http://www.cs.cmu.edu/~jonbrown/Sphinx2-CTAT/.

Syracuse Language Systems (1994). *TriplePlayPlus! User's Manual*. New York, NY: Random House.

Preface to

Developing computer competencies for pre-service language teachers

Is one course enough?

In teacher education programs that are not specifically designed for CALL, it is not easy to know how best to manage and present the knowledge and skills required to use new technologies in language learning. For example, in applied linguistics or TESOL programs – where the value of CALL may be acknowledged, but along with many other priorities and concerns – should there be one course dedicated to CALL, or more, within the time allotted for the degree? Alternatively, should there be a little CALL spread throughout all the courses in the program, given that technologies have now diffused across society and education. Furthermore, how much time should be spent on helping students develop basic computer skills, as opposed to pedagogical issues relating to technology. These questions are not easy to answer. How to treat CALL in relation to a broader program of work becomes especially acute during a period of curriculum reform. In this chapter, Martine Peters considers such a situation in the province of Quebec, Canada, as it proceeds to implement curriculum reform at all levels in the educational system. This major change is affecting every aspect of language teaching and learning, including the question of how teacher education and CALL is managed in the new structure. Peters' study focuses on evaluating the adequacy and effectiveness of one compulsory course on technology for preservice teachers. The discussion is enriched by quotations from students who provide comments on their training, especially as it relates to the organisation and content of the course, and technology integration. Their comments emphasise not only the importance of teacher education and CALL in a more general sense, but also the importance of managing the introduction of the teaching materials and activities in ways that are flexible and effective.

Developing computer competencies for pre-service language teachers

Is one course enough?

Martine Peters
Université du Québec à Montréal

Introduction

Since September 2000, the Province of Quebec has been implementing curriculum reform at all levels of the educational system – primary, secondary, college and university. This reform was prompted by political, social, demographic, economic and cultural changes (MEQ 2001a). These changes have also significantly affected the school population, especially in the Montreal region, with an ever increasing number of immigrants arriving in Quebec. Students are more culturally, religiously and linguistically diverse than they were ten years ago. In order to account for these differences, the Quebec Ministry of Education (MEQ) proposes a socio-constructivist approach for its new curriculum where students are responsible for their learning while the teacher's role, instead of being a transmitter of knowledge, is to guide the students in their acquisition of a second language.

These changes required teachers to modify their ways of teaching, as well as develop new competencies, in order to apply the new curriculum. This compelled the MEQ to modify existing teacher training programs in all Quebec universities. The new teacher training program, implemented in the fall of 2003, proposes twelve new competencies, linked to various teaching functions, with the goal of developing future teachers' ability to adapt to any situation (MEQ 2001b). This new program includes French as a second language teacher training, which now has a very large mandate. Future language teachers must be trained to teach at all levels (primary, secondary and adult) as well as in all language programs existing in Quebec (immersion, core French and welcoming programs) during their four-year undergraduate program (Duquette & Laurier 2000).

Among the twelve new competencies is one that focuses on technology integration in the classroom. This competency is further divided into sub-components or sub-competencies. For example, teachers must themselves become competent in using technology as well as help students make use of technology – not as a superficial or amusing gadget, but as a tool used to develop logical and critical thinking skills. And so the goal of development of these technological competencies in future language teachers is not to train technicians but to train teachers who will be comfortable integrating technology in their teaching (MEQ 2001b).

The purpose of this study was twofold: (1) to determine whether one technology course in a four year program was sufficient to develop technological competencies in pre-service teachers, and (2) to examine whether pre-service teachers, after having followed a course on technology in the language classroom, would have positive attitudes towards technology in schools and would feel comfortable integrating technology in their future classes. The conclusions of this research informed the organisation of a program to include a technological component which would give students the technical and pedagogical competencies necessary to be ready for technology integration in the language class.

Background

Work has already been done in identifying and categorising the competencies needed by a teacher in order to integrate technology in the classroom. Perrenoud (1998) offers a useful list. Perrenoud's categories include the ability to use word processing programs, adapt computer programs to the learning needs of the students, communicate by means of technology, and use multimedia tools in the classroom. Coughlin and Lemke (1999) have developed a continuum of professional competencies with five areas described as core technology skills: curriculum, learning and assessment, professional practice, classroom and instructional management and administrative competencies. Within these areas, the authors have identified specific indicators for each competency. Haeuw et al. (2001) have identified four "families of competencies": (1) communicate and cooperate, (2) organise and manage, (3) document oneself, and finally (4) create and produce tools and services. The International Society for Technology in Education (ISTE) (2000) has also proposed standards for the accreditation of teacher education programs in the US. Twenty-two competencies are identified for prospective teachers in six different categories ranging from technology operations and concepts to social, ethical, legal and human issues.

Desjardins, Lacasse, and Bélair (2001), in an attempt to organise all of these competencies, resort to a four-category grouping. The first category is labelled *technical* competence. Teachers must be able to operate both computer hardware and software. The second category called *social* competence refers to the ability to interact with individuals or groups by using technology. The third category is similar to that proposed by Haeuw et al. (2001). Desjardins et al. (2001) refer to it as *informational* competence and include under this category the ability to document work efficiently using technological tools such as search engines on the Internet and library databases. And finally, *epistemological* competence will enable a teacher to create or modify connections using technology in order to solve problems. We chose to use this categorisation for two reasons. The Desjardins et al. classification is interesting because it has evolved from an extensive literature review and is the result of a reassembly of many existing categories from other authors. As well, Desjardins et al. (2001) have developed and validated a questionnaire on technological competencies to be used in an educational context.

Context

At the Université du Québec à Montréal (UQAM), our four-year language teacher training program consists of 120 credits, among which 90 credits are dedicated to theoretical courses while 30 credits are awarded for practice teaching in primary or high schools or for adult education. The program is part of the Linguistics and Language Teaching Department. In addition, students are required to follow courses in the education, psychology, mathematics and literature departments.

In the Linguistics and Language Teaching Department, where most courses are offered, there are only a few full-time faculty members. As a result, 90% of courses are offered by lecturers. With a few exceptions, most faculty members and lecturers are not interested in using technology within their own courses – even though research (Gurbuz, Yildirim, & Ozden 2000) has shown that pre-service teachers fail to associate technology with their profession and that, therefore, faculty members should demonstrate the importance of technology in their own courses to future teachers. This is why, prior to the reform that took place in 2003, our program had only one course that focused on technology integration in the language classroom and very little technological integration in other courses.

This compulsory course on technology integration in the classroom was taken by the students during their last year of the program. It was the first time students were asked to consider technology for the purpose of language learning and also to develop their own computer skills. This course was offered in a computer lab to a group of approximately 25 students. Students worked individually or in groups of two depending on the availability of computers.

The course content was divided into two separate components. The first part of each class was dedicated to developing competencies for computer integration in the language classroom. The second part was reserved for the students' technological competency development. In the integration component of the course, a variety of topics were discussed such as language learning with technology, development of the four language skills with technology, evaluating with technology, the use of Internet for language learning purposes, etc. Also examined were the advantages and dangers of technology used in learning a second language and how various computer activities and applications can be used in the classroom. Students developed their technical abilities in the second part of the class. They learned about file management, how to use word processing effectively such as creating tables and inserting a table of contents in a document, etc. *Excel* was used to learn how to calculate grades and make charts while *Hot Potatoes* served to create activities to evaluate language skills. Part of the course was dedicated to Internet skills such as downloading and uploading as well as creating a webpage.

Since there was no pre-requirement for this course, students entered the course with a wide spectrum of technological skills. Some students had very minimal technological skills and could not properly manipulate a mouse while others had taken computer courses while in high school or in CEGEP.[1] We observed that the students were frustrated by trying to learn technical and pedagogical competencies in a single course because they had a lack of preparation in the former. This divergence also became frustrating for students and professor alike because too much time was spent on technical skills development rather than on learning how to integrate these skills in one's teaching.

Research

In 2001, we initiated a research project to determine whether the current practice of one technology course in the program was indeed sufficient to develop the technical and pedagogical skills necessary for students to feel confident in their ability to integrate technology in language classrooms. Empirical data was needed to confirm our observations that the students were not getting enough technological training. We knew that all teacher education programs were being recalled by the MEQ. The timing was appropriate for an evaluation of the technology component of our program in order to make the necessary changes for the implementation of our new program in 2003.

Data were collected from one group of students during the fall of 2001 and from another group during the fall of 2002. Both groups followed the compulsory technology course during that period and were tested at the beginning and at the end of the course. For both groups, the course was identical and given by the same instructor.

Instruments

For this research, two questionnaires were used. The first questionnaire elicited demographic data in order to describe the participants and their technological habits. The second questionnaire (Desjardins et al. 2001) was used to obtain students' perceptions of their technological competencies at the beginning and at the end of the course. This questionnaire contained 20 statements, with five statements for each of the competencies on a 5-point Likert scale. For example, pre-service teachers were asked to judge if they completely agreed, somewhat agreed, were neutral, somewhat disagreed or completely disagreed with the following statement on the informational competency: "I am able to use different methods to search the Internet." The score for each competency could vary between 5 and 25, with 15 being neutral. Scores over 15 indicated that the participant felt competent whereas a score under 15 represented a perceived lack of competency by the pre-service teacher. This questionnaire was validated with pre-service and in-service teachers by Desjardins et al. (2001).

In addition, qualitative data consisting of journals kept by the students during their course was analysed. The students had to write four entries in their journal commenting on their perception of the development of their technological competencies and their thoughts on teaching a language with technology.

Participants

From September 2001 to December 2002, data were collected from pre-service teachers (n=43) registered in UQAM's second-language program. There were 37 women and six men. Only 21% of the students were 30 and older, with 37% of the students being 23 and younger while the other students (42%) were between the ages of 24 and 29. Of these participants, 49% wanted to teach primary school, 26% preferred high school, 14% had chosen to teach adults and 11% had not yet decided at which level they wanted to specialise.

When asked if they had previously taken a technology course, half the students responded yes. As for technological equipment, one student (2%) did not have a personal computer, four students (10%) had a computer without Internet access. All the other students (88%) had a computer with Internet access. None of the pre-service teachers reported never using a computer while 28% of them reported using it on occasion, 51% reported frequent use of the computer and the remaining 21% said they used a computer constantly. As for the different uses the students made of the computer, they all reported using the computer for homework, the vast majority used email (91%) and surfed on the Internet (79%) while fewer students played games (35%) and fewer yet chatted (23%) or scanned documents (16%).

Table 1. Pre-service teachers' competencies in September

Competencies	N	Minimum	Maximum	Mean	Std. Deviation
Technical	43	6	25	14.5	4.9
Social	43	9	25	16.3	4.1
Informational	43	9	25	17.5	4.8
Epistemological	43	5	24	13.8	5.2

Table 2. Pre-service teachers' competencies in December

Competencies	N	Minimum	Maximum	Mean	Std. Deviation
Technical	42	9	25	17.4	4.4
Social	42	11	25	19.9	2.9
Informational	42	8	25	20.1	3.6
Epistemological	42	6	24	17.5	4.1

Results

Questionnaire

The competency questionnaire (Desjardins et al. 2001) was used to examine how pre-service teachers perceive their four technological competencies: technical, social, informational and epistemological. Table 1 presents the descriptive statistics for the pre-service teachers' competencies at the beginning of the course.

The descriptive statistics indicate that pre-service teachers perceive their technical and epistemological competencies to be the least developed while their social and informational competencies are perceived to be somewhat developed. The same trend can be observed in December (see Table 2) with the technical and epistemological competencies being perceived as being less developed than the social and informational competencies.

The participants note a definite improvement in all competencies from the beginning to the end of the course. The students report more improvement in the epistemological and social competencies than in the technical and informational competencies.

Journals

The pre-service teachers kept a journal in which they expressed their views about their technological competencies as well as their ability to integrate technology in language classes. Recurrent common themes emerged from the journal entries and were categorised into five findings. These common themes were present in the data collected in 2001 as well as in 2002. For the purpose of this chapter, the participants' quotes were translated from French to English. All the participants' names have been changed to protect their identity.

Findings

Finding 1: Educational character of technology in the language classroom

According to our data, the participants felt that the use of technology in the language classroom had to be well prepared in order for it to be educational. Many expressed a concern that technology use did not contribute to language learning if a specific language goal or objective was not defined and that it could turn an activity into technology use for the sake of technology and not for language learning.

> Technological activities must be linked to language learning activities in order to be worthwhile. They must be integrated within a teaching approach where the student will have a learning intention, a goal which will maximise language learning (Caroline).

> In order for the student to learn, it is not sufficient for him to open windows, to surf, to click in multimedia programs, to dialogue with an intelligent program. These operations must be done by a student looking for information in order to realise a goal which will result in language learning (Sylvie).

> All lab work must be significant and must represent a challenge for the student. The students must realise that they are learning and that what they are doing will help them in their language learning (Guylaine).

Some participants perceived that technology could be used to motivate students and to make language learning easier.

> Technology as I have just explained facilitates linguistic exchanges, very important in language learning. The development of these exchanges also encourages students to write (Chantal).

> Learning must not be perceived as boring by the students. With the Internet, learning can be an interesting activity for the students that approximates authentic learning (Maryse).

Finding 2: Changing roles of the learner and the teacher

The participants generally expressed positive attitudes towards the new roles of the learner and the teacher in a classroom where technology was being used. The preservice teachers felt that students would be more autonomous with technology while still having the teacher at hand to guide the students.

> Technology will let students become more and more autonomous. They will solve problems on their own using knowledge learned along the way (Karine).

> Using technology, students will be less dependent and passive, they will help each other more and they will become the principal actor in their own learning (Élyse).

The participants explained that the new role of the language teacher would be to guide the students, to accompany them in order to facilitate learning.

> The role that I will take will be one of resource person. I will give answers to the students when asked and intervene when necessary. I will also open their eyes to the world which will be theirs (Gisele).

> With technology, the teacher becomes the students' advisor, helping when needed. The teacher is also learning, like the students. The teacher becomes a guide, not a dispenser of knowledge like before (Mathilde).

None of the participants felt threatened by the computer replacing language teachers. On the contrary, most felt that it would be an ally in the language learning process. A few students called for moderation in the inclusion of technology in the classroom saying that it was a valuable tool but that human contact was still and would always be necessary.

> Whether in class or at home, the student will always be motivated by computer activities and that's why it's important to use them as an ally. I am saying ally because the computer must be a pedagogical tool and not a teaching machine (Nancy).

> No matter how intelligent the activities that will be created with technology, the physical presence of others with all it implies of verbal and non-verbal exchanges and human warmth will remain essential (Lucie).

> I will never concentrate my courses on technology because although it can be useful, it is only a tool to support teaching. After all, there is nothing better than human contact to learn a second language or any subject matter (Rachel).

Finding 3: Concerns about the integration of technology in the language classroom

The pre-service teachers had many concerns about the integration of technology. The first one had to do with the lack of equipment or of properly functioning equipment in schools.

> As for the teaching of French as a second language with technology, it is foolish to think that we will be able to use computers like we want. If we think of the local high school, the students have access to computers only during their computer courses. The labs are used to full capacity and it is very difficult for the language teachers to reserve them (Luce).

> I think that the number of computers in classes should be augmented in order to give a chance to all students to use this tool. Because of the budget cuts of the Ministry of Education, a lot of Quebec schools don't have enough computers especially when we compare ourselves to our American neighbours or to our French cousins (Tania).

> I think that if schools want their teachers to use technology with the students, it is imperative that they give appropriate equipment and training (Élise).

Many of the participants also commented on their concerns about the dangers of using the Internet and the spell checker for the language learner.

> One major disadvantage of the computer is that it corrects automatically (almost) the spelling mistakes made by the students when they type. The result: the students don't learn any spelling anymore (Luce).

> I will not go as far as to say that the Internet is dangerous for the students but it can surely give them a lot of false information, present contents that are not suitable for them (pornography) or give them the opportunity to meet dangerous or scary people through the use of chatting (Valérie).

Another concern of the pre-service teachers was the lack of resources in the schools to help them with technology integration.

> Unfortunately, the language classroom is not the best place to integrate technology because there are not enough resource personnel for the number of students (Viviane).

> I believe that in order for technology to be properly implemented in the language classroom the school would need to hire a specialist in technology as is already the case in many schools (Luce).

Finding 4: Confidence in their competencies for technology integration

Most of the pre-service teachers indicated that they felt they had developed basic technological competencies. However, most commented on the fact that they did not feel ready to integrate technology in their language classrooms.

> In general, I can get along all right with technology which I learned by myself. I have always been told that the best way to learn something is to practice and that is what I have done (Marisa).

> I sincerely think that since there is so much importance given in the new curriculum that is starting that even though I can get by with what I know about technology, I am not sure that I could teach that to anybody since I feel I still have so much to learn (Alexandra).

Finding 5: Lack of preparation for technology integration
Many participants felt they had to comment on the lack of proper technology training they had received during their four-year program. These comments were particularly interesting since it confirmed the perceptions of our research team about our teacher training program.

> As a future language teacher, it would be most useful to have more technology training at the university level. I don't feel competent about computers and all the technological possibilities that are offered to teachers (Rachelle).

> I believe that there is a need to worry about our incompetence in technology and I really hope that pre-service teachers and in-service teachers will receive more training about technology in the future (Stephanie).

> Throughout the session, I learned a lot of things but it seemed it all was superficial. There was no time to practice the different techniques that we learned. I am conscious that we had a lot of things to learn but there just was not enough time (Denise).

As we analysed the pre-service teachers' journals, we realised that their thoughts echoed what has been said in other studies as will be shown in the discussion section.

Discussion

Earlier in this chapter, the situation for the fourth-year technology integration course was described as frustrating because many students needed to develop the prerequisite technical competencies to then be able to integrate technology into the language classroom. The data collected with the questionnaire confirms that the pre-service teachers do not feel competent using technology at the beginning of the course. They perceive their technical and epistemological competencies to be underdeveloped while their social and informational competencies are viewed more positively. Desjardins (in press), when looking at in-service teachers, also found that they perceived their epistemological competency to be the weakest while their informational competencies were thought to be the most developed.

This can be explained by the use of technology by the participants. When questioned, the vast majority of the students reported surfing on the Internet and using email. Zhao et al. (2001) found the same results when questioning in-service teachers about their use of computers. This use of technology for communication and searching for information on the Internet seems to have developed in our participants an ease in using the computer and more confidence in those competencies.

The results at the end of the semester show the same competencies being perceived as more developed. These results echo those of Mitra and Steffensmeier (2000) who found that students' use of computers in a classroom setting left them more confident and less apprehensive when using technology. However, in our study it is interesting to note that the highest perceived gain between the beginning and the end of the semester came in the epistemological and social competencies and not the technical competencies, as Mitra and Steffensmeier would suggest. It is possible that the technology integration course showed the participants the multiple ways in which the computer can facilitate their language teaching and this translated into a higher perception of their epistemological competency.

Even though the participants felt their overall competencies had developed during the course, they still had concerns about using technology in the language classroom. The fact that technology could be used as a tool to motivate students was not disputed by any pre-service teachers. However, many pre-service teachers questioned the purpose of using technology, not completely convinced that technology would be used to learn a language rather than solely for learning about technology.

Most students felt comfortable with their new role as language teachers within a technology integration context and did not feel threatened by the computers. Unfortunately, many had concerns about the lack of properly functioning equipment and resources in schools. They felt that the help they would need in integrating technology in their language classes would not be available. As well, the thought of having to deal with the dangers of the Internet with their students worried them. Zhao et al. (2001) also found that in-service teachers fear losing control when students go on the Internet. This need for control is certainly linked to the pre-service students concern about lesson planning in order for learning to occur.

Overall, the students expressed confidence in the technological competencies yet still felt that they were not ready to integrate technology in the language classroom. Many felt that this was due to a lack of training during their teacher training program.

Conclusion

After analysing the data collected over this two-year period, we agreed that our pre-service teachers were not sufficiently prepared to integrate technology in their future language classes. Other research (Benson 2000; Gillingham & Topper 1999; Wildner 1999) confirmed that a single course on technology integration in a teacher education program was not sufficient. It produced quick results but was too often limited to technical aspects, was not distributed over time to guarantee competency development and as a result was quickly forgotten by the pre-service teachers. Furthermore, the message sent to the pre-service teachers is that technology is an add-on rather than an integrated component of the program. Knezek and Christensen (2001: 277) have said that:

> Anxiety tends to be reduced rather quickly with meaningful exposure to ICT. On the other hand, enthusiasm/acceptance of ICT and belief in the utility of ICT for professional productivity is slower to evolve. It appears that older types of attitudes take longer to change, in the time frame of years rather than months.

Consequently, after seeing the results of our study, we revised our language teacher education program and technology was integrated throughout the program in two different ways. All students are now required to take a course during their first semester in the program during which they learn the basic technical computer skills necessary for their studies (see Hegelheimer, this volume, for a similar model). For example, students will learn how to use *PowerPoint* to make an oral presentation, they will learn how to manipulate images etc. As well, students will create a webfolio that will evolve over their four-year program. This webfolio will be integrated in most of the courses of the program.

The second way we found to integrate technology throughout the program is by using discussion forums. Students are now required to use this technological tool to share their opinions with each other but also to do group work. We hope to develop a collaboration which the pre-service teachers will continue to use after they have graduated.

We hope that this infusion of technology throughout the program will develop the technical skills of the pre-service teachers, which in turn will free up the technology course that will be from now on dedicated to learning how to teach a language with technology. We believe that in order to have proper integration of technology in the language classroom of primary and secondary schools, our teacher education programs must have a strong technology component to properly prepare future teachers for this integration. A one-course approach is not sufficient to give the competencies as well as the confidence needed to fully integrate technology. A teacher education program must provide more training and more occasions to use technology and to practice technology integration in the language class if we are to succeed in using technology to teach languages in primary and secondary schools. Further research will show whether these modifications to our teacher training program will result in more competent and more confident teachers that in turn will translate into better technology integration in the language classroom.

Note

1. In Quebec, after high school, students must complete a two-year program in a community college (CEGEP) in order to be accepted in university. A variety of programs are offered from ⸱ sciences to psychology that students choose according to what they want to study in university.

References

Benson, S. J. (2000). Preparing prospective teachers for technology integration: Preparing tomorrow's teachers today at NMSU. Available at http://pt3.nmsu.edu/research.html.

Coughlin, E. & Lemke, C. (1999). *Dimension 3: Professional competency continuum.* Santa Monica, CA: Milken Exchange on Education Technology.

Desjardins, F., Lacasse, R., & Bélair, L. (2001). Toward a definition of four orders of competency for the use of information and communication technology (ICT) in education. In *Proceedings of the IASTED International Conference, Computers and Advanced Technology in Education* (pp. 213–217). Banff.

Duquette, L. & Laurier, M. (2000). *Multimédia et apprentissage de la langue seconde.* Montréal: Éditions Logique.

Gillingham, M. G. & Topper, A. (1999). Technology in teacher preparation: Preparing teachers for the future. *Journal of Technology and Teacher Education, 7* (4), 303–321.

Gurbuz, T., Yildirim, S., & Ozden, M. (2000). A comparison of student-teachers' attitudes toward computers in on-line and traditional computer literacy courses: A case study. In *Society for Information Technology and Teacher Education International Conference: Proceedings of Site 2000.* San Diego.

Haeuw, F., Duveau-Patureau, V., Bocquet, F., Schaff, J.-L., & Roy-Picardi, D. (2001). *Competice: Outil de pilotage par les compétences des projets TICE dans l'enseignement supérieur.* Paris: MEN, Direction de la technologie.

ISTE (International Society for Technology in Education). (2000). *National Educational Technology Standards.* Available at http://cnets.iste.org.

Knezek, G. & Christensen, R. (2001). Impact of new information technologies on teachers and students. In C. Morales, G. Knezek, R. Christensen, & P. Avila (Eds.), *Users Views of New Information Technologies in Education: Studies from multiple nations* (pp. 269–278). Mexico: Instituto Latinoamericano de la Comunicacion Educativa.

Ministère de l'Éducation du Québec (2001a). *Quebec Education Program Languages, Français langue seconde.* Québec: MEQ.

Ministère de l'Éducation du Québec (2001b). *La formation à l'enseignement. Les orientations. Les compétences professionnelles.* Québec: Gouvernement du Québec.

Mitra, A. & Steffensmeier, T. (2000). Changes in student attitudes and student computer use in a computer-enriched environnement. *Journal of Research on Computing in Education, 32* (3), 417–438.

Perrenoud, P. (1998). Se servir des technologies nouvelles. *L'Educateur, 3* (98), 20–27.

Wildner, S. (1999). Technology integration into preservice foreign language teacher education programs. *CALICO Journal, 17* (2), 223–250.

Zhao, Y., Byers, J., Mishra, P., Topper, A., Chen, O., Nfield, M., Ferdig, R., Frank, K., Pugh, K., & Tan, S. H. (2001). What do they know? A comprehensive portrait of exemplary technology-using teachers. *Journal of Computer in Teacher Education, 17* (2), 25–37.

Preface to

Learning in context

Situating language teacher learning in CALL

For pre-service students studying in a CALL course within the rather privileged world of a university, a major hurdle is to relate what is learned in the university context to the cultures and realities of everyday classroom teaching. While a student-teacher is studying, classes are usually well-planned, the technologies they use work and are well-supported, and they have the time to reflect and discuss tasks, projects and scenarios of various kinds with similarly well-motivated classmates. On the other hand, as all in-service teachers know, unfortunately this does not last. In real teaching situations, time is strictly limited, decisions have to be made quickly, priorities have to be juggled and what we might *like* to do is not always what we are *able* to do. The technological infrastructure and support, access, and general resources available may also vary widely between a university and a classroom in a school, for instance. Yet those of us who are involved in teacher education wish our students to apply the knowledge and skills they acquire in real classrooms. How can we bridge this gap? In this chapter Joy Egbert provides some possible solutions by discussing two situated learning contexts: a web-based CALL course and a case-based approach that deals with open-ended, real-world cases relating to CALL issues. The discussion engages with the complexity, diversity and oft-times conflicting priorities that can arise in real classrooms. Egbert explains how a CALL course can be made more authentic and relevant to course participants through situated learning strategies and techniques, providing access to expert performances and modeling of processes, and using technology more broadly to increase contact and engagement between pre-service and in-service teachers and tutors.

Learning in context

Situating language teacher learning in CALL

Joy Egbert
Washington State University, USA

As noted in Egbert, Paulus, and Nakamichi (2002), traditionally most language teacher education programs have worked on the premise that teachers can learn during teacher preparation coursework what they need to in order to teach well, with limited opportunities for practice along the way, and then apply it in classrooms upon completion of their programs of study. Preparation in computer-assisted language learning (CALL), which is often a part of these programs, also occurs within the fairly isolated confines of the teacher education program. However, many teachers from these programs find themselves unprepared for the realities of language teaching and unprepared to challenge and transform institutional dynamics with technology (Cattani 2002; Hargreaves 1994). The result is confusion and stress that teachers can feel once they assume an instructional role and have to apply technology-enhanced content learning to a culturally situated context (Hargreaves 1994).

Research, however, indicates that teacher learning that occurs in the authentic contexts in which the knowledge applies may reduce these tensions. The implication is that teacher change and growth occur through learning that is *situated* in classrooms (Brown, Collins, & Duguid 1989; Lave & Wenger 1991; Feiman-Nemser & Remillard 1995; Putnam & Borko 2000). In other words, for effective teacher understanding and growth, teacher education in CALL should happen in ways that link teachers with students and technology.

This chapter discusses two situated learning contexts – a Web-based CALL course and a case that deals with issues of CALL – to demonstrate the potential of situated learning for providing effective language teacher development in technology use. Situated learning is not presented here as a possible educational panacea, but rather as one proposed reform that warrants close examination. Situated learning is surely not the only useful innovation in CALL teacher education, but it is useful for researchers and teacher educators to discuss its efficacy (Andersen,

Reder, & Simon 1996, 1997; Brown & Duguid 1993). In addressing these issues, this chapter offers a brief overview of teacher learning and a short summary of situated learning and then presents an analysis of the two contexts to demonstrate how CALL teacher learning might be situated.

Teacher learning

A brief discussion of how teachers learn to teach sets up the discussion of the two CALL contexts. Kaufman (1997) notes that many teachers are unprepared to deal with the changes in student demographics that have led to a greater number of children who are underserved. These concerns around preparation and preparedness assume importance for everyone involved in education, but nowhere more than in classrooms with English language learners (ELLs) at every level. For learners to have an effective learning experience, teacher education must prepare teachers who grasp the cultural realities of teaching (Edwards, Gilroy, & Hartley 2002). As part of these realities, technology and its roles must be fully explored.

Most researchers agree that teacher learning combines a mix of *content, task,* and *professional* knowledge. In addition, learning to teach in language and content classrooms requires that teachers transfer course content to school settings across *contexts,* and that teachers continue to learn and grow as practicing professionals (Andersen, Reder, & Simon 1996; Griffin 1995; Hendricks 2001). Those who choose the teaching profession gain many of their attitudes and beliefs about teaching from the teachers and school-related events that they observe and experience throughout their lives (Anderson & Holt-Reynolds 1995; Barnes 1987; Bird et al. 1993; Freeman 1992; Lortie 1975). In many cases, this means that teaching is perceived as something a teacher does *to* learners. In others, it can mean a strongly held view that electronic technologies do not have a place in classrooms. It is these unchanged beliefs that lead teacher education students to discard theories and content about teaching that teacher education programs propose (Anderson & Holt-Reynolds 1995).

In order to move beyond these deep-seated and often ill-conceived views, teacher education students need "alternative experiences" that challenge the validity of these naïve concepts about teaching and learning (Feiman-Nemser & Remillard 1995). To help language teachers learn to teach with technology, teacher education programs must help teachers to understand the relationship between academic knowledge about computer use and its application across a variety of contexts. Learning to teach in this sense means supporting the use of content in teacher-like ways, or by helping teachers to "transform their knowledge into professional activity" (Feiman-Nemser & Remillard 1995: 15). Clearly, CALL teacher education must be more like the contexts in which such language instruction takes place.

Situated contexts and learning about teaching

If teacher change relies on understanding the differences between views, language teachers learning about CALL need opportunities to see different views in action and to reflect on the value of different views and practices. As existing scholarship suggests, coursework alone, devoid of the opportunities to practice, challenge assumptions, apply, and see evidence of student improvement, may lead to theoretical knowledge about teaching, what Kennedy (1999) calls expert knowledge, but not craft knowledge, or the day-to-day active understandings that teachers use in their classroom. As Kennedy explains, expertise arises from the joining of expert and craft knowledge. Learning about teaching (expert knowledge) but not learning to teach (craft knowledge) offers an incomplete scenario and does not empower teachers.

Learning to combine expert and craft knowledge occurs in the authentic contexts in which the knowledge is actually of use (Feiman-Nemser & Remillard 1995; Lave & Wenger 1991; Lemke 1997). This theory of situated cognition/learning has been interpreted in many ways, all with the goal of helping education students to "think and act like teacher(s)" (Feiman-Nemser & Remillard 1995:25). Situating learning is a way to help CALL teachers to focus on inquiry, produce and consider alternatives, and collaborate as they reflect on practices different from their own. Existing scholarship suggests many different ways that this may occur, including involving teachers in more inquiry-based fieldwork (Johnson 1992; Kaufman 1997); helping teachers to become part of a professional teaching community (NCRTL 1994); assisting teachers to frame classroom dilemmas in appropriate ways (Anderson & Holt-Reynolds 1995); and involving teacher-learners in tasks in which they interact with new possibilities for teaching (Bird et al. 1993; Noordhoff & Kleinfeld 1993).

Situating teacher learning online

When discussing situated learning contexts, educators typically refer to learning by participating in instructional experiences in actual classrooms; however, language teacher learning can be situated in a variety of contexts. Part of the problem with providing classroom learning contexts where teacher education students can have extensive access to learners and authentic materials is the availability of such placements. In cases where field experience placements are in short supply, distance learning opportunities can be an effective choice for linking populations. Theoretically, situating learning in teachers' classrooms through distance education gives both pre-and in-service teachers an opportunity to put new ideas into play immediately and to see the outcomes as they happen in authentic settings. Teachers

Course Outline

Mode

Admin | **Normal**

| Home | Course Roster | Course Administration | Exit Course |

About This Course

3/5/2004 - 5/31/2004

About this Course
This document explains the course content and structure and includes due dates for all assignments. Read with care!

Course Format Description

Posting and Discussion Handout
This handout explains how to post to the discussion and journal. Read carefully so that you post correctly.

VTC Discussion Help

New Discussion Features and Interface

Unit 1

3/8/2004 - 3/14/2004

Unit 1 Introduction
Click this link to read about Unit 1 instructions, including activities and readings.

KWLS
This document is for your Unit 1 Focus Reflection. It is formatted in MS Word. You can download it to your desktop by clicking on the link.

Chapter 1: Principles of CALL
This is the second reading for this unit. You can open it on your desktop or download it and print it. It is formatted in MS Word.

Unit 1 Content and Discussion

Figure 1. Outline page from the CALL course.

can thereby test new assumptions as they are presented, see student improvement, and reflect on their practice. In addition, teachers studying to use technology in their classrooms gain additional understanding by working through and with the variety of distance technologies involved in Web-based distance coursework.

One example of a situated learning experience for language teacher education students is a seven-week Web-based course on CALL. In a project funded by a federal grant, Washington State University (WSU, Pullman, WA, USA) developed and implemented six Web-based courses required for the state's K-12 ESL endorsement, one of which was "Technology and Language Learning." The course focus is on goals and standards that K-12 language learners are expected to reach, and the units emphasize the use of technology to support language student learning. For example, units explore production, collaboration, creativity, and communication goals for English language learners. All assignments in the course require course participants to reflect on, investigate, and apply their knowledge to real classrooms, either those in which they are teaching or that they "adopt" for this purpose. In addition, pre-service and in-service teachers work in concert to solve problems and define issues in these classrooms.

Participants in the online CALL course collaborate through a course system called the WSU Virtual Teacher Community (VTC). Like many other courseware systems, the VTC, hosted on a college server, provides users with a course syllabus, detailed instructions for completing the units, the ability to post private and public comments and documents, a grade book, email lists, and a course library (see Figure 1 for an example of the outline from the CALL course). However, the specific software used to situate the learning is not as important as the ways in which it supports situated learning.

Evaluating the situatedness of the online CALL course

A set of questions from Herrington and Oliver (1995, 1999, 2000) can be used to demonstrate the extent to which learning opportunities in the CALL course are situated. These questions are based on situated learning theory and are founded on the work of Lave and Wenger (1991) and other social constructivist theorists such as Savery and Duffy (1995). Although these questions do not refer only to teaching with technology, they provide a useful framework for evaluating opportunities for CALL teacher education.

1. Does it provide authentic context that reflects the way the knowledge will be used in real life?

For Herrington and Oliver, an authentic context is one in which 1) there is an authentic audience, 2) a large number of resources are available, 3) there is complexity, and 4) there is the possibility of collaboration. The online CALL course meets these criteria in many ways. For example, pre-service and in-service teachers meet and work with other teachers in different contexts throughout the course, exchanging views, building off of each others' data, and empathizing with each other during discussions. The participants consistently note the authentic audience of other teachers as one of the most valuable parts of the course. In addition, the course has a library which is available from each unit and from the main menu of the course; the library contains hundreds of resources categorized for ease of use. Additional resources are provided by the instructor and by course participants. The complexity criterion is met through the exploration of teaching problems by participants, and collaboration occurs during activities and discussion.

2.   Does it provide authentic activities?

The focus reflection that serves as the opening task in each of the course's seven units asks participants to reflect on some aspect of their classrooms, from describing a communications task they have used previously to outlining their opinion on how software should be evaluated. Tapping previous knowledge not only models authentic teaching practice but involves participants in reflecting on their own experiences. The unit task and unit activity then build on the reflection, asking students to integrate new knowledge and then apply it in creating or using what they have built. In this way, all of the learning tasks in the units are used directly in real-life situations. For example, the focus task for the course's production unit asks:

> Think of a language learning activity that you have used in your instruction or that you have seen taught. Choose one during which students were asked to create and/or produce a product. List ways you use or see to support/motivate/encourage student production or creativity. What parts of the activity worked well with ELLs? What parts of the activity could have been made more suitable to ELLs?

Students then move on to improve this activity and add technology if and where appropriate.

The activities in the course meet additional criteria in this category by providing students with choices of tasks and choices of how they want to complete the tasks. In addition, the tasks can be adapted across subject areas. This unit activity from the creativity and production unit exemplifies this concept:

> Unit Activity: Select *one* of the following options. With the use of technology (e.g. word processing, graphic software, or other appropriate tools),
> a.   Develop materials to enhance/support the process of student creativity and production, *or*

   b.   Produce something to help yourself as an instructor who encourages
        student creativity and production, *or*
   c.   Produce something to use with your students/potential students during
        student creativity and production.

Students write a one-paragraph summary explaining the reasons for their task
selection, the basis of the materials/documents they have created, the goals for
the document/materials, and how they met their goals. They then share and discuss their products and reflections with their pre-service and in-service teacher
classmates through discussion in the class electronic forum. During these activities, even pre-service teachers without current access to classrooms can reflect
on actual teaching situations, and, with support from the in-service teachers and
the course instructor, make effective and authentic plans for using CALL in their
future classrooms.

3.   Does it provide access to expert performances and the modeling of processes?

"Expert," in this instance, refers to others at various levels of expertise (or "more
capable others"), including the instructor, external guests, and other course participants. Depending on the context, materials, and topic, students may rotate
through the roles of learner, instructor, or coach during a task, a unit, or the course.
For example, a course participant that knows how to use PowerPoint well may act
as an expert in facilitating peers' understandings, or a participant may instruct
and coach others through the process of teaching ELLs production skills or understanding the theory behind such activity. In the CALL class, students access experts
by posting messages to individuals or to the class at any time via the public electronic forum built into the courseware. In addition, the participants are required
to post their unit task and asked to post other activities that they want to share
with others into the public forum. In these ways, the course gives participants opportunities to share their own stories, or areas in which they might be considered
experts, and opportunities to share the expertise grounded in others' stories.

4.   Does it provide multiple roles and perspectives?

The discussion instructions for each unit encourage participants to express their
views and to comment on others'. Through the discussion, the participants work
with classmates to understand the overall task and to complete the task from their
own perspectives. Participants take a variety of roles throughout the course, based
on their knowledge, experience, and context. The following is an example of the
discussion instructions from the unit on student production in CALL classrooms:

> In order to prepare for your Final Unit Activity, refer to the readings and ac-
> tivities in this unit as you read your classmates' postings and discuss with your
> classmates.

> Explore with your classmates the variety of ways that computers can be used by both students and instructors to create and produce materials and activities. Also explore with your classmates ways/materials/activities you can use to support/motivate/enhance/encourage ELLs' creativity and production. Discuss the impact on ELLs when these types of computer activities are introduced in a content or language learning setting. Also examine your classmates' Task summaries. What information is useful to you? What else do you need to know? What other ways can the Web sites be used as the basis of student production?

Because the discussion is asynchronous, and students are required to post two initial comments and three replies per week, they all participate at the same basic level, and they all have a chance to have their voices heard. Participants comment that it is easier for them to be honest and thoughtful at a distance from peers and that by talking about their own classrooms they can approach topics knowledgeably.

5. Does it promote collaboration, reflection, and articulation and provide coaching and scaffolding?

The criteria in this category overlap with those in others. Although only one of the activities in the course specifically asks participants to work together, they have the choice of working together on the other sections. Because participants generally register for the course with colleagues from their schools or districts, they typically take advantage of this to collaborate with local peers. Participants are encouraged to reflect on their own and others' contexts, ideas, and responses both through specific assignments like the discussion instructions and the requirement that they reply to three others' comments each week. The asynchronous nature of the forum gives them time to read and think before responding.

Scaffolding is provided in the background reading for each unit that helps learners to focus on important issues in the unit, but coaching is not built in. When there is a good instructor who can help learners to help themselves, coaching is present. However, this is sometimes a weak area for the course when the instructor does not or does not know how to appropriately facilitate and work with students online.

6. Does it provide authentic assessment of learning within the tasks?

In the first two offerings of the course, this was an area of weakness for situating learning about CALL. Herrington and Oliver's criteria in this area include 1) opportunities for students to revise and polish their task products; 2) assessment that is seamlessly integrated with the task; 3) the presence of multiple indicators of learning; 4) validity and reliability in scoring; and 5) appropriate criteria for scor-

Your overall discussion participation is worth 25 points based generally on 5 points for each of the following criteria:

- reflection (Do you show your thinking process and reflections in your postings? Do you integrate unit readings, resources, and activities? Do you refer to your experiences or others' opinions?)
- quality of comments (Do your comments add something to the discussion?)
- conciseness and clarity of comments (Do you get to the point? Do you use strategies to enhance others' understandings (e.g. give examples)?)
- attitude (Are you a positive and supportive participant? Do you welcome different opinions and perspectives? Do you show respect to others in the discussion?)
- amount of interaction (Do you interact with others or only make isolated comments?)

The Final Unit Activity (Enhancing creativity and production) is worth 40 points based on the following criteria:

- writing and clarity (Is it clear and professional? Is it easy to read and understand? Do you get to the point?) 5 points
- agreement with instructions (Did you follow the instructions? Did you do it on time? Did you post in the correct place?) 5 points
- completeness (Is it complete? Did you answer all the questions?) 10 points
- content quality (Does it show thought? Is it thorough and reflective? Is your evidence, argument, or question well grounded?) 10 points
- unit integration (Did you refer to the readings, activities and discussion? Did you refer to the unit content?) 10 points

Figure 2. Rubrics from the production unit in the CALL course.

ing varied products. Because the course was offered in an intensive seven-week format (what would usually be a 16-week course), students were rarely given the opportunity to revise. In many instances there was only one indicator of learning for a task, for example a short written response; however, each unit contained multiple indicators of learning. There were too many, in fact, for instructors to evaluate in a reasonable amount of time. For example, in one week during the production unit, learners completed a reflection that was a page long, a unit task that asked them to evaluate a Web site or tool, five discussion postings, and a unit activity in which they created and justified a product. Because feedback was expected to be thorough and quick, instructors spent many more hours per week evaluating than they should probably have.

The course did meet two of the criteria for this category more effectively: the rubrics developed for each activity and the discussion were appropriate for a variety of participant products, and the grading using them was reliable and valid. For example, two rubrics for the student production unit are presented in Figure 2.

In the future this course will meet these criteria better by facilitating instructor learning, offering participants more choices and more opportunities for collaboration, and moving toward a system of evaluation that involves more of the students and less of the instructor.

Anecdotal results and more formal preliminary data analysis from the Web-based teacher education courses indicate that on-line distributed learning opportunities may be one effective way to situate teacher learning about students, language, and technology. Self-report and other participant data collected from the pre-service education students, in-service teachers, and instructors in this course suggest that the situatedness of the course facilitates teacher learning, as indicated by changes in knowledge and practice. Teachers report trying new strategies and tools, applying new ideas and techniques, and using more authentic assessments in their classrooms as a direct result of the situations facilitated by the course.

The instructor's role

In making the courses work, we have found that the role of the instructor is crucial. Knowing when to step in, to steer students back on course, to provide important information, and to ask for authentic examples can enhance the situated learning experience. On the other hand, because the course is necessarily highly structured and explicated, it is relatively easy for instructors to let the course move on its own; this lack of expert facilitation can detract from the experience by letting the conversation derail, by leaving students floundering in a plethora of resources that they cannot figure out how to use, and perhaps by failing to bring the knowledge being constructed back to the students' real teaching contexts. Because the instructors of this course are sometimes K-12 CALL experts with no online teaching experience (typically former teachers pursuing their doctorate at the university), we are producing a simple "instructor's guide" to provide examples of ways to interact effectively with the course, the content, and the students.

Cases as situated learning experiences

Not all teacher education programs are equipped or willing to take on the extra work that creating and delivering online situated courses require; however, it is clear from the literature that teachers who can analyze and handle the many different situations that may arise in their technology-enhanced ESL classrooms will be more effective in helping their students learn than those without such preparation. Like Web-based situated classes, cases can help to prepare language teachers in face-to-face classes in these ways. Although we use cases in both Web-based and face-to-face classes, we have found the synchronous face-to-face discussion in onsite classes to facilitate deeper and more thorough case analysis. Open-ended, reality-based cases can stimulate discussion and help teacher education students to examine their knowledge, experiences, attitudes, and skills without accessing physical classrooms. Although typically not as rich or authentic as a real classroom experience, cases can help teachers to see things from different perspectives, learn how to make decisions in messy contexts, learn how to handle conflict, and think about theory and practice connections.

Business, law, and medical schools regularly use cases as a focus of instruction (see, for example, the well-known Harvard Business Cases). There are many approaches to using cases in education; most important is that learners use the same case but bring different perspectives to its analysis. In general, learners go through some variation of these steps in analyzing a case: identify the issues, consider all perspectives, identify professional knowledge, project possible actions and their consequences, and choose the best action. During this process, students should brainstorm the issues in groups, deciding which facts of the case are relevant, which are urgent, and which are neither. Rather than taking the case at face value, students should look deeply into the possible reasons for the concerns expressed by the people in the case and also into factors that may play a role in finding a solution to the case. Students review the relevant literature throughout. The instructor can point out appropriate readings and other resources or require students to discover and share their own resources. Important to case analysis is that students articulate the reasons behind each action that they project. At the end of the case process, the instructor should assist the students in bringing the case to closure. This can include, for example, summarizing the students' findings, having students reflect on the process, debriefing on specific criteria, or inviting guests (for example, school administrators or in-service teachers) to adjudicate.

One of the cases we have used to help students understand issues of CALL in on-site teacher education classes raises many instructional issues and asks learners to think about ways that technology can be used to support course goals. The teacher in the case, Greg, is trying to use technology to help migrant students with their pronunciation/speaking because it has become an issue in both their social and academic lives. In addition,

> because he knows that many of his students have limited time in school each year and that they do not have much English language support at home, Greg has also tried to find ways to support his students' learning throughout and after their school day when they are not in his class. To this end, he has started a technology loan program that lets students take tape recorders home to do oral journal assignments and to record oral reports. He also checks out software to students that they can use independently to study different aspects of language. In addition, he has shown some of his more proficient students how to use a simple audio email program so that they can send spoken questions and ideas to him and to classmates over the Internet when the students have time in the computer lab.
>
> (Egbert 2005: 95)

Participants analyze the case to see what Greg is doing well/could do better and to propose solutions to what he considers the problem of his students' speaking skills. During their analysis of this case, students discuss what actions might be the most effective for the teacher and the students in the case. They can work in groups or individually for the initial analysis and then in small groups or as a class to discuss issues that arise. Teacher education students refer to the literature on how technology might enhance speaking skills, how teachers can use technology effectively with ELLs, and how complex an activity teaching and learning with technology can be. After exploring the issues with the class, students compose an individual reflection discussing their understanding of the case and supporting the solution that they think most effectively helps Greg to solve his teaching dilemma.

Evaluating the situatedness of the case

Herrington and Oliver's (1995, 1999, 2000) guidelines can be used to demonstrate the extent to which CALL learning opportunities during case analysis are situated.

1. Does it provide authentic context that reflects the way the knowledge will be used in real-life?

This case, like all those that we use, is based on a real-life teaching situation in which technology is used, and the participants may come up against the same basic issues of technology use in their teaching.

2. Does it provide authentic activities?

Participants are involved in reflecting, collaborating, making informed decisions, consulting the literature, weighing options, asking for help, and many other tasks that are part of the daily work of teachers who want to use technology effectively.

3. Does it provide access to expert performances and the modeling of processes?

This is not inherently part of the case method but must be carefully planned and integrated into the process. Using the case method well means that participants understand the process because it has been modeled at least once in its entirety. The instructor and any invited CALL expert guests demonstrate how to analyze the case effectively and appropriately. If course participants have expertise in parts of the case process or in knowledge areas needed to arrive at solutions, they too can be considered experts.

4. Does it provide multiple roles and perspectives?

Participants review different perspectives on technology use from the literature, from each other, and from any experts (including the instructor) who are part of the process.

5. Does it promote collaboration, reflection, and articulation and provide coaching and scaffolding?

The teacher's role is to make sure that the case process includes all of these components, although she is not required to provide all of the coaching and scaffolding herself. That participants are able to express themselves, ask questions, and work together for common understanding with any help that they need is crucial to the whole case process.

6. Does it provide authentic assessment of learning within the tasks?

The case process allows for ongoing assessment more clearly than the online course. Indicators of learning include being able to name all the stakeholders and their stakes, supporting a position after collaborating and consulting resources, and making choices that demonstrate understanding and effective technology-enhanced instruction; from these and other indicators, the instructor can evaluate what participants have gained and how they have changed.

Participants in the language courses that use cases like the one described previously report that the cases help them to understand the complexity of classrooms and the multitude of issues and stakeholders that are involved in different situations. They note that working through a case is a difficult task, but that the collaboration, reflection, and inquiry required produce effective understandings. That tasks ask learners to solve problems, reflect on actual classrooms, and use technology in ways that they will use it as teachers does not alone provide situatedness. As is the case with the online course, effective facilitation of the case is central to successfully situating learning. In other words, the instructor plays a key role in scaffolding, encouraging, supporting, and requiring students to reflect. In order to situate learning in CALL, instructors must understand both the goals of the process and the methods through which learning is situated.

Conclusion

Clearly, language teacher education programs have not always been successful at promoting teacher change and exiting students who employ the practices that reflect their teacher preparation programs. Situating teacher learning in CALL can help to prepare teachers to meet the needs of their language minority and other underserved learners, in part by working directly or virtually with underserved learners to improve their chances for school success. Although researchers have clear anecdotal evidence, theoretical support, and a strong belief that situated learning prepares language teachers more effectively than traditional programs, the CALL profession needs less ambiguous evidence. Since many ways of situating learning exist, we must begin to explore how best teacher learning can be situated in appropriate cultural and technological contexts and what effects this has on pre-service teacher learning and on subsequent gains of students. We should also examine the differences that different situations make on instruction and what gains and losses participants experience in each of these contexts. Most important, we need to better understand how situated learning affects teaching and learning outcomes. The results of research on these and other issues can help us to re-think and reformulate situated learning theory, practical applications to language teacher preparation, and the development of programs that prepare technology-using language teachers.

References

Andersen, J., Reder, L., & Simon, H. (1996). Situated learning and education. *Educational Researcher, 25* (4), 5–11.

Andersen, J., Reder, L., & Simon, H. (1997). Situative versus cognitive perspectives: Form versus substance. *Educational Researcher, 26* (1), 18–21.

Anderson, L. & Holt-Reynolds, D. (1995). *Prospective Teachers' Beliefs and Teacher Education Pedagogy: Research based on a teacher educator's practical theory*. Report RR95-6, National Center for Research on Teacher Learning. East Lansing: Michigan State University.

Barnes, H. (1987, April). Intentions, problems, & dilemmas: Assessing teacher knowledge through a case method system. Paper presented at the American Educational Research Association Annual Meeting, Washington DC.

Bird, T., Anderson, L., Sullivan, B., & Swidler, S. (1993). Pedagogical balancing acts: Attempts to influence prospective teachers' beliefs. *Teaching and Teacher Education, 9* (3), 253–267.

Brown, J., Collins, A., & Duguid, P. (1989). Situated cognition and the culture of learning. *Educational Researcher, 18* (1), 32–42.

Brown, J. & Duguid, P. (1993). Stolen knowledge. *Educational Technology, 33* (3), 10–15.

Cattani, D. (2002). *A Classroom of Her Own: How new teachers develop instructional, professional, and cultural competence*. Thousand Oaks, CA: Sage.

Edwards, A., Gilroy, P., & Hartley, D. (2002). *Rethinking Teacher Education: Collaborative responses to uncertainty*. New York: Routledge.

Egbert, J. (2005). *Bridge to the Classroom: ESL cases for teacher exploration, Volume 1: Elementary*. Alexandria, VA: TESOL.

Egbert, J., Paulus, T., & Nakamichi, Y. (2002). The impact of CALL instruction on classroom computer use: A foundation for rethinking technology in teacher education. *Language Learning & Technology, 6* (3), 108–126.

Feiman-Nemser, S. & Remillard, J. (1995). Perspectives on learning to teach. In F. B. Murray (Ed.), *The Teacher Educator's Handbook: Building a knowledge base for the preparation of teachers* (pp. 63–91). San Francisco: Jossey-Bass Publishers. Also available at http://ncrtl.msu.edu/http/ipapers/html/ip953.htm.

Freeman, D. (1992). Language teacher education, emerging discourse, and change in classroom practice. In J. Flowerdew, M. Brock, & S. Hsia (Eds.), *Perspectives on Second Language Teacher Education* (pp. 1–21). Hong Kong: City Polytechnic.

Griffin, M. (1995). You can't get there from here: Situated learning, transfer, and map skills. *Contemporary Educational Psychology, 20,* 65–87.

Hargreaves, A. (1994). *Changing Teachers, Changing Times: Teachers' work and culture in the postmodern age.* London: Cassell.

Harvard Business Cases Online. Available at http://harvardbusinessonline.hbsp.harvard.edu/b02/en/cases/cases_home.jhtml.

Hendricks, C. (2001). Teaching causal reasoning through cognitive apprenticeship: What are results from situated learning? *Journal of Educational Research, 94* (5), 302–311.

Herrington, J. & Oliver, R. (1995). Critical characteristics of situated learning: Implications for the instructional design of multimedia. In J. Pearce & A. Ellis (Eds.), *Learning with Technology, ASCILITE 1995 Conference Proceedings* (pp. 253–262). Melbourne, Australia: ASCILITE.

Herrington, J. & Oliver, R. (1999). Using situated learning and multimedia to investigate higher-order thinking. *Journal of Educational Multimedia and Hypermedia, 8* (4), 401–21.

Herrington, J. & Oliver, R. (2000). An instructional design framework for authentic learning environments. *Educational Technology Research and Development, 48* (3), 23–48.

Johnson, K. (1992). The instructional decisions of pre-service English as a second language teachers: New directions for teacher preparation programs. In J. Flowerdew, M. Brock, & S. Hsia (Eds.), *Perspectives on Second Language Teacher Education* (pp. 115–134). Hong Kong: City Polytechnic.

Kaufman, D. (1997). Collaborative approaches in preparing teachers for content-based and language enhanced settings. In M. A Snow & D. M. Brinton (Eds.), *The Content-based Classroom: Perspectives on integrating language and content* (pp. 175–186). New York: Longman.

Kennedy, M. (1999). Ed schools and the problem of knowledge. In J. D. Raths & A. C. McAninch (Eds.), *Advances in Teacher Education Volume 5, What Counts as Knowledge in Teacher Education?* (pp. 29–45). Stamford, CT: Ablex Publishing Corp.

Lave, J. & Wenger, E. (1991). *Situated Learning: Legitimate peripheral participation.* Cambridge: Cambridge University Press.

Lemke, J. (1997). Cognition, context, and learning: A social semiotic perspective. In D. Kirshner & A. Whitson (Eds.), *Situated Cognition Theory: Social, neurological, and semiotic perspectives* (pp. 37–55). Hillsdale, NJ: Lawrence Erlbaum.

Lortie, D. (1975). *Schoolteacher.* Chicago: University of Chicago Press.

National Center for Research on Teacher Learning (NCRTL). (1994). *Learning to Walk the Reform Talk: A framework for professional development of teachers.* East Lansing: Michigan State University. Available on line: http://ncrtl.msu.edu/http/walk.pdf .

Noordhoff, K. & Kleinfeld, J. (1993). Preparing teachers for multicultural classrooms. *Teaching and Teacher Education, 9* (1), 27–39.

Putnam, R. & Borko, H. (2000). What do new views of knowledge and thinking have to say about research on teacher learning? *Educational Researcher, 29* (1), 4–15.

Savery, J. R. & Duffy, T. M. (1995). Problem based learning: An instructional model and its constructivist framework. *Educational Technology, 35* (5), 31–38.

Preface to

Training CALL teachers online

Online and face-to-face learning are similar in some ways and different in others. They are similar in that they both involve particular learning settings, course goals, teacher-student and student-student interactions, tasks, and assessment instruments and procedures. However, they are also different, especially in that online and face-to-face learning contexts require each course element to be realized rather differently. As far as interaction is concerned, for example, in a face-to-face class most of the interaction will occur perhaps on a weekly basis for a specified time and in a specified place, when the students meet together in class, or in a workshop or seminar. In contrast, the times for online interactions are more indeterminate: for example, online chat sessions between students usually have to be carefully negotiated in order to ensure participants in different time zones can take part. Online interactions are more fluid, and as such the teachers' role and influence becomes crucial in managing the timing of interactions. Clearly, different contexts lead to different pedagogical strategies and techniques in order to ensure that the student remains motivated and engaged throughout a course of study. There are also different challenges to successful learning in each setting. This chapter by Christine Bauer-Ramazani focuses on the approach taken in an online learning course for teacher education and CALL. It describes the evolution of the CALL training course through its transition from face-to-face to online, together with key content and design elements. The discussion pays special attention to the strategies and techniques required to create an effective community of learners. It also includes quotes from those in the best position to assess the effectiveness and success of a CALL course, the learners themselves.

Training CALL teachers online

Christine Bauer-Ramazani
Saint Michael's College, USA

CALL and online learning

The need for an online CALL course

The fastest growing category of new online offerings is in graduate programs, according to a study by the Sloan Consortium (Allen & Seaman 2003). On-line/distance courses allow those pursuing graduate degrees to remain employed, reduce the cost of travel to campus significantly, and customize completion of course work to their own schedule and needs (Ebersole 2004). TESL/TEFL programs have not remained immune to pressures to offer such opportunities. Given that teacher trainees, just like the pupils they are preparing to teach, increasingly expect "just-in-time" or "any-time, anywhere learning" (Dede 2004; Carter 2004), it seems imperative for institutions to make teacher training courses available in a distance/online format, among them Computer-Assisted Language Learning (CALL). It was these trends and demands, in addition to partnerships with institutions of higher learning overseas, which necessitated the transition of an existing face-to-face course at Saint Michael's College (SMC) to a distance mode with online delivery in January 2000. Since then the CALL Online course at Saint Michael's College (see Bauer-Ramazani 2005c) has matured into a regularly taught course in both the Master of Arts program in Teaching English as a Second/Foreign Language and the Master of Education program and has attracted participants from across the United States and internationally, including Greece, Poland, Iran, Switzerland, Germany, Palau, Egypt, Taiwan, Korea, Saudi Arabia, and Japan.

Certificates in CALL and courses in teaching/education and technology
Several institutions offer online certificates or a hybrid program with online CALL-related courses, for example the Certificate in Computer-Assisted Language Learning (CALL) by the Monterey Institute of International Studies, the ICAL On-line TESL/TEFL Certificate, and the International TEFL Corporation – Online

TEFL Certificate. In addition to CALL Online at Saint Michael's College, on-line CALL-related courses are offered at Washington State University (Research and Practice in Computer-Assisted Language Learning), the University of Albany (Using Media in the Language Classroom, and Media in Teaching & Learning), as well as through the Teachers of English to Speakers of Other Languages (TESOL) organization as part of its Principles and Practices of Online Teaching Certificate Program.

Overview

As the CALL course for teacher trainees at Saint Michael's College has been successfully delivered in an online/distance format for several years now, this chapter will discuss some of the criteria that are important for teacher trainers and teacher training programs to consider when implementing such a course. We will briefly examine the approach taken in the CALL Online course, including its evolution from the face-to-face course taught on campus to a fully online/distance course under the guiding premise and goal that teacher training can be conducted successfully online. The chapter will then focus on the content, structure, and pedagogy of the course in terms of the major components that have ensured its successful delivery – interaction, collaboration, and task/project-based assessment. As the course has not been without its challenges, solutions to those and lessons learned will be discussed. Lastly, we will hear about the course in the words of the learners and plans for the future.

The approach of CALL Online at Saint Michael's College

The task faced by the designer/author in the initial stage of development of CALL Online was to counteract the perception that teaching and learning in online courses differs dramatically in effectiveness and quality from that of face-to-face courses. Thus, the design and delivery of the course was based on the hypothesis that an online course can be as interactive, collaborative, task-and project-based as a face-to face course on training teachers in CALL. In other words, the course designer/author deliberately chose not to follow a traditional model of teaching where lectures might be converted to text in an online environment, but instead intended to continue training teachers by establishing a vibrant community of learners and by modeling "how to use technology in the teaching and learning process" (Willis & Raines 2001:56) in an online environment.

Evolution of CALL Online at SMC: The three phases of development (1997–2000)

To become a fully online/distance course, the CALL course at SMC went through several transitions: In Phase 1 (1997–1999), the class met in a face-to-face setting with weekly on-campus sessions for instruction, student presentations, and discussion. The major support element of the course consisted of instructor-created Web pages that integrated the *resources* and *technology tools* used in the course. These contained *Christine's Links to Useful TESL/CALL Web Sites* (Bauer-Ramazani 2005b) and *Christine's How To's: Tech Tips and Workshops* (Bauer-Ramazani 2005a), with links to hands-on tutorials or workshops on *Windows*, *Word, PowerPoint, FrontPage*, Audio/Video, and Distance Learning tools. The Web pages were supplementary, static elements of the course.

Phase 2 began when five Saint Michael's College MATESL students working abroad (in Greece and Switzerland) were scheduled to enter the CALL course in January 2000, thus creating a need for the College to serve a distant learning community through online tools. The previous Web-based course support site was expanded to a comprehensive Web site for CALL Online, integrating the static Web pages with a dynamic and interactive element for communication among the course participants. The new integrated course Web site consisted of the major building blocks for an online course: (1) the *Course Home* page with a picture and Welcome Video, (2) a *Getting Started* file with instructions and orientation to the course, (3) the *Syllabus*, (4) the *Course Calendar* with links to weekly *Tasks* and *Assignments*, (5) *Tools* (How To's), (6) *Communication*, and (7) *Resources*. The asynchronous and synchronous communication during the course took place in a closed *Yahoo! Group*, where the teacher trainees and the instructor discussed the weekly readings and hands-on links, uploaded and downloaded links and files, and conducted five text- and voice-enabled class chats.

Phase 3 took place in December 2000, when CALL Online was migrated to the course management system (CMS) of *eCollege* for integrated, "one-stop" delivery of both content and communication. Today, the CMS is part of the institutional support system of the college, including access to all campus resources, such as registration, electronic databases, student records, the business office, and other campus departments. Figure 1 shows the homepage for the course.

The guiding premise of CALL Online

Although some guidelines and suggestions have been established for transitioning from face-to-face to online learning and teaching (Bourne et al. 1997), the challenge for migrating a face-to-face course to successful online delivery is to provide a similar learning and teaching environment, one that exhibits the characteristics

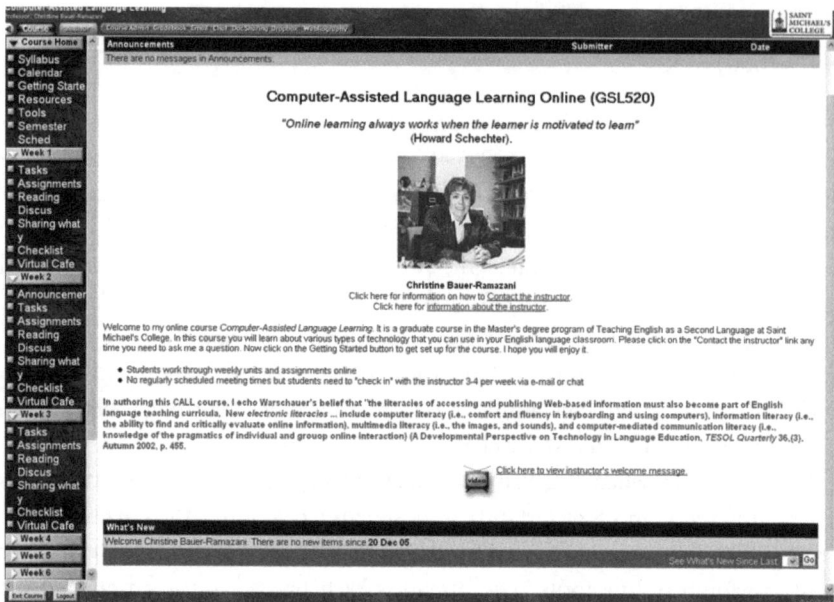

Figure 1. Homepage of CALL Online.

of an active learning community and allows for the assessment of learning outcomes. Thus, the major course components – goals, content, interaction, assessment, outcome, and overall quality – should remain intact. The guiding premise for the author and course designer of CALL Online was, therefore, to maintain the integrity of the learning and teaching experience. To summarize, these goals consist of

– providing a teacher training experience through online CALL that results in active learning as demonstrated by high-quality outcomes;
– finding ways to create an effective, involved, enthusiastic learning community that transcends the boundaries and limitations of the online environment while also taking advantage of the tools and resources available through online delivery;
– modeling effective incorporation of technology into the classroom through hands-on, task- and project-based experiences that follow a constructivist, inquiry-based approach (Butler-Pascoe & Wiburg 2003).

Goals and objectives of CALL Online

With the increasing role of technology in K-12 and higher-education classrooms, the goals of CALL Online have also expanded from the more narrow focus on English language learning to foreign language learning and educational technology in general. As more course participants are pursuing teaching careers in public schools in the United States or abroad, the course goals need to reflect this emphasis and outcomes need to be measurable with respect to standards of technology in education (see the National Educational Technology Standards for Teachers – NETS – developed by the International Society for Technology in Education, 2000–2004). Thus, teacher trainees in CALL Online are expected to develop competencies in educational technology and apply them within their specific teaching and technology environment, be it English as a second or foreign language, other foreign language learning, the educational computer lab, the one-computer K-12 classroom, or the multi-computer K-12 classroom.

Warschauer's four "electronic literacies" (2002) provide the "common denominator" to express these multi-faceted competencies. The goal of CALL Online then is for participants to learn and apply in their specific areas and environments:

1. computer literacy (i.e. comfort and fluency in keyboarding and using computers);
2. information literacy (i.e. the ability to find and critically evaluate online information);
3. multimedia literacy (i.e. images and sounds);
4. computer-mediated communication literacy (i.e. knowledge of the pragmatics of individual and group online interaction).

To satisfy these literacies, CALL Online participants are expected to:

1. establish a vibrant learning community that actively co-constructs knowledge, shares insights and experience, and builds competence as a result of the elements and principles of learning it has interacted with;
2. learn various technological tools, applications, and resources for authoring activities and materials for classes through practical tasks and projects, such as newsletters, e-mail exchanges, presentation slide shows, Internet searches, sound/video recordings, software simulations, concordancing activities, WebQuests, and Web templates to create exercises, quizzes, puzzles, and rubrics;
3. review and evaluate the various technological media, tools, and resources with respect to their effectiveness for language learning and teaching through discussions, peer reviews, and critical reviews;
4. review readings on the history and current research in CALL and discuss the environment of CALL as it is influenced by theories and practices in second/foreign language learning and teaching, applied linguistics, education, educational psychology, and educational technology (see Butler-Pascoe & Wiburg 2003; Egbert 2005; Chapelle 2001; Egbert & Hanson-Smith 1999; Warschauer 1996);

Structure and content of CALL Online

Course design and components
Following the "best practices" for effective online courses (Palloff & Pratt 2003; Phipps & Merisotis 2000; Graham et al. 2001; Wright, C., n.d.), CALL Online incorporates tools of computer-mediated communication (CMC) and follows a teaching approach that encourages collaboration and interaction in an online format. Its design is based on the principles of simple architecture and consistent organization with predictable layout and navigation. Instructions, policies, guidelines, and deadlines are clearly stated and repeated frequently (see the *Getting Started* and *Syllabus* links as well as screenshots on the Training CALL Teachers Online: Support Site – Structure). Consistency and predictability also extend to content and recurrence of the same content elements. The content of the course is divided into weekly topics or modules, each comprised of the following major elements:

1. tasks and assignments
2. communication and interaction
3. collaboration
4. task- and project-based assessment

Tasks and Assignments: Hands-on projects, models, readings, and hands-on links
In the *Tasks* and *Assignments* in CALL Online, the teacher trainees learn the technology tools that guide them toward computer and multimedia literacy (Warschauer 2002) by working through weekly tasks and completing *hands-on projects* that can be short-term (weekly) or longer-term (semester-long). The tasks consist of links to tutorials, workshops, or online "handouts" for learning technology tools, with which the learners work and experiment in order to create a teaching tool, i.e. a hands-on project, that they can employ in their current or future classes. Technology tools can be applications, such as *Word*, *PowerPoint*, or Web editors, links to hands-on tutorials or workshops for these applications, as well as Internet tools, for example online software for marking or for creating exercises, quizzes, puzzles, games, or rubrics. The teaching tools constructed by the teacher trainees are designed for an authentic purpose with a pedagogical focus, e.g. a class or school newsletter in *Word*, a *PowerPoint* slide show that is a lesson plan, a WebQuest lesson, or Web-based rubrics for assessment of student projects. For each teaching tool, the teacher trainees are encouraged to download and review *models* previously constructed by peers and by the CALL course teacher to confirm they are "on the right track."

Through the assigned *readings* of book chapters, articles on the Web or links to electronic databases in the library, the teacher trainees in CALL Online synthesize theory and practice. These teacher trainees review the readings in the online

Reading Discussion Forum in the form of threaded discussions that facilitate the construction of knowledge by the learners and engage them in the learning process through reflection on the technology presented in the context of theory, research, and pedagogy. Participants compose summaries of and reactions to the chapters and articles, drawing on their personal experience and pointing out the strengths and possible limitations or weaknesses of the proposed applications, especially as they relate to the classroom.

As an extension of the tasks, projects, and readings, the learners visit *hands-on links* to outside resources that provide additional illustrations of possible uses of the technology under discussion. These hands-on links are critical to the delivery of content in CALL Online, as they allow the teacher trainees to explore alternative applications of technology tools. This exploration is followed by threaded discussions in the Sharing What You Learned Discussion Forum where participants post their reactions, discussing the strengths, weaknesses, and applications to the classroom (See the Training CALL Teachers Online: Support Site – Content, for an example of the process).

Communication/interaction in CALL Online

The establishment of an online learning community (Palloff & Pratt 1998, 2003; Kollock & Smith 1999) that communicates and interacts is critical to the success of CALL Online and to the achievement of computer-mediated communication (CMC) literacy (Warschauer 2002). As Kim and Moore (2005) report, frequent and constructive interaction as well as dynamic discussions among all participants affect the success of Web-based courses. Thus, the tools and means to facilitate CMC have to be planned for, constructed, and built into the course. Communication in an online environment basically occurs in two forms – asynchronous (delayed) and synchronous (real-time). Due to time and bandwidth constraints, most of the communication in CALL Online is conducted asynchronously. However, CALL Online offers both modes in order to take full advantage of opportunities for interaction with the content, the participants, and the teacher. The learning community in CALL Online interacts and communicates daily and frequently, using the following tools of CMC.

Asynchronous communication

- e-mail: teacher-to-learner(s) or learner(s)-to-teacher
- announcements posted on the course home page
- threaded discussions about the readings in the *Reading Discussion Forum*
- moderators leading the weekly threaded discussions about readings, tasks, and hands-on links by posing questions, fielding responses, and guiding discussions

- threaded discussions about tasks and hands-on links in the *Sharing What You Learned Discussion Forum*
- uploading of individual and group projects for peer review and teacher assessment
- uploading and sharing of individual projects for teacher assessment
- uploading and sharing of text and audio comments on projects (teacher and peers)
- uploading and sharing newly-found links

Synchronous communication

- required class chats in the course site about the pedagogical effectiveness and implementation possibilities of various technology and teaching tools

  - groupings for chats: whole class to start and end the chat; small groups for more in-depth discussion in group chat rooms
  - tools used: text chat, whiteboard, two-way audio broadcast with Web-browsing and desktop(file)-sharing
  - text and audio archives of chat sessions

- conferences with project groups or teams, using text, voice, and Webcam – usually with *Yahoo!Messenger*
- frequent group and individual chat conferences, using text, voice, and web cam – usually with *Yahoo!Messenger*
- virtual office hours in the chat room

The CALL Online course model for interaction is based on a modified version of the "Indicators of Engaged Learning" developed by Jones et al. (1995), in which the student functions as explorer of tools and ideas, cognitive apprentice of a mentor who coaches students to develop ideas and skills, teacher of his/her peers, and producer of projects of real use. The teacher as facilitator monitors the discussions and project work, functions as a guide to help students construct meaning through modeling, mediating, explaining when needed, redirecting focus, and providing options. According to this model, the teacher learns from the students and is willing to take risks to explore areas outside of his/her expertise.

These factors of engaged learning highlight the strong presence and the significance of the human factor in online teaching; however, they do not in themselves guarantee successful online teaching. Thus, in CALL Online these factors have been supplemented by what Palloff and Pratt (2003) call "elements of learner-focused instructional techniques" – openness, communication, commitment, collaboration, reflection, and flexibility. The learner-focus is furthermore enhanced by four interactive elements stipulated by Roblyer and Ekhaml (2000) for distance learning courses. These include social rapport-building activities created by the

Table 1. The "human factor" in CALL Online

Personal contact:	urging participants to call or email the teacher immediately, even on weekends, to avoid frustration; meeting face-to-face with on-campus students to solve problems; exchanging phone numbers to facilitate group collaboration
Visual contact:	teacher-constructed Web page with pictures and biographical information about the participants; use of Webcam by teacher and students during online conferencing
Voice contact:	voice conferences with the teacher and with group members; audio comments in peer and teacher reviews of projects (embedded in documents), audio e-mails, telephone
"Checking in":	checking in with students regularly and briefly, e.g. when they "come online"; being invited to an impromptu audio conference (text/voice/Webcam) with one or more students or students among each other to discuss projects or to counteract reported "loneliness in cyberspace" (see also Kollock's characterization of "online communities as more isolated than 'real-life' groups", 1999)
Q&A forum:	offering a weekly Q&A forum in the course site devoted to student questions and answers, either pertaining to the tasks directly or to technology in general
Virtual Cafe:	a cyber cafe where course participants can discuss issues not directly related to the course
Constant vigilance:	immediately checking in with students who fall behind in their weekly assignments

instructor, instructional designs for learning created by the instructor, interactive technology resources, and interactive quality of learner responses. In the absence of verbal/nonverbal communication mechanisms, the learners in CALL Online want to know that a message was received and that feedback will be given; they also want to be acknowledged, supported, and/or redirected in their discussions (see also Palloff & Pratt 2003; Graham et al. 2001). To implement these interactive elements and to compensate for the absence of the "human factor", i.e. face-to-face communication, the usual verbal and nonverbal cues are substituted through various other means and in as many combinations as possible in CALL Online (see Table 1).

Dede (2004) has called this convergence of different delivery methods "distributed learning," as it combines multiple approaches to meeting the needs and styles of various learners. As Carter (2004) states, the current best practices "point to a combination of the human element, top-notch tech support, a diversity of technologies, a high level of interactivity, and need-to-know topics as essential elements" (36).

Collaboration in CALL Online

The third key factor in establishing an effective learning community among the teacher trainees in CALL Online is collaboration, which was built into the structure of the course in the form of collaborative assignments. Tinzmann et al. (1990) specify four elements of learner-centered collaboration: (1) shared knowledge among teachers and students, (2) shared authority among teachers and students, (3) teachers as mediators, and (4) heterogeneous groupings of students. Learners in CALL Online complete several collaborative and interactive tasks in pairs, groups of three or four, and groups of four or five. Learners may choose partners for the semester-long project but are teamed up in mixed groups by the instructor considering the following criteria:

- current or future teaching focus, e.g. language/non-language focus, K-12, college, adult
- program standing (1st semester, 1st year, 2nd year)
- technical proficiency
- native/non-native speaker
- location (campus, off-campus, abroad)
- gender

As collaborative tasks require the use of CMC, the online environment necessitates the establishment of a diverse group that can utilize the strengths and multiple experiences of its members to its advantage. As Palloff and Pratt (2003) point out, collaborative tasks in an online course "are probably the best way to tap into all learning styles present in the group" (p. 36) as they allow for development of critical thinking skills, co-creation of knowledge and meaning, reflection, and transformative learning.

Group projects in CALL Online are carried out in a variety of ways:

1. peer reviews on class members' short-term projects (text and/or audio comments inserted into *Word* and *PowerPoint* files, AutoShapes, textboxes, font colors, text effects)
2. a collaborative review of three Web sites
3. a collaborative WebQuest about WebQuests
4. setting up a shared class space, e.g. in *Yahoo!Groups*
5. two long-term projects: a CALL lesson for a WebQuest and a WebQuest (see Bauer-Ramazani 2005d for additional free tools and a sample of instructions for a collaborative task)

The collaborative projects fulfill a three-fold purpose in CALL Online. First, they allow the teacher trainees to practice reviewing tools and other technology skills for the purpose of giving feedback to peers on their projects. Secondly, they provide the teacher trainees with a teaching tool that they may be able to implement in their future CALL classrooms. Thirdly, such projects keep the focus on the learner.

Task- and project-based assessment in CALL Online

Following Palloff and Pratt (2003), assessment strategies and instruments are aligned with the overall course structure and course goals of CALL Online. Thus, assessment of teacher trainees in CALL Online is both learner-centered and teacher-directed, as well as formative, summative, and ongoing. As interaction and collaboration comprise vital elements of online learning and are critical to the learning community, over 40 percent of the learners' course grade is dedicated to the completion of interactive and collaborative tasks in which the learners respond to each other's postings in the discussions and provide feedback on each other's work (learner-centered assessment). The learners make adjustments to their projects based on peer reviews and comments from the instructor (formative assessment).

Furthermore, the learners are assessed through performance–based projects and rubrics rather than through exams and traditional paper and pencil testing. Analytical reviews of Web sites and software, as well as the construction of short- and long-term projects make up the remaining 60 percent, which is evaluated by the teacher (summative assessment). Assessment is also ongoing in that learners receive feedback in their threaded discussions in the Reading and Sharing What You Learned forums as well as in email and chat.

As CALL Online has a built-in electronic gradebook, the teacher trainees may receive feedback on their performance as soon as discussions and projects are evaluated. This gradebook indicates how many of the maximum possible number of points per week the learner received, with additional comments posted by the instructor. Peer and instructor feedback on projects can also be downloaded and viewed.

Accomplishment of course goals in the words of the learners

The accomplishment of course goals is best expressed in the learners' own words (used with permission; additional quotes can be found at the Training CALL Teachers Online: Support Site – Quotes):

The following are comments in the first half of the course

> Thanks for being an excellent support! I love this class. It's my favorite, despite being the most time-consuming and nerve-wracking. (3/2005)

> I am more active in the discourse and am more motivated to engage in online discussions than I am in f2f classes. (3/2004)

> The CALL course has completely changed the way I see teaching and learning. Perhaps even the way I see the world and life. It's so carefully organized; it

reveals knowledge, experience and sensitivity. Thank you for the encouragement and care. (2/2004)

The continuum of learning in CALL Online, including the anxiety, the trials and tribulations, the steep learning curve, the sense of accomplishment, and the appreciation of the interactive/collaborative approach taken to CALL are probably best summarized by these learner quotations at the end of the course:

> This course was one of the greatest challenges I've ever had in my education life. Being computer illiterate until recently I felt uncomfortable and inadequate as a language teacher in the age of technology. . . . All of us, however, remember how doubtful and even negative we used to be about the effectiveness of both the CALL and the on-line learning. After a lot of struggle, sleepless nights, stress and frustrations, my doubts have dissolved and my technophobia, my greatest obstacle, seems to have disappeared. . . . Also, I've come to realize that the on-line learning or the distance education in general is based on the same principle: The students take their education in their hands. What they need is the right instruction, proper resources and regular communication with the instructor, who should encourage and appreciate the students' efforts. .. My dear classmates, . . . I feel I've known you for years, although I've never seen the faces of most of you. (5/2002)

> It [the course] ran the full gamut of emotions, from frustration to accomplishment, from anger to surprise to happiness. I'm not sure I like not actually "meeting" my classmates, but I had better interaction in this course than in many of my other "normal" classes. (6/2005)

> I occasionally became very anxious during the course, worrying that I wouldn't be able to finish all the tasks and assignments on time. . .I was/am somewhat of a 'techno-phobe' but this course certainly helped me overcome much of that feeling. It was very empowering to work through so many programs on my own and to develop so many teaching tools. I also felt like I had excellent mentoring support. (6/2005)

> This was my first on-line course, . . . and I now know how students feel when they see all those words come up on a screen and become overwhelmed! (6/2005)

> . . . most importantly, I've been more active in this online class than any of my face-to-face classes. (6/2005)

> This was the freest and possibly the most interactive learning experience I have ever had. I was forced to communicate, not by a teacher, but simply by the nature of the course and online learning in general. Of course, the incredibly dynamic class was critical in this outcome. (6/2001)

Conclusions

Despite some initial trepidation by colleagues and administrators, the CALL On-line course at Saint Michael's College has succeeded in training an online community of teachers in the effective integration of technology into the classroom. Besides meeting the need for technological competence in today's world, the learner-centered design structure and the interactive, collaborative environment have contributed to the demand for the course, both by degree and non-degree students. Mostly due to the dictates of the online environment, the power of teaching has shifted to the learners, creating a more learner-centered and high-quality experience where the traditional lecture mode has been replaced by more effective tools of communication. Based on outcome assessments of semester-long projects, participants have tremendously increased their competency in all four forms of electronic literacy (Warschauer 2002) and are prepared to apply these in their own teaching environments. Authentic and challenging teaching tools that allow for customization to the learners' needs or audience have motivated the participants to be invested in the learning process. They have actively developed their repertoire of CALL and pedagogical theories and approaches, thinking and learning skills, technical problem-solving strategies, and resources for learning and teaching CALL. Tasks, projects, and links have allowed the participants to be autonomous learners, exploring a multitude of possibilities to integrate CALL into different class configurations and constructing meaning and knowledge through the exchanges and collaboration with the online class community.

Over the past five years of conducting teacher training in CALL online, the possibilities for collaboration have increased as new, free conferencing and file-sharing tools have become available. This has also resulted in increased excitement and enthusiasm among the learners to venture into these new areas, and they have enjoyed reflecting on the transformation of learning that happened. Even professed newcomers to the use of CALL are willing to "push the envelope" in their exploration of CMC tools for teaching and learning. In Palloff and Pratt's (2003: 121) words, "when instructors and students alike are able to reap the benefits of a well-designed online course . . . , the result is excitement about what is possible in the online realm and the relationships that are developed."

Challenges in teaching CALL Online and some solutions

Training CALL teachers online over the past six years has not been without challenges. First, such a venture into distance learning combines the fallout from variations in response times, variations in the timing of events, and, very importantly, the lack of visual contact. Scheduling real-time events like class chats or group conferences across several time zones has been difficult and often had to occur for an hour on weekends when all participants were available. Participants were polled at the beginning of the course as to their available times, and the *WorldClock* was used to check times in different time zones. Thus, flexibility on the part of all course members was more necessary than in the face-to-face class. Since the weekend is often the time that participants complete large portions of their projects, difficulties encountered in the process could lead to major frustration unless a group member or the instructor was contacted to help out. It was found to be critical for all participants to be accessible much of the time and in various modes (e-mail, instant messaging, computer-to-computer telephony or Voice-over Internet Protocols (VoIP), and telephone) to provide assistance and support. Secondly, the varying levels of comfort with technology have sometimes presented a challenge to both the instructor and learners. An initial, mandatory interview in person, on the phone, or via email was usually helpful in assessing how steep the learning curve was going to be for the learner and how much additional support was needed. Thirdly, some teacher trainees have found it challenging to balance class work and job commitments. The solution was found in some flexibility around the weekly interaction requirements by allowing students to post additional comments during weeks when they were less busy. Technical problems have, of course, posed a fourth challenge. Round-the-clock access to the Internet and communication tools was not always maintained, either due to the breakdown of students' personal computers or failures of the campus Web or e-mail servers. Participants learned to troubleshoot and get help from the IT staff; often they found workaround solutions on their own and shared them in one of the discussion forums. Furthermore, various versions of the applications used in the course (e.g., *Word 2000* vs. *Word XP*) resulted in some incompatibility issues that raised frustrations temporarily until a solution was found. The constant need for vigilance and readiness to troubleshoot presents another challenge, although mainly for the instructor. Links to Web resources like online tutorials, teaching models, or readings require constant checking and updating. Maintaining links to external Web resources quickly drives home the fact that much of the material on the WorldWideWeb is impermanent and in need of constant updating.

Other lessons learned

The quality of interaction
Even though asynchronous discussions may have lost some of the immediacy of real-time, face-to-face discussions, they have gone far beyond what would be possible in a face-to-face classroom, both in breadth and depth, taking advantage of the expansion of the boundaries of time and space in the online environment, allowing for continuous interaction and thoughtful, cohesive, well-thought-out, and substantive comments. More reluctant or shy participants have become ac-

tive and more vocal in the asynchronous discussions, although at times they have tended to "yield the floor" to more spontaneous participants in whole-class chats.

The instructor's personality and presence

Despite the lack of visual contact, the instructor's personality and "presence" permeate the course in the way it is designed and delivered. In other words, the designer-teacher's organizational skills are reflected in the course structure and navigation and the way interaction and feedback are dealt with. In the words of two CALL Online students, "I could 'feel' [the] presence of this course 24 hours a day ... the course is mostly YOU... I nearly hear your voice...." (last class chat, 4/2001). Thus, online instructors who strive to make interaction paramount in their courses can be assured that their efforts are falling on fertile ground and are rewarded by the interaction of a successful online learning community.

Resource limitations and time

Being exposed to cutting edge technology that is shared on listservs and other online venues may result in a desire for continuous experimentation on the part of both the instructor and the learners. However, both need to remain cognizant and watchful of the limitations of the available resources, for example the hardware involved, cross-platform incompatibilities, institutional constraints, and time constraints. Even though CALL Online has been a tremendously rewarding experience and an opportunity for professional growth, it requires time and effort to revise, maintain, and run the course.

Plans for the future

Demand for teacher competence in "electronic literacies" (Warschauer 2002) is permeating all areas of teaching and has increased the need for CALL courses in the teacher trainees' repertoire. The National Education Standards for Teachers (NETS) and the NETS for students (2000–2004) in K-12 have further increased the need for such courses, mainly as part of continued professional development for practicing teachers. The pressure of on-demand, convenient learning is likely to raise expectations that these courses be delivered online rather than in the traditional on-campus, face-to-face mode. However, depending on the circumstances and the needs of the learners, alternative forms of delivery may also be considered. For example, a hybrid CALL course may have some face-to-face class time but a large portion of the course would take place online. Another alternative, the blended CALL course, would meet face-to-face but offer online threaded discussions and file-sharing, taking advantage of the possibility to expand the limits of the classroom through electronic means. Thus, in the future more CALL teachers may find themselves in the position to design and deliver either partially or fully online courses. Structuring the courses around the core elements of interaction and collaboration will insure the establishment of an effective online learning community.

References

Allen, I. & Seaman, J. (2003). *Sizing the Opportunity: The quality and extent of online education in the United States, 2002 and 2003*. The Sloan Consortium. Available at http://www.sloan-c.org/publications/books/survey.asp.

Bauer-Ramazani, C. (2005a). *Christine's How To's: Tech Tips and Workshops*. Available at http://academics.smcvt.edu/cbauer-ramazani/gsl520_online/howtos2.htm.

Bauer-Ramazani, C. (2005b). *Christine's Links to Useful TESL/CALL Web Sites*. Available at http://academics.smcvt.edu/cbauer-ramazani/Links/useful_sites.htm.

Bauer-Ramazani, C. (2005c). *Computer-Assisted Language Learning (CALL) Online: Demo*. Available at http://academics.smcvt.edu/cbauer-ramazani/gsl520_online/demo/CALL_Online_demo.htm.

Bauer-Ramazani, C. (2005d). *Training CALL Teachers Online: Support Web Site*. Available at http://academics.smcvt.edu/cbauer-ramazani/cb/home.htm.

Bourne, J., McMaster, E., Rieger, J., & Campbell, J. (1997). Paradigms for on-line learning: A case study in the design and implementation of an asynchronous learning networks (ALN) course. *Journal of Asynchronous Learning Networks, 1* (2). Available at http://www.aln.org/publications/jaln/v1n2/v1n2_bourne.asp.

Butler-Pascoe, M. E. & Wiburg, K. (2003). *Technology and Teaching English Language Learners*. Boston: Pearson Education.

Carter, K. (2004). Online training: What's really working? *Technology & Learning, 24* (10), 32–36 (also available online at http://www.techlearning.com/story/showArticle.jhtml?articleID=20300252; free registration required).

Chapelle, C. (2001). *Computer Applications in Second Language Acquisition: Foundations for teaching, testing and research*. Cambridge, UK: Cambridge University Press.

Dede, C. (2004). Enabling distributed learning communities via emerging technologies – Part one. *T.H.E. Journal, 32* (2), 12–22 (also available online at http://www.thejournal.com/magazine/vault/A4963.cfm).

Ebersole, J. (2004). Viewpoint: The future of graduate education. *University Business*. Available at http://www.universitybusiness.com/page.cfm?p=597.

eCollege. Available at http://www.ecollege.com/.

Egbert, J. (2005). *CALL Essentials: Principles and practice in CALL classrooms*. Alexandria, VA: TESOL.

Egbert, J. & Hanson-Smith, E. (Eds.). (1999). *CALL Environments: Research, practice, and critical issues*. Alexandria, VA: TESOL.

Graham, C., Cagtilay, K., Lim, B., Craner, J., & Duffy, T. (March/April, 2001). Seven principles of effective teaching: A practical lens for evaluating online courses. *The Technology Source*. Available at http://sln.suny.edu/sln/public/original.nsf/0/b495223246cabd6b85256a090058ab98?OpenDocument.

ICAL Online Teacher Training. Available at http://www.teacher-training.net/.

Jones, B. F., Valdez, G., Nowakowski, J., & Rasmussen, C. (1995). Plugging in: Choosing and using educational technology. Council for Educational Development and Research, North Central Regional Educational Laboratory. Available at http://www.ncrel.org/sdrs/edtalk/newtimes.htm.

Kim, K. & Moore, J. (November 2005). Web-based learning: Factors affecting students' satisfaction and learning experience. *First Monday, 10* (11). Available at http://firstmonday.org/issues/issue10_11/kim/index.html.

Kollock, P. & Smith, M. (Eds.). (1999). *Communities in Cyberspace*. London: Routledge.

Monterey Institute of International Studies. Available at http://www.miis.edu/gslel-progs-call.html.

National Educational Technology Standards for Teachers (NETS) Documents (2000–2004). International Society for Technology in Education (ISTE). Available at http://cnets.iste.org/teachers/t_stands.html.

Palloff, R. & Pratt, K. (1998). *Building Learning Communities in Cyberspace*. San Francisco: Jossey-Bass Inc., Publishers.

Palloff, R. & Pratt, K. (2003). *The Virtual Student: A profile and guide to working with online learners*. San Francisco: John Wiley & Sons.

Phipps, R. & Merisotis, J. (2000). *Quality on the Line: Benchmarks for success in Internet-based distance education* (April 2000). The Institute for Higher Education Policy. Washington, D.C. Available at www.ihep.com/Pubs/PDF/Quality.pdf.

Roblyer, M. D. & Ekhaml, L. (2000). How interactive are YOUR distance courses: A rubric for assessing interaction in distance learning. *Online Journal of Distance Learning Administration, 3* (2). Available at http://www.westga.edu/%7Edistance/roblyer32.html.

Teachers of English to Speakers of Other Languages (TESOL). Available at http://www.tesol.org.

The International TEFL Corporation – Online TEFL Certificate. Available at http://www.teflcorp.com/ol-home.htm.

Tinzmann, M. B., Jones, B. F., Fennimore, T. F., Bakker, J., Fine, C., & Pierce, J. (1990). What is the collaborative classroom? North Central Regional Educational Laboratory (NCREL). Available at http://www.ncrel.org/sdrs/areas/rpl_esys/collab.htm.

Training CALL Teachers Online: Support Web Site – Content. Available at http://academics.smcvt.edu/cbauer-ramazani/cb/content_ex.htm.

Training CALL Teachers Online: Support Web Site – Quotes. Available at http://academics.smcvt.edu/cbauer-ramazani/cb/quotes.htm.

Training CALL Teachers Online: Support Web Site – Structure. Available at http://academics.smcvt.edu/cbauer-ramazani/cb/structure.htm.

University at Albany – School of Education. Online courses. Available at http://www.albany.edu/education/courses/2005_fall_courses/2005_online_course.html.

Warschauer, M. (1996). Computer-assisted language learning: An introduction. In S. Fotos (Ed.), *Multimedia Language Teaching* (pp. 3–20). Tokyo: Logos International.

Warschauer, M. (2002). A developmental perspective on technology in language education, *TESOL Quarterly, 36* (3), 453–475.

Washington State University at Pullman. College of Education Department of Teaching & Learning. Available at hhtp://www.educ.wsu.edu/tl/ESL/T&L516.htm

WebQuests. Available at http://webquest.sdsu.edu/webquestwebquest-es.html.

Willis, E., and Raines, P. September (2001). Technology in Secondary Teacher Education. *T.H.E. Journal*. Available at http://www.thejournal.com/magazine/vault/A3638D.cfm.

WorldClock. Available at http://www.timeanddate.com/.

Wright, C. n.d. Criteria for evaluating the quality of online courses. Instructional Media and Design Department at Grant MacEwan College, Edmonton, Alberta. Available at http://www.imd.macewan.ca/imd/content.php?contentid=36.

Yahoo! Groups. Available at http://groups.yahoo.com/.

Yahoo!Messenger. Available at http://messenger.yahoo.com.

PART IV

CALL in-service projects, courses, and workshops

Preface to

Training for trainers

Challenges, outcomes, and principles of in-service training across the Irish education system

Most of the chapters in this book deal with courses and programmes run by an individual or a single institution. In this one, however, the focus is on a national programme to prepare language teachers to use technology effectively in their classrooms. Angela Rickard, Françoise Blin, and Christine Appel offer a report on OILTE (Organizing In-Service Training for Language and Technology in Education), a large-scale initiative in the Republic of Ireland. Their account describes the design and evaluation of a pilot programme consisting of two phases. Phase I involved "training the trainer," preparing a group of 18 teacher educators in the primary, secondary and further education sectors. Phase 2 consisted of the implementation and evaluation of the in-service courses developed by the Phase 1 participants. Feedback from participants indicated that the two-phase model was generally successful and worth pursuing further. However, the authors conclude that a number of practical factors need to be improved before OILTE can be scaled up to provide adequate training opportunities to language teachers at all levels throughout Ireland. Among these factors are professional release time for trainers who are themselves classroom language teachers, appropriate compensation for the extensive preparation time, adequate hardware and software support, and formal academic recognition of trainers' expertise. The results of this large-scale pilot are naturally of importance to the setting in Ireland and by extension to national initiatives in other countries. However, they should also be of great interest to any other government or professional entity attempting CALL education programmes on a scale larger than that of the individual institution.

Training for trainers

Challenges, outcomes, and principles of in-service training across the Irish education system

Angela Rickard[a], Françoise Blin[b] and Christine Appel[b]

[a]National University of Ireland, Ireland / [b]Dublin City University, Ireland

Introduction and background

In the Republic of Ireland, the Department of Education and Science oversees the management and evaluation of in-service training for teachers from the primary and post-primary levels. A top-down model of delivery of courses is normally adopted and designed to facilitate the introduction of educational policy or curricular change. An example of a significant educational policy change in recent years is the Irish government initiative in 1997 to invest €50.79 million to put in place a permanent Information Technology infrastructure in Irish primary and post-primary schools and to foster the development of computer literacy among all students. Support was given to teachers to upgrade their professional and computer skills, so that they could integrate the use of technology in the teaching and learning environment of their schools (Schools IT 2000, 1997). However, concern was expressed that the top-down policy for IT development in schools focused on technical matters rather than on pedagogical implications (Mulcahy 1997; see also Lam 2000). In the case of language teaching, local seminars or workshops organised by language teachers associations or national agencies soon became oversubscribed by teachers from the primary, secondary and further education sectors. Feedback from participants to these local or national events suggested that teachers felt ill equipped to make adequate use of the hardware available to them. In particular, primary and post-primary language teachers often reported having difficulties in sourcing and securing funding for CALL related in-service training courses. The National Centre for Technology in Education (NCTE) has addressed some of the above concerns and difficulties by funding initiatives that seek to integrate the upgrading of both pedagogical and technological skills among the teachers of Ireland.

One of these initiatives, OILTE (Organising In-service Training for Language and Technology in Education: *oilte* being the Irish word for 'trained' or 'proficient'), was set up in response to the expressed need on the part of language teachers in Ireland for professional development in the area of CALL. Coordinated by the former Linguistics Institute of Ireland (ITÉ), the OILTE project was funded by the NCTE and the Curriculum Development Unit (CDU), both of which operate under the auspices of the Department of Education and Science. A steering committee made up of representatives of a number of national educational policy-making organisations, language teachers associations, and CALL specialists from the university sector was thus formed under the auspices of the now defunct ITÉ. The remit of the committee was to propose and to pilot a training programme, which would accommodate the needs of language teachers across the education system.[1]

This chapter begins with a description of the overall design and implementation of the pilot training programme developed by the OILTE team. It then discusses the main issues that revealed themselves through the formative evaluation of the programme and proposes principles for the organisation of further CALL in-service training programmes potentially applicable beyond the Irish context.

The OILTE teacher training programme: Overall design and implementation

The OILTE steering committee set out to design a pilot CALL teacher-training programme specifically targeting language teachers (including teachers of Irish) from the primary, secondary and further education sectors. The overall aims of the OILTE Project were twofold. It aimed firstly to provide a teacher-training programme adapted to the professional development needs of language teachers, and secondly to set a firm basis for the establishment of a nation-wide community of practice (Lave & Wenger 1991; Hanson-Smith, this volume) of language professionals who would be in a position to influence and to promote good practice with regard to the integration of ICT in the primary and post-primary language curriculum.

The specific objectives of the OILTE training project were to:

- de-mystify CALL, i.e., to help teachers overcome their fear of computers and to promote a positive attitude towards ICT among language teachers;
- consolidate and enhance the teachers' existing computer skills;
- encourage teachers to explore the resources already available in their schools (e.g., multi-media labs, Internet access, etc.);

- build teachers' confidence in using the above resources and in selecting new ones;
- expose teachers to a variety of software titles, Internet resources and sample projects suitable for the language classroom;
- explore ways to evaluate resources and to disseminate written evaluations through the websites maintained by NCTE;
- promote the effective use of technology and the adoption of appropriate pedagogical applications or approaches (e.g., fostering the development and exercise of learner autonomy, task based learning, use of authentic materials from suitable websites etc.);
- help teachers share and develop classroom activities integrating ICT.

The introduction of ICT in the language curriculum transforms the role of the teacher and of the students (Lam & Lawrence 2002; Blin 1999) and consequently implies changes in classroom management strategies. Therefore, the project also aimed to provide teachers with opportunities to explore the implications of ICT for classroom management strategies (including classroom layout, classroom control, rules of behaviour and management of resources, etc.). Finally, the pilot training programme intended to help language teachers assert their right to access their school computing facilities, often seen as the sole preserve of the science, business or computer departments.

The concepts and principles of learner autonomy (Little 1991; Little, Ridley, & Ushioda 2002), learner-centredness, constructivism (Jonassen & Land 2000) and more particularly situated learning (Lave & Wenger 1991) were to underpin the pedagogical approach. In line with the normal practice for in-service teacher training in the Republic of Ireland, the OILTE programme consisted of the initial delivery of a *Training for Trainers* course (Phase 1, Autumn 2001) followed by *in-service* courses (Phase 2, Spring 2002). Training for Trainers programmes run by the NCTE normally consist of providing future trainers with the knowledge and skills that will enable them to deliver a pre-determined curriculum using set materials. The OILTE approach marked a departure from this established practice insofar as no fixed curriculum or set materials were to be produced by a team of experts: the in-service curriculum and the accompanying materials were to be collaboratively prepared by the future trainers assisted by the project co-ordinator and her team. A colloquium, held at the University of Limerick, concluded the pilot project in September 2002 and provided a forum to reflect on the experience and to further disseminate the principles underlying the OILTE project. Attending the colloquium were approximately 100 delegates representing a broad range of interests within language education, including policy-makers, inspectors from the Department of Education and Science and ICT advisors from a number of Education Centres.

For the initial Training for Trainers phase (*Phase 1*), the OILTE steering committee invited an expert panel of tutors from Ireland and overseas to deliver a series of presentations and to facilitate workshops covering the theory and practice of CALL. The steering committee also nominated 18 practising language teachers with known skills in the use of technology and with considerable teaching experience, to participate in the training for trainers programme. These teachers came from a range of educational contexts across the four Irish provinces[2] (e.g., rural and urban; primary, secondary and further education schools; children, adolescents and adults; girls, boys, and co-ed schools; etc.). The languages covered in this initial phase were Irish, French, German, Spanish, Italian and Japanese. Indeed, it was felt that bringing together language teachers from different contexts and languages would provide them not only with insights into the diversity of language education in Ireland but also with opportunities to share their different experiences, to learn from each other and to construct a coherent national training programme. The course was organised around five sessions, which took place on Saturdays and in a different county each time. Between these sessions, all participants had access to a dedicated *WebCT* course hosted on the Dublin City University server. Discussion forums and additional resources enabled the participants to continue their reflection and exchanges throughout the programme.

In *Phase 2*, trainees became trainers and ran in-service courses between March and September 2002 in their home county or city. As indicated earlier, they were responsible for the choice of materials that they felt would be useful, effective, and relevant to the levels and languages taught by themselves and their colleagues. Three categories of courses were thus developed, which targeted the primary, secondary and further education sector respectively. A total of eleven courses were delivered in eleven different venues to 106 teachers across Ireland as outlined in Table 1 below.

It had been projected that the number of trainees selected for Phase 1 would correspond to the subsequent number of courses in the second phase. Different reasons such as inadequate school facilities, trainers' confidence to deliver a course alone or job changes for some of them led to a different configuration of courses in the end. In the case of the primary sector, the introduction of a new curriculum had resulted in training 'fatigue' among teachers in this sector during the time period in question. Also, given the pilot nature of the project, considerable flexibil-

Table 1. In-service courses delivered in Phase 2

Sector	Number of courses	Number of trainees
Primary sector	1	6
Secondary sector	7	78
Further Education sector	3	22
Total	*11*	*106*

ity was afforded to the trainers in terms of how and when they would deliver their courses. Within each category of courses, individual differences also arose from the trainers' choice of materials and degree of computer expertise. As trainers were encouraged to deliver a course that they felt comfortable with, most of them elected to work with another trainer to plan or to plan *and* deliver their course together. In this case, the most adequate location was chosen, be it a local education centre or a school.

Phase 2 courses comprised approximately 10 hours of tuition and were delivered either through five 2-hour sessions or as a two-day workshop, depending on the local context and the trainers' availability. Courses were non-language specific, except in the case of Japanese, which presented a number of unique technical and linguistic constraints.

Content and pedagogical approach

Phase 1 of the training programme thus aimed to give future trainers the necessary background knowledge, skills and confidence that would help them design and deliver a training course adapted to the wider Irish educational context while responding to specific local needs. This was to be achieved by encouraging participants to share and to reflect on their own teaching practice, by helping them consolidate and improve their computer skills, and by leading them to explore different possible scenarios for the integration of ICT in the language curriculum in a wide range of settings. Five one-day sessions were held between early October and mid-November. Starting with a thorough needs analysis with respect to ICT and language pedagogy, presentations, hands-on sessions, group activities and discussions were designed around the following themes:

- Session 1: Using generic software for language learning (e.g., word-processing, presentation software, etc.);
- Session 2: Sourcing and evaluating CALL artefacts (e.g., authoring tools, courseware, web-based materials, etc.)
- Session 3: Creating a website for language classes and authoring interactive web-based exercises and activities;
- Session 4: Using Computer Mediated Communication (email and chat) and setting up collaborative projects;
- Session 5: Understanding and using electronic reference tools (e.g., on-line dictionaries, corpora, concordancing, etc.).

The pedagogical approach adopted throughout the training programme took the participants' experience and pedagogical expertise as a starting point, and later related it to theoretical concepts when appropriate. Presentation and demonstrations of technologies or artefacts were followed by hands-on sessions and were seen as potentially facilitating and enhancing the participants' teaching methods, while taking into account the actual environment in which they operate on a daily basis. Session 4, on the use of CMC and collaborative projects, provides examples of such an approach. Following a brief introduction to the programme of the day (see Appendix 1), participants were asked to reflect on and to share their views and experience on collaborative language learning as implemented in their own classrooms. Examples of tasks carried out in pairs or group projects were provided by the participating teachers and small or whole group discussions focused more specifically on the actions carried out by students and teachers in their drive to complete the task (i.e., what do students and teacher do, where, when and how?), on the benefits of collaboration as actually observed by teachers (e.g., increased motivation, acquisition of transferable skills, facilitation of cross-curricular activities, etc.), and on the problems encountered. The latter included the appropriateness of group work in relation to the official curriculum and State examinations, individual and group behaviour, plagiarism, and logistical issues such as the availability of resources and, in the case of collaboration between schools, timetabling. Solutions to these difficulties were offered by the participants themselves and emphasised the need to fully integrate collaborative language learning into the curriculum by designing appropriate tasks, while providing adequate learner support and making optimal use of existing resources. The points raised during the group discussions were then taken up by the session tutors who related them to research findings, before exploring the potential role of technology in facilitating and enhancing collaborative language learning, either within the classroom or between schools.

In the afternoon, CMC tools that can be easily deployed in a school environment were presented and demonstrated by an 'expert' tutor who also discussed how these tools could be used for carrying out language tasks involving different configurations of users (e.g., native and non-native speakers, teacher and students, etc.). A simulation organised around the setting up of a tandem email exchange between Brazil and Denmark then allowed participants to familiarise themselves with chat rooms while exploring ways of planning and designing a language learning task suitable to their environment. The session concluded by a discussion on the applicability and feasibility of such tasks in the teachers' own environment.

Each session thus gave participants ample opportunities to jointly explore new ideas and technologies that were immediately applicable in their classroom. In addition, the second half of the last session (Session 5) was devoted to the production of syllabi for the in-service courses that were to take place the following spring. From the material presented and the activities carried out during the five 1-day sessions, the future trainers selected ideas, tools, resources and approaches they thought would be most appropriate for the teaching setting with which they were familiar. For each sector, a general curriculum was thus developed by the trainers,

which was then adapted in accordance with the needs of their colleagues participating in the in-service courses (see Appendix 2 for an example of a course de-
scriptor used for a primary sector in-service course). Although *Phase 2* in-service
courses mirrored the themes covered in *Phase 1*, they also diverged from them to
some extent. For example, the theme of *Creating a Website for language classes* was
not integrated in any of the in-service courses as the trainers felt they needed to
further develop their own skills in that area before training others. Other themes
were integrated in some courses and not in others. For instance, while the theme
of *Using Computer Mediated Communication and setting up collaborative projects*
was explored by all further education in-service courses, it was only touched upon
in less than half of the secondary level courses.

Evaluation

Throughout the development and implementation of the two phases of the training programme, a formative evaluation was conducted, which aimed at uncover-
ing the difficulties encountered by the trainers during the preparation and delivery
of the in-service courses. During *Phase 1*, the participating teachers were asked to
provide some feedback at the end of each face-to-face session. In *Phase 2*, feedback was sought from both the trainers and their trainees. In addition, extensive
discussions with the trainers took place at the end of both phases. Due to space
limitations, the next sections will report some of the results of this evaluation from
the trainers' perspective only.

Evaluation of Phase 1 (Training for Trainers)

Following each session, the participants were asked to take part in an anonymous
survey administered via *WebCT*. The form was kept simple to encourage all participants to respond and was designed to get a sense of what should be improved
for the next session as well as to prompt the future trainers to start building their
own course. The form thus consisted of the four open questions given below.

- Question 1: Indicate three things you liked about today.
- Question 2: Indicate three things you did not like about today.
- Question 3: Indicate what could be improved for a future course.
- Question 4: What aspects, if any, of today's course would you like to replicate
  in *Phase 2* of the project?

All participants viewed the opportunity throughout the course to engage in discussion with peers and tutors as the most positive aspect. In particular, the combination of levels, languages and teaching situations made for lively discussions

and enhanced learning as illustrated by the following examples extracted from the questionnaires:

> Meeting with like-minded people. The opportunity to discuss our experiences with other teachers from different levels. (Session 1)

> I enjoyed meeting other Language Teachers (a few familiar faces, many new ones) with an interest in exchanging and developing new teaching ideas. As my own ICT skills are quite limited (self-taught) the project gives me a great incentive to improve and to learn from others. I found it easy to approach others in the group when something went over my head. (Session 1)

> That through informal discussion with other participants I was able to learn new things about language education in areas different from my own. (Session 2)

> The brainstorming exercise which asked us to define collaborative learning and pin-point where it takes place. A worthwhile discussion followed which offered the chance to hear many interesting ideas from various teachers in the group. Again, nice to actively involve the participants and also provides some affirmation that we are on the right track in our teaching (sometimes!) (Session 4)

Other positive comments relate to the tutors' professionalism and their generosity with the material they had prepared, the clear focus and practical applications of the course, and to the exposure to a variety of materials, many of them freely available:

> That I was introduced to software being used in my own subject area and given the opportunity to take it home and examine it in detail. (Session 2)

> I feel this has been the most important session for me so far, it was practical but realistic. We looked at a lot of issues that I feel will be put to us as facilitators of the course. We left with real resources, e-boards etc. (Session 3)

However, participants also felt disappointed and frustrated at technology breakdowns, which unfortunately occurred in two sessions in a row:

> Technological breakdown was a big disappointment: this session should have been a 'fairly safe one' since we were not relying on communications technology. [I did not like] the argument that such technological problems were a good example for us of what might happen in the classroom (we do know about these problems because we already use IT with our pupils) and the failure to identify strategies for coping with such problems (many of us would have had some experience of such problems) (Session 2)

The technological problems were aggravated by the OILTE committee's decision to decentralise the training and to use different venues each time. While this provided opportunities to sample various educational settings, it prevented organisers and tutors from properly testing the technological infrastructure available in each venue. Long journeys across Ireland were also an issue for most participants, who generally felt that moving from place to place for the training was more effort than it was worth.

Most importantly, the future trainers felt that the time commitment was very onerous and suggested that courses such as this be run during school time rather than weekends. Furthermore, fears about their role and expected contribution in *Phase 2* were also expressed as illustrated by the following example:

> Several members are becoming confused and/or concerned about the expectations of our participation on the course and the level of in-service we are to provide as OILTE trainers. (Session 2)

Notwithstanding the growing realisation of the work involved in becoming OILTE trainers, the *Phase 1* participants continuously related the content of the course they were attending to their own teaching practice as well as to the needs of their colleagues. Furthermore, the strategies used by the tutors and organisers provided a model on which to base (or not to base, as the case may be) their own courses. Some of these strategies proved to be particularly relevant to the group and were to constitute the backbone of the in-service component. In particular, conducting a needs analysis at the beginning of the course, fostering a sense of ownership, focussing on hands-on sessions and providing ample opportunities for group discussions and activities were considered as essential elements of a successful in-service course.

Evaluation of Phase 2 (in-service courses)

The in-service courses designed and implemented by the *Phase 1* participants were indeed successful. Trainees expressed overall satisfaction with the quality and relevance of the particular course they attended. The OILTE steering committee's main concern, however, was to determine whether the training programme put in place was scalable so that adequate training opportunities could be made available to all primary, secondary and further education language teachers. To assess the feasibility of turning the pilot project into a nation-wide initiative, the *Phase 1* participants were once again called upon to provide detailed feedback on their experience as *Phase 2* trainers and to help determine the direction of future training programmes.

The trainers delivered courses mostly to colleagues in their own schools and maintained the ethos and collaborative approach established during *Phase 1*. They also expressed a strong sense of ownership of the training materials, which they had developed in collaboration with other trainers and tailored to the specific needs of the targeted schools. Trainers thus felt confident while delivering their courses as they were operating in a familiar environment. Their in-depth knowledge of the local context combined with a thorough knowledge of the materials, along with a good understanding of the issues that may present themselves to teachers, ensured that the in-service courses met the needs of the trainees.

However, a number of difficulties arose in the preparation and delivery of courses. Although most of the tutors were self-taught users of technology, not all of them had adequate access to computers either at home or in school. This hampered their efforts to practise or further explore the topics covered in *Phase 1*. It also constrained the production of content and materials and added enormously to the pressure they were under. During the delivery of courses, considerable technology-related difficulties were experienced by trainers. In particular, difficulties in installing software and, in some cases, the incompatibility between software and operating systems led to partial or complete failure of software evaluation sessions. In addition, the resources available to trainers in advance of the courses were scarce. Although the OILTE team had hoped to ensure that each trainer would be provided with a sufficient number of language learning software titles in time for the delivery of the in-service courses, this proved to be an unrealistic target for the pilot phase of the project. When software was indeed available, a number of trainers commented on the rigidity of software and the speed at which it can become out of date in the eyes of students.

Finally, lack of time was an area of concern to all trainers. They attended the first phase of training during five Saturdays; the preparation of *Phase 2* courses was also done during their free time on weekends and evenings after work and this put them under considerable pressure. While trainers acknowledged the benefit of their participation to their own professional development, they felt that more could be done to recognise their contribution, both financially and in terms of academic accreditation. The funding mechanisms in place, which facilitate teacher participation in approved courses and pay trainers for the delivery of the training, do not account for the preparation and production of training syllabi and materials. Furthermore, in this model the trainers' potential contribution to the professional development of large numbers of teachers across Ireland does not currently lead to any form of certification, which could enhance their career advancement prospects.

A number of issues thus need to be resolved if the training programme is to be scaled up in the Republic of Ireland or indeed adopted by other small countries or regions: time constraints and limitations, availability of and access to hardware and software, and the trainers' financial and/or academic recognition. These issues are further discussed in the next section.

Discussion and recommendations

In response to the above issues, the trainers formulated a number of recommendations, which can also be applied elsewhere through cooperation between the different actors involved in the provision of in-service teacher training.

Time constraints and limitations. The trainers suggested that time for professional development of this kind be made available during working hours, through the provision of funding for substitution hours. In the case of participation in a *Training for Trainers* programme, these substitution hours should not only cover attendance but also the time needed later by trainers to produce adapted materials and to test the technology prior to the delivery of their course. Financial recognition for preparation time should also be negotiated with funding agencies. Furthermore, in order to maximise teachers' participation in CALL in-service courses, these need to be included in the overall diet of scheduled in-service courses offered under the auspices of the relevant education authority (i.e., the Department of Education and Science in the case of Ireland).

Availability of and access to hardware and software. Difficulties arising from time constraints were aggravated by the lack of adequate access to computer facilities during the preparation phase of in-service courses. The group suggested that a number of laptop computers be made available to trainers from their Education Centres. It also recommended that the NCTE and the Department of Education and Science consider working out an attractive deal for teachers to purchase laptop computers because such an initiative may encourage more teachers to use computers for class preparation and delivery. More importantly however, a suitable technology infrastructure is required if trainers are to apply and deliver what they have learned in *Phase 1*. Such an infrastructure must also be similar to, or at least compatible with, the teaching environment familiar to their trainees. This implies that criteria for the selection of future trainers must include not only the applicants' professional expertise and innovation record but also the capacity of their environment to provide a suitable technological infrastructure. With regard to the availability of software, adequate funding and some agreement with software developers are required to ensure that software packages are available for evaluation by course participants. Multiple copies are needed if hands-on sessions are to be facilitated in different venues across the country.

Trainers' academic recognition. Concrete suggestions were made for ways to better acknowledge the effort teacher-trainers make in developing and delivering professional development courses to their colleagues. For example – and to keep in line with current initiatives on lifelong learning policies in Ireland – teacher-trainers ought to be entitled to submit a portfolio of their work as part fulfilment of the requirements for the award of a university post-graduate diploma or degree under the Accreditation of Prior Learning (APL) scheme implemented in some Irish universities.

The above recommendations point to the central role of national or regional educational policy and of funding agencies in ensuring the scalability and success of an in-service teacher training programme such as the one piloted by OILTE. They also highlight the importance of a close collaboration between a variety of actors, and in particular between the public and commercial sectors (e.g., between the Department of Education and software developers). Notwithstanding the issues discussed thus far, a number of distinctive features promoted by OILTE and recognised by the *Phase 1* participants can nevertheless be integrated in other in-service training programmes. In particular, OILTE succeeded in combining technical and pedagogical training to alleviate teachers' fears regarding the role of technology in the classroom. Throughout *Phase 1*, participants were able to reassert the fundamental role of the teacher as the main facilitator of language learning. In turn, a similar emphasis on the role of the teacher in the technology-supported language classroom underpinned *Phase 2* in-service courses. In both phases, the development of technical skills was therefore rooted in the teachers' everyday practice, which was acknowledged and valued. Through group activities and discussions such as those described earlier, this practice was continuously reappraised by the participants themselves, be they trainers or trainees. New ideas emerged that were immediately applicable by the participating teachers in their given context, such as the use of *PowerPoint* animations to illustrate difficult grammar points or of pinboards to share ideas and materials between teachers and schools.

Furthermore, the expert tutors selected by the OILTE steering committee to facilitate the *Training for Trainers* phase of the programme took great care in sharing their knowledge and skills without making any statement regarding the application in particular settings of the concepts, principles or tools they presented. Rather, they availed themselves of the teachers' expertise and practical knowledge of these settings to assist in the tailoring of the materials for delivery in *Phase 2* courses. This teacher-driven approach ensured that the training programme was relevant to the participants' concerns and to their teaching environment.

The provision of a common *Training for Trainers* programme to teachers from three different levels (i.e., primary, secondary and further education levels) constituted another distinctive feature of the OILTE programme. The tailoring of content and materials to different levels was made possible, and even enhanced, by the sharing and contrasting of experiences. Indeed, throughout *Phase 1*, the participants had to articulate their needs and the challenges they face every day in the classroom in a way that would be comprehensible and meaningful to others. The solutions or pedagogical approaches proposed at one level led teachers of other levels to question their own established practice. Through this collective questioning and reflection, individual participants were able to reappraise their own practice beyond the boundaries of their own local settings.

Conclusion

The pilot teacher training programme reported in this chapter was specifically designed to address the needs of experienced language teachers wishing to harness the potential of ICT for language teaching and learning in the Republic of Ireland. It presented language teachers with an alternative to top-down training programmes, whose content and materials may be developed by external experts with little practical knowledge of the local situation. In fact, one distinguishing feature of the OILTE project was its emphasis on the participating teachers' own experience as language teachers. As a result, it empowered them to make informed decisions on and to take control of their own professional development. The project also brought together actors from every sector of the Irish education system, from national agencies to representatives of schools, further education colleges and universities. As such, it set the basis for the creation of a network of professionals working together towards the development and promotion of good practice in relation to the use of ICT in language teaching.[3]

As the project drew to a close, a number of avenues for future developments suggested themselves. In particular, the move from a pilot in-service programme to a full implementation across the state is being considered by the OILTE steering committee, should adequate funding be provided by the Department of Education and Science. Additional administrative and financial resources are however required to properly evaluate the impact of such a training programme on the taking up of technology supported language learning activities in schools. Indeed, improved in-built mechanisms need to be set up to facilitate the systematic collection and analysis of data on the process and outcomes of both training phases.

If some of the issues raised by the OILTE trainers may be specific to the Republic of Ireland, others are likely to occur elsewhere. For example, time constraints, difficulties in accessing hardware and software, and the need to recognise the trainers' contribution to professional development will undoubtedly manifest themselves in other world regions. Each of these issues will require local responses taking cognisance of the specificity of the social and structural organisation of teacher training.

Notes

1. The authors of this chapter were members of the steering committee, chaired by Angela Rickard. They designed and delivered part of the training programme.

2. Leinster, Munster, Connaught and Ulster.

3. In recognition of the innovative and inclusive approach to in-service teacher training, the OILTE project was awarded the European Label for Innovation in Language Teaching and Learning in September, 2003.

References

Blin, F. (1999). CALL and the development of learner autonomy. In R. Debski & M. Levy (Eds.), *WorldCALL – Global Perspectives on Computer-Assisted Language Learning* (pp. 133–148). Lisse: Swets & Zeitlinger.

Jonassen, D. & Land, S. (Eds.). (2000). *Theoretical Foundations of Learning Environments.* Mahwah, NJ: Lawrence Erlbaum.

Lam, Y. (2000). Technophilia v. technophobia: A preliminary look at why second language teachers do or do not use technology in their classrooms. *Canadian Modern Language Review, 56,* 389–420.

Lam, Y. & Lawrence, G. (2002). Teacher-student role redefinition during a computer-based second language project: Are computers catalysts for empowering change? *Computer Assisted Language Learning, 15* (3), 295–315.

Lave, J. & Wenger, E. (1991). *Situated Learning: Legitimate peripheral participation.* Cambridge: CUP.

Little, D. (1991). *Learner Autonomy 1: Definitions, issues and problems.* Dublin: Authentik.

Little, D., Ridley, J., & Ushioda, E. (2002). *Towards Greater Learner Autonomy in the Foreign Language Classroom.* Dublin: Authentik.

Mulcahy, J. (1997). Information technology in the Junior Cycle curriculum. In *Issues in Education, ASTI Educational Journal, 2,* 143–153.

National Centre for Technology in Education (NCTE). Available at http://www.ncte.ie

OILTE. Available at http://www.oilte.ie

Schools IT 2000 (1997). Department of Education and Science. Available at http://www.oasis.gov.ie

Appendix 1: Programme of Session 4 (*Phase 1*)

Collaborative and email projects
Saturday 10 November, 2001

Objectives

At the end of this workshop, you should be able:

- To design, to plan and to implement collaborative projects within the language curriculum;
- To integrate ICT, and more specifically CMC tools, to enhance collaborative language learning;
- To appraise the benefits of collaborative language learning and to identify the problems and technical/ logistic difficulties relating to it.

Programme

9.30	Welcome and overview of workshop (with coffee)
10.00	**Session 1** – Collaborative learning: what is it and why should we get involved? (Françoise Blin)
11.30	*Coffee break*
11.45	**Session 2** – Computer Mediated Communication (CMC) tools for collaborative language learning (Christine Appel)
12.45	*Lunch*
14.00	**Session 3** – Setting up an exchange: practical considerations (CA & FB)
16.00	*End*

Appendix 2: Example of course descriptor

Level: Primary	**Course duration:** 10 or 20 hour course

Target audience:
- Project Leaders for the Pilot Project for Modern Languages
- Teachers in Gaelscoileanna
- Primary School Teachers

Skills Level:

We would recommend that participants would be comfortable in the use of computers (opening, closing and saving files, copying and pasting, using email and Internet). Ideally participants will have completed the Phase I and II NCTE in-service courses, or equivalent.

Aims:
- Highlight ways of integrating ICT in the classroom in all languages, noting the potential for the development of resources in Irish
- Foster understanding and awareness of the use of ICTs in the language classroom
- Promote skills and confidence to integrate ICTs

Objectives:
- Provide exposure to variety of software titles, web resources, projects
- Discuss management strategies
- See potential for collaborative projects
- Deliver training

Indicative syllabus:

1. Needs Analysis – informal discussion on teachers' experiences & needs
2. Authoring Tools – practical web-based resources for creating materials
3. Standard Applications – exploring features of existing school software
4. Email Projects – the what, why and how of establishing email projects
5. World Wide Web – exploiting the web for authentic resources, references
6. Software – exploring and evaluating some examples of software titles
7. Tools for Collaboration – using web for teacher & student collaboration

Each session or topic will be concluded with a discussion based on its advantages, disadvantages, issues of classroom management and the implications for the role of the teacher. The course will endeavour to refer to software or other authoring tools that may be common to participants' schools e.g., *HyperStudio*, *Clicker*, *Textease*, *Microsoft Publisher*.

Preface to

How WebQuests send technology to the background

Scaffolding EFL teacher professional development in CALL

WebQuests were developed initially as tasks for students in academic subjects involving searching, filtering, organizing and synthesizing information from the web to help them hone research and critical thinking skills. However, they have become increasingly popular in language courses because they put students in contact with authentic materials in a motivating setting structured by the objectives of the quest. In this chapter, Chin-chi Chao shows how the creation of WebQuests can serve as the central project to introduce CALL concepts and know-how in a graduate-level CALL course for K-12 EFL teachers in Taiwan. Her approach, built on the cognitive apprenticeship model of Collins, Brown, and Newman (1989), focuses on the importance of scaffolding at two levels: providing teachers with the support needed to successfully complete their WebQuest projects and helping teachers insure that the WebQuest lessons they ultimately produce include appropriate scaffolding for their own students. The chapter covers two successive years of the CALL course and provides a narrative of lessons learned in the first year that led to improvements in the subsequent offering. For example, in the first year projects were begun in the last three weeks of the course and required teachers to produce web pages from scratch, raising a lot of anxiety. Based on feedback from that year, Chao began the projects much earlier and allowed teachers to use available templates to produce their WebQuests. This chapter provides key advice to educators on anticipating the challenges teachers face in a project-based approach and echoes Egbert (this volume) in emphasizing the value of keeping the learning situated in authentic teaching contexts.

How WebQuests send technology to the background

Scaffolding EFL teacher professional development in CALL

Chin-chi Chao

National Chengchi University, Taiwan

The need to contextualize teacher learning has been discussed widely in teacher education. Schön (1987: 25) characterized teacher knowledge as knowing-in-action, indicating that understanding is a part of the everyday classroom context. However, it is difficult for teachers to distinguish "knowing that" (their knowledge) from "knowing how" (their practice) because the two are fully integrated (Ryle 1949: 25–61). Thus, helping language teachers learn computer skills must be contextualized in their everyday teaching environment, and scaffolding must be provided to aid them in developing computer skills that are closely linked to their everyday practice and to the learners that they work with in a mindful and reflective way (Egbert, Paulus, & Nakamichi 2002; Meskill, Mossop, DiAngelo, & Pasquale 2002).

One way to achieve the goal is through project-based learning (see Debski, this volume), a teaching approach that directs all learning efforts toward a concrete product created by the learner. This chapter focuses on strategies to scaffold teacher learning through projects and also on the challenges faced by teachers while learning to use technology in support of project-based learning. Both of these foci are mediated through WebQuests, a type of inquiry project that can create a meaningful and contextualized language learning experience.

In a graduate-level CALL course for K-12 EFL (English as a Foreign Language) teachers offered by this author in Taiwan, WebQuests were used to help teachers understand the potentials as well as challenges associated with computerized EFL instruction. To use the computer to its optimal potential in the language classroom, computer skills are not the only training that teachers need. Evidence from the previous research is clear that teachers best learn the potential of computers in situated contexts when they can think about learners and classroom implementation (Becker 1994; Egbert, Paulus, & Nakamichi 2002; McKenzie 2001). This implies that a CALL program developing deeper-level beliefs and modeling sound pedagogy, not just teaching technical skills, is likely to have a strong and positive impact on learning and teaching. It also follows that an important task for CALL teacher educators is to demonstrate ways of scaffolding learning in the computer-rich environment through supporting teacher learning situated in real world contexts. To this end, the WebQuest required in this course was intended to focus EFL teachers' attention on providing motivating language instruction, while putting technology where it should be – in the background. Through the experience with a WebQuest project, teachers were expected to see new possibilities and develop a more constructive use of the computer and the Internet with EFL learners.

What is a WebQuest?

The website *WebQuest Central* at San Diego State University has the following definition for a WebQuest:

> A WebQuest is an inquiry-oriented activity in which most or all of the information used by learners is drawn from the Web. WebQuests are designed to use learners' time well, to focus on using information rather than looking for it, and to support learners' thinking at the levels of analysis, synthesis and evaluation (Overview, the *WebQuest Central website*).

The three most important elements of a WebQuest project are inquiry-based learning, meaningful use of web information, and critical thinking skills. These elements are manifested in the five sections of every WebQuest project: *Introduction, task, process, evaluation,* and *conclusion,* presented in the form of web pages as a project plan. Examples of WebQuests can be accessed through the *WebQuest Central* website, maintained by Bernie Dodge, or the *Best WebQuest* website, by Tom March.

Dudeney (2003) pointed out five reasons for using WebQuests in the language classroom, including requiring no advanced technical knowledge for both teachers and learners, fostering interaction among learners, allowing interdisciplinary inquiry, encouraging the use of higher order skills, and motivating learners through authentic contexts. Benz (2001) further pointed out that WebQuests bring out intrinsic interest. The most important benefit of a WebQuest project is that it makes language learning come alive so as to allow learners to experience the use of target language in an authentic and meaningful way.

Scaffolding and cognitive apprenticeship

Using scaffolding as the metaphor for teaching implies that help, guidance, and instructional support are temporary. The goal is for teachers to move forward from their current stages of understanding and eventually become independent and self-regulated in the chosen domain. In practice, many models of scaffolding in education have been developed (see Hogan & Pressley 1997). For the course discussed here, the concept of *cognitive apprenticeship*, developed by Collins, Brown and Newman (1989) was adopted to guide our support of teacher learning because its emphasis on "developing concepts out of and through continuing authentic activity" (Brown, Collins, & Duguid 1989:44) is consistent with the goal of making computer training relate directly to the teacher's everyday work. Cognitive apprenticeship is described as a means of coaching learners through authentic activities, tools, and culture so that they can eventually perform the targeted tasks on their own. Important steps are observation, coaching, and eventually practicing to acquire and integrate cognitive and metacognitive strategies. Specifically, the following six methods are included in designing an ideal learning environment based on the concept of cognitive apprenticeship:

1. *Modeling* – An expert carries out a task so that students can observe and build a conceptual model of the processes that are required to accomplish the task.
2. *Coaching* – Consists of [the teacher's] observing students while they carry out a task and offering hints, feedback, modeling, reminders, and new tasks aimed at bringing their performance closer to expert performance.
3. *Scaffolding* – Refers to the supports the teacher provides to help the student carry out a task... taking the forms of suggestions or help.
4. *Articulation* – Includes any method of getting students to articulate their knowledge, reasoning, or problem-solving processes in a domain.
5. *Reflection* – Enables students to compare their own problem-solving processes with those of an expert, another student, and ultimately, an internal cognitive model of expertise.
6. *Exploration* – Involves pushing students into a mode of problem solving on their own. Exploration is the natural culmination of the fading of supports. (Collins, Brown, & Newman 1989:481–482)

Note that Collins, Brown and Newman regard scaffolding as just one of the six methods; however, the whole system of cognitive apprenticeship can be viewed as scaffolding in a larger sense. This expanded concept of scaffolding was adopted in the present study to support teachers in designing WebQuest projects, with the goal to investigate the challenges involved in EFL teachers' planning, orchestration, and moment-by-moment support of learning with computer-supported projects.

The context

The context for this study was an EFL teacher professional development course which focused on theory and practice in computer-assisted and multimedia-supported language teaching. Developing a WebQuest project for language learners was the final project for the class of two consecutive years (2003–2004).

Teachers attending this course were all practicing Taiwanese teachers working toward a Master's degree in TEFL (Teaching English as a Foreign Language). In the first year, 2003, 23 junior high and high school teachers took the course. In the second year, 2004, 19 teachers from elementary, junior high, senior high, and vocational high schools took the course. The average numbers of years teaching for the two groups were 9.5 and 6.8, respectively. Thus, although the teachers were working toward a language teaching degree, they were not pre-service.

Although they were experienced teachers, few were familiar with using computers in language classrooms prior to the course. According to a survey conducted at the beginning of the course, only five in the first year and four in the second year reported that they had had some experience. From the class discussion in the first two weeks, it was also clear that many teachers had not thought about language-learning computer applications in any way beyond that of the traditional one-computer-to-one-learner model, in which drill and practice or mechanical games were the major activity types. None of the teachers were aware of WebQuests before the course.

Data collection and analysis

In order to understand the teachers' responses to the scaffolding provided in the class and the challenges that teachers faced during the project, data were collected during the course and analyzed qualitatively afterwards. These data included records of class discussion, on-line forum postings, the teachers' final WebQuest projects, and their reflections after the project. The reflection, the forum postings, and the WebQuest projects were originally written in English as part of the course assignment. The teachers were asked in the last meeting for their permission for the data to be used in this study. Each project was examined for the context that the activity was situated in, coherence of activity design, required critical thinking and language skills. Teacher concerns regarding instructional strategies were noted, and by comparing and contrasting all of the concerns discovered, cross referenced with issues discussed in the class, the challenges faced by the teachers were derived. Finally, the challenges were categorized, and the results are presented in the discussion below.

The experience of the course

The experiences the course provided in the two years were somewhat different because, based on the suggestions from the 2003 group, some revisions were made to better support the teachers in the 2004 class. For both years, the structure of the course was designed to support teachers through all aspects of the course experience, including scheduling, brainstorming, specific scaffolding strategies, technical learning, use of the asynchronous forum, and the development of a sample learner product.

Scheduling

In the first part of the course, the teachers of the 2003 group were introduced to a framework for CALL activity design and were shown examples of how the computer and the Internet could support reading, writing, listening, and speaking instruction. They did not start working on the WebQuest until the last three weeks of the course as a final project. One suggestion the 2003 group made after the course was that the project should be moved to an earlier time in the class, because they had experienced anxiety waiting for the project to begin. The anxiety came from their assumption that their grades depended on how sophisticated their webpages would be even though the class discussion emphasized the instructional side of the project design. Following the teachers' suggestion, work on the WebQuest project for the 2004 group started from the second week. The reading discussion, which was originally done before the project, was also carried out side by side with the project. These changes were intended to give teachers ample time to develop their ideas, to reduce anxiety, and to situate conceptual and theoretical discussion in a concrete project experience.

Brainstorming

To help generate initial ideas, the participants in the 2003 group were asked to bring to class one initial proposal for their WebQuests, and those in the 2004 group were asked to bring two. It was also specified for the 2004 group that only one of the two ideas could be of a travel-related theme, since in 2003, nine out of 23 projects were on travel-related themes. It seemed that the teachers chose to stay with travel, a presumably safe topic for the EFL context, rather than really explore other possibilities. Such projects often do not require much critical thinking because learners can just copy and paste information taken from the Internet and complete their projects, a problem noted by March (2003). Given that there were a variety of task types and examples available for the teachers' reference, they were encouraged to collaboratively experiment with different creative task designs and to explore a wider range of possibilities for EFL learning with WebQuests.

After the participants had developed their initial proposals, group brainstorming occurred regularly. Each individual had the opportunity to talk about ideas, no matter how rough or immature they might be, and get feedback from the other participants. This was also a time for the participants to explore new task possibilities and to articulate and reflect on how they thought about language teaching in general, with modeling and coaching provided by the instructor on the side as suggested by the cognitive apprenticeship approach.

During brainstorming, the teachers in 2003 had feedback from their instructor and peers, while the 2004 group also had the unique opportunity to work over the Internet with a group of teachers in the US taking a similar course from the University of Toledo in Ohio. The goal for this international collaboration was twofold: one was to give EFL teachers the experience of working with native speakers over the Internet so that they would understand what could be accomplished with computer-mediated communication, an important focus of the course. The other reason was to allow a wider variety of feedback for their WebQuests, because, based on the 2003 experience, teachers thought that task ideas developed by native speaker (NS) teachers were more creative, perhaps due to the fact that NS teachers were placed in an environment that was rich in the target language and culture. The collaboration with the teachers from the US was expected to encourage EFL teachers to think out of the usual classroom box.

Scaffolding measures

There were many important scaffolding strategies. First of all, the teachers were often engaged in face-to-face and online discussion. At the time when teachers were required to come up with initial proposals, opportunities were provided for them to talk about their ideas in class. As explained earlier, based on the concept of situated cognition, this was for teachers to *articulate* their understanding and assumptions about language teaching as well as technology use in language teaching. These opportunities helped make the implicit obvious to the teachers themselves and to the instructor. Such discussion also fulfilled the purpose of assuring the teachers of the legitimacy of their implicit knowledge in this unfamiliar project.

Discussion in class highlighted key elements in a quality language-learning WebQuest, including a storyline or a scenario to engage the learner in an authentic and meaningful context, the use of critical thinking while fulfilling needs of fluency and accuracy in language use, and the requirement to make the task, the process, and the evaluation components consistent with the scenario. These points are similar to task design in other second language activities (Ellis 2003). Also discussed in class were color coordination, copyrights, and visual and interface design issues unique to the computerized language learning environment.

As the instructor, I often modeled ways to think about the project creatively, helping the teachers to solve problems in task design or to develop interesting contexts, for example, by getting ideas from TV programs. The teachers never adopted my ideas directly. They would strive to add something more to make the idea theirs, mostly based on their understanding of their learners. In addition to face-to-face interaction with the instructor, the 2004 group also relied on a journal article on WebQuests based on the same class in 2003 (Chao 2004). This paper, written in Chinese, discussed the strengths, weaknesses, and concerns found in the previous group's projects. Teachers in the 2004 class were often seen using the article as a handy reference to examine their work throughout the project. The article thus served as another useful tool for scaffolding teacher thinking.

Scaffolding in this class was also provided by invited speakers. One of the presenters in 2004 was a high school teacher who took the course in 2003 and who had had the experience of actually using the project with her students. In addition to introducing the content of her WebQuest, this presenter also talked about her experience and mistakes in both designing and implementing it. For example, she had thought that her high school students would be able to work on the project on their own with some simple introduction to the WebQuest that she had developed in the course. After all, she believed that she had provided everything they would need for the project. But, to her surprise, there were still many gaps to be filled. First of all, being low-proficiency learners, her students showed strong resistance to reading webpages entirely in English. Because this had not been part of their language learning experience, they did not have confidence to read authentic English online all by themselves. The teacher had to teach useful reading strategies by guiding learners to look for specific and necessary information only and helping them give up the habit of reading every single word on the page as in reading a language textbook. With reading strategy instruction in the context of the WebQuest project, the students eventually became unafraid of reading English pages. Similar observations in learner behaviors led the teacher to add more supportive materials to her WebQuest. It was only after repeated revisions that the teacher finally felt satisfied with her project as well as her ways of scaffolding language learning in a WebQuest.

This presentation gave the class a clear picture of what a WebQuest was like in a real language classroom and how it could have an impact on the students' perception of language learning in general. In addition, it showed that developing a successful WebQuest project requires a long process of implementation, reflection, and revising. What the teachers were creating at the time during the class was just the first step. Other presenters inspired the class with information about color coordination on web pages, multimedia applications, and copyright issues. Building on the concept of *cognitive apprenticeship*, these experts were likely to allow a wider and deeper level of reflection and awareness than what one instructor could ever have provided mainly because of the multiple perspectives they brought to the class. In other words, all the presenters enriched the teachers' experience in ways that would not have been possible if the instructor had been the only source of information.

Technical learning

In 2003, although there was only limited time for the project, teachers were asked to create webpages from scratch, using a webpage editor to design, develop, format everything on the page, and publish the finished product to the Internet. Since everything needed to be done in the last three weeks of the course, the teachers experienced great pressure and anxiety. In order to reduce the undue focus on technical skills, the class in 2004 not only started earlier but also used the ready-made WebQuest templates provided by the *WebQuest Central* website. Teachers who did not have any experience with developing webpages could easily open the template in a webpage editor and replace the place-holder content with their own information, in a way similar to using a word processing program. The template guided the teachers to write all the necessary components for a WebQuest, allowing them to concentrate on developing ideas, rather than being daunted by new technical procedures. Those who felt comfortable with their webpage skills still had room to create new pages and challenge themselves technically as they wished.

Using the asynchronous forum

In 2003, the asynchronous forum was used for discussion as in a distance education course. Having many years' experience teaching on-line courses where no face-to-face meetings were involved, I expected that these EFL teachers would continue their class discussion in the on-line forum in a manner similar to my distance education students. However, there was not much interaction in 2003, presumably because using the forum to carry on discussion was not meeting a real need. With the class meeting twice a week for three hours each time, there were already sufficient opportunities for the participants to discuss important issues face to face. It became clear that if an asynchronous forum was to be included as part of the class experience, it must be used very differently from that in a distance education course.

Inspired by the popular *weblog* (or blog) concept, in which people share personal notes, journals, commentary, passing thoughts or links (Blood 2004), I decided to create a "personal space" in the forum for each participant. Like a *weblog*, the space in the class forum was for the teachers to share their thoughts and reflections. It could also be used as a place to hand in assignments or a storage space to transport files back and forth from the computer lab. To demonstrate and encourage use of the space, I posted plans for each class meeting, intended objectives for each activity, responses from the students, and my reflection after class. Because the personal space was open to everybody in class, teachers could see my thoughts about each class meeting. Gradually teachers too used the space for many activities related to the project and the course, including keeping their class notes, recording their thoughts, and keeping continuous logs about their WebQuest project. Interestingly, because the *weblog* on the asynchronous forum was meeting real needs for journaling, communication, and file storage during the project, many teachers mentioned that they would like to set up a similar forum for their learners. This indicated that the use of an asynchronous forum was perceived as a useful strategy for supporting learners during the project.

Developing a sample student product

In 2003, some of the teachers' projects were too complicated, with too many detailed requirements to be fulfilled by language learners; while others provided only simple and broad guidelines, making it hard for learners to understand what was required of them. It was determined that teachers needed to create a sample student product based on their own requirements so that they would understand how much work was involved and what help might be needed. Thus, in 2004, besides the WebQuest webpages, all teachers had to produce and present an example of the kind of final product that language learners were expected to create. This led teachers to examine whether or not their *task*, *process* and *evaluation* were consistent and reasonable. They were encouraged to revise the project and the requirements accordingly, if necessary. Again, the intention for this added assignment was to encourage reflection and self-assessment.

Lessons learned

Although in both years the scaffolding measures and requirements were provided as much as was possible at the time, it is clear that the 2003 group's feedback helped improve the course in 2004. The two groups' responses to the questionnaire at the end of the project did not show much difference: both groups reported that they had a positive experience in the course. However, there are many qualitative differences. First of all, in the process of developing the project, participants in 2004 were indeed more concerned about the instructional design issues than technical skills. Also, while the topics for the 2003 group's WebQuests were mostly traditional language teaching topics, such as travel-related themes or introducing cultures and places, the 2004 group's topics had more variety, including humanistic concerns and other popular topics among teens such as movies. Furthermore, the process and task designs for the 2004 group also had a more consistent look, rather than jumping from an inquiry focus at the introduction back to vocabulary or grammar quizzes. Thus, the 2004 group's WebQuests, in my view, are more interesting and more likely to bring creative language learning experience to learners.

WebQuest as a form of project-based learning presented many challenges to the teachers in both years, but three major ones can be identified: (1) the challenge to their assumptions and beliefs about language teaching, (2) the challenge to develop strategies in supporting student learning, and (3) the challenge to beliefs about technology use in language teaching.

Assumptions and beliefs about language teaching and learning

Presented as a content- and project-based approach, WebQuest was very different from most EFL teachers' everyday classroom experience. For example, although some projects in 2003 had interesting story contexts, language learners were often required to read information and answer comprehension questions, instead of transforming the existing information to create a new piece of information. Some teachers asked expository, fact-searching questions in their projects, rather than open-ended and inquiry-oriented ones, as evidenced in cases where only one answer was possible to the questions. The only reason for the learner to read information to produce such an answer was that the teacher believed it was *important* to know, not because it was needed for solving a problem or developing a product.

During class discussion, one question that teachers often asked was how to design a WebQuest for elementary school EFL classes or lower-level learners. This revealed the teachers' concern that if a learner did not have sufficient input or *the basics*, then it was not clear how the learner would be able to engage in projects that required critical thinking skills or output-oriented performance. This resulted in some of 2003's projects that had the appearance of an interesting context actually being traditional language exercises. The teacher who presented her WebQuest and her experience with low-level learners in 2004 convinced me that the teachers would accept project-based learning only when they have a chance to work with their learners, solve problems along the way, and see low-level learners blossom in the projects.

This brings up another concern related to March's point (2003) that a WebQuest has to be "transformational," which means using the existing information to create something new and useful, such as requiring learners to analyze information based on a new framework. There were questions about whether or not this requirement was really reasonable for EFL learners. Many teachers in the class believed that as long as a WebQuest provided an opportunity for learners to use the target language in an oral presentation, even if learners did not do any higher order thinking with the topic or simply copied and pasted information from the Internet, they still had to speak and use the target language in the final presentation. Because of the use of target language in the final product or presentation, it can be argued that the transformational process might not be a must for EFL learners. In class, there were also discussions on using the learner's native language in the process of developing the project. All of these discussions showed that WebQuest projects challenged teachers' existing views about teaching English as a foreign language. The teachers might not have been able to reach a consensus in the discussion, but WebQuests indeed provided an opportunity for them to think about what really matters in language teaching and learning.

Strategies for supporting student learning

Scaffolding is the most important aspect of the WebQuest project (March, 2003) and figures prominently in the cognitive apprenticeship model of Collins, Brown, and Newman (1989) discussed earlier. In designing the project, *process* and *evaluation* are where scaffolding should be provided. Teachers needed to make sure that the *process* was a natural and cohesive development of the situation presented in the *introduction*. Some teachers had an attractive scenario in the introduction section which provided authentic and interesting context for the project; however, the *process* section switched to unrelated questions that were meant to test reading comprehension or vocabulary. This suggests that there were competing systems of language teaching knowledge at work: While WebQuests encouraged learners to focus on authentic use of language through problem-solving and critical appraisal of information, many language teachers actually wanted to build in opportunities for bottom-up skill training. Thus, keeping all the components consistent and cohesive was very challenging for these teachers.

Teachers also needed to search for relevant web information that could actually be used by EFL learners. However, many of the WebQuests led learners to a complicated webpage without explaining what exactly they should be looking for. Learners with limited language proficiency could be overwhelmed by a complex page layout and have problems figuring out which information was actually the focus. Furthermore, some web sites were provided not to help learners solve problems or develop projects, but because the teacher thought this was interesting background information. In other words, resources did not necessarily go well with task requirements and goals.

Beliefs about technology use

In the process of developing the WebQuest project, the teachers' beliefs about technology use were often challenged. First of all, having the computer skill to create was such an empowering and exciting experience that teachers from both years often wanted to create many computerized tasks for their students once when they knew how to use a computer tool. The case most often observed was with the presentation software *PowerPoint*. Once teachers learned how to use it, they would often create presentations for their learners. However, the intention to create materials for learners risks the possibility of depriving them of the opportunity to use the target language creatively on their own. Students are likely to be left with activities that do not require much critical thinking or that might not support students' creative use of the target language. For example, one participant in the first year who was a technology coordinator in his school developed a series of project webpages that used professional-looking photos of his own creation. However, the project was mostly about having learners respond to factual questions related to his description of the photos, rather than involving them in critical thinking or creating solutions to a problem. His focus on technical presentation was very obvious. It was a challenge to help him become aware of what exactly the learner was doing in the project. Providing more exemplary projects in the second year was helpful in reducing this kind of problem. Nevertheless, one challenge for teachers to design computerized projects was to do just enough for learners, always focusing on their learning opportunities rather than the computer skill that the teacher has acquired.

Another problem that showed up frequently in the teachers' WebQuest designs was animated graphics. In one of the class presentations, the audience could hardly focus on the message given by the presenter because on the screen behind the presenter there was a monster repeatedly swallowing a big red heart down into its throat. It was indeed a funny animation, but it was too distracting.

The problem seemed to be in the teacher's understanding of what visual design meant. As most teachers had limited technical skills, clipart or free graphics on the Internet were often their only source of graphics. When an animated graphic was used, it was mostly for aesthetic reasons: teachers did not take into consideration the possibility of its distracting the learner from the task. One teacher who had had experience making web pages argued forcefully for the need to attract young learners with animated graphics as well as digital background music. She did not change her mind until an invited talk given by a professor specialized in visual design. The professor analyzed many professional websites designed for children, none of which used animated graphics. Instead, a cohesive use of simple and consistent features and bright colors were considered effective to get children's attention. This presentation helped to change the teachers' concept about color usage and visual design. One teacher said afterwards that she had never realized her use of graphics and colors could influence how a learner perceived information. It was clear that developing a WebQuest project challenged them to look at webpage development from the perspective of an educator, rather than simply as an amateur webpage developer.

Conclusion

Creating a WebQuest provided a learning opportunity rich enough for teachers to think reflectively about language teaching. It also allowed them to develop an understanding of CALL in a way different from the past when technical skills were the only focus, making teachers think more like educators rather than webpage developers or technicians. Teachers became more self-directed learners in projects when the teaching context was in their view. The problem is they might be blind to some misconceptions, as was the case with graphics and icons. Supporting teachers learning through the cognitive apprenticeship acts of modeling, coaching, scaffolding, articulation, reflection, and exploration was beneficial in this course, because the teachers had a variety of opportunities to engage in reflection and sense making.

Looking to the future, although the scaffolding measures were improved in 2004, many things remain to be strengthened, including helping the teachers overcome the three major challenges discussed earlier. Support for implementation is also important. As some teachers from both years are still in touch, I know that many of them are not using computers or the projects that they created in this course, for reasons such as a shortage of computers for language classes. Implementation is probably a larger problem than knowing how to create the project itself.

To solve this problem, it is necessary to further integrate the CALL course and the teacher's teaching context. One possibility would be dedicating half of the time to creating the project and the other half to actually implementing it in the teacher's classroom. This way the teachers would be supported in the process of implementation, and they could see how real learners react to their projects. My experience with teachers as well as many existing studies related to teachers' learning of technology (Becker 1994; Egbert et al. 2002; McKenzie 2001) show that those who actually implemented their projects were more likely to continue developing their skills in using the technology and developing a mature understanding of the role of technology in language teaching and learning. Thus, a longer term interaction between teachers and teacher educators, perhaps in a learning community format, will be valuable.

This paper discussed ways to scaffold teacher learning in one form of computer-assisted language learning and suggested that the challenge for teacher educators may not be in helping teachers acquire technical skills only. More importantly, it emphasized the value of educating teachers to use the computer reflectively. Only when teachers become aware of their assumptions and misconceptions associated with computer use can they develop effective solutions to foster language learning and achieve a fruitful learning environment.

References

Becker, H. J. (1994). How exemplary computer-using teachers differ from other teachers: Implications for realizing the potential of computers in schools. *Journal of Research on Computing in Education, 26* (3), 291–321.

Benz, P. (2001). WebQuests: A constructivist approach. Available at http://www.ardecol.ac-grenoble.fr/english/tice/enwebquests.htm.

Blood, R. (2004). Weblogs: A history and perspective. Available at http://www.rebeccablood.net/essays/weblog_history.html.

Brown, J., Collins, A., & Duguid, P. (1989). Situated cognition and the culture of learning. *Educational Researcher, 18* (1), 32–42.

Chao, C. (2004). Designing WebQuests for EFL instruction: An analysis of high school teachers' experiences. *English Teaching and Learning Journal, 29* (4), 1–20.

Collins, A., Brown, J., & Newman, S. (1989). Cognitive apprenticeship: Teaching the craft of reading, writing and mathematics. In L. B. Resnick (Ed.), *Knowing, Learning and Instruction: Essays in honor of Robert Glaser* (pp. 453–494). Hillsdale, NJ: Lawrence Erlbaum.

Dudeney, G. (2003). The quest for practical web usage. *TESL-EJ, 6* (4). Available at http://www-writing.berkeley.edu/TESL-EJ/ej24/int.html.

Egbert, J., Paulus, T. M., & Nakamichi, Y. (2002). The impact of CALL instruction on classroom computer use: A foundation for rethinking technology in teacher education. *Language Learning & Technology, 6* (3), 108–126. Available at http://llt.msu.edu/vol6num3/pdf/egbert.pdf.

Ellis, R. (2003). *Task-Based Language Learning and Teaching.* Oxford: OUP.

Hogan, K. & Pressley, M. (Eds.). (1997). *Scaffolding Student Learning: Instructional approaches and issues.* Cambridge, MA: Brookline Books.

March, T. (2003). The learning power of WebQuests. *Educational Leadership, 61* (4), 42–47.

Meskill, C., Mossop, J., DiAngelo, S., & Pasquale, R. (2002). Expert and novice teachers talking technology: Precepts, concepts, and misconcepts. *Language Learning & Technology, 6* (3), 46–57. Available at http://llt.msu.edu/vol6num3/pdf/meskill.pdf.

McKenzie, J. (2001). How teachers learn technology best. *From Now On: The Educational Technology Journal, 10* (6). Available at http://www.fno.org/mar01/howlearn.html.

Ryle, G. (1949). *The Concept of Mind.* Chicago, IL: University of Chicago.

Schön, D. A. (1987). *Educating the Reflective Practitioner.* San Francisco, CA: Jossey-Bass.

WebQuest Central. Available at http://webquest.sdsu.edu/.

Preface to

Designing and implementing collaborative Internet projects in Siberia

Much of the literature and discussion on modern CALL relates to situations in the developed world, most particularly in North America and Europe. By adopting this perspective, numerous assumptions tend to follow without question or reflection: that the technological infrastructure is stable and reliable; that a wide range of software applications and programs are available to all; that institutions are receptive to the introduction of CALL; and that the practices of language teachers are readily amendable to change if the opportunity for training is provided. At a deeper level, there is a tendency for certain political, social and economic circumstances to be taken for granted; furthermore, within education, particular pedagogical contexts, cultures and approaches are assumed. While much valuable information and expertise can be exchanged between those who share this common ground, it would be foolish indeed to assume that this constituted the whole picture. It is crucial we also look outward, to different CALL settings operating within different parameters and sets of assumptions. Thus, in this chapter Larissa Olesova and Christine Foster Meloni consider teacher education and CALL in a particularly remote area: Yakutia, Siberia. They look in detail at the design of a 20-hour course on CALL for English language teachers in this part of Russia, taking into account the role and status of English in a non-English-speaking country. The chapter considers the challenges faced and the many factors that need to be taken into account when introducing teacher education and CALL in such a context.

Designing and implementing collaborative Internet projects in Siberia

Larissa Olesova and Christine Foster Meloni
Yakutsk State University, Russia / George Washington University
and Northern Virginia Community College, USA

Introduction

In order to utilize technology effectively for pedagogical purposes, teachers of foreign languages need to have appropriate training. They need to learn how the technology works and how it can be used to improve the teaching and learning process. Although language teachers anywhere in the world need to learn these fundamentals, there are special circumstances for those involved in technology training in isolated or less developed regions of the world. This chapter discusses one such setting, English teachers in Yakutia, Siberia. The teacher training course described here can serve as a model for trainers in similar settings; trainers in any situation, however, ought to find many aspects of this model relevant, particularly those in non-English speaking countries.

We begin with a brief description of the context in which this course is situated. The official languages of the Republic of Yakutia are Russian and Yakut; however, the working language in the government and many other spheres is English. The Educational Standards in Training Specialists of Higher Education in the Russian Federation require the preparation of English-language specialists in Yakutia. There is, therefore, an urgent need to prepare individuals who are proficient in English. The skill areas of particular interest are writing and speaking. Individuals are needed who are able to write accurately and appropriately in English (e.g., to prepare reports, business letters, formal e-mail messages) and who can speak effectively at professional meetings where English is the medium of communication, both at home and abroad.

Yakutia is a republic in Northern Siberia, the largest and most remote territory in Russia. The climatic conditions are severe as winter lasts seven months with an average temperature of minus 60 degrees C. Roads are impassable and rivers are frozen. The economic situation is poor. The local economy depends almost exclusively on its natural resources as few other ways to obtain income have been developed in Yakutia. Salaries are generally very low.

How do university professors in this desolate and remote location train their teachers to prepare individuals who are highly proficient in English? Computer technology seems to hold the key to their success although serious problems exist. The cold weather has an impact on the computers: the Internet satellite connection operates in the open air, and it can freeze when the temperature is low. The connection through the regular telephone cables is safer but it is extremely slow. Despite these hardships, interest in computer technology is keen. It is generally acknowledged in all sectors of society that the Internet offers a very attractive solution for bringing the people of Yakutia closer to people beyond their borders.

Yakutsk State University (YSU) is located in Yakutsk, the capital and the largest city in Yakutia. Founded in 1956, it is an educational institution of higher learning in Yakutia with an annual enrollment of more than twelve thousand students. Despite the poor economy in Yakutsk, YSU has modern computer facilities for teachers and students. In 1999 the Soros Foundation installed computer labs with an Internet connection in the university. The Ministry of Education of Yakutia is very interested in the development of educational technology and teacher preparation. It has partnered with YSU to establish three distance education centers within the University: the Yakut Regional Center of Distance Education, the Center of Distance Education (*Sitim*), and the Educational and Methodological Laboratory (*Communikant*). A number of courses have been developed to train teachers in the use of computer software, multimedia, and Internet informational resources. Most of these courses have been designed for the disciplines of computer science and mathematics. Unlike their colleagues in the scientific and technical fields, foreign language teachers at YSU have been reluctant to adopt Internet technology. Those who have utilized the Internet consider it primarily as a source of teaching materials. Few recognize its communicative potential.

One of the authors (Olesova), a professor of English at the Yakutsk State University, was the first foreign language educator to implement a collaborative Internet project there. She designed four projects with two universities in the United States. The objectives of these projects were to improve student accuracy and fluency in writing in English and to develop cross-cultural communicative competence.

She found that her students were very enthusiastic about these projects and felt that the project objectives were reached. However, she was unable to convince her colleagues to implement their own collaborative Internet projects. They were hesitant primarily for two reasons. First of all, they considered the computer primarily as a tool for developing writing skills and felt unsure of their own ability to write well in English as they lacked formal training in writing. Secondly, they lacked computer expertise. As Pilus (1995) wrote of the situation in Malaysia, "Assuming that everybody is able to use a keyboard is a fallacy as it is not uncommon to find some teachers grappling with the keyboard searching for the right button to press. For a novice computer user, using the keyboard can be quite intimidating. . ." [1]

Before attempting to implement collaborative Internet projects, the YSU teachers requested in-service training. They wanted to learn more about writing and about computing simultaneously. These YSU teachers had a very supportive institutional administration and modern computer facilities. The crucial missing elements were instruction in writing and training in CALL. Olesova therefore designed a CALL training course with a focus on collaborative writing projects that was piloted with two groups of teachers. The remainder of this chapter discusses the design of the course, the results of the two pilots, and the implementation of the course.

In-service CALL course: "Teaching with Technology: Designing and Implementing CALL Projects"

Course design

Because collaborative CALL projects are viewed as an effective means of training English language specialists, the YSU administration sees this new course as a very valuable addition to the teacher education in-service curriculum. Given the remoteness of Siberia and the shortage of opportunities for face-to-face contact with native speakers of English, these projects can bring the English-speaking world closer in a way that would not be otherwise possible. As Kasper (1999) points out,

> Recent research has demonstrated that collaborative computer-based learning yields a number of significant educational benefits to ESL students that can empower them in their efforts to gain full access to an English-speaking academic environment.

Dracopoulos (2003) emphasizes the sense of community that collaboration in cyberspace can create:

> Learners have a sense of identity within and a sense of belonging to their virtual community. In a virtual learning environment, the sense of community plays an integral role in education by minimizing the feelings of isolation that learners may experience.

The course has been designed, piloted, and revised; it was added to the curriculum in Spring 2005 as a supplement to two existing courses: "Methods of Teaching Foreign Languages" and "Methods of Teaching English."

The new course challenges the traditional approach to teaching and learning in Siberia. As it introduces a learner-centered approach, teachers need to rethink their basic pedagogical assumptions. Warschauer and Healey (1998) write that teacher roles have changed and what teachers learned in their teacher training courses years ago is no longer adequate:

> The assumption from cognitive theory is that teachers do not pour information from their store into the heads of waiting and willing students, but that students actively interpret and organize the information they are given, fitting it into prior knowledge or revising prior knowledge in the light of what they have learned.

This approach initially seems less appealing to many of the teachers who are satisfied with the teacher-centered classroom because "The first step in a true learner-centered approach is to gain as deep an understanding of the learner as possible" (*Focusing on Learners* 2005). Additional effort on the part of the teacher is, therefore, required. Brown (2003) clearly explains the distinction between the teacher-centered and learner-centered approaches:

> The teacher-centered approach places control for learning in the hands of the teacher. The teacher uses her expertise in content knowledge to help learners make connections. The effort to get to know the learner and how he processes information is secondary. The learner-centered approach, however, places more of the responsibility for knowing individual learner capabilities and creating an environment where learners can make learning connections.

The introduction of technologies such as e-mail and the WWW naturally leads to more student control. "Certainly online instructors are discovering that their role must change from 'sage on the stage' to 'guide on the side' – tutor, facilitator, and coach" (*Focusing on Learners* 2005).

Teachers are grappling with this change in most parts of the world. Walker (1994) points out, for example, that in Saudi Arabia teachers generally view the introduction of CALL as a positive event but some teachers are hesitant about "turning over control to students." In talking about CALL teacher education in New Zealand, Johnson (1999) states that the most widely accepted model is that of students as "passive receivers of knowledge, in the form of lectures, from their teachers, 'the experts.'" Although the concept of autonomous learning is familiar because of its popularity in the literature, many cannot relate to it personally.

The YSU course takes into consideration the potential resistance of the teachers by creating a course that is learner-centered and provides opportunities for collaboration. It consists of both the theoretical and practical training of EFL teachers. It is divided into three parts. Since the majority of teachers are not proficient in basic computer skills, the first two weeks are dedicated to computer basics. The second part, Internet Applications, focuses on search engines and communication technologies. The third part introduces Collaborative Internet Projects in EFL.

The course is undertaken in a traditional classroom (8 hours) and in a computer lab (12 hours) for a total of 20 hours per semester over a 10-week period. Teachers spend additional hours every week in cyberspace completing assignments.

Course syllabus

The first part of the course, *Basic Computer Skills Development and Theoretical Grounding,* takes two weeks and consists of two two-hour lessons. The first lesson is conducted in the computer lab and includes computer fundamentals such as keyboarding and mouse work, along with basic word processing techniques. Teachers begin by filling out a questionnaire to assess their computer skills at the beginning of the course. They then practice keyboarding and mouse use and word processing techniques. The second lesson takes place in the classroom and focuses on the theory and practice of computer-mediated communication. Teachers read and discuss a variety of books and articles that consider the use of asynchronous and synchronous computer technologies (e.g., Almeida-d'Eça 2003; Braunstein, Meloni, & Zolotareva, 2000; Egbert & Hanson-Smith 1999; Fotos & Browne 2004; Gonglewski, Meloni, & Brant 2001; Inman 2004; Robb 1995; Warschauer 1996; Warschauer, Shetzer, & Meloni 2000; Weasenforth, Biesenbach-Lucas, & Meloni 2001; Weasenforth, Meloni, & Biesenbach-Lucas 2005; Wood & Smith 2001). These readings not only provide the theoretical and practical background for the course but also demonstrate the rather large body of literature on the benefits of collaborative Internet projects.

The second part of the course, *Internet Applications,* takes four weeks and includes four two-hour lessons (lessons 3–6). The main purpose of the third lesson, held in the computer lab, is to show teachers how to find, save and store Internet sites. Teachers are introduced to the most appropriate search engines (e.g., *Google*), effective search strategies, and techniques to evaluate websites. They browse content-rich sites, e.g., "Blue Web Content Areas" and "Marco Polo". They read the article "Sorting Strands of the World Wide Web for Educators" by March (n.d.) in which he gives suggestions for effective searching and provides a framework for classifying materials found on the Internet into seven categories. While searching, teachers evaluate sites and bookmark the ones they want to keep in a personal list. Teachers become familiar with the Purdue University Online Writing Lab and locate guidelines and models for writing business letters and essays. They write a comparison/contrast essay in which they compare three Web sites on a topic of their choosing related to English language teaching.

In the next lesson teachers learn/review computer and Internet terms as well as the mechanics of e-mail and become familiar with ways of using e-mail as a communicative means for educational purposes. They discuss the article on using e-mail in the foreign language classroom by Gonglewski et al. (2001). They experience e-mail messages in authentic situations by sending e-mails to each other and to the instructor. In addition, teachers experience chat by meeting in a chatroom to discuss their own views on the advantages and disadvantages of chat for English language learners. They use *Tapped-In*, which offers an easy-to-use chat platform, and discuss Almeida-Eça's (2003) article on the use of chat.

Teachers experience the discussion board as a new means of online communication between teachers and students in the fifth lesson. Popular course management systems such as *Blackboard* are not available in Yakutsk; therefore, *Nicenet* was chosen as the vehicle for the discussion board: it is free and easy to use. Teachers learn the mechanics of the discussion board and engage in a threaded discussion. Teachers return to the classroom for Lesson Six. The discussion topic is the advantages and disadvantages of the discussion board.

The third part of the course, *Collaborative Internet Projects,* takes four weeks and consists of the final four two-hour lessons. The seventh and eighth lessons are held in the classroom. Teachers become familiar with the theoretical background of project-based methodology and discuss selected journal articles that describe Internet projects. The primary article is "The US-SiberLink Internet Project" by Braunstein et al. (2000). It describes a project in detail and is directly relevant to the teachers' situation as it discusses an exchange between YSU students and students in the US. The instructor presents other projects including several carried out by Ruth Vilmi in Finland and ones mentioned in the teacher resource book by Warschauer et al. (2000). Then teachers are asked to find articles or websites that describe other collaborative Internet projects and then study the content and the design of those projects.

The final two lessons of the course focus on the development of individual projects. Teachers work in the computer lab to design their own collaborative Internet project which makes use of e-mail, the WWW, *Nicenet*, and *Tapped-In*. They complete a preliminary version of the syllabus for a project that they intend to implement. This project serves as the teacher's final exam for the course.

Technology focus

In order to develop and participate in a collaborative Internet project, teachers need to be familiar with three communicative technologies in particular, e-mail, the discussion board, and the WWW. All lesson assignments, plans and questionnaires in the course are sent through regular e-mail. A discussion board is established and it becomes the true focal point of the course (see Kamhi-Stein (2000) for a discussion of the use of this technology in a methods course). Teachers are required to participate in weekly discussions on a variety of course-related topics. They soon discover that a discussion board has the potential to bring about dramatic changes in the roles of teacher and students. A teacher who sets up a discussion board automatically creates a more learner-centered environment. The World Wide Web is also important for finding information and for publishing projects.

Chat is introduced as an interesting feature but one that is not necessary for a successful collaborative project. Synchronous communication becomes difficult when you take into consideration the differences in time zones. There is, for example, a nine-hour time difference between Yakutsk and London and a 14-hour time difference between Yakutsk and Washington, DC. This creates scheduling challenges that are sometimes insurmountable. It is worth trying if possible, however.

Special course considerations

Pace
When planning a CALL course for teachers, it is important to keep in mind that the computer skills of the participants vary. In order not to slow the pace of the course unnecessarily, students in this course are divided into small groups for the lessons in the computer lab. Each group includes a teacher with more advanced computer skills who can help the others develop their skills more quickly. In this way the instructor does not have to work with each teacher individually, and the course can proceed more expeditiously.

Slow connection
The most frustrating feature of computer use in Yakutsk is the connection speed. The speed depends to a certain extent on the time and the day, and this reality needs to be taken into account when scheduling lab time for CALL courses. But it is also wise to avoid certain tasks such as downloading audio and video files that take considerable time even with relatively fast connections. Avoiding possible sources of frustration is advisable in order to keep or gain the enthusiasm of the teachers.

Flexibility
In-service CALL courses should be designed to meet the specific needs of the teachers enrolled in the course. As Egbert, Paulus, and Nakamichi (2002:119) found in their survey of the effectiveness of CALL training, "Previous research has suggested that transfer might be more effective if coursework dealt with the needs and circumstances surrounding specific teaching situations." They cite in particular studies by Fisher (1999) and Ringstaff, Yocam, and Marsh (1996). For this reason the final part of the course focuses on the individual teaching situations of the participants. The teachers create a project that is appropriate for their own classroom.

Two pilot studies of the new course and evaluation

The new course "Teaching with Technology: Designing and Implementing CALL Projects" has been involved in two pilot trials. The first pilot of the new course was held for 30 university teachers from the Department of Foreign Languages in Technical and Natural Sciences of YSU in May of 2004. The second pilot was held for 22 EFL teachers from secondary schools of Yakutia in October of 2004.

These pilots were abbreviated versions of the course. The first pilot consisted of two hours per week for five weeks for a total of 10 hours. The second pilot was a two-day workshop of five hours per day for a total of 10 hours. The participants in the first pilot were university EFL teachers between the ages of 25–35 who were considered more advanced computer users. The instructor was confident that it was not necessary to teach keyboarding and Internet browsing skills to teachers in this age group but her assumption was incorrect. After working with these teachers, the syllabus was revised to include instruction in Internet search skills as a mandatory part of the course. The second pilot involved a more intensive format but the total number of hours was the same as the first. The participants were secondary school teachers with minimal computer skills. It was necessary to include lessons to develop basic computer skills such as keyboarding and word-processing. The major focus on collaborative learning through Internet projects, however, was retained.

Most of the time in both pilots was dedicated to Part Three of the course, *Collaborative Internet Projects*. The trainer focused on the Yakutia-USA experience, in particular, and the role of synchronous and asynchronous technologies (i.e. e-mail, the discussion board, and chat) in these projects. Certain lessons from Part Two, *Internet Applications*, were briefly presented, such as the selection of appropriate search engines and ways to find content-rich websites.

Participants in the pilots were not given a formal evaluation form to complete at the end of the course. However, based on her personal observation of the teachers during the course and conversations with them at its conclusion, the trainer concluded that the primary benefits of the course were (1) the change in the teachers' perception of the usefulness of Internet projects in the EFL classroom and (2) the teachers' increased confidence in their ability to use computer technology for these projects.

Teachers became convinced that there was educational value for English learners in the communicative technologies. They decided to implement CALL projects in order to, as one participant commented, "refresh the atmosphere of foreign language learning for my students."

A serious problem that the course creator had faced initially was the lack of conviction on the part of the teachers. She realized that the teachers were not convinced of the effectiveness of CALL projects in teaching foreign languages.

These reservations had to be taken into consideration and addressed in a sensitive manner. Cuban (1996) talks of "techno-reformers" who are unable to convince teachers to adopt computer technology because of "their exaggerated claims for what the technology can do, their disregard for the social organization of schools, their ignorance of classroom realities...".

McKenzie (1999) describes Sally Jane, a typical "technology-reluctant" teacher who is not interested in computers and who wants to focus her energies on being a good teacher. She is popular with her students and she has a reputation for achieving satisfactory results in her classroom. She "has not yet seen much value in two decades of technology promises and products. She is reluctant to fix her class if it isn't broken." However, teachers usually do change if an in-service course meets their needs. As McKenzie (1999) affirms, "The most change occurs when someone 'buys in'. They are most apt to 'buy in' when their personal passions and interests are at stake."

Svetlana was one of the few in the pilot course who had already participated in collaborative projects. She was not satisfied with these projects because she had not understood the theoretical rationale for them. She had felt unprepared and ineffective.

> I experienced two CALL projects between my EFL students at YSU and EFL students at the University of British Columbia in Canada in 2001 and 2002. The problem I felt as an instructor was that I couldn't adjust to the new pedagogical theory. I lost myself in traditional instruction and in the desire to continuously grade the progress of my students. I couldn't combine my traditional way of instruction and the new "computerized" way of instruction in these projects. After attending the new course "Teaching with Technology: Designing and Implementing CALL Projects", I finally understood the rationale of these projects with their emphasis on a learner-centered environment and student autonomy. I think EFL teachers should use Internet projects in their classrooms to make their instruction more effective and interesting but they need training.

In addition to lack of theoretical preparation, lack of confidence in their technical ability was another reason for the teachers' negative attitude toward the use of computer technology. The increase in the teachers' confidence during the pilot courses was very evident. This finding is in keeping with research carried out on the impact of pre-service and in-service CALL courses (e.g., Keirns 1992) that show these courses tend to increase the confidence of teachers. Many see this as the primary benefit of CALL courses.

A few teachers felt they were already familiar enough with technology. They discovered, however, that the course was very valuable for them, both for the technical and the pedagogical training. As Oksana said,

> I heard much about technology in EFL but never tried it practically. Before the course, I used e-mail and was familiar with some websites so I thought that I was experienced enough in using technology. But after taking the new course, I was assured that I knew little about teaching with technology. Not only was I not familiar with all of the necessary technology but I had no idea about the pedagogical rationale for these projects. I am sure that this type of course is necessary to run in Yakutia because Yakutia is situated far from other cities and towns of Russia. CALL projects are the best educational tool that can help foreign language students in Yakutia practice the target language and communicate with native speakers.

The course designer noted some problems that arose during the pilots. The major problem was that the teachers were not accustomed to checking their e-mail every day. As a result, the teaching/learning process slowed down at times. Another problem was the initial lack of participation in the online discussions. It was a new experience for the teachers, and it took a few weeks for them to begin to access and post to the discussion board. The workload was admittedly heavy, and the teachers had to struggle to keep up. Although class time was only two hours a week in the first pilot, considerable time was spent outside of class on cyber assignments.

In revising the course, the designer tried to find ways to alleviate these problems. One suggestion was to make participants more aware of the demands of the course before it started. To eliminate parts of the syllabus was not an acceptable option, but it was noted that it may be possible to distribute some of the reading assignments ahead of time.

The original plan for the course was to focus on both writing instruction and technology. As is obvious from the syllabus, little formal writing instruction was included. The teachers did practice their writing a great deal through their e-mail and discussion board communication, and the designer noted that their messages became longer and more frequent. She also observed that, as they had more practice in writing in English, their writing lost its "Russian style". Their mastery of English syntax improved and thus their writing became clearer and more understandable. However, it was decided that two additional courses would be developed focusing exclusively on writing: one that would teach the participants how to write a variety of text types (letters, essays, case studies, research reports) and another that would focus on the theory and practice of teaching writing.

Current status of the course

The course was added to the curriculum in the spring of 2005. It was offered in the spring and in the fall to a limited number of YSU professors of English. Participation was limited because it was felt that some problems still needed to be worked out.

Parts One and Two of the course went quite well. Problems, however, were encountered in Part Three. The teachers were required to plan and implement authentic collaborative Internet projects. As the trainer felt that the teachers were not ready to carry out a project with a group in an English-speaking country, she found two institutions in Siberia that were willing to participate. The first attempt failed because of the inability of the teachers in the two schools to finalize the project guidelines in a timely fashion. The second attempt failed as well because of problems with the Internet connection.

Two important revisions have been made to Part Three. In the future, the participants will work with teachers outside of Russia who have had extensive experience in implementing collaborative Internet projects, and the planning process will begin several weeks before the project is launched.

Conclusion

Foreign language teachers in Yakutia and throughout the rest of Russia have been largely unsuccessful in providing opportunities for authentic communication to their students. They still use audio and videotapes to try to imitate target language environments in their classrooms. But with collaborative CALL projects teachers do not need to *imitate* the target language environment. They can provide an authentic forum in which their students can practice language online with native and non-native speakers from different countries.

Collaborative Internet projects are an excellent means for teachers and students anywhere in the world to improve their language skills. They are especially useful in remote and isolated areas as they help teachers and students become more a part of the global community. Teachers are optimistic that this new in-service course will prepare English teachers in Yakutia to create citizens proficient in the English language. By designing and implementing collaborative Internet projects, teachers will help their students develop the crucial skills needed to communicate in English with native and non-native speakers accurately, appropriately, and sensitively.

Note

1. The reader should be aware that this and other quotations in the present chapter appear without page numbers because they were taken from articles on unpaginated Web pages. These

articles either had no corresponding print version or that version was not accessible to the authors.

References

Almeida-d'Eca, T. (2003). The use of chat in EFL/ESL. *TESL-EJ, 7* (1). Available at http://www-writing.berkeley.edu/TESL-EJ/ej25/int.html.

Blackboard. Available at http://www.blackboard.com.

Blue Web Content Areas. Available at http://www.kn.pacbell.com/wired/bluewebn.

Braunstein, B., Meloni, C., & Zolotareva, L. (2000). The US-SiberLink Internet Project. *TESL-EJ, 4* (3). Available at http://www.kyoto-su.ac.jp/information/tesl-ej/ej15/a2.html.

Brown, K. L. (2003). From teacher-centered to learner-centered curriculum: Improving learning in diverse classrooms. *Education, 124* (1). Available at http://www.findarticles.com/p/articles/mi_qa3673/is_200310/ai_n9332034.

Cuban, L. (1996). Techno-reformers and classroom teachers. *Edweek.org.* Available at http://www.edweek.org/ew/articles/1996/10/09/06cuban.h16.html?querystring=techno.refor.

Dracopoulos, E. (2003). E-Learning *ESL*: Bringing the world together. In T. Varis, T. Utsumi, & W. R. Klemm (Eds.) *Global Peace Through The Global University System.* Available at http://www.friends-partners.org/GLOSAS/Global_University/Global%20University%20System/UNESCO_Chair_Book/Manuscripts/Part_III_Global_E-Learning/Levy,%20David/Dracopoulos_web/DracopoulosD10.htm.

Egbert, J. Paulus, T. M., & Nakamichi, Y. (2002). The impact of CALL instruction on classroom computer use: A foundation for rethinking technology in teacher education. *Learning and Technology, 6* (3), 108–126. Available at http://llt.msu.edu/vol6num3/egbert/.

Egbert, J. & Hanson-Smith, E. (Eds.). (1999). *CALL Environments: Research, practice and critical issues.* Alexandria, VA: TESOL.

Fisher, T. (1999). A new professionalism? Teacher use of multimedia portable computers with Internet capability. Paper presented at SITE 99 (ERIC Document No. 432268).

Focusing On Learners (2005). Epsilon Learning Systems. Available at http://www.epsilonlearning.com/focus.htm.

Fotos, S. & Browne, C. M. (Eds.). (2004). *New Perspectives on CALL for Second Language Classrooms.* Mahwah, NJ: Lawrence Erlbaum.

Gonglewski, M., Meloni, C., & Brant, J. (2001). Using e-mail in foreign language teaching: Rationale and suggestions. *TESL Internet Journal, 3.* Available at http://iteslj.org/Techniques/Meloni-Email.html.

Inman, J. A. (2004). *Computers and Writing: The cyborg era.* Mahwah, NJ: Lawrence Erlbaum.

Johnson, M. (1999). CALL and teacher education: Issues in course design. *CALL-EJ Online, 1* (2). Available at: http://www.clec.ritsumei.ac.jp/english/callejonline/4-2/johnson.html.

Kamhi-Stein, L. (2000). Looking to the future of TESOL teacher education: Web-based bulletin board discussions in a methods course. *TESOL Quarterly, 34* (3), 423–456.

Kasper, L. F. (1999). Collaborating at a distance: ESL students as members of academic learning communities. Paper presented at the Conference on Teaching Online in Higher Education. Available at http://members.aol.com/Drlfk/tohe99.html

Keirns, J. (1992). Does computer coursework transfer into teaching practice? A follow up study of teachers in a computer course. *Journal of Computing in Teacher Education, 8* (4), 29–34.

March, T. n.d. Sorting strands of the World Wide Web for educators. Available at http://www.ozline.com/learning/webtypes.html.

Marco Polo. Available at http://www.marcopolo-education.org

McKenzie, J. (1999). *Reaching the Reluctant Teacher.* Available at http://www.fno.org/sum99/reluctant.html.

Nicenet. Available at www.nicenet.org.

Pilus, Z. (1995). Teachers' interest in CALL and their level of computer literacy: Some implications. *On-CALL, 9* (3). Available at http://www.cltr.uq.edu.au/oncall/pilus93.html.

Purdue University Online Writing Lab. Available at http://owl.english.purdue.edu/owl.

Ringstaff, C., Yocam, K., & Marsh, J. (1996). Integrating technology into classroom instruction. An assessment of the impact of the ACOT Teacher Development Center Project (ACOT Report #22). Cupertino, CA: Apple Computer.

Robb, T. (1995). Web projects for the ESL/EFL Class: Famous Japanese personages. Available at http://www.kyoto-su.ac.jp/~trobb/projects.html

Tapped-In. Available at http://www.tappedin.org.

Walker, B. (1994). EFL teachers' attitudes about CALL. *CAELL Journal, 5* (3), 12–15.

Warschauer, M. (1996). Comparing face-to-face and electronic discussion in the second language classroom. *CALICO Journal, 13,* 7–25.

Warschauer, M. & Healey, D. (1998). Computers and language learning: An overview. *Language Teaching, 31,* 57–71. Available at http://www.gse.uci.edu/faculty/markw/overview.html

Warschauer, M., Shetzer, H., & Meloni, C. (2000). *Internet for English Teaching.* Alexandria, VA: TESOL.

Weasenforth, D., Biesenbach-Lucas, S., & Meloni, C. (2001). Realizing constructivist objectives through collaborative technologies: Threaded discussions. *Language Learning &Technology, 6* (3). Available at http://llt.msu.edu/vol6num3/weasenforth/default.html

Weasenforth, D., Meloni, C., & Biesenbach-Lucas, S. (2005). Learner autonomy and course management software. In B. Holmberg, M. Shelley, & S. White (Eds.), *Distance Education and Languages: Evolution and change* (pp. 195–211). Clevedon, UK: Multilingual Matters.

Wood, A. F. & Smith, M. J. (Eds.). (2001). *Online Communication: Linking technology, identity & culture.* Mahwah, NJ: Lawrence Erlbaum.

Preface to

In-service CALL education

What happens after the course is over?

Many chapters in this volume provide reports of successful implementations of CALL courses and workshops, but little is known empirically about the differences in teachers' subsequent performances. What are teachers able to do with the material they acquired in a CALL course once it is over? And what factors may explain individual differences in success with transferring CALL knowledge and skills to their own classrooms? These are particularly interesting questions to ask with respect to teachers who have been plying their profession without much use of technology for years. In addressing issues such as these, Lillian Wong and Phil Benson present an 18-month case study contrasting the performances of two experienced EFL teachers in Hong Kong during and after a 15-hour in-service CALL training course. The two were introduced to technology for language teaching rather late in their careers, at ages 55 and 56, and provide a striking illustration of how teachers who begin at a similar level can show quite different long-term outcomes due to individual characteristics. In particular, the authors suggest that the internalised views of language teaching the teachers bring into a technology course may play a significant role in how successful the eventual integration of CALL concepts into language teaching practice is. Although they are careful not to overgeneralise, in their study the teacher who was more comfortable with a student-centred approach seemed to be the more successful in integrating technology into her class. For the less successful one, the authors identified a number of factors – some of which correlated with her more teacher-centred approach – that negatively impacted her performance. Accompanied by a rich review of relevant literature and enlightening excerpts from interviews with the two teachers, this study is worthwhile reading for any CALL teacher educator but should be particularly valuable for those working with language instructors who have been teaching without technology for a long time.

In-service CALL education

What happens after the course is over?

Lillian Wong and Phil Benson
The University of Hong Kong, China / Hong Kong Institute
of Education, China

Introduction

This chapter reports two case studies from a longitudinal project investigating how five Hong Kong teachers attempted to put into practice what they had learned during a 15-hour in-service CALL training course. The course aimed to enhance the participants' IT knowledge, skills and strategies with a particular focus on the integration of IT into the curriculum (IT integration). Expecting that the participants would apply what they learned to their own classrooms, we also recognised the difficulties involved in fostering the kind of changes implied in IT integration through a short in-service course. The project discussed in this chapter was designed to investigate how some of the teachers who took the course used IT after the course was over. We focus on what is actually involved in IT integration from the teacher's perspective, by examining the contrasting experiences of two teachers, both of whom were coming to grips with IT relatively late in their careers. Although the experiences described are specific to Hong Kong, insights from them may be more widely applicable, especially to language educators engaged in IT training of teachers in the later stages of their careers.

Integrating IT into teaching

A number of recent studies in the field of computers and education have pointed to what Pope, Hare, and Howard (2002:191) call a "gap" between what teachers are taught about IT and the ways they are expected to use IT in the classroom. In the conclusion to their review of the research, Egbert, Paulus, and Nakamichi (2002:111) observe that although IT courses can change teachers' attitudes, increase their confidence and provide them with IT skills, "coursework alone, devoid of the opportunities to practice, apply, and see evidence of student improvement, may lead to technology learning but not necessarily to its use." The keyword here is 'integration', which is for Ertmer (1999:50) not a matter of the number of computers in a classroom or how often they get used, but a matter of "the extent to which technology is used to facilitate teaching and learning." There is currently a strong expectation in many educational systems that teachers should be capable of taking the lead in IT integration, and it is in preparing teachers for this leading role that pre- and in-service IT courses have been found most wanting. The research suggests, however, that any expectation that this could be achieved through pre-service or in-service technology courses conducted outside the contexts of the teachers' daily work may well be unreasonable. Meskill, Mossop, DiAngelo, and Pasquale (2002:54), for example, emphasise the importance of conceptual change, and argue that "training may not be sufficient for the needed conceptual development that leads to the kind of ease and repertoire characteristic of expert users" (see also Parr 1999). Some researchers stress the value of IT integration within the training experience itself (Mitchem, Wells, & Wells 2003; Pope et al. 2002; Strudler & Wetzel 1999), while others emphasise the value of situated learning experiences (Egbert et al. 2002; Swan, Holmes, Vargas, Jennings, Meier, & Rubenfeld 2002) and mentoring by teachers with IT experience (Franklin, Turner, Kariuki, & Duran 2002; Parr 1999; Swan et al. 2002; Ward, West, & Isaak 2002).

The balance of the research tends to focus on the failure of teacher education to prepare teachers for IT integration. It sometimes appears, however, as if it is teachers themselves who are the main obstacle to this goal. As Franklin et al. (2002:26) put it: "As educational institutions acquire more sophisticated hardware and software, the need arises for teachers to obtain the necessary skills to implement these tools into the classroom curriculum." Mitchem et al. (2003:397) argue similarly that "society is currently experiencing great technological momentum," but "many teachers have not demonstrated an adoption of such advances." These formulations of the problem suggest that technological progress imposes a responsibility of adoption upon teachers, independently of the pedagogical relevance and utility of new technologies to the contexts of their work. From this perspective, a well-grounded decision to reject a particular technology in a particular situation can easily be misinterpreted as a more general 'failure' to achieve the goal of IT integration.

Studies of teachers' rationales for the non-adoption of technologies introduced during IT training courses are, in fact, relatively rare, but those that we have tend to suggest that there are often good reasons behind teachers' decisions (Bullock 2004; Egbert et al. 2002; Lam 2000; Strehle, Whatley, Kurz, & Hausfather 2001; Willis & de Montes 2002). Egbert et al. (2002), for example, conclude that lack of time for preparation, inadequate resources and insufficient support are prominent among the factors that can discourage teachers' use of IT in the classroom. Lam's (2000) study of 10 Canadian language teachers points to the importance of personal beliefs about the benefits of technology: some teachers are simply not convinced that IT integration is worthwhile. Qualitative studies, especially, have pointed to the importance of localised contextual factors. Strehle et al.'s (2001) study of their own experiences of IT integration shows, for example, that it is important that IT serves the instructional goals of the teacher and makes pedagogical tasks less, rather than more, complicated. Bullock's (2004) study of field placements shows how contextual factors concerned with relationships between the trainees and their mentors caused one 'pro-technology' teacher not to use IT, while another, who was initially resistant, used it regularly.

Above all, these studies raise questions about the sense in which the more general process of IT integration is mediated through teachers' experiences of using IT in specific contexts. We are beginning to understand, in other words, that IT integration is not simply something that teachers must 'learn how to do,' but a *process* that potentially involves changes at many levels, including pedagogical beliefs. The present study attempts to contribute to a better understanding of what this process may involve from the teachers' point of view through two case studies of Hong Kong secondary school teachers who struggled to integrate IT into their work with different degrees of success.

IT integration in Hong Kong schools

In recent Hong Kong education policy, IT integration has become a priority and has been viewed as making important contributions both to the development of Hong Kong as an internationalised technology-intensive knowledge economy and to educational reforms focused on student-centred learning (Benson 2004). In view of the importance of English language skills within the Hong Kong education system, English teaching has been a major focus of IT initiatives, and in 1999 a new English syllabus was released, in which preparing learners for the changing socio-economic demands resulting from advances in information technology was specified as one of the two overall aims. As a consequence of this policy, many English teachers report that they are the main users of newly-installed Multimedia Learning Centres (MMLCs) after the computing teachers and that up to 20% of their timetables may be allocated to CALL activities. The SeeIT (Secondary English Education IT) course discussed in this chapter was specifically designed for secondary-level teachers of English with little or no CALL experience in response to an invitation from the Education and Manpower Bureau. The course consisted of five 3-hour sessions in an MMLC, which introduced the teachers to potential classroom uses of IT resources, including CALL CD-ROMs, the web, bulletin boards, chat rooms, *D-Film*, *PuzzleMaker*, *Blackboard*, *HyperStudio* and *Hot Potatoes*. The course was taken by approximately 1,800 teachers (around 25% of the total number in Hong Kong) between 2000 and 2002.

Research design

The aim of this study, which forms part of the first author's ongoing doctoral research, was to investigate how Hong Kong secondary school English teachers used IT in their teaching over an 18-month period following the SeeIT course. A case study approach was used in order to gain an in-depth understanding of the process of IT integration in the particular contexts in which the teachers worked. Data collection instruments included pre- and post-course questionnaires, video-recorded classroom observations and post-observation interviews over the six months immediately following the course, a round-up interview following the analysis of this data and a follow-up interview one year later. The data collection was completed in August 2004. The five teachers who remained in regular contact throughout the 18 months of the study were volunteers from a group of 120 who took the course in late 2002. In this chapter, we focus on two of these teachers, who were coming to grips with IT relatively late in their teaching careers, because their contrasting experiences offer particular insight into the nature of IT integration as a process.

Case studies

Penny, the subject of the first case study, is a New Zealander who was 55 years old, with over 20 years of teaching experience when she took the SeeIT course. Cathy, the subject of the second case study, is a local Cantonese-speaking teacher who was 56 years old, with 36 years of teaching experience. Penny had been teaching in her school for three years, having previously taught in New Zealand, while Cathy had been teaching in hers for her entire career. Both chose to try out IT initially with one Form 3 (Grade 9) English class. Penny's school was a lower band Chinese-medium school while Cathy's was a higher band English-medium school, which meant that Penny's class had a lower range of abilities in English than Cathy's. The two schools were, however, subject to the same IT policy and had similar facilities, including an MMLC that was available for booking on a voluntary basis.

Responding to questionnaire items eliciting ratings of self-confidence in using IT on a scale from 1 (not confident at all) to 5 (very confident), Penny gave herself a 2 at the beginning of the SeeIT course and a 3 at the end, while Cathy gave herself a 1 at the beginning and a 3 at the end. In interviews conducted 18 months after the end of the course, however, Penny described herself as being "on the high side of

3", while Cathy described herself as "between 2 and 3". Responding to a modified version of Russell's (1995) model of six stages of adaptation to new technology, Penny and Cathy both placed themselves at Stage 2 ("I am currently trying to learn the basics. I am often frustrated using computers. I lack confidence when using computers.") at the beginning of the course and at Stage 3 ("I am beginning to understand the process of using technology and can think of specific tasks in which it might be useful.") at the end of the course. Eighteen months later, however, Penny placed herself at Stage 4 ("I am gaining a sense of confidence in using the computer for specific tasks. I am starting to feel comfortable using the computer to enrich the curriculum."), while Cathy placed herself between Stages 3 and 4.

These self-ratings give some indication of the different trajectories of Penny's and Cathy's experiences of IT integration during and after the course. Penny began from a higher level of self-confidence and reported steady gains in confidence both during and after the course. Cathy, on the other hand, began from a lower level of self-confidence and reported a much higher gain during the course than she did in the 18 months that followed. As we will show in the case studies that follow, this reflects the fact that Penny experienced more success than Cathy in her efforts to apply what she had learned from the course.

Penny

As noted above, when Penny began the SeeIT course, she had been teaching English in her current school for three years. Before this she had taught English in New Zealand for around 20 years. At the beginning of the course, she reported that she had some experience of using *Word*, email and chat and that she had used the web to search for teaching materials, but not in the classroom. Penny also reported strong explicit beliefs about language teaching. In response to a request for information on her teaching background and IT experience at the beginning of the project, she provided a detailed CV, including a section in which she stated:

> I am skilled in the communicative approach to language and stress student involvement, participation and interaction....I am committed to the use of authentic materials in the classroom and aim to ensure all ESOL teaching is appropriate, relevant and focused on student needs and abilities.

In the 18 months following the course, Penny used a limited range of IT tools, focusing on the use of web searches to extend topics covered in the school textbook. She held a total of 12 MMLC lessons, divided into four topic-based units, in the first six months of the project. In the three lessons on the fourth topic of "Visiting Hong Kong", for example, the students worked in small groups to locate web sites on travel to Hong Kong, noted information on weather, hotels, restaurants, shopping, etc., and made *PowerPoint* presentations for the class. Penny usually prepared task sheets for MMLC lessons and generally appeared comfortable in the MMLC, giving clear instructions and guidelines, moving freely around the classroom, and frequently sitting down with students to help them with their work.

In the interview conducted 18 months after the SeeIT course, Penny reported that she was continuing to use IT regularly and suggested that IT was now well-integrated into her teaching as a whole:

> I don't want to move right away from what we usually do as we don't get time. And I'm focussing on the topic we are doing in class anyway, it's an extension of the vocabulary, giving them a chance to get used to what we've been using.

In addition to MMLC lessons, Penny had also begun to use a laptop computer in her regular classes, to give *PowerPoint* presentations on grammar points, and said that she wanted to use bulletin boards and *Hot Potatoes*, but she had not yet found the time to master them.

Penny seems to have assumed that the use of IT would add interest to the students' learning:

> Oh, because I've been thinking about IT when I'm designing the [teaching] program... and I think adding something to what they've been doing with the textbook. I think, it adds to the enjoyment, to the interest they have and their willingness to work.

Her familiarity with the Internet, however, appears to have been the main factor in her choice of web searches as a focus for units of work:

> It's not that difficult actually, once you get into it, you start thinking about it, I did the same thing, I thought I need somebody to give me a [software] program to use. After the IT course I realised I could actually do things with IT, that don't involve spending money...

Interestingly, Penny credited the SeeIT course for the realisation that she did not need to use specially designed software, but could instead build upon the limited IT knowledge and skills that she already had.

Penny also had a fairly clear idea of the role that the Internet could play in her students' learning as an extension of topics covered in the classroom. Following the fourth observed session, for example, in which the students searched for information on jobs, she commented:

> You can find so much more if you go online, a newspaper is, is limited ... and there are new jobs coming up online... I mean they are not really looking for jobs here, what they are eventually doing is practising using a very useful tool to find real information.

Her expectation also tended to be confirmed by the outcomes that she observed in the MMLC, which contributed to a fairly rapid growth in her confidence with IT. After the fifth observed class, for example, she commented:

> The use of technology definitely improves motivation and more successful pair work. Students were relaxed and appeared to enjoy the activity. Some of the students were developing some creative and imaginative presentations using a variety of well developed skills. Most students were on task and using initiative to create interesting presentations. ... Most students were positive about the activity – they were interested and enjoyed having the chance to be creative.

Penny was, nevertheless, confronted with obstacles, including technical break-downs, frustration with the layout of the MMLC, problems associated with the difficulty of the language that students found on the web and a lack of interest and collaboration from other teachers. She appears, however, to have overcome these obstacles relatively quickly. Her attitude to problem solving in the MMLC was reflected in a series of self-evaluative comments that she wrote at the end of the first six months, which included the following:

> Development of confidence in my use of MMLC and the use of IT with the students. From my observation of the videos, I felt there was a definite change in my ability to present the lesson to the students, to explain what I wanted from them and to actively participate in helping students in a positive way.

> Improved programme planning as I developed the different units. I think I was unrealistic in what I expected students to complete in a lesson at the beginning of the programme and at first very little was actually finished. I need to improve further on this and keep the units of work simple and short while remaining challenging for students.

These comments show that Penny viewed obstacles and failures as opportunities for learning and that she had a clear perception that she was making progress and of the nature of the progress that she was making. As we will see in the next section, Cathy appears to have experienced similar obstacles more intensely and was less successful in her attempts to overcome them.

Cathy

When Cathy began the SeeIT course, she had been teaching in the same school for 36 years. She taught English for eight years in the early part of her career, then switched to teaching Geography through the medium of English, returning to English teaching in 1998. At the beginning of the SeeIT course, Cathy reported that she used *Word* for school administrative work and for setting tests and examination papers and *Excel* for recording student grades, but had no experience of using IT in teaching. In response to the request for background information, Cathy provided only a brief summary of her working experience. In contrast to Penny, she did not articulate a coherent set of beliefs about teaching at any time during the project.

In the six months following the course, Cathy used the school MMLC on seven occasions, including five observed classes. On each occasion, she brought an IT technician to the class as an assistant. In contrast to Penny, Cathy used a variety of the tools presented during the SeeIT course, including a bulletin board, *D-Film*, web searches and voice recording. Eighteen months after the SeeIT course, Cathy reported that she had used the MMLC several times over the previous year for web-searches, student writing and poster design activities, voice recording and CALL activities based on a commercial package related to the school textbook. Summing up her experience over the 18 months, Cathy said:

> I can see certain results and I can see that I can carry out some of the lessons quite er ... quite well may be. However, it's sometimes... disorientating and sometimes frustrating. Disorientating ... I just have no idea what I'm going to do and what direction I should go. And the frustrating thing is I myself haven't got the expertise to use various kinds of software or in different ways.

What we see, then, is that although Cathy continued to use the MMLC and re-tained some enthusiasm, her use of IT was not exactly integrated into her teaching as a whole. She was still using the MMLC sporadically and for a variety of pur-poses, none of which was sustained over any period of time. IT activities had not become a regular part of the learning routine for her students and she acknowl-edged her own lack of direction in regard to IT.

Cathy's description of the first four classes, in which she used a bulletin board (E-class), and a web-based animation programme (*D-Film*), reveals a pattern in which she would try out tools and activities and then abandon them fairly quickly:

> I found that out of 42 students, about 10 of them really responded to E-class, the rest of them didn't really respond to it, so I tried D-film and I found that creating a dialogue in reported speech seems to be a good choice for the D-film, so I chose D-film for them to create dialogues, make the lesson more interesting, because I know that D-film is quite exciting for the students, but I can't use it many times, it's only once every now and then, so next time I shouldn't be using D-film again, they won't be interested in it anymore...

Cathy appears to have been particularly sensitive to any lack of interest displayed by the students and to her own feeling that the motivation aroused by the tools that she had chosen would not be durable.

Cathy reported four other obstacles in her IT work. These were similar to the obstacles Penny had experienced, but it seems that Cathy found them much more difficult to deal with. Firstly, she referred on a number of occasions to her lack of expertise. In the first observed class, for example, she noted the difficulty of managing the threads of discussion on the bulletin board:

> I'm not familiar with the E-class, some of them, when they started up a new topic for discussion, I have no idea of whether this is a new topic, or are they really commenting on what I posted up, I'm not familiar, and then the IT technician told me that these are the new topics they posted up.

Cathy is referring here to a familiar problem for first-time users of bulletin boards – that of posting and responding to messages in the appropriate thread. She also acknowledges that she was the source of the problem in this case and that it was the IT technician who solved it. Cathy experienced a number of technical or quasi-technical problems of this kind in her early classes, which she tended to attribute to her own lack of technical expertise.

Secondly, Cathy frequently referred to issues of classroom control. Describing one lesson, for example, she said:

> It was rather out of control (smiles) ..., I got stuck in the front and just couldn't walk around and supervise, I have to concentrate on how to control the discussion, so I can't provide them with any supervision, I was walking around and encouraged them to talk among themselves.

She was also concerned that students did not listen to her during MMLC classes:

> I found myself getting a bit annoyed when students were not responding to my questions. My tone started to change and I was rather blunt in my questions.

While the students were working on tasks, Cathy tended either to walk up and down the central aisle or stand at the back of the room, rarely looking at the students' screens unless they asked for assistance. In fact, she never seemed entirely comfortable in her interactions with the students in the observed MMLC lessons. She tended to address the students from the front of the class, at one point adopting what she called the "rather severe approach" of 'locking' the students' computers so that they would pay attention to her.

This loss of a sense of control appears to be linked to the third obstacle, concerned with the quality of the students' language work in the MMLC:

> I cannot control how they type, they keep ignoring me and keep typing phrases, short sentences, I have to keep scolding them, you can't do that, in a way ... free response is a good thing but I have no control of it.

In particular, she was concerned about their use of non-standard English, saying that she worried that "they are doing this as if they are doing ICQ". Lastly, Cathy felt that she was somewhat isolated in her efforts:

> I have limited knowledge of different websites, I myself am not very keen on surfing the Internet, old people like me. Every day at home after school, I arrive home at about 7 o'clock, after dinner I will also spend some time, I don't have much time, just check email, I seldom surf the Internet, so I'm still learning a lot of basic skills, and sometimes, as I said, I am sort of forcing myself try hard to find out more, and also I don't have a lot of connections with the colleagues at school, and I don't know what they are doing and they don't know what I'm doing.

We note that both Penny and Cathy saw the need for cooperation among colleagues and sensed a lack of collaboration among the teachers in their schools. Unlike Penny, who began to use the web frequently herself after the SeeIT course, Cathy also seems to have seen herself as being somewhat isolated from the community of those who "surf the Internet", which she attributed to her age. This may well have contributed to the intensity of the other difficulties she experienced.

Cathy also recognised that lack of preparation contributed to some of the difficulties she experienced. In the third observed class, she took up the researcher's suggestion to extend a recent classroom activity by asking the students to do a web search on the life of Einstein. The transcript of this class shows that this was a less than satisfying experience, however, with a good deal of confusion over what exactly was to be done and a rather indefinite conclusion. After the class, Cathy observed:

> As I did not tell them what I expected them to do afterwards and did not have questions for them to do, they did not have a clear idea of what to look for and just read. I realised my mistake in not telling students my expectations and not giving them enough guidelines.

Summing up her experiences after the first six months, Cathy also showed awareness of the need to prepare for MMLC classes in the longer term, commenting that she had "no real definite plan" for when to use the MMLC because "the lessons that we're using in the textbooks seldom need the involvement of computers". She added that "unless I really do a topic with them, at the moment, it seems that I'm using the MMLC for the sake of using it". As we saw earlier, a year later, Cathy still had this sense that her IT work lacked "direction".

Cathy showed no lack of awareness of the need to integrate her IT work with the curriculum as a whole. It appears, however, that the repeated and interacting obstacles that she experienced in the MMLC made the task of IT integration particularly difficult in practice. In the face of these multiple obstacles, she never-theless maintained a positive attitude in the final interview:

> Sometimes I have a feeling that I'm trying to force myself to use IT to teach English but it's the only chance that I can see whether I can, you know, put what I have learnt into practice and see whether students can gain something from using this. . .

Although Cathy appeared to have made relatively little progress in regard to IT integration eighteen months after the SeeIT course, she had not given up trying.

Discussion

Penny and Cathy both learned a great deal from their experiences during and after the SeeIT course. By the end of the eighteen months, however, Penny had clearly been the more successful of the two in terms of the goal of IT integration. While Penny appeared to have reached a zone of relative comfort in regard to IT integration, Cathy was still struggling with many of problems confronting her in the first weeks of the project. For teachers adopting IT relatively late in their careers, IT integration may involve deep processes of change at both the professional and personal levels. In this respect, Penny seems to have been far more open to change than Cathy was. It is important to recall, however, that both took on the task of IT integration willingly and enthusiastically and that they saw similar potential benefits for their students and themselves. While it is possible that Penny was simply more 'adaptable' than Cathy, we also want to consider two senses in which the obstacles to IT integration may, in fact, have been greater in Cathy's case.

Especially relevant here is the fact that educational policies in Hong Kong and elsewhere explicitly link IT integration to a shift towards more student-centred learning. Penny's data show that she already had strong explicit commitment to student-centred learning and a communicative approach to language teaching involving the use of authentic materials. Her decision to focus her MMLC lessons on web searches was informed by an understanding that materials on the web could be used as an authentic supplement to textbook materials. She also welcomed the opportunities for pair and group work and for interaction with students at their workstations that the MMLC provided. She was, in other words, able to fit IT into an existing framework of beliefs and practices. Although Cathy was not overtly resistant to the idea of student-centred learning, she was less experienced in it and her data show that she faced particular problems in working out how the MMLC could fit with her teaching style. Although she saw benefits in terms of student motivation, she found it difficult to see how IT-based activities could complement the curriculum and was not entirely convinced that the students were really learning

English in the MMLC. She also experienced difficulties in organising MMLC activities, which were related to a sense of loss of control in the classroom. In this sense, Penny and Cathy may have been engaged in very different processes of change. In Penny's case, IT integration seems to have been a matter of coming to grips with the ways in which IT could support clearly conceptualised pedagogical purposes. In Cathy's case, however, it was a matter both of coming to grips with IT *and* finding a pedagogical purpose for its use. IT integration may in this sense have been a far more complex task for Cathy and this complexity may well explain the feelings of 'disorientation' that she continued to feel 18 months after her training course had ended.

The fact that Cathy was engaged in a more complex process of change may well explain the greater subjective intensity with which she experienced technical problems. Cathy consistently connected these problems to her own lack of expertise with IT and tended to rely on an IT technician for their solution. In contrast, Penny adopted the view, consistent with principles of student-centred learning, that the students were the 'experts' on IT and that she could rely on their expertise in the MMLC. Also, in the early weeks of the project, Cathy's main difficulty seemed to lie in the sheer number of technical and logistical problems that she faced in the MMLC. Switching tools and activities in the face of these problems also meant that she regularly encountered both new problems and new contexts for old problems. Penny, on the other hand, seems to have experienced fewer problems in the early weeks, in part because she was able to recycle tools and activities with which she was becoming progressively more familiar. Why did Cathy not simply adopt some of the solutions to logistical problems that Penny adopted, such as the use of task-sheets for web searches? The answer may be that she fairly quickly found herself in a 'vicious circle' in which problems seemed to pile up on each other rather than diminish. It is possible that what Cathy lacked most in the early weeks of the project was simply a positive experience in the MMLC, which would have allowed her to recycle activities, reduce the number of problems she was facing, and begin to develop her skills using tools which she felt served a clear pedagogical purpose.

Conclusion

Earlier studies of pre-service training have concluded that a short course is likely to be insufficient preparation for teachers to successfully integrate IT into their classrooms. This chapter suggests that this is also likely to be true of in-service training, but in a somewhat different way. In-service teachers, especially those encountering IT late in their careers, may face the particular problem of integrating IT with deep-rooted beliefs about teaching and learning. Given that current thinking on IT integration tends to favour a student-centred approach over a teacher-centred approach, this problem may be more acute for some teachers than for others. Our case studies also suggest that the process of IT integration is one that involves the teacher as a whole person and tends to develop its own momentum within the unique context of the teacher's work.

This suggests to us that a more comprehensive professional development for IT integration should include not only technical skills and knowledge, but also strategies for technology-enhanced teaching and classroom management. It should also involve discussion of beliefs about teaching and learning and the ped- agogical implications of IT integration. In addition, active steps may need to be taken to help teachers gain positive experiences in the process of transition to new modes of teaching with IT and to assist them to explore and understand the im- plications of technological innovation for their own beliefs and practices. Further research is clearly needed, however, to examine how the process of IT integration works for teachers at different stages of their careers. This chapter suggests that relationships between the adoption of IT and teachers' pedagogical knowledge, beliefs and practices will be one important focus in such research.

References

Benson, P. (2004). Autonomy and information technology in the educational discourse of the information age. In C. Davison (Ed.), *Information Technology and Innovation in Language Education* (pp. 173–192). Hong Kong: Hong Kong University Press.

Bullock, D. B. (2004). Moving from theory to practice: An examination of the factors that preservice teachers encounter as they attempt to gain experience teaching with technology during field placement exercises. *Journal of Technology and Teacher Education, 12* (2), 211–237.

Egbert, J., Paulus, T. M., & Nakamichi, Y. (2002). The impact of CALL instruction on classroom computer use: A foundation for rethinking technology in teacher education. *Language Learning & Technology, 6* (3), 108–126.

Ertmer, P. A. (1999). Addressing first- and second-order barriers to change: Strategies for technology integration. *Education Technology Research and Development, 47* (4), 47–61.

Franklin, T., Turner, S., Kariuki, M., & Duran, M. (2002). Mentoring overcomes barriers to technology integration. *Journal of Computing in Teacher Education, 18* (1), 26–31.

Lam, Y. (2000). Technophilia vs. technophobia: A preliminary look at why second language teachers do or do not use technology in their classrooms. *The Canadian Modern Language Review, 56* (3), 389–420.

Meskill, C., Mossop, J., DiAngelo, S., & Pasquale, R. K. (2002). Expert and novice teachers talking technology: Precepts, concepts, and misconcepts. *Language Learning & Technology, 6* (3), 46–57.

Mitchem, K., Wells, D. L., & Wells, J. G. (2003). Effective integration of instructional techno- logies (IT): Evaluating professional development and instructional change. *Journal of Technology and Teacher Education, 11* (3), 397–414.

Parr, J. (1999). Extending educational computing: A case of extensive teacher development and support. *Journal of Research on Computing in Education, 31* (3), 280–291.

Pope, M., Hare, D., & Howard, E. (2002). Technology integration: Closing the gap between what preservice teachers are taught to do and what they can do. *Journal of Technology and Teacher Education, 10* (2), 191–203.

Russell, A. L. (1995). Stages in learning new technology. *Computers in Education, 25* (4), 173–178.

Strehle, E. L., Whatley, A., Kurz, K. A., & Hausfather, S. J. (2001). Narratives of collaboration: Inquiring into technology integration in teacher education. *Journal of Technology and Teacher Education, 10* (1), 27–47.

Strudler, N. & Wetzel, K. (1999). Lessons from exemplary colleges of education: Factors affecting technology integration in preservice programs. *Education Technology Research and Development, 47* (4), 63–81.

Swan, K., Holmes, A., Vargas, J. D., Jennings, S., Meier, E., & Rubenfeld, L. (2002). Situated professional development and technology integration: The Capital Area Technology and Inquiry in Education (CATIE) program. *Journal of Technology and Teacher Education, 10* (2), 169–190.

Ward, J. R., West, L. S., & Isaak, T. J. (2002). Mentoring: A strategy for change in teacher technology education. *Journal of Technology and Teacher Education, 10* (4), 553–569.

Willis, E. M. & de Montes, L. S. (2002). Does requiring a technology course in preservice teacher education affect student teachers' technology use in the classroom? *Journal of Computing in Teacher Education, 18* (3), 76–80.

Preface to

Teacher preparation for online language instruction

Increasingly, we are seeing the development of language courses that are conducted either partly or wholly online. How do we prepare today's classroom teachers for the transition to the effective use of both the online environment and dedicated online applications and content? In an institutional environment, what kinds of training and support need to be in place for the migration of parts or all of an existing course to the online setting? In this chapter Christopher Jones and Bonnie Youngs describe a hybrid foreign language course developed at Carnegie Mellon University containing both face-to-face and online elements, though with an emphasis on the latter. The focus, however, is not on the course but on the challenges facing the developers in preparing the teachers who implemented it. The first part of the chapter reviews three interdependent areas that have been identified as keys to success in online teaching and learning: socialization to the online environment to build both student-teacher and student-student relationships, stimulation of active participation, and collaboration. The authors go on to describe the Language Online project, initially developed to replace "self-paced" courses at Carnegie Mellon that made limited use of technology. Their discussion includes lessons learned from early implementations, for example, recognizing differences between regular and adjunct instructors and between those with stable broadband connections as opposed to those dialing in to the campus system from off site. Excerpts from case studies of four French and Spanish instructors give further insight into the implementation and training process as well as individual differences in teacher adjustment to this new environment. In addition to the analysis offered in the chapter, Jones and Youngs provide links to training checklists and teacher questionnaires that can be adapted by others engaged in making the move to online language instruction.

Teacher preparation for online language instruction

Christopher M. Jones and Bonnie L. Youngs
Carnegie Mellon University, USA

Introduction

Though literature in the area of general online instruction is now widely available, the preparation required of teachers for an online language instructional environment is little understood. The multiple definitions of "online" are part of the issue, in that the instruction described varies from enhancements of classroom teaching, to hybrid courses (mixed online and face-to-face), to fully Internet-based distance teaching, though this last is still relatively uncommon for languages. The technologies in use change annually, at the very least, and often require new learning from instructors and students. Certain technologies imply new methodologies; others require no more than a transfer of an existing methodology into a new medium.

This chapter combines an overview of the issues involved in preparing teachers to teach languages online with a report and case studies based on the Language Online project at Carnegie Mellon University in Pittsburgh, Pennsylvania. Language Online is a grant-funded project to deliver basic French and Spanish language instruction via the Web.

Teacher preparation in CALL

Evidence of teacher preparation for teaching online, distance, or hybrid language courses is difficult to find in the United States, to the point where NCATE (The National Council for Accreditation of Teacher Education) has specifically indicated that technology methodology training for K-12 foreign language teacher candidates needs to be added to their preparation. Indeed, for a study in which 19 countries responded to a questionnaire on technology use to enhance language learning, one universally cited success factor was rigorous teacher education in the forms of the integration of language and content learning, communicative teaching methods, and a focus on language learning strategies (Pufahl, Rhodes, & Christian 2001:3).

As indicated above, many countries are already prioritizing technology in teacher training programs, and European teacher trainers advocate a mandatory set of teacher education standards by describing a first recommended benchmark for a European infrastructure of language teacher training for technology that would "...compare modes of delivery and access, the structures of training, and its content. It also needs to set out information on pedagogic matters, methodology, and theoretical perspectives in second language teaching and learning" (Grenfell, Kelly, & Jones 2003:211). In addition, the authors note that benchmark number 17 urges the use of ICT (Information and Communications Technologies) approaches for interactive use with pupils in the classroom, and while agreeing that much good practice in teacher education training programs exists, there is no consistency (Grenfell et al. 2003:240).

Just as Europeans see a need for improved teacher education in technology, Americans could improve in this field. Spector and de la Teja note: "It is...quite clear that our capacity to make effective use of information technology in educational settings is impaired by inadequate preparation of teachers..." and furthermore that changes in information technology mean that "...the development of competencies for online teachers [is] a continuous process and demands continuing professional preparation and training for online teachers" (2001:4). Glatz states that

> [i]n addition to the traditional methodology course, [a] second course exploring the critical nature of the mediated social context of multi-media, perhaps even specific to one language of instruction, would then also be required, one in which students started creating MBC (Multi-media-based content) and TELL (Technology-enhanced language learning) materials (2001:232).

Teacher education in technology is not optional, due to the obvious differences between traditional language teaching and online teaching. Issues such as course design, how the content is delivered, and how the instructor interacts with the students (Meyen, Lian, & Tangen 1997:168), as well as redesigning teaching strategies and learning activities, especially where visual cues are absent in text-based environments (Harasim 1987:119, 131) all must play a major role in teacher education programs. Moreover, the

> ...online instructor does not have the advantage of being able to make changes in lectures, resources, or even assignments on a routine basis, as might occur in traditional instruction...Revisions are possible, but difficult and time-consuming.
>
> (Meyen et al.:168)

In many delivery systems, even a basic requirement like writing class plans, therefore, can be a major obstacle to teaching well, if a teacher cannot learn to prepare well in advance for possible glitches in online delivery.

Key target areas for teacher training

There is agreement among researchers that key areas need to be addressed by teachers learning to use technology in their online environments: socialization, active participation, and collaboration (cf. Harasim 1987; Hiltz 1988; Carlson 1997; Glatz 2001; Grenfell, Kelly, & Jones 2003). This is undoubtedly a novel aspect of online instruction: combining pedagogical goals with a course's technological underpinnings.

Creating socialization is an important skill for teachers to learn in the online arena (Carlson 1997; Meyen et al. 1997). Initial contact between teacher and students is vital (Carlson 1997:6). Especially with respect to an online course, Meyen et al. observe that

> ...online instruction is a hybrid approach to distance education that incorporates many of the features of independent study with the structure of an organized class. That is, students have classmates to interact with, and communication with the instructor is an integral part of online instruction (171).

Group activities can also foster socialization (cf. Harasim 1987; Hiltz 1988; Mason 1988; Carlson 1997; Li 1999; Glatz 2001). Teachers can be taught how to use CMC (computer-mediated communication) as it deals directly with two issues related to translating traditional pedagogical methodology to a technology-rich learning environment, thereby increasing socialization: by facilitating and monitoring interactions with students, and by facilitating and monitoring interactions between students (Glatz: 230). Moreover, the immediate feedback and the stimulation provided through CMC can provide models of language use from student to student, and perhaps help maintain a continued interest in the subject matter and learning (Glatz: 224, 230).

Stimulating active participation by all students can be one major pathway to success in an online course (Hiltz 1988; Carlson 1997). Hiltz states that

> [t]echniques related to success in the Virtual Classroom have to do with stimulating a form of participation which is very difficult within the traditional classroom: the active engagement and participation of all students in a collaborative learning community... [T]hat communication is asynchronous...opens up new possibilities for enabling all students to actively participate, at their own pace, in dealing with the concepts, skills, and ideas in a course (27).

Carlson supports this idea by observing that "...[I]n an online class, students have to participate to stay in the class; passive students must quickly become active students to succeed in an online class" (7). Glatz describes small group discussions in a forum as "...the natural interaction of people at a social gathering" (231). This type of natural interaction, promoted by a teacher educated in technology use, could stimulate successful active participation.

Collaboration is the third key area of successful online technology use, and it can be improved via the socialization techniques described above and through active participation by as many students in the course as possible. Teachers collaborate with students regarding course materials, technology use and difficulties, and course requirements, in addition to posting comments related to student contributions in chat or group forums. Collaboration between and among students in chats, posting responses to each other's comments, and in group projects will contribute to socialization and participation, as all three areas are necessarily interrelated and interdependent.

Online language learning at Carnegie Mellon

Language Online (LOL) was initiated in 1999 with the award of a grant from the Mellon Foundation toward the costs of creating online courses in basic French and Spanish. Four-semester sequences were created and written with the participation of over fifty faculty, staff and consultants, and by 2005 had been in regular rotation for three years. The courses have been extensively evaluated (Chenoweth & Murday 2003; Chenoweth, Jones, & Tucker 2006) and appear to fall within the targeted zone of "no significant difference" in terms of both student achievement and student and instructor satisfaction when compared with conventional classroom instruction. Two doctoral dissertations have also been completed based on data collected on LOL students (Murday 2004; Ushida 2004). A major upgrade to the French course is scheduled for fall 2006, in the context of the Hewlett-funded Open Learning Initiative as well as the new NSF-funded Pittsburgh Science of Learning Center. In this next round we hope to integrate significant student tracking and modeling in a proprietary course management system, cognitively informed tutorials, enhanced media content, and research-driven iterative development.

The LOL courses were intended to solve a general education problem of scheduling conflicts for students in studio and lab-intensive majors who found it almost impossible to register for beginning language courses meeting four times per week. In the process the new courses altered the focus of the department in the domain of technology-enhanced learning from the computer as a "teaching machine" (Fleming & Hiple 2004: 70) to distributed or web-delivered instruction.

With this change, technology became inseparable from the course, as opposed to previous partial or modular (and often optional) integration. Stand-alone websites with JavaScript enhancements and *Hot Potatoes* exercises are used for the delivery of course materials and practice, while testing and communication for both instructional and administrative purposes occurs through *Blackboard*. Face-to-face interaction continues to be part of the course delivery through a single weekly class meeting and flexibly scheduled one-on-one meetings with the instructor and a language assistant. Online modular work plans that can be easily altered by individual instructors allow for customizing of the learning sequence according to instructor preference. From the instructor's point of view, the primary changes in teaching the new courses were an altered definition of the instructor's role and technology training that could no longer be avoided without consequences.

Early history of LOL teacher preparation

Noting the trends regarding teacher preparation, teacher education courses, and the needs that teachers have to teach well with technology, it is obvious that training at a professional level, scattered until now, is increasingly recognized as vital to the success of students in an online language course. At Carnegie Mellon University, we have attempted to base online instructor training on preferred instructional strategies with an eye toward student learning styles. This has not been by any means a seamless process.

Several factors made the first offerings of the online courses the most difficult of all. Since LOL courses took the place of "self-paced" courses in French and Spanish, courses which had few technical enhancements and relied primarily on assignments done individually and submitted in hard copy for correction, the transition to managing an online course proved to be daunting for many of the instructors primarily used to dealing with a traditionally organized self-paced course. The first instructors were the least prepared and technically adept, and at the same time the LOL courses were in a beta state with imperfections and technical failings, leading to a high level of frustration in many cases.

The initial training sequence for instructors was not substantially different from what it is today: mailings of a pre-semester checklist of preparatory steps and necessary skills,[1] followed by one or more workshops to work through aspects of course preparation which had not been mastered. In the case of adjuncts who had other full-time jobs or were only marginally available for out-of-class training, this system was not successful. In one notable case, a valued instructor missed all the training and was hesitant to ask for help with the result that important online course components were never used. Another adjunct needed to dial in long-distance through a telephone modem to access *Blackboard* and course materials. The page loading was glacial in speed, and the department needed to make a one-time concession to pay the substantial phone bill. Difficulties of this nature were unforeseen, but in retrospect were normal changes and to be expected when instituting an online program of this scope.

The technological reputation of Carnegie Mellon University can lead to the assumption that technological literacy is universal throughout the university community. This assumption is often unfounded for students, and even more frequently for instructors. One difference from the first offerings of these courses is that instructors who are judged to have little technical background are not offered teaching assignments in LOL. Even those with some technical experience make a substantial effort to become comfortable with the various technologies which make up the course underpinnings. A questionnaire was originally proposed to determine an individual's technological capabilities, but a conversation between the Coordinator and a potential instructor was found to be sufficient (see the NETS and Michael Coughlin sites for further information on technological literacy).

An additional problem arises with instructors who have gone through one training sequence, mastered several technologies, then assume that nothing will have changed in the technical environment since the last course offering and skip the training sessions. A major example of this occurred when LOL changed from an early use of *WebCT* to the institutionally-supported *Blackboard*. Virtually every associated technology had a different look-and-feel, while the testing environment had significant differences that made porting the tests from one management system to the other a major adventure.

Beyond technical training, meetings of online instructors to discuss pedagogical issues have been unfailingly fruitful. Issues such as how to structure chat sessions (or not), the number of participants in such sessions, and the need for consistent and timely feedback on everything from online tests to submission of writing assignments, are among those discussed in this context. These discussions have the advantage of being peer-driven, rather than top-down (as in the technical training), and often create lines of communication that remain useful throughout the online teaching experience. Even these must be carefully dosed, however, so as not to overburden instructors; training at the beginning and a group wrap-up at the end of a semester seem to be more than adequate. Online teaching is anything but a free ride: our predictions that instructional time requirements would *not* be reduced in an online context have proven to be correct (see Chenoweth, Jones, and Tucker (2006) for this and other summative research findings on LOL).

Case studies: Four online instructors

Training is an important aspect of learning how to teach online courses. More crucial, however, is beginning the process of teacher training with instructors who have been grounded in sound pedagogy and methodological practices. The case studies described below may help to illuminate instructors' perceptions of the differences between the methodologies required for the two environments.

In spring 2003, four limited case studies were done on four online instructors. The case studies involved the observation of one class, an electronic questionnaire,[2] and a follow-up interview based on the questionnaire. Three of the instructors had taught an online course more than once; one instructor was new to the online environment. The instructors will be designated as FR2 and SP2 (second semester French and Spanish respectively), FR4 and SP4 (fourth semester French and Spanish respectively). The impetus for the study was a comment made by the SP2 instructor during a department meeting. Even though this instructor is an excellent instructor (as are the other three instructors in this project), having won a graduate student teaching award at Carnegie Mellon, she reported having difficulty handling the material in her online course, stating that she did not know how to create the same atmosphere for learning and speaking as she was able to in her traditional courses. For the purposes of this study, in addition to the instruments noted above, observations were done on the SP2 instructor's two traditional SP2 classes. It is important to note that for both French and Spanish, the content of the online courses is different from that of the traditional courses.

The questionnaire was written to highlight the SP2 instructor's comments and insecurities. The interest in the study stemmed from two very distinct points of view: that of the FR2 instructor's perspective that teaching the online course is similar to teaching her traditional courses as opposed to the SP2 instructor's opinion that the two environments are not at all similar. The research's focus was to understand how these instructors approached the management of their online courses, most specifically as related to the handling of the one hour weekly class, and with respect to all possible combinations (student-student, teacher-student, student-teacher) in the second language acquisition research areas of interaction, community building, and feedback.

Prioritization becomes a major issue in the hybrid sections, as the need to choose which topics to practice or review in class is primary. The SP2 instructor found that she spent more time scaffolding her students' oral abilities, a need she found much less evident in her traditional sections, and was therefore unable to focus on exploring and expanding the content of the online course via oral exercises. She felt too that one of her priorities in the online class hour was to explain the Spanish language to the students in a much more concrete manner than in the "exploratory" mode that she favored in the traditional classes. This led to her speaking Spanish much more slowly, thus for her, inauthentically, and using more English than was her norm.

One of the central interview questions posed was to ask the instructors what they would teach new online instructors. There were no strong themes to the replies, although the issue of teaching online instructors how to use and adapt the technical aspects of the course was certainly essential. Online instructors need to feel able to change the course to suit their personalities and the needs of their students; lack of this ability can lead to frustration for the instructor. This major aspect was noted by Meyen et al. (1997): online instructors must feel in control of the teaching and learning situation. Moreover, our online instructors indicated that the students need to be trained in the technical aspects of the course as well, in order to limit frustration all around: for the instructors when students do not accomplish their tasks, and for the students when they do not know how to accomplish their tasks.

During the electronic and face-to-face interviews of the methodology study, the key areas of socialization, active participation, and collaboration, as discussed above, were also in evidence. Getting to know the students, and in fact, the ability to get to know students more easily in the online context, became a theme throughout the responses. Instructors felt that it was easier, given the smaller classes but also the intimacy of one on one conversations with the students, to know students and understand who they were as individuals. This would lead, as discussed in the literature review, to increased socialization between the students and teacher, but also perhaps to increased active participation as the students felt more comfortable in the online learning environment. Knowing one's students can also create a more intimate classroom atmosphere, perhaps leading in turn to a more familiar environment which would enable the students to feel comfortable in getting to know each other, to socialize, and to participate in online activities such as chat in a more personal manner.

The methodological research issues of interaction, community, and feedback then, appear to relate directly to the discussion at hand. Collaboration and community, as the instructors felt a more direct connection with their online students, seem to be established by the instructor in a successful online context. The FR2 instructor noted that the online course design fosters "...community by group and paired activities both in and outside the classroom... it may be the need to keep in touch by a variety of means that leads to an increased sense of community..." (Youngs 2004). This effect of community would create a desired participation in collaborative activities, and perhaps more collaboration as exercises were assigned to be done in an online environment, as in chat. In fact, even the SP2 instructor noted that her online students found it difficult to change chat buddies, as the students had developed relationships that they felt loath to relinquish.

Interaction and feedback are related to the issue of active participation. As students feel more in tune with the class and with their classmates, interaction becomes more open and feedback between and among students, and between the instructor and the students, becomes facilitated. The FR4 instructor in this research project found teacher-student interaction to be much more personal in the online format, and there was increased interaction between the SP2 instructor and her students as she felt more able to get to know her online students. Interaction was also a factor in the community building of the SP4's online classroom as her students would bring their chat topics to class and laugh about their chat conversations, continuing the discussion in the online class hour. This improved interaction, as students must participate in the class hour and in online activities in order to succeed, echoes the ideas presented by Carlson (1997) and Glatz (2001). Feedback therefore plays a major role, as collaborative activities, active participation, interaction, and community all lead to increased and hopefully improved feedback. Feedback must take place electronically as class time is limited, but the large amount of feedback in the form of questions during chat (student-student), in the personal time with the language assistant and the instructor (teacher-student, student-teacher), in addition to class time, can increase the sense that the student is indeed part of a larger group, and not alone in the technological wilderness of an online course.

The evolution of pedagogical practice in Language Online

The literature review and case studies above highlight common issues confronted by online instructors, including the need for socialization of the students (often referred to as building a community of learners), and fostering active participation and collaboration. Related questions include the need and methods for furnishing feedback to learners and the potential for individualization in a technology-enhanced environment. We will discuss each of these items as they apply to the concrete context of LOL, which aspects of course design were intended to address each issue, which teacher behaviors were encouraged in each case, and what the near-term evolution is likely to be in each of these aspects of the online arena.

Building a community of learners

As in classroom-based instruction, building community in a large group of learners by a single instructor is also a concern in an online context. Reduction in contact hours, however, could lead to the alienation of individuals from a sense of a collective endeavor, thus resulting in high dropout rates due to this lack of a sense of community and the cohesion that such a sense can bring to the class

(Galusha 2004). Some sections of LOL have addressed this issue by requiring student homepages within *Blackboard*. The unsatisfying nature of this technology within *Blackboard*, though, coupled with hesitancy on the part of instructors, has meant that the webpage option is not often exploited. There is also little indication that other students are intrinsically interested in the homepages of their classmates.

Other collaborative aspects, including asynchronous response to classmates' postings on discussion boards and synchronous chat in pairs or small groups with rotating partners, are more effective, in that they involve creative and active language use, although there is no single instructional design concept that should be imposed on learning to teach online courses. There are, however, examples of possible modes of interaction – in pairs or small groups, using role plays, prepared discussion topics, or free discussion – which instructors can experiment with and adapt. If there are class meetings, for example the LOL weekly classes, class time should be student-centered and minimally teacher-centered to maximize exposure of students to each other and deepen the sense of community. Though this format is emphasized during instructor meetings, it is clear that certain instructors have developed a teacher-centered methodology that has relatively serious consequences in the LOL context.

Fostering active participation

Many (if not most) college students live in an information continuum where communication via messaging and voice is nearly always available, through cell phones or computers. For older generations of instructors, this style of "active" participation in an electronic environment is difficult to sustain. Nevertheless, a high priority must be placed on prompt response by the instructor to e-mail queries, acknowledgement of electronic submissions, and the posting of up-to-date evaluations. Prompt response is vital to the success of any language course, but most especially to one without continued access to an instructor, as in a traditional classroom. Not maintaining a high level of contact with online students sometimes leads to a decrease in their active participation in the course. Additionally, students must be committed to taking class and meeting preparation seriously or the flow of interactive language during contact hours will be limited or wasted in remedial study or drill.

The current state of LOL courseware is such that it is not possible for the instructor to verify that the student has done the necessary preparation other than through an in-class quiz that wastes precious time for interaction. The new version of the course under preparation will remedy this problem by being fully "instrumented," i.e. capable of collecting individualized data on each student's use of the materials, so that it will be feasible for instructors to verify student preparation and offer appropriate responses to foster full participation by all students. This is an aspect of online instruction that cannot be duplicated using traditional materials. It is critical, therefore, that instructors feel comfortable with the tools supplied to examine this information in order to facilitate their use of student participation data.

Innovation in collaborative technologies

As mentioned in the above section, students are more attuned to the social use of communication technologies than are instructors. In LOL training, the primary focus has been to introduce *Blackboard*'s chat and discussion forum components and to make instructors aware of the key to successful instruction using those components. The use of chat, especially, has now been documented as having communicative importance (Blake 2000; Toyoda & Harrison 2003). As mentioned above, in LOL, instructor intuition as well as student preference and feedback have guided the use of these technologies, and have been reflected in the structuring, or not, of these interactions. The central training element appears to be the liberating effect of impressing upon instructors that there is not a single correct way of exploiting the potential of the medium; we tell them rather that any assignment that stimulates a sufficient volume of targeted student discourse is valid.

It appears clear that subsequent course designs will integrate audio conferencing, either synchronous (Hampel & Hauck 2004) or asynchronous (*Wimba*). Instructors who have let the email, messaging and cell phone revolutions pass them by may well have difficulty making instructional use of paired and group audio-conferencing. For language-based courses, the added benefit of shared whiteboard or browser technologies is less obvious and is likely to remain the exception in course design and instructional practice.

Individualization for students and instructors

The notion that computer-based learning intrinsically allows for individualization of the amount of input and practice for students is a long-standing one. Inherent in this notion are assumptions that students will naturally perfect areas of weakness through additional listening, study, repetition of exercises to mastery, and so forth. Research indicating that such student behavior is the norm has yet to be done; contrary indications that students will tend to avoid areas of weakness are abundant. Thus students who are weak in oral production tend to speak less, those with easy fluency may ignore grammatical correctness, whereas those who are fixated on grammar tend to be unable or unwilling to express themselves authentically in either written or oral form.

Analysis and exploitation of such individual profiles are rarely done. The current version of the course, while offering plentiful opportunities for practice, listening, and production, records almost no student interactions with the exception of exams, which are of marginal instructional use. As mentioned above, the LOL courses within the year will have the capacity to offer sufficient data to instructors on student performance to allow for very targeted individual meetings and an increased understanding of actual time-on-task. This latter is critical when an instructor needs to decide whether an individual student has a legitimate deficiency in listening comprehension, or a more generalized "homework" deficiency.

Learning styles can also be a critical element of online instructor training. The notion of multiple intelligences, that individuals learn better via different methods, is essential, as online learning takes the form of fixed modes of input: listening, reading, and writing, and mostly in an individual mode. If a student prefers group learning situations, hands-on in the sense of performing and doing or in the sense of speaking, an online course might not be the best option. On the other hand, elements of the online course can be supplemented with the weekly class hour, and students who feel a great need for socialization can profit from the hybrid approach via the personal interviews with the language assistant and the instructor, and to a lesser degree, the online chats with classmates. In any scenario, an instructor who intends to teach online must be aware or made aware through training that different student personalities and learning styles must be accommodated to the greatest extent possible in order to create a successful learning environment for all members of the class. This may only mean offering extra chat hours, or suggesting additional practice exercises, depending on the student. The improved data collection mentioned above will allow an increased focus on learning styles in that certain components of the course can serve as diagnostic tools pointing toward specific learning sequences based on learning style. This is in the future, however. At the moment, instructors must use traditional means to identify students with marked differences.

The concept that the instructor can change the course of instruction according to his or her preferences is one that has already been implemented. As mentioned above, a work-plan generator allows the instructor to choose from content pages in the course, re-order them at will, and integrate external resources from the Internet, presenting a links sequence to the student which becomes an alternate gateway to the course. While instructors are given training in using this tool, our feeling is that its use will increase as instructors gain experience and confidence in this form of teaching and its associated tool set.

Conclusion

While training for online language teaching is in the early stages of development, the need for it is not likely to diminish. Human intervention and guidance in online language instruction will be a constant for the foreseeable future, even with the accelerated technological innovation that has characterized the last few decades. The major methodologies for language instruction in this new environment will continue to be a mix of those which characterize effective classroom teachers with others that build on the potential for flexible and responsive learning communities in cyberspace. Concurrently, courseware will increasingly exhibit adaptive characteristics reflective of student learning styles.

The time of thinking of technology as "just another tool" and thinking that "students will adapt" to an online environment has passed, as courses become entirely dependent on technology for their delivery. Elements of good teaching practice relating to interaction, community and feedback can often be transposed seamlessly to the new environment, but important differences in methodological potential are emerging through the combination of what we have called the societal information continuum and technology-enabled tracking and modeling of student performance and participation in online courses. Maintaining currency with these developments is a new demand on language instructors, and negative characteristics of the information society, including stress or frustration relating to rapid change, may become more common unless training finds a more permanent place in both initial and continuing teacher education.

Notes

1. The checklist is available at http://ml.hss.cmu.edu/facpages/cjones/TrainingChecklist.pdf.

2. The questionnaire is available at http://ml.hss.cmu.edu/facpages/cjones/TeacherQuestionnaire.pdf.

References

Blake, R. (2000). Computer-mediated communication: A window on Spanish interlanguage. *Language Learning & Technology, 4* (1), 120–136.

Carlson, R. (1997). Educating online: Creating the virtual classroom community. ERIC ED 412 934.

Chenoweth, N. A. & Murday, K. (2003). Measuring student learning in an online French course. *CALICO Journal, 20* (2), 285–314.

Chenoweth, N. A., Jones, C. M., & Tucker, G. R. (2006). Language Online: Principles of design and methods of assessment. In R. Donaldson & M. Haggstrom (Eds.), *Changing Language Education Through CALL*. London: Routledge.

Coughlin, M. (2004). Facilitating online learning. Available at http://users.chariot.net.au/~michaelc/olfac.html.

Fleming, S. & Hiple, D. (2004). Distance education to distributed learning: Multiple formats and technologies in language instruction. *CALICO Journal, 22* (1), 63–82.

Galusha, J. M. (2004). Barriers to learning in distance education. Available at http://www.infrastruction.com/barriers.htm.

Glatz, L. F. (2001). Technology in language teacher training: The new challenges of multimedia based content, technology-enhanced language learning, and computer-mediated communication. In Gerd Bräuer (Ed.), *Pedagogy of Language Learning in Higher Education. Advances in Foreign and Second Language Learning*, Vol. 2 (pp. 221–36). Westport, CT: Ablex.

Grenfell, M., Kelly, M., & Jones, D. (2003). *The European Language Teacher: Recent trends and future developments in teacher education*. Bern: Peter Lang.

Harasim, L. (1987). Teaching and learning on-line: Issues in computer-mediated graduate courses. *Canadian Journal of Educational Communication, 16* (2), 117–135.

Hampel, R. & Hauck, M. (2004). Towards an effective use of audio conferencing in distance language courses. *Language Learning & Technology, 8* (1), 66–82.

Hiltz, S. R. (1988). *Teaching in a Virtual Classroom. A Virtual Classroom on EIES: Final evaluation report*, Vol. 2. ERIC ED 315 039.

Li, L. (1999). The Delivery of Foreign Language Instruction via the Internet: A survey of online foreign language instructor and program providers. MA thesis, Sonoma State University.

Mason, R. (1988). Computer conferencing: A contribution to self-directed learning. *British Journal of Educational Technology, 19* (1), 28–41.

Meyen, E. L., Lian, C. H. T., & Tangen, P. (1997). Teaching online courses. *Focus on Autism and Other Developmental Disabilities, 12* (3), 161–174.

Murday, K. (2004). Individual Differences and Student Adaptation to Online Language Learning. PhD dissertation, Carnegie Mellon University.

NETS (National Educational Technology Standards). Available at http://cnets.iste.org/teachers/t_stands.html.

Pufahl, I., Rhodes, N. C., & Christian, D. (2001). What we can learn from foreign language teaching in other countries. ERIC ED 456 671.

Spector, M. J. & de la Teja, I. (2001). Competencies for online teaching. ERIC ED 456 841.

Toyoda, E. & Harrison, R. (2002). Categorization of text chat communication between learners and native speakers of Japanese. *Language Learning & Technology, 6* (1), 82–99.

Ushida, E. (2003). The Role of Students' Attitudes and Motivation in Online Language Courses. PhD dissertation, Carnegie Mellon University.

Wimba. Audio b-boards and other educational products. Available at http://www.horizonwimba.com.

Youngs, B. (2004). Methodological issues in online courses. Paper presented at CALICO Symposium. Carnegie Mellon University.

PART V

Alternatives to formal CALL training

Preface to

Expert-novice teacher mentoring in language learning technology

A number of authors in this book address the critical issue of bridging the gap between the knowledge and skills that the learners seem able to acquire in formal CALL courses in a university or college, and the knowledge and skills they actually need in everyday teaching in the classroom. Clearly the two contexts are very different. In the university setting, with carefully organized classes and an effective teacher, students can be helped through the problems they encounter. In many ways the students are protected from some of the harsher realities of regular classroom teaching. In contrast, in the school situation, teachers are required to operate within a complex environment of opportunities and constraints. Constraints may include low levels of access to new technology and support, time pressures, diverse proficiency levels within the class, technical problems and so forth. Many of these constraints are context bound so they are difficult to predict, especially when viewed from the perspective of the relatively "still waters" of the teacher education course. In this chapter, in a three year project, Carla Meskill and her colleagues present an innovative approach to bridge the gap for pre-service teachers in CALL. It centers upon a very carefully devised mentoring plan which links more experienced educators – doctoral students and in-service teachers – with preservice teachers. Exposure to real teaching situations, collaborative activities, and the creation of a learning community are emphasized in the approach taken. The dynamics and effectiveness of expert-novice mentoring provide the focus of the research study and reflections on the experience from members of each of the three groups involved are reported.

Expert-novice teacher mentoring in language learning technology

Carla Meskill, Natasha Anthony, Shannon Hilliker-VanStrander,
Chi-Hua Tseng, and Jieun You
University at Albany, USA[1]

Perspective

Becoming a teacher means being a learner. Likewise, to teach is to learn. To be a learner means to produce new knowledge in interaction with the world, especially within the communities of practice where the target learning/expertise resides. From this perspective, effective learning occurs when participation begins at the periphery of these contexts and gradually increases until there is full engagement and co-participation with those more knowledgeable within the target context (Lave & Wenger 1991; Samaras & Gismondi 1998). The design of the Technology Assisted Language Learning (TALL) ESOL teacher professional development project was based on the notion that to be a learner one needs to apprentice in real contexts and be guided to recognize effective practices (Vygotsky 1978). It was also understood that practices are dynamic, socially constructed and are changed by direct contact and experience. When a pre-service teacher is included and apprenticed in a more experienced teacher's classroom, for example, the dynamic interaction of new, old, and evolving knowledge can be powerful (Grove, Strudler, & Odell 2004).

In terms of instructional technologies, recent studies in teacher education have shown that, although a technology-specific course can develop basic computer skills, it does not prepare educators to integrate technology into everyday teaching and learning in ways that are supportive of learning (Abdal-Haqq 1995; Cuban 2001; Dunn & Ridgway 1991; Karchmer 2001; Lam 2000; Meskill, Mossop, DiAngelo, & Pasquale 2002; Mullen 2001). Effective integration after all is a complex, situated activity. What educators need to know when it comes to effective integration is in large part developed experientially in real institutional contexts. For these reasons, mentoring has been found to be a viable approach to teacher education in technologies (Kagan 1992; Kariuki, Franklin, & Duran 2001; MacArthur, Pilato, Kercher, Peterson, Malouf, & Jamison 1995). One approach that has been suggested whereby contextualized mentored experiences can be provided is the integrated field experience design during which pre-service teachers learn to use technology via mentoring by experienced educators in their classrooms (Grove et al. 2004; Strudler, McKinney, & Jones 1999). In this way, novice teachers with practical knowledge concerning technology and language learning can experience firsthand the supports, constraints, logistical demands, and instructional impact of technologies in use.

The three-year TALL Project consisted of a series of activities with the aim of closely examining the anatomy and effectiveness of expert-novice mentoring that involved veteran in-service educators, doctoral students with expertise in instructional technology, and novice, pre-service educators. Fundamental to the design of TALL Project activities is the belief that teacher development is optimally a collective, interactive process made up of modeling, mentoring, apprenticing, dialoging, and scaffolding with the goal of transforming novices into active participants, inquirers, and critical thinkers (Feiman-Nemser 1996; Furlong & Maynard 1995; Nespor 1987; Tharp & Gallimore 1988) and that this becomes especially important when considering the integration of technology in teaching and learning (Becker & Riel 2000). The project consequently sought to orchestrate professional mentoring experiences that would involve new and experienced teachers working in tandem in classrooms – the novice bringing practical, up-to-date technology skills, the experienced teacher bringing her pedagogical expertise, with doctoral students in instructional technology serving as mentors and guides to both parties. A series of professional development activities were thus undertaken to achieve these aims with mentoring between novice and expert educators playing a central role. Our aim in tracking and documenting these professional development experiences was to pinpoint 1) intersections of expertise; 2) consequent generative dialog that ensued; and 3) coalescence of technical and pedagogical knowledge that might further similar initiatives in CALL teacher education.

TALL professional development activities

Given our aim to provide optimal professional development experiences in language learning technology for a cohort of novice ESOL educators, a group of in-service mentors, and doctoral students in instructional technologies, a number of intersecting activities were designed and undertaken. Figure 1 indicates the many interacting components of the TALL Project. Each of the three points of the triangle represents project participants with the pre-service teachers at the apex. Running horizontally across the triangle are the major activities undertaken

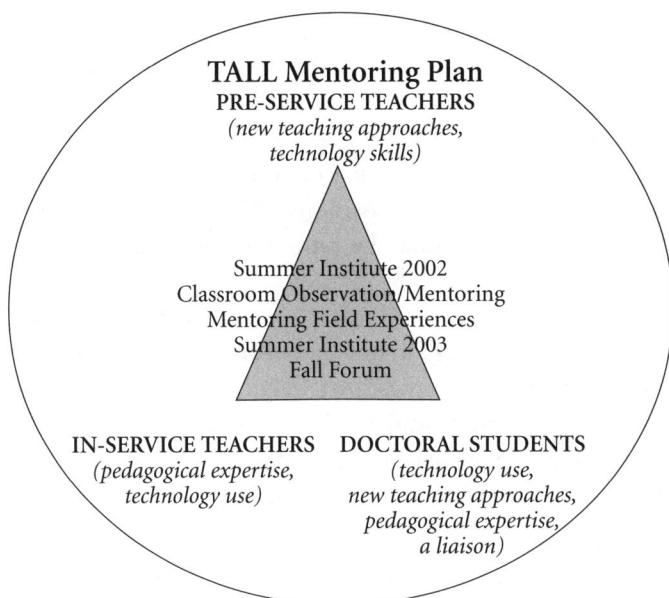

Figure 1. TALL mentoring plan.

by participants as part of the project. These activities are explicated below in chronological order (1–5).

1. Summer Institute 2002: An intensive ten-day summer workshop for experienced in-service professionals, the purpose of which was to orient them to the TALL Project, augment their technology knowledge and skills, and prepare them to work with their mentees during the coming school year.
2. Classroom Observations/Mentoring: project doctoral students followed through with in-service participants by observing their uses of technologies in their classrooms and providing assistance as needed.
3. Mentored Field Experiences: Pre-service teachers were placed with TALL-trained in-service ESOL teachers to collaborate in developing and implementing technology applications for that classroom.
4. Summer Institute 2003: The same teams of in-service and pre-service teachers worked together with the assistance of the project doctoral students to develop additional web-based materials for use in the classroom during the coming school year.
5. Fall Forum: The same teams of in-service and pre-service teachers presented both the materials they developed and ESOL learner reactions to using these materials at a regional conference for ESOL professionals.

Doctoral student mentors were from Korea, Russia, the US, and Taiwan and had strong interest in CALL. Project design and implementation decisions were made collaboratively by the doctoral students under the guidance of the faculty director. Each of the four doctoral students[2] was assigned to mentor each of four in-service teachers and the pre-service teachers placed in the four in-service teachers' K-8 (elementary and early secondary) classrooms. The ratio of doctoral students to in-service teachers was one to one; the ratio of doctoral students to pre-service teachers was one to one, or one to two.

The six pre-service teachers, through their mentoring partnership with four in-service teachers, were required to implement and develop technology activities for ESOL classrooms and present these materials at a regional conference for ESOL professionals. Also they were required to keep reflective journals on their experiences with technology use in their in-service teachers' classrooms. The purposes for asking them to maintain these journals included:

1.   to reinforce and enrich their mentored experiences and keep them on track;
2.   to inform the design of future mentoring systems for pre-service teachers;
3.   to inform others in the teacher training field (especially in instructional technologies) of working models for teacher development – the strengths, weaknesses, pitfalls, and successes of this particular approach.

The doctoral mentor's task was to keep the pre-service teacher focused, actively reflective, and consistently submitting journal entries for review and further discussion. Over a nine-month period, pre-service teachers met with, observed, and co-taught with their in-service mentors, developed web-based instructional materials and activities for use in the classroom, and communicated on a regular basis with their doctoral mentors via their electronic journals.

Data gathering

The dataset consists of pre and post project questionnaires, interviews, and written reflections on the part of the mentored novices. Pre-service journals included records of classroom observations focused on technology use and served to provide the doctoral students with information on the technological needs of both in-service and pre-service teachers as they prepared topics and activities for the Summer Institute. In addition, interactive journals were used to collect data to inform the design of future mentoring systems for teachers and to inform others in the teacher training field of working models for teacher development – the strengths, successes, and weaknesses of this particular approach and directions for future research. Written and oral reflections on the part of the mentoring teachers and doctoral mentors regarding their experiences with their mentees were also analyzed. Field notes of observations during technology workshops where novice and mentor worked in tandem to develop web-based materials for the mentor's classroom also served in our analysis of processes and outcomes. The following is a breakdown of data collection techniques by participants.

In-service teachers: Questionnaires and written reflections from the 2002 and 2003 Institutes; interview data and in-class observations; final reflections on the mentoring experience.
Pre-service teachers: Questionnaires and written reflections from the 2003 Institute; reflective journal entries; interview data; final reflections on being dually mentored. It should be noted also that prior to participating, all pre-service teachers were required to have completed their core course requirements for the M.S. TESOL degree as well as an intensive online course in CALL.

The CALL course guides students in developing their understanding of how electronic media can enhance language instruction. Practical, hands-on activities with media resources, with lesson plan development, and with web page design are the main components of the course. The overall goal is for students to be prepared to implement media-assisted activities that are informed by current theory and research. Correspondence between language teaching practice and learners' media use inside and outside classrooms is also considered.

Doctoral Students: Written reflections from Institutes and observations; these documents were reviewed by the author/participants individually and as a group on several different occasions.

Themes and salient mentoring events or conversations were identified in developing the following descriptive analyses of the TALL mentoring activities.

Results and observations

Across participants and activities, attitudinal outcomes were uniformly positive. Positive attitudes toward technology use, however, do not ensure that teachers will be able to use technology and use it well in the classroom. Teachers reported the many constraints that obstructed their wish to use computers in their teaching. Time pressures, both outside and during class, and lack of support, resources, and technical support were frequently cited as impediments by all three groups of participants. Schools, in short, were not easy places to use technologies. When teachers managed to persevere, not all could make as much use of their web-based materials as they wished due to poor or intermittent connectivity. As one teacher commented:

> Teaching teachers is one thing but where do they get the support from when they are bringing that to the classroom, that is another thing to pay attention to.
> In-service participant Jenn

Such reports of contextual and logistical constraints were prominent, underscoring the need for novice teachers and doctoral students in instructional technology to have first-hand experience in actual contexts of use – the pre-service teachers to understand what to expect and how to troubleshoot, the doctoral students to understand the constraints that the teachers in training they research and instruct are subject to as they try to implement innovative technology uses in their professional contexts.

The following sections summarize participants' reflections on their experiences throughout the TALL activities. The predominant theme in these reflections is that of collaboration: all three groups found that the collegial peer collaborations they undertook were mutually beneficial to each cohort's professional development aims.

Pre-service teacher reflections on mentoring

Work with in-service mentors

Pre-service participants reported on both the successes and failures of technology implementations in their in-service mentors' classrooms. Many expressed surprise at the quantity and tenacity of constraining factors when it came to the logistics of teaching in public schools in general, and teaching with technology in particular. They uniformly expressed admiration at the flexibility and good natures of their mentors as they faced these daily glitches (scheduling changes, disappearing equipment, equipment in disrepair, interruptions, and the like). As one pre-service participant expressed this:

> I now know what to expect when I walk into an ESL classroom and I know what the teacher has to deal with.
> Pre-service participant Linda

From the novices' perspective, working with seasoned experts who could answer their questions regarding the everyday logistics of the classroom was very helpful in their quest to conceptualize the technology integration they had learned about in the abstract through university coursework. As one pre-service participant noted about working with her in-service mentor:

> Working in my mentor's classroom benefited me mostly because I could ob-
> serve technology being used within the context of teaching ESL and then
> practice using it myself. I was free to ask questions and get solid feedback
> from my mentor.
> Pre-service participant Lynne

Moreover, pre-service journals enthusiastically reported incidents of their learning
from their in-service mentors:

> I learned a little about the software known as Inspiration, April loves it –
> doesn't have time to develop what she wants, but depending on the needs of
> the elementary teacher, she'd like her True Story curriculum somehow linked.
> Pre-service participant Kent

They also report having influenced their in-service mentors:

> I mentioned that I would like to create a map, that when you click on different
> parts of the world, would take you to information about that particular part
> of the world in relation to immigration. My teacher said she didn't know that
> it was possible to have a graphic bring you to more than one location. So, I
> think in regards to new ideas, I might have influenced my [mentor] teacher.
> Pre-service participant Chris

The benefits derived from contextualized, in-service mentoring were clearly com-
plemented by the supporting work of the project doctoral students.

Work with doctoral student mentors

The doctoral students played a number of mentoring roles for the pre-service cohort. They worked intensively with them and with their in-service mentors during
the Summer Institute to support the development of a jointly designed set of web
resources and activities to be implemented in the in-service teachers' classrooms.
In addition, they supported the pre-service teachers' conceptual and practical
development on an on-demand basis during and after the intensive, week-long
institute. When a novice had questions, concerns or quandaries they were quick
to turn to the doctoral students for advice and assistance. Novices also reported
having benefited from having a doctoral mentor to journal with throughout the
field experience. Doctoral student mentors helped to keep novices' journaling on
task, focused, and reflective. Additionally, the pre-service participants reported
that they learned specific strategies from their doctoral mentors and in some
cases passed this learning on to their in-service mentors. This type of learning
is reflected in the following journal excerpt:

> Pre-service Teacher: Jenn (in-service participant) expressed an interest in In-
> ternet websites for activities for low-level learners where she could sit her
> students down for independent ESL work while she works with students at
> a different level. I suggested a resource guide with listings of appropriate web-
> sites, their web addresses, and a brief description and evaluation of each, i.e.,
> what skills they will develop.
>
> Doctoral Mentor: Have you ever looked at MERLOT? . . .It is basically a site
> with a whole bunch of sites that are useful in 12 disciplines. World Lan-
> guages is the discipline you and Jenn would be interested in. If you go to
> www.merlot.org then click on "communities" then "world languages" you
> will find ESL sites as well as sites in other languages that Jenn may be able
> to use for English as well as native language literacy. If you have not been to
> MERLOT and want more information let me know.
>
> Pre-service Teacher: Thank you, yes what a wonderful site! I'm sure Jenn will
> like hearing about this site.

Important connections were thus made between the expertise of all three cohorts:
the pre-service teachers, the in-service teachers, and the project doctoral students.
Pre-service and in-service teachers worked collaboratively with project doctoral
students thus enhancing one another's experiences by sharing knowledge and
ideas. Interviews with both pre-service and in-service participants served to confirm that while educational theory and technical skills are critical to implementing
CALL, guided practical experience is equally critical.

In-service teacher reflections on mentoring

In-service teachers provided feedback to the project chiefly through the project
questionnaires, where they were asked to reflect on their mentoring experiences
with the pre-service teachers and the doctoral students.

Work with pre-service teachers

The in-service teachers and the pre-service teachers worked together to develop
and implement technology materials for the in-service teachers' classrooms. Although they did not always know every aspect of using technology, they did learn
that they could solve problems by working together. One in-service teacher expressed the value of co-teaching with her assigned pre-service teachers in her
classroom.

> We needed to share our own expertise and knowledge with each other. The
> work we did together was beneficial and a great learning experience for

all... Overall, I enjoyed the collaboration and the "feeding off" each other's style/method of teaching and ideas.
In-service participant Rachel

Another in-service teacher expressed the benefits of working together with the pre-service teachers. In her case, her partner was an expert in using the computer.

It was beneficial to learn more creative ways to use technology from another person. It was also helpful to discuss together ways to use technology to en-hance what the kids were learning. We became good friends since the mentor experience and I still ask him periodically for his tech support.
In-service participant Venus

The in-service teachers and pre-service teachers helped one another, shared their ideas, and problem-solved together. Eventually, they developed synergistic visions about technology use and integration in the classroom.

Work with the doctoral students

The in-service teachers reported that the doctoral students were useful in help-ing them integrate technology more effectively in their teaching and invaluable in making classroom implementation easy and successful. The doctoral students assisted them in developing a website to fit the needs of their students, locating technology applications for language teaching, and developing technical skills such as recording/editing visual/audio files. The following in-service teacher statement was typical:

Kim encouraged and inspired me to use technology in my classroom. Her positive remarks stimulated me to continue to try ways to use technology. It made me reflect on how I use technology in my class. This prepared me to think about how I would like my pre-service teacher to use technology. It was also helpful to know that I had a group of people (doctoral students) that would support me if I had questions or issues on projects that I did with technology.
In-service participant Jenn

The in-service teachers gained confidence and expertise in the use of technology and their attitudes towards technology improved through the mentoring expe-riences with the doctoral students. The doctoral students played a central role in supporting the in-service teachers not only for theoretical and pedagogical background of language learning with technology, but also for more practical classroom applications and fostering positive attitudes toward technology use.

Doctoral student reflections on mentoring

According to a recent Survey on Doctoral Education and Career Preparation (Golde & Dore 2001), more than 60% of doctoral candidate respondents indicated that they were "not prepared" or "somewhat prepared" to teach college students. Additionally, the majority reported being inadequately prepared for such higher education duties as supervising, advising, and mentoring their students. Moreover, in 1999 about 38% of all students enrolled in the graduate programs were foreigners (Johnson 2000). Indeed, nearly 20% of all doctorates granted in the US in 1998 were awarded to non-U.S. citizens with almost 75% stating their intention to remain in the U.S. (National Opinion Research Center 1999). Needless to say, the lack of familiarity with the US school contexts on the part of foreign-born educators is a potential weakness. An integral component of the TALL mentoring project involved both international and native-born doctoral students studying technology in language teacher education. For the project, they worked closely with in-service teachers and pre-service teachers as they implemented technologies in real classrooms. This represented multiple opportunities for them to merge their theoretical knowledge with the complexities of US schools and classrooms.

Work with pre-service teachers

Analysis of the pre-service teachers' reflective journal entries indicate that the doctoral students not only took an active role in teaching pre-service teachers how to use technologies for ESOL, but they also learned some tips from them as well. For example, the following exchange took place between a pre-service teacher and a doctoral student:

> Pre-service teacher: Her (In-service participant Venus') web site was very impressive and it gave us ideas about what we could include in our own site.

> Doctoral Mentor: I took a look at this site. It's gorgeous. I like that it provides the glossaries of terms. I think it helps. I liked Hot Potato quizzes. Virtual Paper Dolls is an excellent activity. WebQuest is great. I've never seen website worksheets before. I think it would help children to concentrate better.

It is notable that conversations between doctoral students and pre-service teachers exceeded the frames of the topic of using technologies in teaching ESOL and spread over different pedagogical issues such as grading policies, "pull-out" vs. "push-in" classes, new methods of teaching, students with special needs as ESOL learners, parent involvement, etc.

Work with in-service teachers

Understanding pedagogical issues in the abstract versus what actually happens in a real US classroom was a powerful lesson for the doctoral students. TALL activities included doctoral students observing the use of technologies by in-service teachers. This helped them to understand the context, the practical constraints and supports, and consequently better ways of implementing technologies in real ESOL classrooms. One of the doctoral students wrote:

> As expert technology users and not very experienced ESL teachers, we had ideal uses for technology in the classroom in our minds. When we suggested any of these uses to the in-service teachers, the reality of what went on in the classroom was realized as our ideal lesson had constraints such as those involved with time and equipment.
> Doctoral student Jamie

In-service teachers also had an impact on doctoral students' pedagogical beliefs and understandings. For example, one of the international doctoral students (Tonya) wrote in her evaluation of the project, "It was great to work with in-service teachers because we learned teaching experience and know the current ESL issues from them." In addition to conveying their experiences to doctoral students, in-service teachers provided models of in-context teaching that was unique for many of the doctoral students. One wrote, "I gained invaluable experience in teaching diverse cultural students from the in-service teachers."

Three of the doctoral students in the TALL Project were from countries where teacher-centered approaches are the only reality (Korea, Russia and Taiwan). Through their TALL experiences they developed new understandings of classroom dynamics. One of the doctoral students wrote in her reflections:

> Before the mentoring project began, to me (as an international student who is familiar with authoritative teaching styles), mentoring implied a one-way relationship, in which one person (who knows more than the other) provides some information for the other to help him or her become knowledgeable... Having this kind of perception on my mentoring experiences, I thought I needed to be the person who takes a lead and provides a model that the mentees (in-service teachers and pre-service teachers) could follow to be a successful learner. However, as the Project went on, I noticed that my mentoring experiences should be a two-way-relationship rather than a one-way. The mentors and the mentees would be learning partners for one another so that they are able to share their own expertise and help each other to construct their own learning in meaningful ways. With the changed perception on the role of myself as a mentor, I could react differently to the in-service teachers and pre-service teachers who were assigned to me for the mentoring partners.

> Rather than figuring out any problems confronting them and providing every detail in every step for them, I could step aside and let them figure out their problems and share each other's expertise.
> Doctoral student Kim

A balanced, complementary synergy thus evolved between TALL Project participants through productive, focused conversations. Evidence that classroom learners benefited from the technology implementations these collaborations bred was also clear in reports by both novice and expert participants and via classroom observations.

Suggested improvements

Like most human endeavors, not everything in the project worked exactly as planned and TALL participants came up against challenges. One of these was related to both in-service and pre-service teachers' reluctance to participate in the TALL online text-based discussion forum, an activity set up on the TALL website and intended for extended collaboration. The usefulness of online text-based discussions in teacher education is a relatively new subject in the field of teacher professional development and few studies have been devoted to this topic (Bonk 2003–2004). Some studies report discouraging results when attempting to involve teachers in reflective conversation on teaching/learning through the means of Computer Mediated Communication (CMC) (Stephens & Hartmann 2004). As Stephens and Hartmann (2004) speculate, one of the reasons why teachers do not adopt CMC in their professional development activities is that they have "simply not yet become comfortable with this combination of discussion content and medium" (71).

Participants and our own observations also underscored the fact that pre-service learning in real classrooms is markedly different from that in university lectures: hands-on, contextualized experiences were a must. In-service teachers reported a need for more time to learn, to experiment, to try things out, and to integrate. This need aligns with the results of other contemporary studies on teacher technology integration (Becker 2000; Kirkwood 2000; Meskill, Anthony, Hilliker-VanStrander, Tseng, & You, in press) where teachers around the U.S. point to time as the greatest obstacle to using technology in their teaching. In the case of the TALL Project, pre-service teachers' help and support in the classroom supplied some of that needed time to confer with peers. These teachers, like teachers across the globe, need that additional time to develop best practices.

Implications and importance

To recap, the TALL Project brought together three groups of teaching professionals who worked collaboratively around CALL implementations in K-8 ESOL classrooms. Participating in-service teachers provided the pre-service teachers with a real-life classroom and context in which to see the craft of teaching supported by technology. The pre-service teachers brought to these contexts fresh ideas and new forms of technical expertise that they had learned in their university coursework. Through constructive, professional dialog, they designed, implemented, and shared with their regional colleagues informed applications of CALL and their outcomes. The doctoral mentors, with their expertise in CALL and curriculum, supported both the pre-service and in-service teachers in this undertaking. In exchange, they received invaluable experiences as mentors and, for the international students, experiences in U.S. schools. Processes and outcomes that evolved out of the TALL activities are captured in Figure 2.

The instructional conversations that ensued through these mentoring collaborations were consequently rich, productive, and of mutual benefit. Moreover, the learning was as beneficial to those ostensibly in the role of mentors as it was to those being mentored. Keeping the novice teachers' eyes keenly focused on the intricacies and complexities of classroom cultures in their reflective observations via doctoral mentors was additionally an effective strategy in helping these new teachers make sense of what they were experiencing within the frameworks of their university coursework and their personal experiences.

We can conclude that linking pre- to in-service education is critical to successful growth of teaching professionals (Bullough & Gitlin 2001; Freeman 1996)

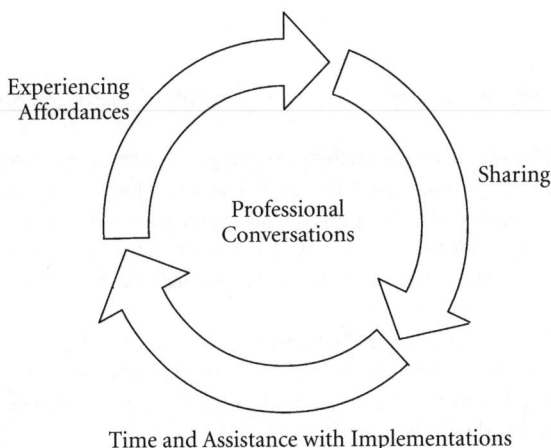

Figure 2. Professional development processes.

and that such structures facilitate the important linking of procedural knowledge with theoretical knowledge (Kagan 1992). The success of using field experiences and guided reflection as complements to university coursework in instructional technology, in conjunction with the orchestrated exchange of critical knowledge between novice and seasoned educators, was evidenced in the responsiveness of TALL participants to these experiences. Matching novice technology-learning teachers with experienced classroom teachers therefore appears to be a ripe venue for constructive, collaborative, and productive conversations about teaching and learning with technology. Indeed, technologies can serve as a source of shared and divergent experiences upon which generative conversations can be constructed. In this case, mentoring has been shown to be a viable approach to teacher education in technologies and the professional conversations that evolved out of the TALL Project affirm this.

Note: This project was supported in part by the U.S. Department of Education's Office of English Language Acquisition (OELA, Award #T195A970024-99). The views expressed herein are those of the authors and do not necessarily represent the views of the Department.

Notes

1. After the first author, names appear in alphabetical order.

2. The co-authors of this chapter consist of the faculty director, Dr. Carla Meskill, and the four doctoral students who participated in the TALL project.

References

Abdal-Haqq, I. (1995). Infusing technology into preservice teacher education. *ERIC Digest 389699.*

Becker, H. (2000). Findings from the teaching, learning and computing survey: Is Larry Cuban right? *Education Policy Analysis Archives* 8(51). Available at http://epaa.asu.edu/epaa/v8n51/

Becker, H. & Riel, M. (2000). Teacher professional engagement and constructivist-compatible computer use. *Center for Research on Information Technology and Organizations University of California, Irvine and University of Minnesota.* Available at http://www.crito.uci.edu/tlc/findings/report_7/startpage.html

Bonk, C. (2003–2004). I should have known this was coming: Computer-mediated discussions in teacher education. *Journal of Research on Technology in Education, 36* (2), 95–102.

Bullough, R. & Gitlin, A. (2001). *Becoming a Student of Teaching: Linking knowledge production and practice.* New York: Routledge Falmer.

Cuban, L. (2001). *Oversold and Underused: Computers in the classroom.* Cambridge, MA: Harvard University Press.

Dunn, S. & Ridgway, J. (1991). Computer use during a primary school teaching practice: A survey. *Journal of Computer Assisted Learning, 7*, 7–17.

Feiman-Nemser, S. (1996). Teacher mentoring: A critical review. *ERIC Digest, ED397060.*

Freeman, D. (1996). The 'unstudied problem': Research on teacher learning in language teaching. In D. Freeman & J. Richards (Eds.), *Teacher Learning in Language Teaching* (pp. 351–378). New York, NY: Cambridge University Press.

Furlong, J. & Maynard, T. (1995). *Mentoring student teachers: The growth of professional knowledge.* London: Routledge.

Golde, C. M. & Dore, T. M. (2001). At cross purposes: What the experiences of doctoral students reveal about doctoral education. Available at http://www.phd-survey.org

Grove, K., Strudler, N., & Odell, S. (2004). Mentoring toward technology uses: Cooperating teacher practice in supporting student teachers. *Journal of Research on Technology in Education, 37* (1), 85–109.

Johnson, J. (2000). Presentation on the Survey of Earned Doctorates. Available at http://www.grad.washington.edu/envision/resources/earned_docs.pdf.

Kagan, D. (1992). Professional growth among preservice and beginning teachers. *Review of Educational Research, 62* (2), 129–169.

Kariuki, M., Franklin, T., & Duran, M. (2001). A technology partnership: Lessons leaned by mentors. *Journal of Technology and Teacher Education, 9* (3), 407–420.

Karchmer, R. (2001). The journey ahead: Thirteen teachers report how the Internet influences literacy and literacy instruction in their K-12 classrooms. *Reading Research Quarterly, 36* (4), 422–466.

Kirkwood, J. J. (2000). The status of technology education in elementary schools as reported by beginning teachers. *Journal of Industrial Teacher Education, 37* (3), 93–114.

Lam, Y. (2000). Technophilia v. technophobia: A preliminary look at why second language teachers do or do not use technology in their classrooms. *Canadian Modern Language Review, 56*, 389–420.

Lave, J. & Wenger, E. (1991). *Situated Learning: Legitimate peripheral participation.* New York: CUP.

MacArthur, C., Pilato, V., Kercher, M., Peterson, D., Malouf, D., & Jamison, P. (1995). Mentoring: An approach to technology education for teachers. *Journal of Research on Computing in Education, 28* (1), 46–63.

Meskill, C., Mossop, J., DiAngelo, S., & Pasquale, R. (2002). Expert and novice teachers talking technology: Precepts, concepts, and misconcepts. *Language Learning & Technology, 6* (3), 46–57.

Meskill, C., Anthony, N., Hilliker-VanStrander, S., Tseng, C., & You, J. (In press). CALL: A survey of K-12 ESOL teacher uses and preferences. *TESOL Quarterly.*

Mullen, L. (2001). Beyond infusion: Preservice students' understandings about educational technologies for teaching and learning. *Journal of Technology and Teacher Education, 9* (3), 447–466.

National Opinion Research Center (1999). Summary Report, 1998. Doctorate Recipients from the United States. Survey of Earned Doctorates.

Nespor, J. (1987). The role of beliefs in the practice of teaching. *Journal of Curriculum Studies, 19* (4), 317–328.

Samaras, A. & Gismondi, S. (1998). Scaffolds in the field: Vygotskian interpretation in a teacher education program. *Teaching and Teacher Education, 14* (7), 715–733.

Stephens, A. & Hartmann, C. (2004). A successful professional development project's failure to promote online discussions about teaching. *Journal of Technology and Teacher Education, 12* (1), 57–73.

Strudler, R., McKinney, M., & Jones, P. (1999). First-year teachers' use of technology: Preparation, expectations and realitities. *Journal of Technology and Teacher Education, 7* (2), 115–129.

TALL Project Website. Available at http://www.albany.edu/faculty/meskill/TALL/home/home.htm.

Tharp, R. & Gallimore, R. (1988). *Rousing Minds to Life*. Cambridge: CUP.

Vygotsky, L. (1978). *Mind in Society*. Cambridge, MA: Harvard University Press.

Preface to

Communities of practice
for pre- and in-service teacher education

The chapters in the preceding two sections of this volume have covered a variety of perspectives on what both pre-service and practicing teachers in various settings need to be able to learn to do with technology in teaching. Collectively, they have made a strong case for the importance of formal training. However, Elizabeth Hanson-Smith begins this chapter with the sobering observation that within months after leaving their formal educational settings teachers may find that most of their knowledge and skills in CALL have become obsolete. To address this dilemma, she notes that teachers increasingly have the opportunity to continue developing their knowledge and skills through participation in communities of practice, or CoPs, which in this context represent groups of technology-using language teachers who connect with one another and collaborate in pursuing their common goals and interests. Besides providing "just-in-time" situated support, CoPs serve the purpose of allowing teachers to connect and interact with like-minded peers and avoid the isolation that often comes from being the only CALL practitioner in a given language program. Regular participation in online CoPs has the added advantage of building teacher experience and confidence in using computer-mediated communication applications, know-how that will be valuable in developing CMC activities with students and training them in tasks that support language learning objectives. In addition to offering a set of criteria for distinguishing CoPs from other professional and social groups, Hanson-Smith provides extended descriptions for several CoPs and a number of resources for those interested in learning more. Perhaps the most important lesson from this chapter, however, is that whatever else may be offered in formal pre-service or in-service education, providing teachers with both the foundational knowledge and the skills necessary to discover and participate in relevant CoPs is among the most effective ways to support continuing professional development.

Communities of practice
for pre- and in-service teacher education

Elizabeth Hanson-Smith

California State University, Sacramento, USA

What are communities of practice?

Virtual worlds are *real worlds.*
(Galarneau 2004)

One of the most significant problems facing computer-using teachers is that no education curriculum can prepare them for the swift and continuing changes that take place in the world of technology. Within months of obtaining certification, teachers find that most of what they studied about using computers and the Internet for language learning has become obsolete. A second major and little recognized problem is their isolation from other technology-using teachers. Often technology-trained instructors are hired as the sole *expert* in the area of technology. Not only are they given charge of the lab and the students using it, but also they are asked to help other teachers who possess widely varying levels of computer skill and computer phobia. Each day may be spent answering calls for help with lost passwords, frozen screens, page not found messages, virus infestations, firewall rigidities, or server crashes. After helping the more venturesome teachers who may tentatively stick a toe into the sea of teaching with computers, little time remains for the technologically competent to explore and expand on their own knowledge and skills through exchange with like-minded, sympathetic peers.

Communities of practice (CoPs) may present a significant means to overcome both of these problems for the teacher who uses computer-assisted language learning (CALL) and Internet communication tools (ICT).[1] Lave and Wenger (1991) are thought to have coined the term *communities of practice* (CoPs), which they describe as occurring in a variety of settings where social groups naturally form to solve problems, share knowledge, mentor or assist apprentices, and collaborate to practice the skills of a domain. *Community* is often loosely used to describe any online course, particularly those based on structured course management software such as *Blackboard*, regardless of lifespan or purpose. The term *collaborative* is also often loosely used to refer to any set of resources where several people contribute to a collection. However, as will become clear in the course of this chapter, short-term, individual courses or workshops are not truly CoPs, particularly when unequal power or authority structures pertain, as in a typical student-teacher-school setting.

In order to define teacher CoPs more clearly, the author proposes the following criteria, which will be used throughout the chapter:

- A common *purpose* or *domain* of knowledge (Wenger 2004)
- The generation and discussion of *ideas*, the creation and sharing of *skills*, and *reflection* on these operations (but unlike a simple discussion list, this aspect is carried out through *experimentation*)
- *Collaboration* in the active practice with and exploration of skills or knowledge, often through reciprocal *mentoring* or apprenticeship – *praxis* as opposed to talk
- *Social support* (referred to as "social *scaffolding*" by Johnson (2003))
- Appropriate *tools* for communicating, archiving, and collaborating on projects while sustaining the social community (especially important for CALL or ICT specialists, who, being isolated, must communicate over distance; see Stevens (2000) and Hanson-Smith and al-Othman (2004))
- *Longevity* – while a CoP might be formed with a short-term goal in mind, if the analogy to a real-life community holds, an online community must also display stability and staying power as a social entity (see Jones 1997); student "communities" generally do not meet this criterion

Links to numerous articles about CoPs and their formation, including graphical visualizations by Wenger (2004) and Johnson (2002), have been collected at the author's Web page, *Community of Practice Resources*, (Hanson-Smith 2006), which also includes a section on definitions. This chapter discusses the most crucial of the above criteria in the context of several teacher communities, some of which the author belongs to and/or moderates. Suggestions will also be provided for creating and maintaining communities as extensions of pre-service or in-service programs, and for using technologies that can make the virtual online environment a real world for community building.

Purpose or domain

Several electronic discussion lists focus on CALL for teachers as a domain, for example, *NETEACH-L*, the *LLTI* forum, EUROCALL's electronic lists for language processing and speech technologies, and *TESLCA-L*; however, while these are long-lived, they do not necessarily promote the more substantial kinds of practice, collaborations, and social support that genuine CoPs sustain. Several other "communities" have emerged more recently that make fuller use of newer technologies and offer a richer mix of online tools than simple e-mail. For instance, *Cyber-Langues*, a European association for teachers of modern languages who use information and ICT technology, has an RSS (really simple syndication) feed for items about language and hosts a yearly colloquium on land in France. As with many self-denoted "communities," one receives the impression that its Website is still mainly a passive information source rather than a community where knowledge is generated and practical teaching applications are shared through mentoring. However, recent developments include a blog (Web + log) and a photoblog, signs of increasing social life.

One example of an authentic community with a very specific domain is *Real English Online* (REO 2003), based in a *Yahoo! Group* (*Y!G*) that provides peer help for the many teachers around the world who use video and audio media on the Internet. The group was formed by the author and Mike Marzio to assist teachers in using free online videos created by Marzio and to discuss the pedagogy of media use. As word spread, instructors around the globe began to collaborate in devising online exercises and activities for the videos, located at The Marzio School's *Real English* Website (2005). They created Web pages with video-based interactive quizzes and WebQuests (Internet-based research projects, see Chao, this volume), and assisted each other in experimenting with a wide variety of free online video and audio technologies. Currently, the *REO Y!G* provides a place to archive files and links, and its electronic list is the main communications resource. One month the discussion may focus on compressor/decompressor rates, and in another month attention will turn to free video sources, points of grammar, how to write HTML, or culture and pedagogy. Students may join the group in order to use the free videos independently.

Because of the wide range of technical literacy in the group, *REO* provides an annual introductory workshop in January-February at the *Electronic Village Online* (see Hanson-Smith & Bauer-Ramazani 2004) to familiarize newcomers with the group's operation and resources during hands-on, mentored practice. Members may also join the regular Sunday chats of its sister group, the *Webheads in Action* (described below), where immediate live help can be provided. The highly international nature of *REO* leads to interesting discussions about varieties of English and the language and culture of users: Marzio is based in France and the author is in the U.S.; members have had discussions about and in Polish and have created Websites and video exercises in several major languages besides English, including French, Spanish, and Portuguese.

As is typical of most online discussion forums, busy teachers selectively participate in *REO* activities, as determined by their own needs, their current level of domain knowledge, the time available to them, and their own highly individualized interests in technology or pedagogy. While teachers in online courses invariably worry about student "lurking" (reading messages but not contributing), most researchers perceive it as a legitimate aspect of authentic online communities (Lave & Wenger 1991; see also Preece, Nonnecke, & Andrews 2004). With a group like *REO*, teachers know they can bring forth a problem at the moment it needs attention and expect to find an answer and hands-on help quickly, even if they have been silent for weeks or months before: This *just-in-time* knowledge building is a significant aspect of teacher communities and is quite different from periodic land-based teacher training workshops that speak to pre-ordained topics on pre-set schedules. Arguably, online in-service is far more efficient and far more cost-effective. Naturally, this type of knowledge construction is difficult for students in pre-service programs, who will be pressed to complete marked and graded assignments in the time frame of an academic term.

Practice through experiential collaboration

Peer mentoring has been identified as an important aspect of technological education for teachers (see Valdez, Fulton, Blomeyer, Glenn, & Wimmer 2004). However, few teacher-training institutions make provision for ongoing peer-to-peer mentoring after graduation. And while a number of learning centers around the world sponsor collaborations between students, usually class-to-class (see, for example, the GLOBE project (Kennedy 2006)), far fewer have been able to create teacher-to-teacher collaborations that would serve as apprenticeships in the practice of new technological knowledge or skills. *Webheads in Action*, founded in its present form in 2002 by Vance Stevens (2005; and *evonline2002_webheads* 2001), comes close to being an ideal in-service teacher community in that its members consistently volunteer to mentor, create, or share in online presentations, and they sustain frequent explorations in new technologies with colleagues and their students. Knowledge is put into practice not only in land-based presentations, for example, the Pre-Conference Institute (PCI) at TESOL 2004 offered by six Webheads from different countries (Stevens et al. 2004), but in numerous online collaborations both with their students and with pre- and in-service teachers (see the *Index* to the Webhead archives (Almeida d'Eça 2005)). The Webheads recently organized their own free, wholly online, 3-day conference to showcase their work (see *WiAOC 2005*).

Voluntary assistance among teachers in CoPs takes place in a just-in-time setting. Often mentoring begins with a call for help; one teacher will begin, for example, "I'm going to try blogs with my students. What's the best blog to use?" Other members respond, and eventually someone in the group summarizes the information. *WiA* is particularly notable in its encouragement of this type of reflective practice. Once a member has tried out a new tool or pedagogical strategy with students, it is almost obligatory – yet voluntary – to report back on the experiment, usually by creating a Web page or blog with photos or video. (See for example, González's (2003a) testimonial to how her skills in technology developed, al-Othman's (2003) vivid examples of how her class Web pages evolved, and Almeida d'Eça (2004) discussing her participation in an Annenberg-sponsored course.) Trials with new tools often involve the direct participation of *WiA* members online, as they model responses and techniques during a live chat or video conference (see Stevens et al. 2004; Yeh, González, & Mühren 2004). The voluntary self-evaluation and feedback on *What I have learned* has become an important part of the *WiA* experience, and often results in a published article. (See for example, González (2003b), Suzuki (2004), and the comprehensive *Index* of experiments in Almeida d'Eça (2006)).

The role of mentoring and reflective *praxis* in online collaboration may be summarized as a recursive operation:

1. Query about practice or tools (or call for participation in an event)
2. Rapid member response
3. Live chat demonstration and/or walk-through of a tool
4. Summary of information
5. Live collaborative trial with students (or event presentation)
6. Further discussion
7. Reflective summary and report (and/or possible publication)
8. Repeat as needed

Essential tools

Most research about online "communities" before 2002 deals primarily with electronic forums or message boards. However, ongoing, just-in-time collaborations require tools that allow rapid feedback both synchronously and asynchronously. For technology-using teachers, good online tools are crucial to hands-on mentoring and the community building that fosters the trust needed to ask questions and experiment. Below is a short list of the tools the author perceives as the most important to CALL-based CoPs. (See Preece and Maloney-Krichmar (2003) for more on the implications of various tools.)

Virtual community space. Virtual CoPs must have a locus. *Y!G* is an essential free tool that allows groups to build their own community space online (see Figure 1). *Y!G* has e-mail distribution, space to store files and links, a calendar to distribute reminders, polling software, and a database that can function as a wiki

Figure 1. The *Yahoo! Groups* interface provides a free, easy-to-use set of tools (see left window) to start and maintain a community online (*Real English Online* 2003).

(collaborative online editing software), for example, where members can edit a paper together or self-select into teams. The *Y!G* interface is so user-friendly that members of *REO* and *WiA* regularly start *Y!Gs* for specific short-term purposes, such as a collaborative course or publication planning. One *REO* member set up a *Y!G* just to hold copyright-free photos for student projects.

While many Webheads are also familiar with and use *Moodle* for courses, this structured online course environment has certain limitations for community building. As in other course management systems, such as *Blackboard*, messages are threaded into different forums, a feature that has the advantage of dividing a class into specific topics for discussion groups, but the disadvantage of splitting a community into small pieces. For long-term community building, this feature can become very inconvenient, especially if several discussion threads are active at one time and deliver multiple daily digests. *Y!G* has only modest threading ability, but access at the Website allows messages to be viewed in threads. *Moodle*'s structure quickly reveals its purpose as a teacher-friendly classroom space, but *Y!G*, having been designed specifically for informal communities, remains superior in many respects for voluntary CoPs, which are not graded, hierarchically ordered, or directed by a sole teacher.

Another virtual locus, *Tapped In* (*TI*), is both a tool and a community of communities. It addresses a much broader range of domains than *WiA* or *REO*: librarians, administrators, and teachers of all the age/grade levels and all content areas, including science, art, physical education, K-3+, and ESL/EFL. *TI* provides educators with their own virtual offices where they can conduct chat sessions privately with students, archive resources and assignments, and in effect hold virtual classes online with the help of experienced live facilitators. Many teacher groups, including *WiA,* hold regular monthly or weekly meetings live online at *TI,* an important desideratum for community building. *TI* allows teachers themselves to create any grouping they desire. An annual virtual festival brings all the communities together to share ideas. One might think of it as a large town with many neighborhoods or clubs, rather than as a single-purpose structure.

Live chat. While *TI* is the main text chat locus for Webheads, *WiA* also uses *Yahoo! Messenger* (*Y!M*) extensively, both for individual messaging, and as a back channel in case of technical problems with other venues. *Y!M* allows Webcamming while chatting. Since the group promotes inclusion and many members use Macintosh computers, which *Y!M* does not currently support in voice chat, *TI* and *Y!M* are often combined with other voice and video chat locales, for instance, *Alado* or *LearningTimes* (*LT*). Because of *WiA*'s leading role in experimenting with technology, group members are allowed to use these two platforms for free online conferencing; however, many institutions will no doubt soon have courseware management systems that support their own versions of Web conferencing. Like *TI, Alado*'s and *LT*'s purpose is to foster communities, though they are usually of shorter duration, more like mini-courses or conferences on specific subjects. *LT*'s Web-based voice chatroom allows users to upload pictures, display electronic slide presentations, write on the whiteboard with a variety of drawing and text tools, operate a simulated laser pointer, "push" Web pages into local browsers, take a real-time poll, give a quiz, etc., all while text, voice, and single-user Webcam chatting. The facility is thus a full-featured classroom as well as a richly furnished meeting place with multimedia archiving. *LT* also supports bulletin board discussions so that groups may have longer-term contact.

Although asynchronous sharing of information via e-mail list or bulletin board is important, synchronous text and voice chat, especially at regularly scheduled intervals, are important tools to solidify collaborations, mentor new technologies in real time, and share personal and family tidbits – the "social glue" that holds a group together. Most voice chat facilities provide multimedia recording so that permanent archives can be maintained of both synchronous and asynchronous communications. Webcasting and podcasting (iPod + Webcast) are also increasingly being used for voice communications online. (See for example, *WorldBridges,* whose Ed Tech Talks have become a regular meeting place for the Webheads.)

Web pages and/or blogs. CoPs may be formed without a dynamic Web presence; however, online records of group work and spaces for individuals to reflect on their own development seem to be a natural accompaniment to the creation of real communities. We come to know others in real life through their housing and dress; likewise, in a virtual world, we become acquainted through our home pages and blogs, which give far more information than the member profile space typical of some courseware. Generally, the CoPs discussed in this article are sustained by individuals' virtual homes. For example, Webheads' pages may be found in the frequently updated *Index* (Almeida d'Eça 2006); *REO* places member Web page and blog addresses in its *Y!G* Links area. *TI* provides virtual offices that may be decorated with photos and personal messages as well as links to scholarly work.

Social scaffolding

As intimated above, a unique element of CoPs, as defined by Lave and Wenger, *Situated Learning: Legitimate Peripheral Participation* (1991), is their social aspect: Learning takes place by participation in a social entity; learning is itself a social activity, hence *situated* in a community. Group members may participate to varying degrees, depending on outside demands on their time and their degree of interest or expertise in an area, hence, *legitimate peripheral* participation. One difference between teacher CoPs and learner CoPs is the voluntary nature of their social climate: Students in a course are constrained to participate; teachers join a CoP because they want to.

In the realm of CALL, virtual social support is of particular importance because technology-trained teachers may be isolated in their own departments or institutions. Further, regardless of their initial training, they may have quite a range of expertise, and changes in technology arrive at a rapid pace: Teachers are always trying to keep up. They generally have a great deal of authority in their classrooms, but may feel vulnerable in situations such as CALL, where they may be more ignorant than their students. The joy of meeting friends regularly on the Internet and making new ones in the context of a group whose purposes are clear and whose strategy is welcoming may be of special importance to them. As Ebeltoft and Nyrop put it, in a study examining four teacher communities: "It is a safe feeling to meet a patient guide on the net, a live person who is able to introduce, explain and give positive feedback on your first fumbling tentative participation" (2001: Section 9, ¶3). Since *WiA* members are for the most part teachers, many with advanced degrees and expertise or interest in sociolinguistics, several aspects of learning as a social activity are intentionally reinforced by long-standing members, who purposefully reach out to and socialize with newcomers. These techniques are worth exploring, particularly if the reader is interested in forestalling problems that may arise in creating a successful, self-sustaining CoP, whether for students or in-service teachers.

Getting to know others. As in real life, entry into a virtual group demands social recognition, some form of welcome. *REO* and *WiA* encourage newcomers to write a short self-introduction and upload a picture to the *Y!G*. *WiA* maintains a Web page with photos, introductions, e-mail and chat addresses, home page addresses, recent presentations, etc. This allows other group members to quickly find someone and recognize them online and off (see Stevens' portal page 2005). Other groups use searchable member profiles, or a *Frappr* map, which gives a visual location, a photo, and a brief message. (See Motteram and Forrester (2005) on the importance of social induction in distance learning.)

Regular periodic meetings are a second strategy to integrate newcomers. Professionally, an annual session at the *Electronic Village Online*, mentioned above, serves as the means for *WiA*, *REO*, and *Webloggers* (see below) to induct new members in the appropriate technologies. Socially, scheduled weekly live chats create interconnections among members that are not possible in communications to the larger e-list. Chat topics rarely have an agenda, and most sessions include many personal exchanges – sympathy when a relative is ill, news of travels on a recent vacation, congratulations on a birthday (a group member keeps an electronic birthday list), comments about the weather, celebration of holidays (Mardi Gras and Halloween are special favorites), etc. Celebrations and small talk form an important part of the social cement that holds any community together, whether real or virtual. If more serious business, such as a joint presentation, is looming, members can retreat to an individual office for private discussion.

Cheerleading. Recognition by one's peers is a powerful group cement. In *WiA* especially, members are expected to report on recent achievements, particularly when they involve collaborative activities or face-to-face meetings with other members, and to comment on each other's work. In most cases, members will create a Web page or blog to link from the *WiA Index* (Almeida d'Eça 2006). In *REO*, members bookmark their students' projects in the Links area. Thus, an ongoing public history of the group provides community continuity. Reading each other's work and responding to it is an important element in CoP formation and stability.

Face-to-face meetings. Since *WiA* and *REO* are global communities, meeting one another face-to-face is a special treat. Again, both groups document such encounters and often go out of their way to connect in person, for example, to attend a member's PhD defense in Spain, or to travel to a conference where someone is presenting on land (see Almeida d'Eça (2006) Face to Face Meetings).

F.U.N. (*Frivolous Unanticipated/Unorganized Nonsense*). A term coined by Vance Stevens, F.U.N. refers to the fact that, just as in a "real" community, members arrange surprises and small acts of kindness, often seasoned with humor. On

April Fools' Day, one *WiA* member created an extraordinarily complex spoof of the *Index* of achievements, including links to odd videos, morphed visages, wacky names, and outrageous titles. At a Halloween chat at *TI*, members wore virtual "costumes," that is, text descriptions attached to their handles (online names). Costumes were judged on originality and extravagance, and virtual prizes were awarded. F.U.N. is especially important when the tensions of learning become too great: After a frustrating day trying to install an application, someone mailed the group a "symphony" based wholly on computer desktop sounds.

Mentoring. Land-based teacher training courses or in-service workshops generally present material, inform, and possibly provide some simulated practice. Among peers, especially in-service teachers, training is better shaped by reciprocal mentoring and sharing areas of expertise. Also, online mentors can directly participate with mentees in projects and classes with live students; simply being present is often an important contribution from a newbie. The emotions of gratitude for help received become mingled with the pleasure of encountering friends; the thrill of achievement is celebrated; the potential failures may be anticipated before they become disasters. As Garber summarizes: "Growing a *virtual learning community* therefore requires that we understand and embrace the social aspects critical to learners as they engage (and influence) each other across time and space" (2004:¶6). The knowledge that is generated is strengthened by the social network that surrounds each exploration.

Future prospects

The Webheads are an exceptional group in many ways. Fast friendships have formed over the five years of its existence, and yet the group remains open and exceptionally welcoming to new members. *REO* has a shorter history, but is continually evolving, adding new members, and exploring multimedia collaboratively. The *TI* and *LT* collections of communities support some very dedicated teacher groups in a wide range of content areas and continue to expand their outreach globally. However, somewhat less intense and personally engaging CoPs are gradually developing around the world, in part owing to the introduction of new online tools – or old tools put to new educational uses – and the spread of open source materials; and in part because of the growing recognition of the importance of connecting with others socially as knowledge is shared and created. The movement has even spawned a new approach to pedagogy, *Connectivism* (Siemens 2005). An examination of growing online communities indicates a steady movement from simple resource archives toward true CoP status as they add new ways of communicating and functioning. Teacher-training institutions would do well to encourage their pre- and in-service teachers to join one of these free communities (or create their own) as a way of meeting the challenges of technology. To outline just a few examples in ascending order of community-building:

MERLOT (*Multimedia Educational Resource for Learning and Online Teaching*), primarily an online journal and archive of peer-reviewed, open source, member-created materials. Members, mainly in higher education, connect with each other through a search of interests and specialities tagged in their profiles and at an annual international conference in North America. A survey in Fall 2005 indicated interest in adding communicative features.

The *SANTEC* network was organized to promote educational development and e-learning in the African context. A discussion board and e-newsletter are enhanced by monthly online colloquia on topics suggested by members. *SANTEC* serves as a channel for development grants, and regularly puts out calls for proposals and requests for consultants. With over 500 members representing most African states, the network seems to have the potential to develop an authentic community with a history, a focused geographic domain and purpose, and potentially great effectiveness in developing the continent through social networking.

The Reading Matrix, for teachers of reading, has, like other online journals, gradually shifted from a traditional academic format to a developing Internet community. It held its first wholly online conference in 2004, in a format that allowed participants to read papers and view and hear slide presentations beforehand, and then chat live online with presenters at specific times throughout the conference. The Website regularly has added features, such as a monthly poll on a hot topic accompanied by a bulletin board to discuss results, and offers useful links, free interactive reading lessons, a free quiz-scripting tool, and an e-newsletter. It has potential as a CoP, yet so far offers little means for teachers to communicate directly with each other. This will be an interesting site to watch as it develops further community-building aspects.

Australian Flexible Learning Framework, open to global members as well as Australian teachers, provides free electronic tools, connections to leaders in the field of e-learning, short-term training courses, and annual online conferences. It focuses on both people and supportive technologies in the vocational education and training sector, offering live facilitators in its COMMUNITY FORUM and an issues-focused bulletin board. Like *TI* and *LT* (where it has a voice chat room), the *Framework* is a home for many diverse CoPs or potential CoPs. Flexible e-learning makes obvious economic sense in a country the size of Australia, and the *Framework* appears to offer a significant model for Internet-driven, community-powered educational development.

Webloggers, another community on the Webheads model, originated with an *Electronic Village Online* session in 2005 and has since developed into a strong CoP, including an *EVO* induction session (the 2006 session focused on podcasting), weekly live meetings at *TI* (the Blogstream Salon), and asynchronous communications through the *weblogging Y!G* and RSS feeds. Community student projects include the group blog, *Dekita.org*, devoted to outstanding work in Web-publishing by English learners and peer-to-peer contact around the globe. *Dekita.org* received an Edublog Award in 2005.

Internet tools that support community creation are fast becoming free and standardized for universal adaptation: text, voice, and video chat, online interactive whiteboards, RSS feeds, blogs, podcasting and Internet radio, mobile accessibility to the Web, and reusable and open source course materials – these are just some of the technologies that foster the growth of global communities. Eventually, the one constraint on developing CoPs will be the time and energy of the participants. Teacher-training institutions would do well to encourage their students to join a CoP; if an institution wishes to form its own, the criteria for success should be kept in mind:

– *Domain and purpose.* A CoP created as an extension of your own workshop or online course may provide more extended and coherent assistance to new teachers over several semesters as they move from pre-service to in-service. Ensure that newbies have an initiation period to familiarize themselves with the technology and workings of an e-group, as well as the specific purpose of the community. Seek out international CoPs for your student-teachers to join. These will help with an understanding of their students in second language settings and the target culture in foreign language settings.
– *Collaborative praxis:* Create online teams to complete assignments and ensure a way to permanently archive the information they generate, for example, in Web pages, blogs, and *Y!Gs.* Archives provide reference points to steer newcomers to what has already been learned and to prevent the tedium for old hands of repeating explanations. Share reusable learning objects and encourage formative self-reflection in blogs or Web pages that can be referenced by future generations of students.
– *Tools:* Find out what Web conferencing tools are available at your institution, or take advantage of free tools such as *Y!G, Y!M, TI,* and *LT.* Tools must be cross-platform, and include real-time communication, such as live chat and/or video conferencing, in order to help student-teachers maintain contact throughout their careers. Use these tools to put student teachers in touch with each other and with the global community.
– *Social support and peer mentoring*: Seek out the most sociable student-teachers and encourage them to mentor others online. Be aware that relationships may take longer than a single class or workshop to develop. Plan for regularly scheduled meetings online, as well as asynchronous bulletin boards or e-lists. Model socialization and community-building in your own communications with novice teachers.

A local CoP may well become an important feature of an institution's total program and carry over into in-service life, particularly as more institutions offer online distance education and international programs (for several examples of local institutions' CoP formation, see Hanson-Smith 2006). If an expected part of teacher education is membership in a CoP, whether one of the international communities described here or a local class or content-based group, instructors will be far better prepared to stay knowledgeable and comfortable with technology throughout their careers. CoPs are the most economical way for classroom teachers, the front line of the education battle, to maintain and improve the skills demanded by the fast-changing world of technology their students will inhabit. CoPs can do so just-in-time, when teachers need a particular piece of information, skill, or guided practice. Consequently, teacher trainers should include in their curricula the information and encouragement needed for new instructors to step into a global, online community of practice. The virtual world has become a real community.

Note

1. ICT is used here to refer specifically to "Internet communication tools"; however, ICT is also widely used in CALL and elsewhere as an abbreviation for the much broader concept of "information and communication technologies".

References

al-Othman, B. (2003). How participation in a CoP informs and influences personal teaching. Presentation at the TESOL Convention, Baltimore MD, USA, March 26, 2003. Available at http://www.geocities.com/esl_efl_ku/projects.htm.

Alado (2005). Available at http://www.alado.net and http://www.digibridge.org.

Almeida d'Eça, T. (2004). *Teresa's Blog for The Learning Classroom Course.* Available at http://teresa-engvenblog.blogspot.com/.

Almeida d'Eça, T. (2006). *Index of "Webheads in Action" Web Pages and Related Sites.* Available at http://64.71.48.37/teresadeca/webheads/wia-index2.htm.

Blackboard (2006). Available at http://www.blackboard.com.

Australian Flexible Learning Framework (2005). Commonwealth of Australia. Available at http://www.flexiblelearning.net.au/.

Cyber-Langues (2005). L'association des enseignants de langues vivantes qui utilisent les Technologies de l'Information et de la Communication pour l'Enseignement et l'apprentissage des langues. Available at http://cyber-langues.asso.fr/.

Dekita.org: P2P in EFL/ESL Exchange (2006). R. Amman, A. Campbell and B. Dieu. Available at http://www.dekita.org.

Ebeltoft, N. & Nyrop, S. (2001). Cooperative cultures in sociotechnical communities. (Trans., S. Nyrop). *Dansk Paedagogisk Tidssdrift, 4*. Available at http://home19.inet.tele.dk/susnyrop/helpful.html.

EUROCALL (2006). European Association for Computer-Assisted Language Learning. Available at http://www.eurocall-languages.org.

evonline2002_webheads (2001). V. Stevens. Available at http://groups.yahoo.com/group/evonline2002_webheads.

Frappr (2005). Available at http://www.frappr.com.

Garber, D. (2004). Growing virtual communities. *International Review of Research in Open and Distance Learning* 5(2). Available at http://www.irrodl.org/content/v5.2/technote4.html.

Galarneau, L. (2004, 19 July). Virtual worlds *are* real worlds. *Relevancy*. Available at http://www.oddwater.com/relevancy/index.php.

González, D. (2003a). *My Journey with Webheads*. Available at http://dafnegon.tripod.com/myjourneywithwebheads/.

González, D. (2003b). Teaching and learning through chat: A taxonomy of educational chat for EFL/ESL. *Teaching English with Technology, 3* (4). Available at http://www.iatefl.org.pl/call/j_review15.htm.

Hanson-Smith, E. (2006). *Community of Practice Resources*. Available at http://webpages.csus.edu/~hansonsm/CoP_Resources.html.

Hanson-Smith, E. & Bauer-Ramazani, C. (2004). Professional development: The electronic village online of the TESOL CALL interest section. *TESL-EJ* 8(2). Available at http://www-writing.berkeley.edu/TESL-EJ/ej30/int.html.

Hanson-Smith, E. & al-Othman, B. (2004). Tools for online collaboration. Paper presented at the Reading Matrix First International Online Conference on Second and Foreign Language Teaching and Research, September 25–26, 2004. Available at http://www.geocities.com/ehansonsmi/reading_matrix/Tools_for_Collab.html.

Johnson, C. M. (2002). *CoP Theory Overview*. Available at http://sites.inka.de/manzanita/cop/.

Johnson, C. M. (2003). Establishing an Online Community of Practice for Instructors of English as a Foreign Language. PhD dissertation, Nova Southeastern University.

Jones, Q. (1997). Virtual communities, virtual settlements and cyber-archaeology: A theoretical outline. *Journal of Computer-Mediated Communication, 3* (3). Available at http://jcmc.indiana.edu/vol3/issue3/jones.html.

Kennedy, T. (2006). Making content connections online via the GLOBE Program. In E. Hanson-Smith & S. Rilling (Eds.), *Language Learning through Technology*. Alexandria, VA: TESOL.

Lave, J. & Wenger, E. (1991). *Situated Learning: Legitimate peripheral participation*. Cambridge: CUP.

LearningTimes (2006). Available at http://www.learningtimes.net.

LLTI (The Language Learning and Technology Information Forum) (1999). Available at listserv@listserv.dartmouth.edu. Archives available at http://listserv.dartmouth.edu/archives/llti.html.

MERLOT (Multimedia Educational Resource for Learning and Online Teaching). (2006). Available at http://www.merlot.org.

Moodle, Version 1.4.5 (2005). Available at http://moodle.org.

Motteram, G. & Forrester, G. (2005). Becoming an online distance learner: What can be learned from students' experiences of induction to distance programmes? *Distance Education, 26* (3), 281–298.

NETEACH-L. Rev. (30 June, 2004). J. Falsetti and S. Moody (co-owners). Available at listserv@hunter.listserv.cuny.edu. Homepage available at http://www.ilc.cuhk.edu.hk/english/neteach/main.html.

Preece, J., Nonnecke, B., & Andrews, D. (2004). The top five reasons for lurking: Improving community experiences for everyone. *Computers in Human Behavior, 20* (2), 201–223.

Preece, J. & Maloney-Krichmar, D. (2003). Online communities. In J. Jacko & A. Sears (Eds.), *Handbook of Human-Computer Interaction* (pp. 596–620). Mahwah, NJ: Lawrence Erlbaum.

The Reading Matrix (2005). Available at http://www.readingmatrix.com/.

Real English (2005). The Marzio School and Real English LLC. Available at http://www.real-english.com.

Real English Online (2003). E. Hanson-Smith & M. Marzio. Available at http://groups.yahoo.com/group/Real_English_Online.

SANTEC: Educational Technology and eLearning for Development (2005, July). Available at http://www.santecnetwork.org.

Siemens, G. (2005). Connectivism: A learning theory for the digital age. *International Journal of Instructional Technology and Digital learning, 2* (1). Available at http://www.itdl.org/Journal/Jan_05/article01.htm.

Stevens, V. (2000). Developing a community in online language learning. *Proceeds of the Military Language Institute's Teacher-to-Teacher Conference: Tools of the trade, May 3–4 2000,* Abu Dhabi, UAE. Available at http://www.geocities.com/vance_stevens//papers/webheads/t2t2000.htm.

Stevens, V. (2005, November). *Webheads in Action: Communities of practice online.* Available at http://www.geocities.com/vance_stevens/papers/evonline2002/webheads.htm.

Stevens, V., Freed, A., González, G., Hanson-Smith, E., Jones, C., & Yeh, A. (2004). *Enhancing Online Communities with Voice and Webcams: Webheads in action. Pre-Convention Institute (PCI) at the Annual TESOL Convention, Long Beach, CA, March 30, 2004.* Available at http://www.geocities.com/vance_stevens/papers/evonline2002/pci2004.htm.

Suzuki, R. (2004). Diaries as introspective research tools: From Ashton-Warner to blogs. *TESL-EJ, 8* (1). Available at http://www.kyoto-su.ac.jp/information/tesl-ej/ej29/int.html.

Tapped In (2005). SRI International. Available at http://www.tappedin.org.

TESLCA-L (2004, August 15). Available at TESLCA-L@CUNYVM.CUNY.EDU.

Valdez, G., Fulton, K., Blomeyer, Jr., R., Glenn, A., & Wimmer, N. (2004). Effective technology integration in teacher education: A comparative study of six programs. *Innovate, 1* (1). Available at http://www.innovateonline.info/index.php.

weblogging (2004). A. Campbell, B. Dieu, & G. Stanley. Available at http://groups.yahoo.com/group/weblogging.

Wenger, E. (2004). *Communities of Practice: A brief introduction.* Available at http://www.ewenger.com/theory/index.htm.

WiAOC 2005: Webheads in action online convergence (2005, December). Available at http://wiaoc.org.

WorldBridges (2006). Available at http://worldbridges.com/livewire.

Yahoo! Group. Available at http://groups.yahoo.com.

Yahoo! Messenger. Available at http://messenger.yahoo.com.

Yeh, A., González, D., & Mühren, A. (2004, February). *Let's Get Physical!* Available at http://dcyeh.com/sy0304/2ndsem/groupa_projects/tpr.

Preface to

Training ourselves to train our students for CALL

There is a widespread and credible view within education that collaborative tasks offer a productive means of achieving learning goals. As is evident from other chapters in this volume, formal courses in teacher training programs and CALL professional development can be built around collaborative projects, and communities of practice clearly provide opportunities for collaboration with peers. Another way to harness the power of collaborative learning is to build a team within an institution, language department, or language program that pursues a curricular objective or CALL project together. In this chapter, Marinna Kolaitis and her co-authors chronicle the first three years of an ongoing initiative at a community college-based ESL program to train the language learners to be more effective users of CALL. Although assisted by an external consultant and guided by a set of learner training principles, the group of nine faculty engaged in this project ended up largely training themselves and one another collaboratively in order to develop and implement the learner training materials and strategies. The chapter documents how in the process the teachers transformed their views of CALL and became more reflective about their language teaching in general. It also shows how they adapted the set of learner training principles to accommodate both general and specific characteristics of their teaching environment. The chapter discusses the challenges they addressed in putting together combinations of workshops, group meetings, and mentoring systems to refine their own approach to training their students to use technology more effectively and to assist other interested faculty in the process.

Training ourselves to train our students for CALL

Marinna Kolaitis[a], Mary Ann Mahoney[a], Howard Pomann[a], and Philip Hubbard[b]

[a]Union County College, USA / [b]Stanford University, USA

Today, multimedia and the Internet are widely accepted in the second language-learning field, but their potential to improve students' language proficiency is yet to be realized. In the early years of the computer revolution, the primary concern was simply attempting to get computers into the system and to find software that "comfortably" fit into the curriculum. Eventually, it became obvious that the effective use of computers for language learning would be even a greater challenge for both faculty and students. The Institute for Intensive English (IIE) at Union County College (UCC) in New Jersey accepted that challenge by integrating computer-assisted language learning (CALL) into its curricula and by training its faculty in CALL.

Over the past 25 years, through state-funded grants, faculty have purchased hardware and software, established computer classroom labs and open Academic Learning Center (ALC) labs, trained faculty, and created computer lessons to incorporate CALL into the program (currently more than 2000 ESL students from 83 countries). From the beginning of CALL integration, our experience has been largely collaborative, one of learning by doing and sharing our successes and failures. The collaborative efforts of the faculty focused on ways to provide a stronger link between the classroom and lab by developing a series of content lessons to be used in class before and after the computer lab sessions. While in some instances it appeared that CALL was successfully being incorporated with the content, a number of faculty questioned the time, effort and effectiveness of integrating the software into the curriculum. As faculty read and discussed related research, they began to expand the CALL approach to include training for both themselves and their students in ways to achieve language goals. The centerpiece of this chapter is an account of the collaborative efforts of our most recent college-funded project involving CALL, based on five learner training principles taken from Hubbard (2004). Specifically, this chapter will describe how a group of faculty worked together on a project to train ESL students in using CALL software more effectively and in the process trained themselves to become more informed and effective CALL teachers.

Identifying the problem

With the advent of more sophisticated software and Web access, the faculty showed the students the basics of the new software and provided curriculum study guides so that students would be able to work on their own in reinforcing their language skills. The assumption was that the students would want to work independently, especially with all the combined features of listening, recording, video and color. However, over time the instructors came to realize that the students' use of technology as an extension to language learning was minimal. That realization led to the project described in this chapter.

Specifically, faculty found that students did not follow through with lab assignments and that classroom activity did not carry over to independent study. They noted that students, and in fact many teachers, did not know how to use the software to its fullest potential, thus reducing student motivation to work independently as well as teacher incentive to take them to the computer classroom labs and train them on the computers. Students often rushed through the programs without applying language-learning strategies because neither they nor the instructors were appropriately trained beyond the mechanical aspects of the program. In addition, students did not know how to pace themselves. Many students moved through a program quickly just "to get through it", while others stared at the screen apathetically not knowing what to do next. Some faculty simply blamed the software, and many students simply switched to word-processing or e-mailing when they thought the teachers were not looking.

Teachers voiced a number of concerns over these issues, including the following.

- How can we help students to be more selective in their activities and to reflect on identifying a language learning goal?
- What strategies can students use to go about achieving their goal?
- How can students learn to extend these selective strategies outside the classroom, so they can become independent learners?
- How can students learn to approach a task in a way that best suits their language needs, their learning styles, which in many cases are determined by their cultural backgrounds, and their individual motivation?

Learner training

In response to these problems, in 2002, a team of seven Union County College ESL instructors (including chapter authors Kolaitis, Mahoney, and Pomann), one Academic Learning Center Educational Support Specialist[1] and an external consultant (Hubbard) began a project to develop pedagogically-centered CALL strategy materials along with faculty workshops, both modeled on a set of learner training principles linking networked software and Web-based ESL activities to learner goals (Hubbard 2004). These principles were initially developed and refined in the context of a single classroom, and this represented the first attempt to scale them up to a program level.

The rationale for CALL learner training and the consequent development of the principles stemmed from the realization that there is a disconnect between the realities of the CALL environment and the ideals of learner control and autonomy. As noted in Hubbard (2004: 45):

> A fundamental quandary in CALL is that learners are increasingly required to take a significant amount of responsibility for their own learning, whether that learning is taking place through the programmed teaching presence in tutorial software or the unstructured spaces of the world wide web. They are expected to do this despite the fact that they know little or nothing of how languages are learned compared to an appropriately trained teacher. And they are expected to do this within a domain – that of the computer – that is still relatively unfamiliar as a language learning environment to most of them.

The paper continues with a call for integrating learner training into any language course with a significant technology component, offering a proposal for guiding such training with five principles, summarized below (Hubbard 2004: 51–55). The first of these is aimed just at teachers rather than their students:

Principle 1: Experience CALL yourself

This principle is based on the following observation: although they may use computers regularly, many language teachers have not had firsthand experience as learners with either CALL instructional software or other uses, such as computer-mediated communication (CMC) or even browsing the web in a foreign language. With a little experience in this domain, they can understand their students' challenges and frustrations better and be more empathetic and realistic in their expectations. Further, they can see for themselves what kinds of learning opportunities and limitations the computer environment actually provides and adjust their plans for learner training accordingly.

The four remaining principles in that paper are devoted to guidelines for promoting and sustaining learner training in language classrooms.

Principle 2: Give learners teacher training

If learners are expected to take on more of the teacher role, as they do in any autonomous learning situation, then they will clearly be better prepared for that role if they have some of the same knowledge regarding language learning that their teachers possess. One part of such training lies in the linking of an activity with a specific learning objective. To accomplish that connection requires providing learners with guided practice in identifying objectives and an awareness of the need to determine a path to realize them. A related aspect involves emphasizing the importance of *deliberation* and *consolidation* in the CALL learning task or exercise. Basically, deliberation refers to the cognitive steps a learner goes through in a CALL activity, such as preparing to respond to a comprehension question or thinking about the feedback when an item is missed. Consolidation refers to the additional cognitive steps that follow the final feedback on an item or activity before the learner continues to the next one, ideally linking any new material to what has been previously learned. Taken together, deliberation and consolidation simply imply an intent to learn: for a typical tutorial CALL exercise, this means you think before you answer, especially if you are uncertain of that answer, and you reflect on the feedback after you receive it.

Principle 3: Use a cyclical approach

This principle acknowledges that few things are learned by a single exposure. Most computer programs today embody a range of controls and features that cannot be mastered all at once. All too often, technical training takes place only at the beginning, and pedagogically-oriented training does not occur at all. For language learners to get the most from CALL training, it needs to be done on a regular basis both to avoid information overload and to reinforce previously learned concepts. In addition, it is recommended that learners be given an opportunity to "play" with software or experience the web or CMC environment before being given training so that some degree of familiarity is established on which to hang the instruction. As noted in McDonough (1995: 101–102), there are a number of problems with training in strategy use for language learning in general, among them the lack of evidence for the strategies' persistence over time. Assuming this observation carries over to the type of learner training proposed here, consistency and ubiquity in training through the repetition inherent in a cyclical or spiral approach appears the most promising way of promoting long-term positive changes in how students interact with their CALL applications.

Principle 4: Use collaborative debriefings

It is widely recognized that collaborative learning has a number of advantages. When students are on a computer, typically they are alone. Whether engaged in using tutorial software or in some use of the computer as a communicative tool, learners will probably engage more fruitfully if they regularly share information about what they did and why they did it. Such "collaborative debriefings" can occur either at the end of a group lab session or at the beginning of a class session following a CALL homework assignment. Ideally, students are divided into small groups for a short reflective discussion focusing on what they did and why they did it – how they saw their actions as linked or not to an identifiable learning objective.

Principle 5: Teach general exploitation strategies
As mentioned in the introduction, students using software tend to move through it mechanically, without considering the high degree of control they actually have. Through training, they can learn how to adapt to the software, leading it to support not only the language skills and subskills it was designed for, but often others as well. This is typically a later stage of learner training, as it represents the most creative and individualized of the principles and assumes learners already have the ability to make informed choices in selecting among a range of potential learning objectives that a given piece of instructional software or other computer-based activity or task may afford. Key concepts in this area that can be taught somewhat earlier are techniques that may be applied across a range of programs for making hard material easier, such as judicious use of the "pause" button, or making easy material harder, for example, by hiding the list of possible answers to multiple choice questions and trying to answer them first as open-ended ones.

It is worth noting that this approach to learner training has clear links to the development of autonomy (Healey 1999; Benson 2001: 136–141) and that some of the metacognitive and cognitive strategies suggested for learner training are similar to those presented in Oxford (1990) and elsewhere, though with an added technological twist.

Project faculty training

During the first year, to implement learner training in their computer classes, the project team reviewed the existing networked programs available to the students and analyzed the various meaning aids and other support features that the programs offered.

At the same time, a set of strategy guidelines was developed so students could follow through using the program activities for their independent study. The team met monthly for their own collaborative debriefings and conferenced by phone and e-mail with the project consultant to revise the student materials, to plan faculty workshops, to get and give feedback on student reactions, and more importantly, to share their classroom implementation of learner training. In the process, the team members came to recognize how important it was for their own training to be cyclical and collaborative, which an understanding of language learning principles.

In order to engage in CALL learner training more fully, the group met twice to experience CALL on their own (Principle #1) to gain insight from the learner's perspective. Using the online *Rosetta Stone* software program, team members each chose a language that they had little knowledge of or were completely unfamiliar with. The results were enlightening as they discussed the various strategies used to reach their individual goals. One participant wrote on the workshop evaluation sheet:

> I realized that if I were a student, how I used this program in the ALC would probably vary according to my purpose and how much time I had. On some days I might want to focus just on pronunciation, for example, while another day I might want to really concentrate on prepositions. I think I would probably use it a bit differently each time depending on my focus.

At the end of the first year, the team began to revise its approach to strategy development. After several months of implementing the software suggestions in the classroom labs, they observed that the students' primary focus was still to complete the activity rather than to improve in their language skill. It then became evident that the development of effective strategies needed to be taken a step further by first identifying the language goal, a core element in strategy development, and understanding the language learning principle behind that goal.

However, when the team met, there was little agreement at first on matching goals with various software activities. In regard to listening, for example, recommendations from members were often based on the perceived outcome of the activity rather than on the specific goal. Several members viewed listening instruction as answering comprehension questions and completing dictations correctly. Separate goals for listening had not been delineated in terms of listening for main ideas, listening to process language, and listening for individual grammar structures and vocabulary. The team questioned: "Should students look at the transcript as part of their listening practice?" "When should students read and listen simultaneously?" "When do students move from one goal to the next?" The problem seemed to be that individuals had not clarified the relationship between certain language learning principles and the various goals in any consistent way. At this point, the consultant assisted the group in connecting the language principles to each associated goal. Once language learning assumptions and goals were connected, consensus on suggested strategies was reached. With the goal and language principles in mind, the team was able to help students select strategies more effectively and manipulate the various controls and meaning aids more skillfully.

As part of this process, the strategies for listening and grammar were organized into four categories: language learning goals, language learning principles, deliberation (pre-response) strategies, and consolidation (post-response) strategies. A "CALL journal" for students' independent study was devised, also based on the learning principles of deliberation and consolidation. The team intended the journals to serve as note-taking guides to assist students in consolidating important language points for their listening, grammar, and vocabulary goals.

By utilizing a CALL journal, students are trained to keep notes from session to session, understand why they selected an answer, and reflect on what they have done and how it relates to their goals and class work. Applying deliberation and consolidation strategies to a specific language goal allows students to become more effective in their choices, more adept in using the various controls and meaning aids, and more reflective in their responses. As an added benefit, teachers can use the journals as records of how students apply strategies throughout the semester.

The following outline for grammar is a sample of the strategy material that was developed by the project team.

Goal: Grammar – language learning principles
1. Understand context of an item.
2. Understand why you are choosing a particular item (form and function).
3. Reflect and understand why a form which you chose was incorrect.
4. Take notes in the CALL journal to remember new and important forms and functions.

Based on these language learning principles, the following suggestions are offered to students to guide them through deliberation and consolidation processes.

For deliberation strategies
1. Read instructions carefully to determine form(s) being practiced.
2. Review grammar explanations and/or charts to clarify the use of a form before starting.
3. Read the entire sentence or paragraph to understand the context. Use dictionary resources if necessary.
4. Reflect on why you are choosing a particular response before answering.

For consolidation strategies
1. Reflect on incorrect responses before answering a second time.
   Why did I make the mistake?
   What is the correct form, and why is it correct?
   What points do I need to review?
   What questions do I have for the teacher?
2. Take notes in your journal, explaining why forms are correct or incorrect. In some cases, print out screens with incorrect forms and then correct later, noting why your answers were wrong.

As the team began the second year of strategy training with their students, they felt comfortable with the cyclical implementation of the training (Principle #3) and with the introduction of general exploitation strategies (Principle #5). However, they generally felt much less comfortable with raising their students' awareness of language learning principles (Principle #2), and with conducting/finding time for collaborative debriefings (Principle #4). A major focus of the team meetings was on how students can be trained to express their strategy choices in debriefing sessions and ultimately apply these strategies independently.

To address these issues, the team explored ways to conduct collaborative debriefings before, after and during lab sessions. They shared classroom discussion questions, which encouraged students to reflect on their strategies. Faculty who taught advanced levels had more success in conducting collaborative debriefings in which students discussed strategy use. Teachers at beginning levels saw that their students could summarize content learned, but in many cases did not have the language to express their goals and strategies. With this in mind different formats for debriefings at each level were discussed. Debriefings at the beginning levels concentrated on mechanical strategies and content, while the advanced levels focused on identifying their goals and explaining their choice of strategies. By the end of the second year, the team realized that such debriefings were more successful when student training was also extended into the classroom as well as in the lab.

Training faculty outside the project group

One of the key points of this collaborative approach is that those in the project group became the "learner training experts" for the program and both formally and informally shared their experiences, techniques, and materials with other faculty members. In the first year, a full-day workshop was given by the consultant to introduce the learner training principles and strategies to interested UCC faculty who were not in the project group. In the second year, training continued with a full-day workshop given by the project team and consultant and three additional in-house sessions to continue learner training discussion, share suggestions for classroom implementation and receive feedback from other faculty. In these in-house sessions the training procedure was similar to that of the project team: the teachers were given a pre-workshop task of identifying ways they used the *Rosetta Stone* to meet specific language goals. During the workshops, participants were introduced to applying language learning principles to the activities in our networked grammar software. Working in groups, they identified various types of strategies and reflected on why they chose those strategies. Subsequent workshops were given specifically to concentrate on listening goals.

Additional training took the form of team members meeting individually with full-time and adjunct faculty to introduce strategies for software used at their course levels. To accommodate the adjunct faculty's varied schedules, a software fair was set up for two weeks in which team members were available in the lab for faculty to come in at their convenience. Faculty discussed the mechanical aspects of the programs along with specific strategies. About fifteen teachers attended over a two-week period. During these hands-on sessions, teachers became familiar with software suitable for their class levels. They practiced how to use the menu systems, hints, etc. and discussed various strategies to use for listening and/or grammar goals. Although this format provided more individual input and discussion while working with a specific program, most participants did not get beyond the "how to" level. Similar one-on-one training sessions were given by the Educational Support Specialist in the Academic Learning Center throughout the semester.

These all day workshops and individual drop-in training sessions were somewhat successful but clearly had their limitations. The team realized that the training approach needed to be cyclical as with the project team and students, i.e., to introduce the learning principles, discuss strategies to meet the goal, practice hands-on both on their own and in the classroom, and provide opportunities for debriefing/reflecting on the strategies.

Consequently, in the third year, the team attempted to provide one-on-one training with follow-up meetings and/or team teaching for full time and part time faculty. Experience with this form of training has varied, depending on the faculty member's interest, CALL experience, and teaching style.

At the beginning of the semester, faculty members were invited to meet with a project mentor to go through the different software programs available for their classes. Teachers chose a program based on the language learning goal they wanted to stress in the lab. Basic deliberation and consolidation strategies to meet the goals for the chosen software were introduced, and the concept of using CALL journals for grammar, listening, and vocabulary development was presented, as well as the CALL website. Mentors also discussed ineffective behaviors that students typically demonstrate if they are not trained, i.e., running through programs. They focused on demonstrating to the teachers how and why the suggested strategies can help their students to become more successful learners.

Although it was an effective approach for some faculty, especially those who were experienced in CALL and already had some understanding of the role of strategy training in other domains, for many this initial session was too overwhelming. The team encouraged other faculty to continue working with a mentor and even to have a mentor assist them in the lab; however, most faculty were reluctant to go beyond the first meeting, given that it was voluntary and no additional compensation was provided. The project team is currently working on ideas to increase the effectiveness of this initial mentoring session and the subsequent retention rate.

With the faculty who did continue with mentoring, each was approached differently. One faculty member teaching intermediate students was interested in teaching her students how to use various programs on the web to improve listening. A mentor followed up the initial meeting by discussing listening goals, associated learning principles, and specific software and journal strategies to achieve the goals. The mentor taught with the teacher for two lab sessions, introducing the initial principles and strategies to her students. The faculty member and mentor met a few weeks later to discuss the application of journal strategies to a different web-listening program.

A second faculty member teaching a beginning level class was interested in strategies for *Live Action English*, a multi-skill video-based program. Over the course of several weeks, the mentor and the instructor discussed the strategies for the multiple templates in the software and strategies for training the students. Eventually, through the on-going discussion and occasional observation of students in the classroom lab, the project mentor began to see students utilizing new strategies that the teacher had developed on her own, such as sitting in pairs retelling the video actions.

Another faculty member teaching a beginning level class was interested in learning strategies for a networked listening/grammar program. Although the teacher met with the mentor several times, he did not go beyond the "how to" level in using the software. In the classroom lab sessions, he remained fairly inactive, only getting up to help students when asked. It was surprising to the team that the faculty member was very open to the mentor coming in and working actively with the students. At times, even with a more extended introduction of the learner training principles, it is difficult for some faculty to get beyond a preconceived assumption that students left on their own will use the software effectively and efficiently, needing assistance only with basic usage and content questions.

These subsequent mentoring sessions were undoubtedly more effective than the one-time sessions. However, it is important to note that they did not seem to offer the depth of learning and transformation that the collaborative approach provided for the project team.

Changes in teacher implementation

With implementation of learner training principles in computer labs, the project team made changes in their approach to teaching CALL strategies. The cyclical approach was used throughout the semester to train students in the learner principles and strategies, allowing them to become familiar with the software and to practice choosing specific strategies that suited their individual learning styles. Faculty realized students needed time during class and on-going training over a period of time. As a result, teachers became more interactive with students in labs by guiding them in making effective choices. As one teacher observed:

> Before I just walked around and as long as they didn't look stuck, I left them alone and assumed they were learning. But now I try to figure out what they are doing, what they are learning. Very important to circulate during the lab sessions the entire time and get feedback/give advice to students.

During the time students were working, teachers were able to coach them while allowing them to take more control. Student training was being directed toward autonomous learning. As another teacher noted:

> Training/encouraging students to be independent learners is not an easy task, but it is worth the effort. Self awareness of learning strategies is a gradual process that will develop over successive semesters.

Faculty helped students go beyond the mechanical aspects of CALL by showing them how to mesh the mechanics with their goals, as reflected in the following comment:

> My approach has changed completely. I didn't use to train students to use the CALL software in an active way, so I didn't like to take students to the lab because I thought it was too similar to using the book and that students weren't really paying attention or learning. Now I feel that students are using the lab time in a more focused, active way.

An important aspect of the strategy training was the incorporation of discussion and reflection sessions into the curriculum. Allowing time for these essential discussions was best done during or immediately following the lab sessions. When students were given a task for these collaborative debriefings, such as completing questionnaires about strategy use, it was found that their responses were more reflective and specific.

Through these small-group discussions, students become aware of how and why they are using a strategy and begin to take control over their strategy use and choices. The debriefings provide a chance for students to reflect on their own strategies, learn the language needed to talk and write about strategies, expand language acquisition knowledge, learn from other students, and review content of lessons. While listening to various responses, faculty can monitor the students' selection of strategies and thus adapt the training accordingly. One faculty member commented on the value of reflection sheets:

> Class discussions were based on their reflection sheets. Students shared advice and we discussed some common errors that they'd reported on their sheet.

Changes in student implementation

As a result of CALL learner training, observations of the students show that many are utilizing strategies to exploit different capabilities that a program offers. Rather than following the direct menu path of a program, students will often take the lead by choosing a particular activity, related directly to their goal. Furthermore, many are slowing down and moving away from the goal of quickly running through a program. It has also been noted that they are taking some notes in their journals, printing out charts, screens and pages with their work, and analyzing incorrect responses. One faculty member reported about her students in an end-of-semester evaluation form:

> Increased confidence and independence. For example, as the semester continued, I noted that many of my weaker students began to take control of their learning by checking Grammar Notes, checking their class notes, copying difficult items, and asking software-related questions in class.

Nevertheless, a few challenges remain: some students still spend time on activities that are not beneficial and that are time consuming for a small return; some go through every activity in order of the program menu; some need constant monitoring; some need to be reminded of their goal; others resist taking notes. And then there are those who do not wish to be interrupted while doing a computer activity. These challenges need to be addressed by continuous training of students to understand what they are doing and why.

What we have learned

Redirect the teacher's approach from focusing on a specific task to identifying the learning goal first.

One of the most critical changes in the project team's approach has been the shift from focusing on the best ways to complete an activity to exploring the best ways to achieve a specific language goal using an activity. That is, the activity changed from being the "end" to becoming the "means to the end". This shift occurred in both the development of strategies (as described in previous section) and with classroom implementation.

Shift emphasis from simply reinforcing content taught in class to training students in strategies for independent learning.

Another major area of discussion in the team meetings has been related to the balancing of content instruction with strategy training for independent learning. Prior to the project, the main focus of the lab was on supporting the content of the classroom. With the shift to an emphasis on strategies for independent learning, however, the focus has become "how to learn" and "how to teach yourself." To summarize, the instruction included teaching students to a) identify the learning goal, b) choose appropriate programs/activities, c) choose the appropriate level of ability/interest, and d) use appropriate strategies on their own.

This shift has not been fully accepted by some faculty because of their orientation toward content teaching and their perceived time constraints. In one-on-one training sessions, for example, several teachers have been reluctant to use web-listening sites unless the sites include comprehension questions. In these training sessions, it is pointed out that although questions may be a component of listening activities, they are not the goal. Rather, the emphasis is on showing students how to achieve their listening goals independently by selecting an appropriate listening passage and by using the audio/video clip, the script, and other features.

Extend to regular classroom activities.

As a continuation of the cyclical approach, strategy training was extended to other classroom activities. The project team realized that when applying the language principles to everyday activities, students became aware that strategy selection applies to all their learning. For example, while doing a fill-in-the blank grammar activity, students can learn to reflect on their wrong answers by circling the incorrect answers rather than erasing them. With the same activity, they can discuss with another student the reason their answers were incorrect or correct. With listening activities, students can be introduced to the different listening goals and practice the various ways of using the audio transcript to support their listening. Beyond the specific strategies, discussion on how they approach their overall studies throughout a semester helps students realize which strategies are best for them. Not only has this extension been beneficial to the students' teaching themselves, but it has also had a dramatic impact on the project team's teaching in class.

Consultant's perspective

The project began with a set of principles (Hubbard 2004), but the experience in applying them had previously been limited to the consultant's own classes. In scaling up first to the small group (project team) and then to the larger group (other interested faculty) level, there were some important lessons learned. First, it came as something of a surprise that principles for *learner* training, such as using collaborative debriefings, were adapted by this group so readily for their own *teacher* training. Second, it became clear that these principles are guides, not prescriptions. For instance, the suggestion to spend significant amounts of class or lab time on collaborative debriefings was difficult to implement for some of the project members and even more so for the other faculty. Instead of following the principles dogmatically, this group adapted ideas selectively, building more strongly on the concept of strategy development, which seemed to be more in line with their setting and teaching approaches. They also made adjustments to the principle of providing the learners with teacher training to fit the language level differences, with lower proficiency students generally receiving less in this area. Third, groups of teachers engaged in collaborative self-training are put again in the role of students to some degree, and as such they are more likely to see the world from a student's perspective, opening their eyes to new possibilities. The addition of the CALL journal was just one example of an innovation for CALL learner training to come out of this experience. Being on the opposite coast, the consultant often was not engaged in the project for several months at a time, and most of the training was being done by the teachers – training themselves and one another. This collaborative approach, though not always smooth, appears to have led to more profound changes in practice than would have occurred otherwise.

Conclusion

At the end of the third year, the team continued with five members from the previous group and four additional members. The new group proceeded in strategy training by conducting monthly meetings following the model of learner training principles. In the first meetings of the semester, the team discussed the learning principles in relation to their class implementation with emphasis on deliberation and collaboration strategies for listening and grammar. Questions and prompts used in their classroom debriefings were shared and further adapted to make them appropriate for each instructor's style and class level.

In addition to monthly meetings, a *WebBoard* forum was established for faculty to share their suggestions, guidelines for student use and classroom materials. This tool has served as a cyclical resource for the training of the team, and in the future for other interested faculty. Faculty and students also have access to a new ESL website with links to the developed strategy materials and CALL journals along with links to various listening, grammar, pronunciation, and language reference websites.

In the future, the three facets of training will be continued: the project team collaborative group training, full faculty workshops, and one-on-one mentoring. Of the three formats, the collaborative approach based on the learner training model has been the most effective at UCC. Moreover, such training can be organized more informally with a small group of faculty with minimal funding and flexible scheduling.

At the time of this writing the team has extended the training by emphasizing learning CALL on their own (Principle #1) as a collaborative group for the current year. Using CD-ROM and on-line materials to practice a second language, a group of eight faculty and the consultant are exploring their individual learner strategies while achieving their language goals. Keeping a weekly learning journal through an online discussion board (*WebBoard*) and meeting regularly, faculty discuss what they have discovered about their strategy use and classroom implementation. Through this process, faculty have noticed that strategies they had previously suggested to students may be more effective in some cases than others. This experience has also been helpful in training students to discover how they learn. Additional initiatives include developing on-line tutorials based on the strategy guidelines, classroom implementation, and suggestions from the faculty CALL journals. Further grant funding will be sought to replicate the collaborative approach of the "CALL on Your Own" project, and to extend the strategy training program-wide.

The project has been an enriching and enlightening experience for the nine-member team. During meetings, the team has questioned each other's rationales for using certain approaches and strategies; in classes, the process of incorporating the language learning principles has challenged each member's own approach to language learning, not only with software programs, but also in general classroom instruction. The process of reflecting on the learner training principles made the team members more aware of *why* and *what* they are teaching, as well as *what* students need in order to be autonomous learners. Through this team effort, they have gained renewed respect for each other's approaches while thinking about their own approaches in new ways.

We anticipate that the collaborative approach the project group applied to CALL learner training at UCC can be extended to future technology initiatives there. This is clearly a promising area for additional research and development, and others are encouraged to consider it as an alternative or supplement to formal CALL training for their own language programs.

Note

1. The authors would like to thank Lewis Cohen of the Union County College Academic Learning Center for his assistance on this project.

References

BBC Languages (2005). Available at http://www.bbc.co.uk/languages.

Benson, P. (2001). *Teaching and Researching Autonomy in Language Learning*. London: Longman.

Healey, D. (1999). Theory and research: Autonomy and language learning. In J. Egbert & E. Hanson-Smith (Eds.), *CALL Environments: Research, practice, and critical issues* (pp. 391–402). Alexandria, VA: TESOL.

Hubbard, P. (2004). Learner training for effective use of CALL. In S. Fotos & C. Browne (Eds.), *New Perspectives on CALL for the Second Language Classroom* (pp. 45–67). Mahwah, NJ: Lawrence Erlbaum.

Live Action English (2001). Berkeley, CA: Command Performance Language Institute.

McDonough, S. (1995). *Strategy and Skill in Learning a Foreign Language*. London: Edward Arnold.

Oxford, R. (1990). *Language Learning Strategies: What every teacher should know*. Boston, MA: Heinle & Heinle.

The Rosetta Stone (2006). Available at http://www.rosettastone.com.

WebBoard (2006). Carlsbad, CA: Akiva. Available at http://www.webboard.com.

Preface to

Helping teachers to help themselves

If we were to ask current language teachers and researchers how they had learned about CALL, most of us would not be surprised if the vast majority replied they had educated themselves, through attending conferences and workshops, reading the literature, investigating software, and holding discussions with similarly inclined peers and colleagues. Independent learning has almost been the norm. In fact it is a testament to the initiative, commitment and resourcefulness of contemporary CALL practitioners that much has been achieved without the support, in the main, of formal teacher education programs and courses in the field. Although we believe we have reached a stage where a more systematic approach to teacher education and CALL needs to be contemplated seriously, we also acknowledge the strengths of independent learning and the capacities this approach brings to an individual language teacher who faces rapid and continuous technological change. Furthermore, even if we were to have a wide ranging network of teacher education courses in CALL, we would still need individuals who can continue to respond confidently to innovation and change after the more formal part of their CALL education has been completed. In this chapter, Thomas Robb provides an overview of the literature on autonomy and self-directed learning as it relates to CALL, and clarifies and distinguishes the meaning of these terms. This important discussion also helps us to understand the interrelationship in teacher education and CALL between the development of purely technical skills and the development of the pedagogical skill, knowledge and expertise necessary to be able to teach a language effectively in a learning environment that involves technology. He also explores some subtle points on how an instructor's background, intuition and knowledge of resources lead to certain actions in a CALL setting and ultimately, certain understandings of problems and their solutions.

Helping teachers to help themselves

Thomas N. Robb

Kyoto Sangyo University, Japan

The preface to the inaugural issue of the *International Journal for Self-Directed Learning* begins by saying that,

> The proliferation of information and technology and the accelerated rate of change in all aspects of our lives have led to increased recognition of the importance of lifelong self-directed learning. Educational institutions at all levels have added the development of lifelong self-directed learners to their mission and goal statements, as have professional associations of nurses, physicians, and engineers, among others. (Long & Guglielmino 2004: ii)

This need is felt even more strongly in a rapidly developing field such as CALL, where the skills and content encountered in training programs could well be outdated in a matter of months. Teacher preparation programs must thus look beyond the mere teaching of today's software and skills to ensure that teachers can act autonomously to upgrade their knowledge and be able to apply new technologies to their teaching in a timely manner. Language teaching programs in schools and universities must likewise do whatever possible to encourage their instructors to keep up with changes in technology and their many applications to more effective language teaching and learning.

The language teaching profession today is keenly aware of the need to foster autonomy among its students, but little has been said about the need for autonomy in our professional development programs. To this end, Warschauer states that,

> [T]he concept of autonomy must be extended beyond self-directed use of language and today's technology to the ability to develop, explore, evaluate, and adapt new technology as it evolves. This ability requires the development of metaskills of critique and innovation beyond the skills of deploying any particular technology....Teachers should be able not only use today's CALL software, but should have successful strategies for evaluating and adapting the new waves of software that will surely come. (Warschauer 2002: 457)

Autonomy and self-directed learning

While such learning activity has been discussed in the language training field under the rubric of *autonomy*, in other fields it is more commonly referred to under the closely-related term, *self-directed learning* (Hiemstra 2004: 3).

Autonomy, in its basic dictionary meaning, simply refers to the ability of an entity (originally, a political entity) to act free of restraint from outside forces. In the field of second language education "teacher autonomy" as discussed in Smith has two very distinct connotations, one being the ability of the teacher to act without constraint and the second, with which we are concerned here, the ability to extend one's learning for oneself (Smith 2003). It is perhaps due to the potential ambiguity of the term *autonomy* that *self-direction* is used more often when discussing the continued learning of instructors, rather than students.

Confessore and Park (2004: 42) define "functional learner autonomy" as:

> ...a range of ability and willingness to participate in selecting and shaping learning projects in which the learner may function independently or in concert with others. The degree to which an individual is engaged in functional learner autonomy is expressed in the extent to which the learner optimizes the learning process by making efficient and appropriate use of personal resources and *the resources of others*... (italics mine)

Thus for a learner to act autonomously does not mean to act alone, but rather to be able to decide how to use one's own resources and those of others appropriately.

Guglielmino, Long, and Hiemstra (2004), in their review of self-directed learning in the United States, quote Knowles, who defines self-directed learning as

> a process in which individuals take the initiative, with or without the help of others, in diagnosing their learning needs, formulating learning goals, identifying human and material resources for learning, choosing and implementing appropriate learning strategies, and evaluating learning outcomes. (Knowles 1975: 18)

Another important distinction between *autonomy* when referring to language learning and *self-direction* in the acquisition of technical skills and CALL methodology is that the degree of self-direction required and the learning goals for technical skills are often much narrower in scope and more easily attained than the overall goal of learning a language. For example, a technical goal might be as simple as "find a way to search for line break characters and replace them with spaces" whereas almost no goal in language learning can be so easily defined or attained.

Traits related to autonomous, self-directed learning

Confessore and Park (2004) present a discussion of the various psychological constructs that are related to autonomy and self-direction. In their paper, they report on Ponton (1999) who has developed a five component construct for learner initiative which I summarize below with extracts from their longer descriptions:

1. Goal-directedness: "The behavior of a learner establishing a learning goal that will lead to a valued level of learning and subsequently working to accomplish this goal."
2. Action-orientation: "An action-oriented individual creates and enacts learning plans quickly."
3. Overcoming obstacles: "The learner's continual engagement in a learning activity despite the presence of impediments" such as "a lack of confidence in learning ability, lack of resources, time constraints. . .."
4. Active approach: A learner that "does not wait on someone else to solve his or her problems."
5. Self-starting: "The self-starting learner will not wait on others to create learning goals." (Confessore & Park 2004: 45–46)

Ponton, Carr, and Derrick (2004) see resourcefulness, initiative and persistence as intentional behaviors that underlie motivation and self-efficacy. Self-directedness occurs when an individual believes that self-directed learning will lead to the attainment of a goal, that goal only being created when the individual believes that he or she possesses the capability to achieve it (62). Performing a "path analysis" of the relationship of desire, resourcefulness, initiative and persistence, they found that resourcefulness, that is, the subjective judgment that an individual had concerning his or her ability to access the materials or information required to attain a certain goal, was a strong predictor of the degree of initiative and persistence shown (67). Thus, it would appear that the key to encouraging initiative and persistence would be to extend the resourcefulness of our teachers and teachers-to-be.

A simple scenario

To see how resourcefulness and the other factors above might come into play in an actual opportunity for learning, let us expand on the example mentioned briefly above. In this scenario based on an actually observed situation, the instructor realizes the need to acquire a small piece of technical knowledge:

> The instructor copies a page of text from a web page into a blank *Word* document. The text is pasted in with a line break character at the end of each

line and thus appears on the page as a series of alternating full lines and half lines. He knows that he can make the paragraphs whole again by deleting the line breaks one by one, tediously clicking at the beginning of each line, pressing "Delete" and then pressing the space bar to insert a space instead. With a full page of tedious repetitive work ahead of him, he thinks "There must be a better way...", then goes to the search and replace dialog but realizes that he doesn't know how to specify that he wants to search for line breaks, so gives up. He then goes back to removing the line break characters manually, finishing the task in 2–3 minutes.

1) When the instructor made the decision to look for a better way, he probably did so because he already had some knowledge that a search and replace might be possible. This could be because he had seen someone perform this operation at some point, learned about it and forgot it, actually performed this operation with different word processor software and thus assumed that *Word* might have this function as well, or some other possible reason.

2) Once he became motivated to find an easier way, he had several options on how to proceed. In this case, the user made a feeble attempt via trial and error and then quickly gave up. Had he been more persistent, he might have discovered the button that reveals the advanced menu features, noticed that there was a pull down menu for special characters and found the line break symbol ("^p") there. He might have tried a number of other alternatives such as checking the built-in help function, consulting a third party manual on *Word*, searched the web via a keyword search, or called up a colleague whom he knew possessed more advanced knowledge.

3) Another issue is the degree of persistence itself. How willing was he to invest time now to learn something which might make his future word processing more efficient? Perhaps by the second or third time he confronts the same problem, he might decide to invest more time in discovering the correct procedure, or ask a colleague during a casual encounter later on.

In the ensuing parts of this chapter we will look more closely at these issues. First we will define who the target of the discussion, the "CALL instructor", is. Next we will examine more closely the reasons why, apart from trivial examples like the one above, self-direction is required and then proceed to explore avenues to empower our instructors to become self-directed acquirers of technical and pedagogical CALL skills.

Defining the CALL instructor

CALL, as an academic specialty, has no explicit licensing requirements. Anyone can become a "CALL teacher" merely by applying some aspect of CALL to their current teaching. The trend for teachers with no CALL-specific training to use CALL activities in their classes will continue as computers and other forms of technology become more accessible and understandable.

Given that any instructor may freely use CALL in his or her teaching often without the explicit consent or knowledge of the teaching institution, then training via pre-service programs will reach only a fraction of teachers – those new to teaching who took a sufficient number of hours of CALL-related classes while in their preparation program. The onus thus falls upon the language program administrator to see that instructors have access to the knowledge they require to use CALL effectively. We must look beyond formal training courses and consider ways to support and encourage all instructors to continually experiment with and implement new technologies in their language classes.

Why course work is not enough

In addition to the rapid development of technology, which has already been acknowledged, there are other reasons why the content of formal courses is insufficient to prepare instructors for the real challenges of using CALL in the classroom.

- Mismatches between what has been studied and what is actually needed in the classroom. While instructors may understand the technology, they might not be able to use the functions they have learned in a relevant teaching context.
- Instructors typically having little control over either the hardware or software made available to them. Furthermore, they might well be assigned classes where the software they are familiar with is inappropriate. Other factors, such as the orientation of the school towards technology and the level of mastery of the students and other staff, may conspire against effective CALL use.
- Teachers without training needing to pick up skills on their own. As mentioned earlier, many CALL practitioners are self-trained. This trend will continue as the use of technology becomes "normalized" (Bax 2003). In the future, the use of audio, video, computers and the Internet may become generalized to the point that all teachers implicitly use technology as a matter of course, much in the same way that chalk is used today. This of course, does not imply that it will be used effectively.
- Few opportunities to practice and review what has been learned. Just like learning a language, considerable practice is required to "get it right", yet we

cannot possibly build sufficient practice into all of the technical functions that we teach. If instructors do not have the opportunity to prepare and use software under real class conditions there is a strong likelihood that they will forget their training.

- A lack of local support that forces teachers to do their own troubleshooting. The tendency for schools to invest in hardware with little regard for the training of personnel in its effective use is widespread (see Norman 1999; Technology Alliance 1998). Despite the recommendation of the U.S. President's panel on Educational Technology (cited in Feldman 2005), the trend to spend money on hardware at the expense of human support continues:

> ...[a]t least 30% of the technology budget should be used to provide teachers with ongoing mentoring and consultative support, and with time to familiarize themselves with available software and content, to incorporate technology into their lesson plans, and to discuss technology use with other teachers. (5)

The question is then, "How can CALL teacher trainers equip their students with the strategies, know-how and confidence to accommodate themselves to technological change?"

Preparing autonomous CALL teachers – Train for the future, not just the present

An important component of any CALL program is learning some of the basic applications and resources available to instructors along with how they can be used to advantage in the CALL class. With the realization that most of what we teach will soon change, we need to equip our students with the basic components that promote self-acquisition: 1) a solid knowledge base; 2) the confidence to attempt to use new technology and extend their use of the technology they are already using; and 3) an awareness of available resources. Now, let us examine each of these elements in turn.

A knowledge base that removes some of the mystery of the technology

The more aspects of technology and CALL that teachers have had experience with the greater the chance that they will be able to cope when a new challenge presents itself. Since we cannot easily predict the future teaching environments of our students, the more applications that they have had exposure to, the more likely it is that one of the applications taught will be usable in the future. To this end, Duhaney (2001: 27) states:

> [i]n order to ensure that prospective teachers are capable of integrating technology in classroom activities, faculty within teacher education institutions should model appropriate uses of technology for teaching and learning. This should not only be restricted to teaching methodology courses but should involve courses in the different disciplines.

A project approach (Debski, this volume), whereby teacher trainees create a product that is potentially useful in the classroom, or which emulates a project that they might have their students do in class (Chao, this volume), is a useful learning device. Seeing a project through from start to finish helps to build confidence and provides a sense of completeness and fulfillment. Nevertheless, when one considers the premise that we cannot predict what may be useful for any specific individual, a strong argument can be made for a balanced approach that also teaches just the basics of a wider variety of applications. While the basics may not be sufficient for students to quickly apply the software to their future teaching, some familiarity will: a) give them some idea of how it might be useful in the classroom, b) give them the confidence to attempt to use it later on their own, but most importantly c) allow them to see the commonalities between various applications and thus deepen their general background knowledge and understanding of technology, and thereby add to their overall ability to be resourceful. Hughes (2004) espouses the teaching of many technologies: "...offering only a few technology options will reduce the number of technology-using teachers in the school, due to a lack of connection between the available technologies and the teachers' needs" (354).

As important as knowing how to use any specific technology is an awareness of pedagogically useful ways that it can be applied. By consciously using a variety of technologies in all courses being studied, the pre-service instructor will have a greater bank of experiences to draw upon and apply in the future. For example, using a computer projection system, lecture courses can demonstrate "on the fly" searches for answers to questions that come up in class. Teachers can use *PowerPoint* animations to illustrate complex processes, brainstorming sessions can be done with overhead projection and *Word* which allows the various concepts to be easily rearranged and categorized by drag and drop. The result of the activity can then be readily saved and posted on the class website for future reference, thus demonstrating another use of technology. See Teclehaimanot and Lamb (2005), and Marra, Howland, Jonassen, and Wedman (2004) for a deeper discussion of methods to encourage the modeling of technology in teacher education courses.

The confidence to try something new

As discussed at the outset of this chapter, more important than learning any one piece of software is the ability to learn how to learn for oneself. The more background knowledge self-directed learners have, the better they will be able to judge whether a self-directed solution is likely to lead them to the desired goal without recourse to outside help.

A survey by Robb (2005) explores the role that trial and error plays in the acquisition of skills by CALL instructors. The results reveal that for some teachers, particularly for those who have had no formal training, trial and error plays a major role in their skills acquisition process. The growing literature on technology and professional development, however, is testimony to the fact that most instructors require active encouragement and nurturing in order to become more technologically proficient (Technology Alliance 1998).

With technological novices, confidence can be gained by using "fail safe" applications with detailed, supportive instructions that avoid frustration and the negative attitude that more open-ended applications often engender. Nevertheless, it is equally important for instructors to build "challenges" into the applications, perhaps by intentionally skipping some "help" so that the teachers in training will have the opportunity to solve the problem for themselves. Similarly, rather than showing a single way that an application might be used, we need to encourage suggestions on creative ways that a specific technology might be applied and to discuss the pedagogical pros and cons. One instructor (personal communication) requires teachers to pull down every menu in *Word* and discover for themselves what each item does.

Just as we look forward to the errors that students in the language classroom make as opportunities for learning, we need to capitalize on the problems that teachers encounter while working with the application under study. We need to observe problems as they occur, allow teachers to struggle to find a solution, and then as a group review the strategies used to solve the problem. A case study approach that ferrets out the strategies they have used to solve their own problems will provide inspiration to colleagues to do the same.

Building an awareness of the range of available resources

Robb (2005) showed that for the respondents to the survey, trial and error was often the preferred method of skill acquisition. Trial and error would seem to imply a somewhat messy, random approach to problem solving, but this need not be the case. Trial and error is not applied in isolation, but rather in conjunction with other strategies such as those outlined below in an attempt to discover what to try next.

-   Software manuals and built-in help function. Although the manuals and on-line help provided with most software would seem to be the most obvious resource to turn to, it appears that most users are reluctant to use them. Carroll and Rosson have termed this the "paradox of the active user":

> Designers of reference and help systems count on users to recognize opportunities for new methods, and to search out the information needed to implement them. Instead, users often figure out how to use what they already know to achieve new goals. They have little desire to explore new functions, or to search out information, if they can use methods they are already comfortable with to achieve the same goal. (Carrol & Rosson 1987:82)

– Third party manuals. Commercially available self-help books often take a project or problem-oriented approach and are thus more useful than the original manuals which must cover all functions regardless of their potential utility for novice users.
– Web searches. Effective web searching is a fundamental requisite for autonomy. The best way to find an answer to a specific question or problem is often to "Google" it. Internet searches can be time-consuming and frustrating if poor keywords are used, but used well, the answer will appear in the text cited under each hit. Teachers can benefit from targeted training in obtaining quick results. For example, a short snippet of text from an error message will often be sufficient to pull up the needed solution to the problem.
– Membership in associations and mailing lists. CALL associations now exist in many parts of the world, EuroCALL, CALICO (US) and PacCALL to name a few. Their discussion lists, as well as independent ones such as NETEACH-L or TESLCA-L, can be a great source of stimulation since they often discuss problems dealing with new technologies or possible applications of the technology to language learning.
– Communities of Practice (see Hanson-Smith, this volume). Communities of practice are normally thought of as groups of individuals dedicated to the cooperative discovery and use of some approach to teaching. Having such a group of individuals on tap can provide a quick fix when an instructor runs up against a technical wall. One excellent example is *Moodle* where some 4000 active users post over 200 messages daily concerning their problems, ideas and aspirations with *Moodle*, an open-source learning management system (LMS).

Post-course follow-up and support

Assuming that that the completion of any course or workshop is only the first step towards proficient use of the software, techniques or approaches studied, trainers should endeavor to provide a framework for post-course support. This need not be elaborate. It is likely that most participants will eventually find other means of local or network-based support, but the existence of a means for continued dialogue with the trainer and other participants offers reassurance that they will not be alone in their future efforts. Three such measures would be to:

- Create a course discussion list for post-course information exchange.
- Establish a list of links to support forums for software and systems explicitly taught in the course.
- Encourage continuing education through participation in other formal courses and learning opportunities. For example, for-fee online courses such as TESOL's "Principles and Practices of Online Teaching Certificate Program" or those from Monterey Institute of International Studies and other respected institutions, as well as shorter "Online Academies" can provide useful, in-depth training with experienced teachers. The TESOL CALL Interest Section sponsors free, less formal sessions annually on a wide range of topics such as these from the 2006 Electronic Village Online program: Video and Editing for ESOL, Podcasting for ELT, Collaborative Blogging in ESL/EFL, and Creating WebQuests.

Supporting autonomy at the program level

So far, we have looked at developing CALL autonomy for teachers from the perspective of pre-service and in-service educators. However, program administrators also have an important role to play. A nurturing environment in the workplace, where high priority is placed on the integration of technology into the curriculum, is more important that any training course, hardware, or software. While those instructors with a keen interest in CALL may be able to thrive even under adverse conditions, most instructors require overt measures of support such as those offered below.

- Survey your institution's technical support environment. Do instructors have access to resource people who can answer their questions? Are manuals readily available? How easy is it for teachers to gain access to the hardware or software that they require and for them to be able to experiment and practice with it? What support is available at the district level? Is it easy for teachers to arrange to attend specialized workshops outside of the school? See Gahala (2001) for a deeper exploration of these issues.
- Hire a CALL specialist (see Kessler, this volume). The local availability of someone who can advise others, help solve problems and encourage the implementation of CALL related activities may be of more benefit than an intensive training program. Not all schools can, of course, hire a CALL or educational technology specialist on a fulltime basis, but even part-time or irregular availability can be helpful. Hopefully, schools will be able to avoid situations such as the one voiced by the respondent to Robb (2005): "...there is no technician

so computer maintenance is an issue. Plus constant battle to spend money to fix/upgrade. Only support for other teachers is in sessions done by myself."

- Recognize and reward self-training. The talents of those who have become experts in aspects of CALL through their own effort are often not formally recognized yet those that have learned for themselves are probably in a better position to help others to become autonomous. One instructor in Robb (2005) lamented, "I don't have any papers or certificates. I have helped many teachers informally on a daily basis, but at school the administrators do not acknowledge my work...and will not pay me for helping other teachers as I do not possess the papers or 'formal instruction." Instructors who have a high level of technical expertise can be rewarded with release time or other perks in exchange for their willingness to share their knowledge with others.
- Reward innovation. Set up an annual award for "Technological Innovation" allowing teachers to nominate themselves by presenting documentation of their efforts.
- Set up a faculty development program. A formal faculty development program can take many forms, from formal in-house workshops, to team projects (Kolaitis et al., this volume), to the funding of study outside the home institution.
- Allocate a sufficient amount in the budget for training and resource personnel. Roughly equal amounts should be spent on hardware, software and human resources. "A common error ... is to invest most of the available resources in equipment and virtually ignore the need to allow teachers to become comfortable and competent with the hardware, software, and the pedagogy implicit in the innovation" (Mandinach & Cline 1994: 184).
- Encourage networking. Schools vary considerably in the degree that staff see each other and have opportunities to converse. A central staff room equipped with a computer, frequent staff show and tell sessions, and class observations are some ways a school can foster more frequent cross-fertilization.
- Provide release time and funding. Many instructors neither have the time nor can afford to participate in technology-related conferences and other events. "The lack of sufficient discretionary time in the overcrowded schedules of teachers also influences the extent to which technology is used in classrooms. ... Therefore, release time and the use of paraprofessional staff to accomplish the many non-teaching duties assigned to teachers can greatly facilitate the level of effective technology use in the innovation." (Mandinach & Cline 1994: 183)
- Finally, the brute force method. Requiring the use of technology in the classroom, required workshops or targeted proficiency levels may well "encourage" all but the most reluctant to learn in a "reactive autonomous mode" (Littlewood 1999: 76). Such steps are only meaningful, however, if instructors can see significant ways to apply technology to their teaching and the means to use

it (hardware and software) are already in place. For further insights into how specific institutions have encouraged professional development, see Bates and Epper (2001).

Conclusion

As instructors in pre-service and in-service programs, or as coordinators of working language programs, we need to see that our teachers have suitable knowledge and a positive attitude towards implementing CALL technology in their classes. In order to successfully implement CALL, we cannot count on a few technically adept individuals. Technology is no longer the exclusive realm of specifically trained CALL instructors, but something which all instructors will be increasingly incorporating in their classes.

We therefore need to maximize the opportunities for our teachers to experiment with technology, both new and old, to interact with their colleagues and to access other sources of information on technology. We need to foster, in the classroom and the workplace, a positive attitude towards technology by providing multiple examples of good practice, as well as the printed, digital and human resources that are required to attain this goal.

References

Bates, A. W. & Epper, R. M. (2001). *Teaching Faculty How to Use Technology: Best practices from leading institutions.* Phoenix, AZ: Oryx Press.

Bax, S. (2003). CALL – past, present and future. *System, 31* (1), 13–28.

Carroll, J. M. & Rosson, M. B. (1987). Paradox of the active user. In J. M. Carroll (Ed.), *Interfacing Thought: Cognitive aspects of human-computer interaction* (pp. 80–111). Cambridge, MA: The MIT Press.

Confessore, G. & Park, E. (2004). Factor validation of the Learner Autonomy Profile (Version 3.0) and extraction of the short form. *International Journal of Self-Directed Learning, 1* (1), 39–58. Available at http://sdlglobal.com/journal.htm

Duhaney, D. C. (2001). Teacher education: Preparing teachers to integrate technology. *International Journal of Instructional Media, 28* (1), 23–30.

Feldman, D. (2005). Technology and early literacy: A recipe for success. Available at http://www.pbs.org/readytolearn/resources/2005_summer_institute/Feldman_Success.pdf.

Gahala, J. (2001). Critical issue: Promoting technology use in schools. North Central Regional Educational Laboratory. Available at http://www.ncrel.org/sdrs/areas/issues/methods/technlgy/te200.htm.

Guglielmino, L. M., Long, H. B., & Hiemstra, R. (2004). Self-direction in learning in the United States. *International Journal of Self-Directed Learning, 1* (1), 1–19.

Hiemstra, R. (2004). Self-directed learning lexicon. *International Journal of Self-Directed Learning, 1* (2), 1–6. Available at http://sdlglobal.com/journal.htm.

Hughes, J. (2004). Technology learning principles for preservice and in-service teacher education. *Contemporary Issues in Technology and Teacher Education, 4* (3), 345–362.

Knowles, M. S. (1975). *Self-Directed Learning: A guide for learners and teachers.* New York, NY: Association Press.

Littlewood, W. (1999). Defining and developing autonomy in East Asian contexts. *Applied Linguistics, 20* (1), 71–94.

Long, H. B. & Guglielmino, L. M. (2004). Preface to the inaugural issue. *International Journal of Self-Directed Learning, 1* (1), ii. Available at http://sdlglobal.com/journal.htm.

Mandinach, E. B. & Cline, H. F. (1994). *Classroom Dynamics: Implementing a technology-based learning environment.* Hillsdale, NJ: Lawrence Erlbaum.

Marra, R. M., Howland, J., Jonassen, D. H., & Wedman, J. (2004). Validating the technology learning cycle: In the context of faculty adoption of integrated uses of technology in a teacher education curriculum. *International Journal of Learning Technology, 1* (1), 63–83.

Moodle. Available at http://moodle.org

Norman, M. M. (1999). Beyond hardware. *American School Board Journal* July 1999. Available at http://www.asbj.com/199907/0799coverstory.html

Panel on Educational Technology. *Report to the President on the Use of Technology to Strengthen K-12 Education in the United States (1997).* President's Committee of Advisors on Science and Technology: Executive Office of the President of the United States, Washington DC: Sections 1, 2 and 8.

Ponton, M. K. (1999). The Measurement of an Adult's Intention to Exhibit Personal Initiative in Autonomous Learning. Doctoral dissertation, The George Washington University. Dissertation Abstracts International, 60(11), 3933A.

Ponton, M., Carr, P., & Derrick, G. (2004). A path analysis of the conative factors associated with autonomous learning. *International Journal of Self-Directed Learning, 1* (1), 59–69.

Robb, T. (2005). The role of trial & error in the informal acquisition of skills. Unpublished manuscript. Available at http://tomrobb.com/trialerror.doc.

Smith, R. C. (2003). Teacher education for teacher-learner autonomy. In J. Gollin, G. Ferguson and H. Trappes-Lomax (Eds.), *Symposium for Language Teacher Educators: Papers from Three IALS Symposia* (CD-ROM). Edinburgh: IALS, University of Edinburgh, November 2001. Available at http://www.warwick.ac.uk/~elsdr/Teacher_autonomy.pdf.

Teclehaimanot, B. & Lamb, A. (2005). Workshops that work!: Building an effective, technology-rich faculty development program. *Journal of Computing in Teacher Education, 21* (3), 109–115.

Technology Alliance (1998). Report and recommendations from the Technology Alliance's Educational Technology Task Force. Available at http://www.technology-alliance.com/pubspols/studies/teched_report1998.html.

TESOL CALL Interest Section (2006). Electronic Village Online 2006. Available at http://darkwing.uoregon.edu/~call/.

Warschauer, M. (2002). A developmental perspective on technology in language education. *TESOL Quarterly, 36* (3), 453–475.

CALL teacher education resources and professional organizations

Note: Because websites change rapidly and URLs are often long and difficult to type in, most of the online teacher education resources mentioned in this book, along with others gathered by the authors, will appear on the *Teacher Education in CALL* website. Two other particularly noteworthy teacher education sites and a listing of major CALL professional organizations are provided below.

http://www.stanford.edu/~efs/callted. This is the support site for *Teacher Education in CALL*, containing links to course and resource pages collected from the contributors to this volume and other relevant information.

http://www.ict4lt.org. The home of the Information and Communications Technology for Language Teachers Project, this site has the most comprehensive set of online materials available for both teacher trainers and independent learners. There are five modules each for basic, intermediate, and advanced level training in CALL, a separate module on assessment, and a resource center.

http://www.solki.jyu.fi/tallent. The TALLENT site (Teaching and Learning Languages Enhanced by New Technologies) has course outlines, sample projects, and reference lists for nine modules designed for in-service training.

PROFESSIONAL ORGANIZATIONS: following is a list of some of the leading international and regional organizations focused on technology and language learning.

http://www.apacall.org. The Asia-Pacific Association for Computer-Assisted Language Learning.

http://www.calico.org. The Computer-Assisted Language Instruction Consortium.

http://www.eurocall-languages.org. The European Association for Computer-Assisted Language Learning.

http://www.iallt.org. The International Association of Language Learning Technologies.

http://www.iateflcompsig.org.uk/. The Learning Technologies SIG of the International Association of Teachers of English as a Foreign Language.

http://www.paccall.org. The Pacific Association for Computer-Assisted Language Learning.

http://www.uoregon.edu/~call/. The CALL Interest Section of Teachers of English to Speakers of Other Languages.

Index

In the series *Language Learning & Language Teaching* the following titles have been published thus far or are scheduled for publication: